Women Vaudeville Stars

Women Vaudeville Stars

Eighty Biographical Profiles

ARMOND FIELDS

McFarland & Company, Inc., Publishers
Jefferson, North Carolina, and London

The present work is a reprint of the illustrated case bound edition of Women of Vaudeville Stars: Eighty Biographical Profiles, *first published in 2006 by McFarland.*

ALSO BY ARMOND FIELDS AND FROM MCFARLAND: *Tony Pastor, Father of Vaudeville* (2007; paperback 2012); *Maude Adams: Idol of American Theater, 1872–1953* (2004); *Sophie Tucker: First Lady of Show Business* (2003); *Fred Stone: Circus Performer and Musical Comedy Star* (2002); *James J. Corbett: A Biography of the Heavyweight Boxing Champion and Popular Theater Headliner* (2001); *Eddie Foy: A Biography of the Early Popular Stage Comedian* (1999; paperback 2009); *Lillian Russell: A Biography of "America's Beauty"* (1999; paperback 2008)

Frontispiece: Opened in 1913, the opulent Palace Theater at Broadway and 47th Street became the most famous venue for high-class vaudeville. No performer believed she had reached stardom until she played at the Palace (Museum of the City of New York).

LIBRARY OF CONGRESS CATALOGUING-IN-PUBLICATION DATA

Fields, Armond, 1930–
  Women vaudeville stars : eighty biographical profiles / Armond Fields.
     p.   cm.
  Includes bibliographical references and index.

  ISBN 978-0-7864-6916-1
  softcover : acid free paper ∞

  1. Vaudeville — United States — History — 19th century.
  2. Vaudeville — United States — History — 20th century.
  3. Women entertainers — United States — Biography.
  I. Title.
PN1968.U5F54 2012
791.092′2 — dc22   2006006087

BRITISH LIBRARY CATALOGUING DATA ARE AVAILABLE

© 2006 Armond Fields. All rights reserved

No part of this book may be reproduced or transmitted in any form or by any means, electronic or mechanical, including photocopying or recording, or by any information storage and retrieval system, without permission in writing from the publisher.

Cover photograph: Ethel Barrymore (author collection)

Manufactured in the United States of America

McFarland & Company, Inc., Publishers
Box 611, Jefferson, North Carolina 28640
www.mcfarlandpub.com

Acknowledgments

Conducting the research and compiling the information for 80 women vaudeville headliners required the assistance of many talented people. Theater historians Frank Cullen, Herb Goldman, Mark Dworkin, L. Marc Fields and Joe Marchi helped me determine which performers should be included. They were given a list of performers to evaluate, added new names or subtracted others. I thank my colleagues for their contributions, but I take full responsibility for the final choices.

To obtain genealogical information for each performer, I called upon Mary Jane McIntire, who has assisted me in previous searches. Her ability to unearth and discover accurate birth dates, deaths, marriages, divorces, family history, siblings, occupations and educational data was outstanding.

My particular thanks to John Ahouse and Claude Zachary of the University of Southern California Special Collections and Ned Comstock of the University of Southern California Cinema Library who assisted in my research. I also wish to thank the following institutions for their cooperation:

New York Public Library, Performing Arts Division
The Museum of the City of New York
The University of Texas at Austin, Harry Ransom Humanities Research Center
University of Rochester, Rush Rhees Library
University of California at Los Angeles, Theater Arts Division
Houghton Library, Harvard University
San Francisco Public Library, Historical Center
Houdini Historical Center, Appleton, Wisconsin
British Music Hall Society
British Theater Museum
Academy of Motion Picture Arts and Sciences
Library of Congress
National Archives
Princeton University, Theater Collection
Yale University, Sterling Memorial Library
Friars Club
Los Angeles Central Library
Newberry Library, Chicago, Illinois

My wife, Sara, took on the task of editing the manuscript. I thank her for her efforts on my behalf.

Table of Contents

Acknowledgments   v
Introduction: Women in Vaudeville   1
About the Arrangement of This Book   11

PART ONE : THE SINGERS

Maggie Cline	13	Aileen Stanley	63
Lottie Gilson	16	Texas Guinan	65
Eva Tanguay	18	Lillian Russell	69
Anna Held	22	Florence Mills	73
Stella Mayhew	25	Rae Samuels	77
Bonnie Thornton	28	Alice Lloyd	80
Vesta Victoria	30	Bessie Wynn	82
Ada Reeve	33	Ruth Roye	85
Emma Carus	35	Sophie Tucker	87
Blanche Ring	38	Belle Baker	92
Grace La Rue	42	Olga Petrova	95
Yvette Guilbert	45	Ethel Waters	98
Nora Bayes	47	Frederike "Fritzi" Scheff	102
Marion Bent	51	Irene Bordoni	105
Ethel Levey	53	Isabelle Patricola	109
Louise Dresser	56	Adelaide Hall	110
Blossom Seeley	59	Ruth Etting	114

PART TWO : THE SINGER-COMEDIENNES

Irene Franklin	118	Trixie Friganza	132
Fay Templeton	121	Mae West	136
Marie Dressler	125	Molly Picon	140
Ina Claire	130	Marie Cahill	142

Part Three: The Comediennes

May Irwin	147	Florence Moore	162
Cissie Loftus	151	Nan Halperin	164
Kate Elinore	154	Fanny Brice	168
Elsie Janis	157	Winnie Lightner	172

Part Four: The Dancers

La Carmencita	176	Gertrude Vanderbilt	195
Bessie Clayton	177	Adele Astaire	199
Ruth St. Denis	181	Mlle. Dazie	202
Bessie McCoy	186	Charlotte Greenwood	204
Gertrude Hoffman	189	Janette Hackett	208
Florence Walton	192	Irene Castle	210

Part Five: The Sister Acts

The Cherry Sisters	214	The Duncan Sisters	220
The Dolly Sisters	216	The Hilton Sisters	224

Part Six: The Actresses

Valeska Suratt	226	Ethel Barrymore	233
Fannie Ward	229	Sarah Bernhardt	235
Mrs. Patrick Campbell	231	Fifi D'Orsay	237

Part Seven: The Male Impersonators

Vesta Tilley	240
Ella Shields	242
Kitty Doner	244

Part Eight: The Novelty Acts

Anna Eva Fay	247	Evelyn Nesbit	254
Carrie Nation	249	Helen Keller	257
Annette Kellerman	251		

Part Nine: Headliners' Heritage   259

Selected Bibliography and Source Materials   265

Index   269

Introduction

Women in Vaudeville

In the early decades of the 1800s, women were rarely seen on the American stage. Touring was almost unheard of. A few dramatic actresses like Fannie Kemble and Mrs. John Drew visited cities and towns in the East, reciting the lines that had made them famous dramatic performers. Most stage entertainment was provided by resident companies, bringing theater to local patrons. Showboats, operating on the Erie Canal and Ohio River, included a few women entertainers, mostly singers and dancers.

Between 1840 and the early days of the Civil War, there were dramatic changes in the amusement landscape. Train travel offered performers the opportunity to visit more cities. During this time, the population of the United States doubled, with the influx of immigrants and rurals seeking a living in urban areas. Almost overnight, small towns became big cities. Large, concentrated, diverse populations created an increased demand for popular entertainment, the kind of theater that was shaped to meet the tastes of its diverse audiences. Such amusements had to be simple, cheap, easy to understand and designed to delight men, because they represented the majority of the audience. If women happened to be found in places that presented entertainment, like concert halls and beer saloons, it was as "hostesses," serving drinks or selling their wares. Minstrel shows had become popular, but they consisted of white men performing in blackface before predominantly male audiences. In the minstrel show, male performers dressed and acted as women.

Within the structure of Victorian society, women were obliged to be dutiful homemakers, educational guides for their children, and the family's spiritual and moral leaders. The stage was surely not an occupation for a woman, nor would she consider being seen at the theater.

As saloons and concert halls increased in popularity, astute entrepreneurs saw an advantage to having women appear on the stage, if for no other reason than to increase sales. Male audiences stayed longer and drank more. Women's presence added a suggestion of sexual excitement new to these venues. Women performers consisted mainly of chorus lines, their ranks usually filled by the saloon's "hostesses." Soon most concert saloons featured chorus lines. Social arbiters considered these spectacles indecent. To male patrons, the choruses were enjoyable and exciting.

In the early 1860s, the New York legislature passed a law forbidding "hostesses" from working in saloons. The law helped some women, since those interested in performing wished to earn their living solely from stage work. However, in other states, women continued to serve men in saloons, for both drinks and stage performance. Women affiliated with saloon and concert hall life were viewed by society as pariahs.

The first major breakthrough of this moralistic barrier came in 1866 with the presentation of the play "The Black Crook." In this production, women acted in leading roles and wore provocative dress. Managers Henry Jarrett and Harry Palmer spent a lot of money importing from Europe a large ballet group and opulent scenery. The production was scheduled to appear at the Academy of Music, one of New York's more respectable theaters. Unfortunately, the theater was consumed by a devastating fire, threatening the managers with a sizable loss of money and prestige. In desperation, they offered the ballet to William Wheatley, manager of a rival theater, Niblo's Garden. Wheatley quickly accepted the offer and added the ballet to a production he was mounting, a melodrama (based on the Faust legend) which he called "The Black Crook." The play was advertised as a lavish production filled with beauty, due to its scenery and its large cast of women performers.

"The Black Crook" opened in September 1866. It was an outstanding success, running for 15 months. Within a few weeks after the play opened, other enterprising managers produced their own versions of the play. Some historians cite "The Black Crook" as popular theater's first "leg show," a dubious label. They overlook the fact that the show was significant because it was the first time women performers had taken leading roles on the popular stage.

Women wore common tutus at knee length with tights underneath, a major revision in costuming. Several of the dances were viewed as sensual. In daily life, any dress showing flesh above the ankle branded women as having "no proper taste" or maybe having "gone astray." Other women on stage wore tights only and served as statuettes, stationed at the sides of the stage. A theater rule dictated that women in tights could not move about the stage.

Although ballet was an accepted form of entertainment, the shorter costumes and the appearance of statuettes publicly raised the issue of the questionable display of women's bodies. The publicity helped sell more tickets. But what made the play so important was the fact that it attracted men and women. Women went to the theater to see women performers. For the first time, this opened up opportunities for them to participate in the entire theatrical experience.

About the same time, Adah Isaacs Menken, a well-known melodramatic actress, appeared in "Mazeppa." Portraying the role of the hero, she wore a provocative costume, described as pink silk tights and a short tunic. The play's crowning scene displayed her capture by her enemies, "stripped naked" (meaning tights and tunic) and tied to the back of a horse, there to die slowly from exposure. The play was an instant success, primarily because of this scene and secondarily because it was staged in a legitimate, high-class theater. Like "The Black Crook," the play attracted an audience of men and women in almost equal numbers. Adding to the excitement of the play was Menken's reputation; she had had several husbands and lovers. Menken, a shrewd marketer, turned her notoriety into a profitable stage enterprise.

Though these shows were momentous episodes for freedom from the sexual limitations of Victorian life, women did not rush out to become actresses, nor was the concert saloon transformed into a woman-friendly environment. Yet, the barriers had been lowered for more enlightened and emancipated women. During this period the woman's suffrage movement was established, the new and exciting concept of the "New Woman" was receiving sizable press attention, and popular magazines published solely for women were being launched.

Several months after "The Black Crook" closed, Lydia Thompson, an English actress and manager, brought her all-woman company to New York. Her production, "Ixion," opened in September 1868. Included in her company was a chorus of "British Blondes" who inspired women's interest in the production. The play was a satire on society, politics and Victorian morals. Women performers wore tights and short skirts that exposed the lower thigh. Dances featured wiggles, shakes and high kicking, exposing even more of the performer's body. Women had the leading roles, some of which included parodies of male masculinity.

Like the other shows mentioned, this production was an immediate success. It also generated substantial public moral indignation. The show was moved to Niblo's Garden, a larger venue, and continued to fill houses through the spring of 1869. As many women were seen in the audience as men. According to *The New York Times,* women's enjoyment of the play seemed even to surpass the men's. "Ixion" featured women in charge. It suggested a sensuality never before seen on the legitimate stage. Of course, it played on male sexual interest as well. The show also demonstrated that women had stage talent and could command attention with their performing skills.

The early to middle 1870s saw the emergence of popular theaters as venues for entertainment. On their bills, theater managers offered a variety of individual acts. Many were borrowed from minstrelsy and the circus, like animal acts and acrobats. A few performers graduated from dime museums. Managers often visited these venues to seek new acts which, when discovered, were signed to appear for one week, long enough to prove themselves as crowd pleasers. Several performers came from shows like those put on by Menken and Thompson. Talented women now had acts good enough to be seen on the popular theater stage.

Choruses remained a popular feature and the new theaters quickly incorporated them. The increasing popularity of the two-man act, primarily Irish, soon led to the formation of male-female teams, a decided innovation in stage presentation. Their roles were quite defined: The men performed the comedy and the women danced and sang. Their repertoire was borrowed from minstrelsy and included dancing, pantomime and dialect exchanges. The recent heavy immigration and the preponderance of variety acts featuring Irish performers advanced dialect comedy and it rapidly became an audience favorite. By the turn of the century, dialect acts were the most popular form of comedy.

Male-female teams opened the door for women to act on their own. By the late 1870s, a theater bill featured at least one woman on the bill, usually a singer. Managers named female singers "soubrettes" (French for "ladies' maid"). It was not a complimentary word, but women had not yet been accepted on the stage as equals; the singers did what they could to separate themselves from this label. When preparing their routines, they attempted to inject novel features that would highlight their name rather than their act. It might include a unique costume, the selection of specific song themes, or stage antics that helped individualize them.

Male-female teams might have originally been created by managers for the sole purpose of adding sex appeal to the program. Audiences, however, did not tolerate passive performers; both members of the team were expected to act. As women took on more active roles, they helped attract more female patrons to the theater. Many even performed on their own, offering a few minutes of solo material.

Yet women continued to receive second billing. Men devised the routines; they negotiated the bookings; and they retained most of the salary. The safest and most secure teams were those who were married. Usually, when the team broke up, so did the marriage. The unmarried teams had a harder time convincing audiences of their respectability. Still, audiences went to see them, likely savoring the feeling that they were participating in a behavior that society interpreted as questionable. Even as women performers gained stature in teams, men still dominated the tandem. It was not by chance that mixed teams named the man first, i.e., Harry Day and Daisy, Rooney and Bent.

Tony Pastor was the first theater manager who recognized the drawing power of women performers. He offered Saturday matinees that women and children could attend. He gave away gifts to attract more women patrons to his theater. He featured more women on his programs, attracting more women in audiences. Other managers quickly copied Pastor's marketing efforts.

In the 1880s, the role of women in urban society was in transition. With the introduction of innovative household appliances, women had more leisure time at their disposal. "Clean" popular theaters were thriving. Saturday afternoon matinees provided the opportunity for women to come to the theater without escorts. They soon represented about 70 percent of the matinee audience.

More women were inclined to choose acting as a profession. Coincidentally, the increasing demand for women to appear at variety houses gave young performers a greater opportunity to break into the business. Working in the theater was a grind for women, full of barriers and prejudices, but success seemed attainable.

Of equal import was the publicly recognized success of women variety performers like Lottie Gilson, the Irwin Sisters and Maggie Cline. Their triumphs encouraged other women to consider jobs in theater. These performers became icons to emulate. Often, their unorthodox behavior on and off the stage was newsworthy, and their star power served as additional influence over the feminine public. May Irwin was advertised as "the funniest stage woman in America." She introduced "coon shouting" (belting out songs in a Negro dialect). She tailored her songs to suit her persona, a daring decision for a woman performer at the time.

Lottie Gilson, who moved up from the Irish ghetto of New York's Bowery to popular theater stardom, was the best-known "single woman" (the term for a solo performance) on the popular stage. Billed as "The Little Magnet," she had an attractive personality and sang tearjerkers and risqué songs with equal verve.

Probably the most groundbreaking woman performer was Lillian Russell, who made her singing debut at Tony Pastor's Theater in 1881. The night before her first performance, Tony anointed Helen Louise Leonard with her soon-to-be-famous stage name. She was a pretty young woman who sang songs with sensual feeling and appeal. Lillian was immediately accepted by the audience, women and men. In San Francisco, while on tour, she appeared in tights and smoked in public. "Frisco" audiences applauded her behavior.

By 1883, Lillian was starring in comic opera at the Casino Theater in New York, had married a second time, and had several public disputes with managers, most of which she won. If any actress at the time encouraged other women about opportunities in popular theater, it was Lillian Russell. By the late 1880s, more women were applying for theater jobs than men. Nevertheless, male agents interviewed them and male managers employed them.

Variety expanded its popularity by playing to the needs and desires of its audiences. For example, ethnic dialect comedy catered to the wishes of immigrant audiences who lived in the crowded, ghetto-like urban areas. The diversity of variety's acts made shows exciting, startling and entertaining. New performers, new acts and new songs gave the variety show relevance and vibrancy. Astute managers formed traveling companies filled with various acts to tour the country. Train travel had become easier, faster, cheaper and more comfortable. Touring companies were discovered to be quite profitable. Women now represented a formidable presence in these touring companies.

Women also were displaying an assortment of talents: in acrobatics, skits, choruses, ensemble singing and dancing, and as individual performers. Managers saw to it that a goodly share of any touring company consisted of "pretty" women. Such performance could lead to greater opportunities: better class theaters, higher salaries, and increased recognition. Many women performers began their careers as part of the low end of a traveling company's program and moved up the career ladder.

During the early 1890s, vaudeville replaced variety as the country's premier entertainment. Popular entertainment had become a business, with emphasis on attractive programs and profitability. As vaudeville gained in popularity, more theaters were built, more performers were hired and more business relationships prospered. Most important, vaudeville welcomed women, and managers saw to it that they were treated with greater equality. The vaudeville theaters that operated during the late 1890s and into the twentieth century were carefully operated businesses that recognized the value of women performers. Women had now become an acceptable part of any stage company; and they represented half of every theater audience, including those from the better social classes.

Irwin, Gilson and Russell initiated a trend toward women's emancipation on the popular stage. The trend was quickly augmented by such performers as Nora Bayes, Elsie Janis, Anna Held, Marie Dressler, the Dolly Sisters, Blanche Ring, Eva Tanguay and Fay Templeton, all whom attained headliner status.

Most of these headliners began their careers in a vaudeville theater in their hometown. They may have appeared at an amateur night or auditioned for a role in a local show. Some got their start appearing in melodrama. Still others were lucky enough to be referred to managers of traveling companies, always on the lookout for fill-in talent. (Turnover among the chorus or bit players was quite common in traveling companies.) These women started in secondary roles, often performing in ways unrelated to the skills that would ultimately make them headliners. Most worked their way up as they honed their craft, gained precious acting experience, and obtained audience approval for their efforts.

A few advanced quickly because they had unique skills, like La Carmencita, an exotic dancer, and Annette Kellerman, a swimmer. Most spent several years learning the business, putting in hours of practice each day, touring, and playing secondary houses until they were noticed. Performers with specialties usually had short careers because they were unable to change their routines and found that audiences tired of their act. Performers with wide skills usually had extended careers because they had the intelligence and ability to modify their routines to meet changing audience tastes.

Women performers' early years were spent in companies that were lucky enough to finish a season, or on tours that were perennially threatened with unexpected closure or natural disasters. They faced cheerless housing, at best edible food, low salaries, boredom and its degrading escapes. They had to be prepared to play any role and go anywhere to perform. The women who survived these apprentice years were better prepared to take advantage of better times.

Successful careers also meant rewarding benefits: more high-class theaters and appreciative audiences; dressing rooms with hot water; proper meals and comfortable hotels; maids; private rooms on trains; a manager and advance man; expensive costumes; and, of course, satisfactory salaries.

To maintain their headliner status, these women had to work especially hard to remain attractive to audiences. It was as much a battle to retain one's position as headliner as it had been to become one. For women who were determined to lead a life outside the home, the theater offered opportunities for independence, self-direction and self-gratification. For those not entirely committed to this new way of life, the stage was full of barriers, wickedness and ultimate failure.

For headliners, performance was their life, and pleasing audiences was their goal. The satisfaction they felt when audiences cheered and applauded their work was sufficient motivation to continue to entertain patrons to the best of their ability.

By the early 1900s, vaudeville was approaching its height as a popular amusement for millions of America's theatergoers. At the same time, vaudeville had matured as a business and its impresarios and managers were astute entrepreneurs. Stage action was being crafted into carefully calculated acts, their sophistication equal to that of the audiences. Top entertainers were corporations unto themselves, with agents, managers, advance men, makeup people and costumers all part of the performer's entourage. While women headliners may have accumulated a substantial following, high visibility and generous salaries, male managers and impresarios still controlled their careers.

On the positive side, many women performers had become as well-known as men. They commanded top salaries, ranging from $1,000 to $2,500 for eight appearances a week. They hired personal agents to gain favorable bookings and to negotiate satisfactory contracts. Music publishers of Tin Pan Alley made arrangements with singers to promote their new songs. In turn, singers were given a royalty for every piece of sheet music sold. Specific songs were identified with a given singer, which helped to embellish their reputation.

Success on the popular stage persuaded a number of versatile performers to expand their careers. They moved to a new and growing entertainment form called musical comedy, a play with coherent plot and dialogue, interspersed with songs, dances and comedic routines. Performers chose the roles that fit their styles, or they could invent new roles for themselves. But the decision to play musical comedy was risky. A popular show could last several seasons; a poor play lasted a few days to a few weeks. No one knew how successful the play would be until it was introduced to the audience. A failure in musical comedy allowed the performer to return to her vaudeville roots, usually at a price. Acting in musical comedy may have been easier than vaudeville, but one's vaudeville status might be jeopardized.

During this time, there were plenty of newly opened theaters and the demand for women performers was great. Ads in the theatrical newspapers were filled with requests for acts, a few even for untrained people with the promise that they would be trained for the stage. In those days, it was easy to break into popular theater and fresh actors often attained recognized status in a short time. Few women had to face the barriers and ordeals that their predecessors had so bravely confronted.

Several of the headliners were attracted to Los Angeles and moving pictures, but only those whose routines lent themselves to silent film pantomime were successful. They earned substantial salaries but soon found that shooting pictures was very different from stage work. The requirement to follow a prescribed script, the long hours for movie "takes," and the boredom of waiting for something to happen convinced many performers to return to the greater freedom offered by stage work.

While the suffrage movement was vigorously recruiting members to support its drive to implement voting rights for women, many women performers had already embraced its tenets. Headliners like Marie Dressler, Blanche Ring and Lillian Russell spoke at suffrage rallies and were quoted in the newspapers supporting the movement. For them, suffrage represented the kind of freedom they fought for as performers. The synergy between suffrage and women performers would increase in coming years as they lobbied for passage of the Nineteenth Amendment. It was another example of the new freedom women sought as the traditional boundaries between the sexes were reformulated.

On the negative side, much of vaudeville had become a veritable "closed shop." Theater managers Keith, Albee, Klaw, Erlanger, Proctor, Beck and Meyerfield combined forces to control most of the country's theaters and many of the performers. Called the Syndicate, they dictated where performers played, how long they played, and how much salary they earned (with a 5 percent kickback). If a performer refused to sign with the Syndicate, jobs were difficult to find. In spite of their disdain for the Syndicate rules, women performers had no other alternatives if they wished to further their careers. A brief strike by the White Rats, a group of male performers who fought the Syndicate, assisted by several women headliners, failed to break the Syndicate. Instead, those who spoke out publicly against the Syndicate had to turn to independent managers for work. The Syndicate held power over most performers until the Actors' Equity Strike in 1919.

The growth of vaudeville and its promotion of larger-than-life women headliners strongly contributed to the intrusion into their private lives. Newspaper and magazine gossip columns proliferated, with reporters and informers attempting to uncover every bit of information on all performers, and especially women. Rumor, innuendo, accusation and "inside scoops" relentlessly exposed performers' "behind-the-scenes" behavior, truthful or not. A weekly gossip paper, *The Town Tattler,* notorious for its "revelations," contributed its share of unsubstantiated material. Some headliners contributed to this frenzy by having multiple marriages, sensational divorce suits and acknowledged lovers.

Yet, such gossip may have helped women. Although a few women were embarrassed by the information, many found that it gave them more visibility and increased their drawing power. The message seemed to fit well with public perceptions of the new, more emancipated woman.

The years before World War I saw vaudeville at its peak and women performers at their most popular. Vaudeville brought in millions of dollars of revenue each year, more than any other amusement, sport or commercial business activity. Box office prices had risen because the entertainment itself had matured commercially. There were high-class shows, opulent theaters, well-paid performers and high ticket prices. Performers' star power raised their salaries to previously unheard of numbers; it was not uncommon for women performers to receive $3,500 a week. There were more solo acts by women than by men, and their salaries were competitive.

Some historians claimed that the era represented the "feminization of popular theater," not only financially but also because of the quality of performance women brought to the stage. Their assessment of the situation appeared to be accurate.

The women who now appeared on the vaudeville stage were of acknowledged professional caliber. They were pretty and wore expensive costumes. Their singing had been enhanced through voice training, and their dancing learned under the guidance of theater's most talented dance managers. Those who went into comedy had learned well from their male counterparts how to make audiences laugh. Many of these women displayed multiple accomplishments: They played instruments; they performed kid routines; they could sing and dance well; and they were excellent impersonators of other actors. A number of the more flamboyant performers, like Eva Tanguay, Mae West and Gertrude Hoffman, played the role of the "different woman," that is, women who projected the sexual image of free spirits.

Women also brought more provocative business into the theater. Their manner of dress was more sensual. Their song and dialogue topics included male and female relationships, marriage, and a hint of extramarital activities. Songs were filled with double-entendre meanings and audiences loved the novelty. Some singers, like the Duncan Sisters, Blossom Seeley and Sophie Tucker, changed the lyrics of familiar tunes to elicit laughter, with great success. Women performers were the first to introduce jazz numbers into their acts. They helped bring the new music into the mainstream for theatergoers.

Their star power created a myriad of admirers. Performers were avidly followed by the public, from theater appearances to every word attributed to them appearing in the press. Products were named after them. Children were named after them. New businesses, like cosmetic companies and beauty shops, sprang up due in part to the influence of these larger-than-life artists.

Fresh women performers were greeted with equal enthusiasm from audiences and from their professional colleagues. There was plenty of room on the stage for newcomers as well as "old timers." Newcomers quickly learned that if they joined the ranks of their more seasoned colleagues they would reap the benefits of audience appeal. With the beginning of World War I, their theatrical world would expand to even greater heights.

In 1913, the opulent Palace Theater opened on Broadway, promoted as the premier of the nation's vaudeville houses. At first, attendance was spotty. Patrons were not convinced that the programs were worth the higher ticket prices. Even headliners were unable to fill the house. However, when management risked signing nonvaudeville stars like Sarah Bernhardt and Ethel Barrymore to play at the Palace, audiences jammed the theater. No performer had reached "real" headliner status until he or she played at the Palace. Such was its exalted position in vaudeville until the Depression.

Regrettably, World War I and its aftermath signaled the gradual decline of the vaudeville phenomenon and, likewise, the erosion of the dominance of women performers. The war took more than 5,000 vaudeville actors out of theater. Women partly filled the void. Some managers just shut their theaters or played movies. Most women performers were "persuaded" to include stage material related to the war and patriotism. Women performers who refused to be a part of this agenda found it hard to be booked, due to the power of the Syndicate.

Theaters continued to draw full houses although under more restricted conditions. The government limited their use of electricity, so marquee lights were out several times a week. Shows were begun earlier to conserve coal. A 10 percent war tax was placed on all ticket sales, requiring managers to raise ticket prices. This combination of factors forced the reduction of performers' salaries. Touring was discontinued because the government took control of the railroads.

Relations between management and actors had been fractious for several years. Strikes were threatened; legal actions initiated. But the war put all of these activities on hold. Actors patiently waited for the war to end to make long-overdue demands on management to improve working conditions. In the meantime, they maintained a patriotic stance. Women headliners were at the forefront of the war effort at home. They entertained the soldiers; they appeared at bond rallies; they introduced patriotic songs; and they donated their time to knit socks and sweaters for the boys "over there." In fact, George M. Cohan's quintessential patriotic song, "Over There," was promoted by women performers, including Nora Bayes, Elsie Janis and Blossom Seeley.

Immediately following the end of the war, stage work was struck by two significant jolts. Shortly after the soldiers returned home, a virulent epidemic, called the Spanish flu, spread rapidly across the country and closed theaters for several weeks to several months. All performers were out of work. Headliners could assimilate the temporary loss of salary since they were usually on contract. Those performing at secondary outlets or playing supporting roles were profoundly affected. Some women dropped out of the profession and returned home. Some obtained other non-theatrical jobs. The remainder returned to the stage after the epidemic had passed. In the meantime, the men who had left vaudeville because of the war had returned to take up their former jobs. Almost overnight, women's domination in vaudeville had vanished.

The second shock was actor-inspired. In September 1919, actors mounted a significant strike against management. The strike cost theater managers more than $1.5 million in ticket sales. It was a month before managers agreed to the actors' demands. Several women, including Marie Dressler and Lillian Russell, were on the actors' negotiating team. Even though the agreement had stipulated that no performers would be singled out for their opposition to management, blacklisting did occur. Russell could not be punished because she had retired. Dressler, on the other hand, found no work available and went to Hollywood to appear in movies. The strike improved working conditions for actors in general, but did little for women specifically.

While popular theater was making a comeback, vaudeville found itself with increasing competition from musical comedy, cabarets, burlesque (leg shows) and revues that emulated the Ziegfeld Follies. Some women vaudeville performers moved to other venues that offered long-term contracts and good salaries. Touring, which had been an excellent training ground for women, had been curtailed during the war, and its recovery was slow. Booking agents were more likely to rehire actors returning from the war than women, even those recognized as attractive performers. Due to a recession in 1921 that substantially reduced audience attendance, even more pressure was put on theaters featuring vaudeville. Theater managers turned to showing full-length movies instead of stage acts. Movie studios announced plans to expand their distribution by building theaters exclusively for motion pictures.

Popular theater was obviously in transition, and no one had any idea of the effect on vaudeville and especially on its women performers. Women headliners retained their status but they were forced to increase their efforts to remain in the limelight. In their favor, they believed, was the fact that few new women were entering the profession. This could also be interpreted as a sign that the amusement was no longer as attractive to "new blood" as in previous years.

Now, even old-time headliners went in search of new venues in which to perform. Some gave up vaudeville altogether to go into the movie industry, now turning out full-length films by the hundreds each year. With the explosion of radio and recordings as a family-style entertainment, singers used the medium to expand their recognition and promote new songs for music publishers. As radios became common in U.S. homes, music publishers and vaudeville managers were concerned that the new medium would steal business from them. Actually, the opposite occurred for music publishers. The exposure of new music persuaded more people to purchase music sheets and records. Women vaudeville performers discovered that they had to learn all of the new songs being released to satisfy their more knowledgeable audiences. Unfortunately, this detracted from their own specialties.

By the mid–1920s, women performers saw their audiences declining. Musical comedy was fast becoming a permanent fixture on Broadway and successful shows were sent on extended tour. Burlesque attracted a predominantly male audience, the same men who at one time had been enthusiastic vaudeville theatergoers. Cabarets and nightclubs, catering to a more elite audience by virtue of their higher prices for tickets, drink and entertainment, attracted people who enjoyed more intimate and risqué programs, adding new excitement to their leisure-time pursuits. Radio had opened a new venue for entertainers that did not require person-to-person interaction with an audience. Singers and comics, especially, found radio to their liking. The opportunity to reach thousands of listeners at one time with minimal effort was an attractive benefit.

During this period, moving pictures were quickly becoming a viable commercial medium. Astute observers of the theatrical scene saw movies as direct competition to vaudeville. Many theaters split their programs; they began with three or four vaudeville acts and followed with a full-length movie. For women headliners, the end results were mixed. Those who performed in these theaters received higher salaries. At the same time, there were fewer spots open for them to perform.

With changing audience tastes and the tremendous increase in competitive entertainment, theater owners saw an opportunity to inhibit the more assertive and independent women vaudeville performers. It seemed a regressive move against the status that women entertainers had enjoyed during the previous decade. Women's vaudeville performances were being forced into more limiting stereotypes. The women who rebelled, like Mae West and Sophie Tucker, sought other outlets and continued their successful careers. Others, like Fanny Brice, the Duncan Sisters and Charlotte Greenwood, retreated into familiar specialties — kid roles and physical humor — that appeared to satisfy managers and audiences. They performed with success, but women's star power had all but disappeared. Vaudeville was undeniably dying, as was women's once predominant role.

The arrival of talking pictures finally killed a glorious artistic period in which women vaudeville performers dominated popular entertainment and, at the same time, helped change the roles of women in our society.

About the Arrangement of This Book

The biographies in this book have been divided into the following parts.

The Singers

About one-third of the performers were singers. It was the easiest way to enter vaudeville: Any woman who had a pleasant voice and was considered good-looking had the chance. The opportunities were also greater. Every vaudeville bill needed soubrettes and, if their singing styles were different, a bill might contain more than one. Vaudeville touring companies needed singers, not only to play primary roles but also to serve as choruses. Musicals and revues needed chorus girls to back up headliners. As vaudeville expanded in popularity, opening more theaters and creating more touring companies, opportunities for women swelled. At vaudeville's height, there were more women on stage than men, and women headliners commanded higher salaries than their male counterparts.

The Singer-Comediennes

A small group of women entertainers combined their skills to be known as singer-comediennes. Their routines were comedy delivered in songs. They may not have had fine voices, but their renditions put over the comedic content in an appealing manner. Some performers did not begin their careers as comediennes but later added that ability to their acts.

The Comediennes

Women comediennes were usually comics from the beginning of their vaudeville careers. Beauty and a fine voice had little to do with their success. In fact, the lack of these features probably helped them to succeed. Some of these performers extended their careers because they adjusted their routines to meet the changing audience tastes. Some lasted only as long as vaudeville remained a viable amusement.

The Dancers

Dancers usually entered vaudeville early in their careers because most of them had previous dance training. They were required to constantly develop new material to keep audiences interested and extend their own stardom. Some went on to invent new dance techniques. Others developed unique "gimmicks" in their acts that gave them greater identity and prolonged audience approval. Vaudeville audiences tended to accept a new dancer about every three years. Interestingly, no new dancers entered vaudeville after 1914. The ballroom craze, the inclusion of professional dance in musicals, the introduction of the big band era and moving pictures diverted dancers from the vaudeville stage.

The Sister Acts

Sister acts were more prevalent than they seemed, but few of them became headliners. Several stars began their careers in sister acts but went solo as they honed their performing skills. Those sister acts that achieved success and longevity offered novel artistry. The Dolly Sisters were a pretty, provocative duo. The Duncan Sisters played Topsy and Eva for years, making a travesty of *Uncle Tom's Cabin*. The Hilton Sisters were Siamese twins, a stage oddity. The Cherry Sisters were so bad that a screen had to be placed in front of them to avoid missiles thrown by the audience.

The Actresses

At a time when vaudeville was at its apex and paid large salaries to proven headliners, some dramatic actresses decided to appear in the medium "for the money." Many high-class bills featured a dramatic skit. The appearance of a Bernhardt or Barrymore was a highlight and easily filled theaters. Other dramatic actresses who played vaudeville soon found their way into moving pictures.

The Male Impersonators

Male impersonators seemed to be almost exclusively British, and only a few of them were gifted enough to make it in vaudeville. None of the performers who became male impersonators began their careers in that way. Various circumstances and events convinced them to select that particular routine. American audiences, particularly those outside the large urban areas, were uncomfortable with these acts.

The Novelty Acts

Every vaudeville bill contained its novelty acts. Few ever made it to stardom. Most novelty acts were meant to elicit laughs or demonstrate a sensational skill. Those who were headliners were usually successes before they played in vaudeville. The exception may have been Evelyn Nesbit, who used her notoriety to attract audiences for no other reason than out of curiosity for the fallen woman.

Within each of these categories, we have listed the performers according to the date that they entered vaudeville. Most of the performers began vaudeville early in their lives. A few were successful in musicals and revues before choosing vaudeville. By ordering them in this fashion, we can trace the chronology of individual performers as vaudeville proceeded through its life cycle as America's favorite entertainment.

Part One : The Singers

Maggie Cline

The golden era of vaudeville was a great era for Irish songs, and Maggie Cline was a vigorous proponent of both. Tall, hefty and red-haired, the "Irish Queen" captured theater audiences with her booming voice and snappy dances. "Now, ladies and gentlemen," Maggie shouted, pretending to hitch up her trousers like a boxer ready for a fight, "I will sing the dainty and pathetic little ballad that drove me into this business."

"T'row him down, McCloskey" was the cry from the stagehands and orchestra. Loud crashes of whatever was loose backstage emphasized the song. And Maggie would launch into one of her most famous signature tunes.

For more than 30 years, Maggie was one of the most popular Irish performers in vaudeville. No matter what play she appeared in or what she sang, audiences paid to see Maggie and were enthralled by what one reviewer labeled "a unique microcosm of Hibernian lyric art."

When Maggie walked on the stage, she was firm-footed, leisurely and composed. She looked squarely at her audience and smiled, cheerful, friendly and familiar. She walked to the front of the stage and her broad smile embraced the entire audience, and especially the "boys in the gallery." Before she sang her first words, clapping hands and stamping feet greeted her, in enthusiastic appreciation. With fun in her voice and eyes a-twinkle, Maggie captured her audiences as few other performers could do.

Maggie Cline was born January 1, 1857, in Haverhill, Massachusetts, the third of six children. Both her father, Patrick Cline, and her mother, Anne Degman, arrived in America from Ireland prior to the Civil War. Patrick was alternately called a laborer or peddler, his true occupation obscured by an acquired nickname, "The Irish doctor," which in the vernacular of the times suggested that he was a versatile merchant. Patrick served in the 1st Massachusetts heavy artillery during the Civil War and distinguished himself as a fine example of an Irish soldier. Anne did all she could to maintain a home for the children, which was a difficult task. As was common at the time, when children reached five or six years of age, they were sent into the streets to earn a few pennies for the family. Maggie was no exception. At the age of 12, with several years of work experience, she got a job in a shoe factory. Shoe and hat manufacturing were Haverhill's primary industry and Irish youth dominated the labor force. Except for the usual neighborhood leisure time activities, the saloon and church hall, there was little else in the town to entertain young people.

Maggie was impatient and dissatisfied with her life. At 16, she ran away from home to join a burlesque troupe in Boston. Her Irish beauty, stage presence and strong voice gained her entrance to the "wicked world" of variety touring.

During the 1870s, Maggie traveled across the country as a member of various companies, playing in every town that happened to have a theater and in many places where theaters had not yet been built. She appeared in mining towns like Leadville and Butte and in railroad junctions like Omaha, St. Joseph and Duluth. Dime museums and concert halls were the primary venues for touring companies. Audiences were primarily made up of men; liquor, smoke and gambling dominated. When vaudeville houses were built, performers shared dressing rooms, cold water troughs and uncomfortable sleeping accommodations at boardinghouses or on rocking trains on their way to the next engagement. The road was full of hardships, but for Maggie they offered a freedom and independence not available to her elsewhere. Maggie was successful because she appealed to the popular audiences of the day, Irish men who enjoyed her rough-and-tumble songs, Irish brogue and comic skits.

Maggie often appeared in the New York variety houses, typical stops for a traveling company. As one of the headliners, she earned $50 a week. Featured with nine other acts on the bill, Maggie frequently occupied the fourth position, the star. Audiences were primarily made up of Irish immigrants, and Irish women entertainers were their favorites, especially Maggie and Lottie Gilson.

In the early 1880s, Maggie made an instant hit with "Mary Ann Kehoe," a song that became her trademark and was demanded by audiences wherever she appeared. The song was a typical brash Irish story (a young girl sought by two lovers) that ended in a fight. To put across the song, Maggie used the entire stage, prancing back and forth, swinging her arms and legs and expending unbounded energy to recite the story. A reviewer called Maggie "the great, big, bouncing darling of the gallery boys," which indeed she was. Her zest for performing attracted all the patrons. After such a rousing song, she would walk over to the wings and get a glass of liquid from a stagehand. "And this is what they give me when I'm dying for a glass of beer," she remarked to the audience, and they cheered her in recognition. At theaters known for their more liberal attitudes, she would comment to the audience, "When I go to a place to sing, there's nothing can stop me but the police, and they're on my side." This always elicited cheers and applause. Maggie had become a show unto herself.

Tony Pastor's 14th Street Theater in New York was the epitome of vaudeville houses during the late 1880s, and Maggie was one of Tony's perennial stars. Normally, Pastor changed his bill each week. He kept Maggie on contract for more than three years because of her popularity and drawing power. She introduced new Irish tunes

Maggie Cline (Museum of the City of New York).

and appeared in skits and satires, heading a bill of high-class performers. Pastor's theater was "clean," that is, it forbade smoking and drinking and invited whole families to attend the shows. This arrangement helped to broaden Maggie's appeal and reputation, and tended to soften her otherwise rough renditions. When Pastor went on tour he featured Maggie, and she gradually developed a national following. Along with being labeled the "Irish Queen" of vaudeville by New York reviewers, she was often called "The Bowery Brunhilde."

After a break with Pastor due to an argument about salary, Maggie went on her own, playing vaudeville houses wherever she could. However, good engagements and good salaries were hard to obtain because vaudeville was attracting more performers than there were theaters. Competition among a growing roster of women headliners was fierce, and Maggie's act was getting stale to the better class of audiences. New material, new songs and new shows were needed to replenish her career.

Maggie tried musical farce but this proved to be too limiting to her style. Melodrama, no matter how Irish or how comical, did not suit Maggie either. She returned to a vaudeville business now being consolidated by a number of theater owners, soon to be called the Syndicate. Maggie's chance came in 1890, when she happened to meet comedian and songwriter John T. Kelly in Philadelphia.

Maggie asked Kelly if he happened to have any "loose songs about him." He replied that he had one that no one wanted to use and she could have it, "but not for a cent less than two dollars." The song was "Throw Him Down, McCloskey." It was Irish, musical, red-blood roughhouse, scored for a piano and a strong voice. It quickly became Maggie's signature tune.

> T'row him down McCloskey was to be the battle cry,
> T'row him down McCloskey, you can lick him if you try.
> And future generations with wonder and delight
> Will read in history's pages of the great McCloskey fight.

When the song was announced, audiences would whistle and stamp their feet. Before Maggie sang a note, the stagehands would make noise by throwing tin cans against the walls. The gallery sang along with Maggie, and when she reached the chorus, the stagehands again made such a clatter that the orchestra was insignificant. Maggie claimed newsboys originated the noise. They would crowd around the entrance to the theater until they heard the chorus. It was the sign for them to make as much noise as they could on the sidewalk. Maggie brought the stagehands out on the stage for audience recognition. Like the audience, she treated them as "the sons, brothers and cousins of Blarney."

By World War I, audience tastes had become more sophisticated and the Irish knockabout routines had all but disappeared from the high-class vaudeville houses. Maggie knew that her career had ended and gracefully retired from the stage in 1917. She purchased a home in Red Bank, New Jersey, and lived in solitude with her husband. She had married John Ryan, a cafe owner, in 1888, although the marriage was unknown to her admirers.

In 1928, Maggie bought an estate at Fair Haven, New Jersey, a farm where she could garden and tend sheep. On June 11, 1934, 17 years after she left the stage, she died of a stroke. She was 77 years old. A mass was said in Red Bank and burial was in Holy Cross Cemetery, Brooklyn, in her parents' plot.

Maggie gained her fame before vaudeville had become high-class popular entertainment. She paved the way for women performers to attain star status. Her act and her persona reflected the Irish influence in vaudeville and she was one of the most important headliners of her day.

Lottie Gilson

As a teenager, Lottie Gilson became a headliner of the variety stage in New York. With vitality and youthful maturity, she sang both tearjerkers and comic ballads with equal abandon. Audiences enjoyed her selections and often enthusiastically sang along with her.

At the same time that her career was reaching star status, her personal life was self-destructing. She had quick marriages and disagreeable divorces, and suffered from bouts of alcoholism and mental breakdowns. These issues led to her disappearance from the theater and ultimate death.

Lydia Deagon was born in Philadelphia, Pennsylvania, in 1869. She may have been an illegitimate child. There is no information available about her parents or where and with whom she lived during her early years. How she learned to sing and act is unknown. In her early teens, she was reported to have appeared at variety houses and concert halls in New York.

At the age of 16, Lydia made her vaudeville debut as a soubrette, singing tearjerker songs to her mostly male audiences. Reviewers liked her act and stage presence and her ability to almost instantly gain rapport with the audience. For the next several years, she performed at various theaters in cities on the East Coast to popular acclaim. Such songs as "The Old Turnkey," "The Old Sexton," "The White Squall" and "The Little Lost Child" left audiences weeping. In the late 1880s, Tony Pastor engaged Lottie—she was no longer calling herself Lydia—and had her headlining bills at his 14th Street Theater. Pastor called her "The Little Magnet," because she had become a guaranteed draw, and had Lottie return to his theater frequently. Lottie was earning $20 a week when she came to Pastors. By the time she was headlining his shows, she was earning $60 a week, a considerable sum for a young talent.

Lottie's almost instant popularity also contributed to her appeal among stage door Johnnies. There were several reports of engagements and possible marriage to local young dignitaries, but such news quickly disappeared from the newspapers. According to newspaper reports, Lottie supposedly married a man named Gilson around 1887 and immediately changed her stage name. Their relationship ended around 1890.

During the 1890s, Lottie toured on the vaudeville circuits, mostly in Eastern cities. Her brand of songs changed as audience tastes changed, from tearjerkers to comic ballads, some of them bordering on the risqué. The song with which she was particularly identified was "The Sunshine of Paradise Alley." The song was demanded at every performance, and audiences leaped at the opportunity to sing it with her. Other popular songs she introduced were "She's Such a Nice Girl, Too" and "Military Mollie." She also made an Edison cylinder, "Can't You Take It Back and Change It for a Boy."

Lottie became famous for three stage skits that most audiences hailed but critics deplored. She was the first to accept money to plug a Tin Pan Alley song. However, she was not very selective what songs she plugged and they did little to help her act or improve her reputation. She also introduced the "singing stooge" and the "come-on-boys" routine. Playing at the Brooklyn Theater, Lottie was singing "My Best Girl's a New Yorker" when a boy in the gallery began singing the tune along with her, which got a large response from the audience. Lottie incorporated the episode into her act and, at appropriate times, a person in the audience would begin to sing along with her. It prompted the entire audience to follow. The "come-on-boys" exclamation was used to get the audience to join her in song. Soon, other singers adopted these tactics, so much so that everyone forgot that Lottie had been the first to use them.

While Lottie was gaining in popularity, she was adding and discarding husbands. About 1892, she married Thomas J. Ward. A year later, he was arrested and put in jail for a year for attempting to set fire to his wife's apartment. They divorced a short time later. In 1895, Lottie married Lemuel Sloss. Three years later, he shot himself in what was described in the press as an accident. Rumors suggested that he was attempting to shoot his wife. The marriage was terminated shortly afterward. Her fourth marriage, to Jack Westly, quickly followed. It ended in a 1900 divorce so that Lottie could marry J.K. Emmett, actor son of the great J.K. Emmett of "Fritz" fame. J.K., Jr., was taking the "Fritz" legacy and producing his own versions of his father's melodramas.

Lottie Gilson

After her marriage to Emmett, Lottie joined him in a succession of "Fritz" plays in which she had the female lead. For several years, they toured the country with some degree of success. However, with the changes in audience tastes for musicals instead of melodramas, the couple found fewer engagements. In 1904, because of heavy financial losses, Lottie claimed bankruptcy. Her return to the vaudeville stage, without Emmett, was undistinguished and she obtained few opportunities to perform. She turned to alcohol for solace. In 1907, she was picked up on the street and arrested for public drunkenness. Newspapers reported the incident but mentioned only that she was the wife of actor J.K. Emmett. There was no mention made of her career.

A year later, Emmett divorced Lottie, declaring in his suit that she was living with actor William Hart and calling herself Mrs. Hart. A few months later, Lottie voluntarily entered the Bartonville Asylum for the Insane. Hospital physicians reported that Lottie was not insane but, rather, was suffering from nervous prostration. They claimed she would be completely cured in a few months.

Nothing more was heard of Lottie until 1910, when she appeared at a cheap vaudeville theater in Fort George, New York. She had obtained the engagement through a friend. She was quickly dropped from the bill. It was her last appearance on the stage. Friends got her a room on Thirty-Ninth Street. A few weeks later, she was admitted to Bellevue Hospital, suffering from gastritis and neuritis. Doctors expected she would soon die, but she recovered to live another two years, although in constant discomfort.

On June 10, 1912, Lottie Gilson, 43 years old, died alone in a boardinghouse room on 43rd Street. Her obituary was short, the newspapers briefly mentioning that she had a great vogue as a popular singer several years previous. Her funeral was arranged by Maggie Cline, an old friend, and the White Rats, the actors union. She was buried in the Actor's Society plot in Evergreen Cemetery.

Lottie had been considered "one of the greatest soubrettes in show business." In the 1880s and 1890s, her cute songs entertained audiences and made her a popular star on the vaudeville stage. Unfortunately, the events of her personal life cut short a promising career.

Eva Tanguay

Eva Tanguay billed herself as the "Cyclonic Comedienne." *Variety* called her "The Girl Who Made Vaudeville Famous." Audiences loved her while critics hated her. On stage, she was aggressive and raucous with a "don't-give-a-damn" attitude. Off-stage, she was just as tempestuous, breaking contracts and managers' rules, fighting with rivals and having numerous lovers. Her extravagant persona was translated into extensive advertising and promotion that preceded her every appearance. She performed provocative dances and sang suggestive songs. Her costumes were revealing, and her stage prancing exaggerated all of her physical attributes. She was said to have commanded the largest salary of any vaudeville performer.

Eva did not have outstanding talent, the usual means to stardom. Instead, she capitalized on her boisterous behavior, shapely figure and strong determination to become, as many critics reluctantly acknowledged, the single biggest star in vaudeville history.

Eva Bessy Mayflower Tanguay was born August 1, 1878, in Marbleton, Quebec, Canada, Her father, Joseph-Octave Tanguay, was a physician from a family that had lived in Canada for generations going back to the middle 1700s. Eva's mother, Marie-Adele Pajeau, was born in Keeseville, New York. Joseph and Marie were married in Quebec in 1860. They had four children. Eva was the second daughter and the youngest child.

In 1884, the family moved to Holyoke, Massachusetts. A year later, Joseph died, leaving the mother and four children destitute. As was usual in such circumstances, the children were sent out to work—all except Eva, who was only six years old at the time.

Discovered to possess a good singing voice, eight-year-old Eva made her first stage appearance at Parson's Hall, Holyoke, a vaudeville theater, at an amateur night. She won first prize.

Eva continued to make frequent appearances at the theater and often won prizes. On one of these occasions, the Fransesca Redding Company, a traveling company of actors putting on various melodramas, was in town. A juvenile lead fell ill, and Eva was asked to replace the ill child. She and her mother joined the company. A portion of her salary of eight dollars a week was sent home to support the family. Eva was affiliated with the company for five years and played all the child parts, including an extended role as Little Lord Fauntleroy. During her teen years, Eva played in the familiar and well-liked drama, "A Celebrated Case," presented by the E. P. Sullivan Repertoire Company. By this time, her mother had returned home. Eva had developed into a competent performer who understood the delights and disappointments of touring.

During her teen years Eva found work in vaudeville, appearing as a chorus girl and acrobat. Her work as an acrobat would turn out to be a great asset for her in the near future.

In April 1896, 18-year-old Eva was playing Kaloma, a Fiji king's daughter, in a musical farce, "Hoo-Doo." In the middle of one dancing number, she broke away from the chorus line and innovated her own dance steps, which included shimmies and shakes. The audience responded with cheers and applause. However, another chorus girl criticized Eva for her unwarranted display. Stagehands had to intercede before Eva hurt the girl.

In the late 1890s, Eva had displayed sufficient singing and dancing talent to appear in Koster & Bial's production, "In Gotham." A brief stint in a George M. Cohan farce, which introduced Eva to New York audiences, quickly folded. Eva joined a vaudeville touring company in the Midwest and became a leading soubrette. Her act included several suggestive songs and vigorous dancing in revealing costumes. She had begun to develop her own style of performance and audiences were very receptive.

On February 11, 1901, Eva opened at Hammerstein's Victoria Theater in "My Lady." The show featured Clifton Crawford, Lotta Faust and Charles J. Ross. Eva was in the chorus and had one song to sing. The show was a satire of Dumas' "The Three Musketeers." Although it had a dubious plot and music contributed by an assortment of writers, the show ran for 93 performances. While Eva was singing her number, one of the girls in the chorus threw an object to her boyfriend in the audience. He threw it back and caused the audience to laugh. At the end of the act, backstage, Eva attacked the girl and threw her against a wall. Again, stagehands separated the women before any damage occurred. From that point on, it was known that Eva would not tolerate anyone distracting the audience during her act.

Eva Tanguay

Newspaper coverage of theatrical activities was in its early stages, and reporters were attracted to any episode that might appeal to readers. The incident reached the press and, in some cases, made front-page headlines. The result was a public relations bonanza for Eva. Taking advantage of the situation, the manager featured Eva more prominently and the theater was crowded during the remainder of the play's run. Eva had become newsworthy. And she must have realized that her out-of-the-ordinary behavior had been amply rewarded.

After two years, Eva was earning $1,200 a week. She put together her own touring company, the "Eva Tanguay Comedy Company," with the aid of B.F. Keith. Keith was a founder and leader of the Syndicate, which controlled most of the theaters in the country and many of the actors. Although Keith was known for his Puritan rules and regulations, he put up with Eva's antics because she was a box office success. Their history was spotted with periodic arguments, threats, and accusations, all of which made great publicity for Eva, and profit for Keith. She was being proclaimed "the youngest star on the American stage," a gross exaggeration, but it made headlines and filled theaters.

Eva's role in "The Chaperons" (1903) was small but the show's song hit, "My Sambo," made Eva a star on the New York stage. She also introduced a song called "I Don't Care," with lyrics about a woman unconcerned about what people thought of her. The song would become Eva's trademark, and an extensive publicity campaign made her famous as the "I Don't Care" girl.

In 1903, Eva appeared in "The Office Boy," in a dancing role that earned encores and good reviews. Reviewers called her dancing "abandoned." In the same year, she played in "The Sambo Girl." The show had originally been called "The Blonde in Black," starring Blanche Ring, but lasted only 30 performances. Harry B. Smith and Gustave Kerker wrote new songs especially for Eva, but this did not help the show and it closed after six weeks. Nevertheless, the show expanded Eva's reputation and her highly identifiable style of acting.

Eva appeared in her last musical, "A Good Fellow" (1906), a show that never reached New York. After a second unsatisfactory experience playing musical farce, Eva moved to vaudeville, where she would become an uncontested headliner for more than two decades. In 1908, her rendition of Salome delighted audiences and brought out all of the social reformers who denounced the act as obscene. Just months before, the Metropolitan Opera had produced the production, but it played only one day. Members of New York's social elite, like the Vanderbilts and Morgans, demanded the opera be stopped because it was "revolting and disgusting." Almost deliberately, Eva created an act out of Salome's dance of the seven veils. The act caused a riot of reactions, from audience delight to threats of censorship and closure. Eva prevailed. The publicity made the act a fad and many performers did burlesques of Salome's dance for several years.

New York's mayor threatened to close Eva's show if she did not wear a less revealing costume. Actually, the costume was not that revealing, as Eva wore tights and jewelry over the veils. The mere act of discarding the veils one by one as she danced was enough to send the censors into a tizzy. The controversy enhanced her reputation even more.

In 1909, Eva was recruited by Flo Ziegfeld to fill in for the departing Nora Bayes and Jack Norworth from his "Follies of 1909." She demanded top billing and a top salary. Ziegfeld had no recourse but to meet her demands. Her performances made the Follies a continuous sellout, justifying Ziegfeld's decision. A young Sophie Tucker had one song in the show, which Eva took as her own. Tucker was unceremoniously dropped from the cast, but a week later she was on her way to stardom, having been selected by William Morris for his vaudeville theaters.

By 1910, Eva was the top performer in vaudeville, getting a salary of $3,500 a week, more than any other woman on stage, popular or legitimate. Quite apart from her stage delivery, Eva had become an excellent self-promoter. She spent her own money to advertise her openings at theaters. She initiated stunts that garnered considerable press coverage. Once, she sold newspapers on a street corner shared with an elephant. She appeared at an amateur night under an alias and won the prize. She wore outlandish costumes covered with sparkly sequins, feathers and furs. She had a dress covered with $1, $5, $10 and $50 bills and another covered with pennies. Other costumes were dotted with sugar, coal, pens and pencils. It was reported that she employed four press agents at one time. The newspapers loved her; the public loved her; and she loved whatever was said about her. When Eva came onto the stage, she was welcomed with a trombone salute.

Her episodes off-stage were equally noteworthy. Stories periodically flew about her jewels being stolen or about her sexual indiscretions, but they never seemed to harm her. Eva was reported to have thrown a stagehand downstairs. When taken to court, she paid him off with $1,000 bills. Her arguments with managers and agents were duly reported in the press. She slept through matinees and walked out on shows. When she toured on the UBO circuit, Keith and Albee worried that her behavior would embarrass them, and it often did. In some cities, her posters were banned and theaters closed. The forces of morality forbade "indecent" advertising, attempted to boycott her shows, and prevented certain suggestive songs from being performed on stage. Eva ignored them all, sang what she wanted and bounded across the stage with her usual explosive energy.

Along with the song "I Don't Care," Eva introduced others that became hits because she alone put them over. In 1913, her repertoire included "I Want Somebody to Go Wild with Me," "It's All Been Done Before, But Not the Way I Do It" and "Go As Far As You Like." Others that titillated audiences were "That's Why They Call Me Tabasco," "I Can't Help It," "I've Got to Be Crazy" and "I May Be a Nut, But I'm Not a Crossword Fan." Audiences shouted to have her sing all of her personal hits every time she appeared on stage. Critics called her vulgar, ugly, and overweight. Perry Hammond, of the *Chicago Tribune,* stated that he "could think of no entertainer who entertained him less." Another critic wrote that "the only cheerful song ... was one in which she hinted that some day she would retire." Often, Eva responded with a defense of a woman's right to star on stage against a male-dominated business.

Eva was married three times, and all her marriages seemed to be incidental to her career. The first, to John Ford, a dancer in her traveling company, occurred November 24, 1913. Eva was 35. They separated 13 months later and were divorced in 1917. Several years later, she married Roscoe Ails, a vaudeville actor. This marriage also ended in divorce. A third marriage, on July 22, 1927, to Alexander Booke, her pianist, was annulled on grounds of fraud.

Eva had only a brief fling with moving pictures. In 1902, the American Motoscope and Biograph Company filmed her "Sambo Dance" from "The Chaperons." In 1916, she appeared in "Energetic Eva," a five-reel film that she paid for herself. It may never have been distributed. The following year, she made "The Wild Girl." Again, she put her own money into the picture and Selznick Studios distributed it. In the picture, she played a gypsy girl who wins the love of a newspaper editor after being pursued by various villains. She danced several times but otherwise played a dramatic role.

Through the war years and into the early 1920s, Eva remained the top woman performer in vaudeville. In December 1920, booked at the Coliseum Theater, New York, she played to full houses for the entire engagement. The next year, while on tour, Eva appeared at the Palace Theater, New York, her act as boisterous as ever and her audiences as enthusiastic. But she seemed to be acting more on nostalgia, as audiences called for her to sing all of the old favorites.

During 1924, Eva's appearances were limited due to frequent illness. This continued until 1927, when she announced her retirement and moved to Hollywood. She had amassed enough resources to live comfortably. However, when the stock market crashed in 1929, Eva lost her entire savings, and returned to vaudeville. Her opening number, accompanied by the familiar trombone overture, was "Back Doing Business at the Old Stand." Although Eva was 58 and had little to offer the audience, they greeted her with cheers and applauded the entire act. In 1931, Eva toured with the Fanchon and Marco Company as vaudeville played out its dying days.

In 1933, Eva was struck by blindness due to cataracts. Sophie Tucker paid for the operation to restore her sight. Due to arthritis, she could barely get around. In the final years of her life, Eva developed a phobia about meeting people, even her friends. She claimed that she would rather have them remember her as the vivacious "I Don't Care" girl than as an invalid. An interview she gave on her sixty-eighth birthday was conducted through her bedroom window, the interviewer standing outside. "Don't come in," she said. "Eva Tanguay is not here."

On January 11, 1947, Eva died of a stroke after years of suffering from various physical ills and living in virtual poverty. At her bedside were a niece, a nurse, and a neighbor. The walls of the bedroom were papered with photographs of Eva at the height of her career. During the last few years of her life, she spoke only of the past.

Eva had once claimed that her success on the vaudeville stage was due to the capitalization of her personality, nerve, and salesmanship rather than any special talent. When people attempted to flatter Eva on her artistry, she would laugh at them and say, "I've just been lucky." Whether through luck or talent, Eva had been one of the most dynamic performers in vaudeville.

Anna Held

Flo Ziegfeld was not the first to create stage myths for his headliners, but he contributed his share, especially for Anna Held. His most famous publicity stunt was the claim that Anna bathed in cow's milk each day to maintain her schoolgirl complexion. The ruse worked and made her an instant sensation. While some of Anna's success came from Ziegfeld's publicity, she was already an audience-pleasing actress in her own right.

Helene Anna Held was born on March 18, 1873, in Warsaw, Poland. Her father, Maurice Held, was a German–Jewish glovemaker; her mother, Yvonne Perre, who had been born in France, worked at various jobs to keep the family out of poverty. At nine, Anna curled feathers after school hours. When her father became ill and her mother was out of work, Anna helped to support the family by working as a seamstress. The family moved to Paris in 1880 to escape the anti–Jewish pogroms taking place in Poland. Maurice died in 1884, and Anna and her mother moved to London to live with relatives. A year later, when Anna was 12, her mother died. Relatives cared for Anna for several years.

While a teenager in London, Anna got a job as a chorus girl. She was selected to appear in Yiddish plays, led by the well-known actor Jacob Adler. Her acting abilities got her a job with a company touring Holland, Germany and Denmark for three years. During this time, Anna developed her own stage presence. Now a 16-year-old girl, with a piquant face, large brown eyes, red-brown hair and a narrow waist, Anna was a beauty with a provocative delivery of risqué songs. When she returned to London, she quickly became a popular singer in London music halls. Trips to Paris established Anna as an upcoming headliner who easily captured the attention of audiences.

Anna Held

Anna's popularity in Paris brought her to the attention of a South American businessman, Maximo Carrera. Their affair was common knowledge; it was brought to a turning point when the couple decided to marry only months before Anna gave birth to a daughter. Liane Carrera was born May 23, 1895. She was placed in a convent when Anna returned to the stage. Within a few years, the marriage faltered and the couple separated. Anna converted to Catholicism, primarily to protect herself from the anti–Semitism spreading across Europe. To aid her public image, she told of being born and raised in France.

Anna continued her career in the music halls of Western Europe. Her song and dance routines, helped by her fresh beauty and provocative stage behavior, helped to make her a headliner. As part of her "independent" life, she rode horses astride and was one of the first women to use bicycles and automobiles.

In 1896, while Anna was starring at London's Palace Music Hall on a vaudeville bill, she was seen by Florenz Ziegfeld, Jr., a young producer from New York. He had been looking for a woman to star in his new production, "A Parlor Match." Anna's beauty and her enticing French accent persuaded Ziegfeld to offer her the job, supposedly at a salary of $1,500 a week. Anna accepted the engagement and traveled to New York, leaving behind her husband. Ziegfeld's publicity campaign made Anna a celebrity before she appeared on the United States stage.

Charles Hoyt's revival of "A Parlor Match" opened at the Herald Square Theater, New York, on September 21, 1896. Anna made her debut to American audiences. Her role was not especially large. Reviewers remarked about her good looks and stage demeanor, although her acting was less than impressive. Her delivery, French accent and suggestive dress made her an instant hit with audiences. This was the beginning of a rapid rise to stardom. Anna and Ziegfeld planned to marry after the opening of the show, but her husband refused to give her a divorce. So Anna and Ziegfeld lived together as husband and wife until their relationship became a common law union in 1904.

For the next several years, Anna appeared as a headliner on various vaudeville bills with a commanding salary. As a singer she was only average, but as a delineator of sensual and exciting lyrics she was very popular. Her vaudeville tours were profitable and established Anna as one of the top women headliners on the popular stage, comparable to Nora Bayes and Lottie Gilson.

Anna had to learn English to appear in Ziegfeld's new play, written just for her. "Papa's Wife" (1899) was Anna's first big musical hit. The story, written by veteran Harry B. Smith, told how an innocent bride finds out that her husband cannot be faithful on his honeymoon and how she cures him. Anna highlighted her role in the show with the song, "I Wish I Really Weren't, But I Am." Also appearing were 16 young chorus women elaborately dressed; Ziegfeld called them "The Anna Held Girls." This was the first time he featured decorous women on stage. The show ran for 147 performances and then went on tour. It proved to be a very profitable venture for Ziegfeld.

Several other musicals followed, all designed around Anna's stage attributes: "The Little Duchess" (1901); "Mlle. Napoleon" (1903); "Higgledy-Piggledy" (1904); and "The Parisian Model" (1906). "The Little Duchess" lasted for four months and an extended tour due solely to Anna's allure and Ziegfeld's gorgeous chorus. The play had no plot, just a series of vaudeville routines. "Mlle. Napoleon" never reached New York but did well on the road. It again featured a beautifully costumed Anna and an equally elaborate chorus. In 1904, Ziegfeld combined with Joe Weber to put on a typical old Weberfields production, "Higgledy-Piggledy," featuring Anna. However, just before the show went on the road, Ziegfeld and Weber parted company and Anna was replaced by Trixie Friganza. Anna returned to vaudeville for almost two years, increasing her popular appeal as one of the top women stage stars. Ziegfeld spared no effort to keep Anna in the public eye with mythical stunts. He revealed to the press about her daily bath in cow's milk and the apparent theft of her jewels — anything to build the reputation of his wife.

"The Parisian Model" opened at the Broadway Theater on November 26, 1906, starring Anna in a lavish production. The scenery was outstanding and the chorus costumes sumptuous. In one scene, Anna sang a song with six verses and wore a different gown with each verse. Two of Anna's songs became identified with her for the remainder of her career, "It's Delightful to Be Married" and "I Just Can't Make My Eyes Behave." Ironically, it was at this time that the Held-Ziegfeld relationship began to disintegrate. Ziegfeld's reputation as a gambler and womanizer had finally affected Anna.

"Miss Innocence" (1908) became another triumph. Admirers bought tickets well in advance, ensuring that the show would be a profitable enterprise for Ziegfeld, even better than his "Follies of 1908." Audiences saw a risqué story surrounded by beautiful girls and elaborate scenery. The show played for 176 performances in New York and toured for two years. A rumor had preceded the show suggesting that Ziegfeld had forced Anna to have an abortion so she could star in "Miss Innocence." This was probably another myth.

In 1910, Anna returned to London's Palace Theater as an accomplished star on her own, at a salary of $2,500 a week. She played for almost a year to full houses. In early 1912, Anna reentered the vaudeville circuit, appearing in a skit that featured songs from her repertoire of hits and beautiful gowns. A year later, she starred in a musical, "Mlle. Baby," that never reached New York.

Ziegfeld was now openly courting a Follies beauty, Lillian Lorraine. Anna took the European view, allowing her husband his infidelities. But when Ziegfeld escorted Lorraine to dinners in New York's fashionable restaurants and put her in an apartment two floors above his own, Anna sued for divorce, naming Lorraine as one of the co-respondents. They divorced in 1912. (Even common law marriages needed divorces in New York.) Anna traveled to Europe to continue her career.

In 1914, when World War I began, Anna went to France to entertain the troops, often appearing in shows near the front lines. In October 1915, she returned to the United States and vaudeville, appearing at the Palace Theater, New York, with great success, although she sang only three songs and a verse of "I Just Can't Make My Eyes Behave." Audiences still regarded Anna as a headliner in spite of her lack of recent appearances on the American stage.

Anna had a brief experience with motion pictures. In 1913, she appeared in a Kinemacolor short. In 1916, she starred in a full-length film, "Madam La President." Anna's acting seemed appropriate for film work but she never appeared in films again. Also in 1916, Anna starred in a musical, "Follow Me," produced by the Shuberts. Anna scored well, as did the showgirls and the usual vaudeville turns, typical of Shubert shows during the war years. The show toured but Anna also found time to raise funds for relief charities.

Upon her return from a long tour, Anna was ill. Doctors diagnosed that she was suffering from multiple myeloma, a form of bone cancer. Anna died at the Savoy Hotel, New York, on August 12, 1918. She was 45 years old. At her bedside were Susan Westford Allen, a sister of Lillian Russell, and Beatrice Buonchi, a maid. Anna left an estate estimated to be more than $250,000 to her daughter, with whom she was reconciled before her death. Liane Carerra had had a theatrical career; she changed her name to Anna Held, Jr., after her mother's death. Anna was buried in Woodlawn Cemetery, New York, in a private ceremony. Hundreds of floral tributes were received from Europe and America.

When told by her doctor that she had only a short time to live, Anna was said to have remarked, "It is the last curtain. I have lived and I will hold out to the last — it is the spirit of Joan of Arc and the spirit of my parentage — to the unconquerable French." The myths surrounding Anna lived long after her death, as was her wish.

Stella Mayhew

Stella Mayhew first gained fame singing coon songs in blackface. She and her husband, Billee Taylor, performed a song-and-dance act that made them headliners on the vaudeville circuits. Stella interspersed vaudeville with musical comedy, featuring her renditions of the latest ragtime songs. After she made a grand performance in the musical "Hit the Deck," the Depression and the decline of vaudeville left her unemployed and penniless.

Stella Mayhew was born in Waynesburg, a small town in eastern Ohio, in 1874. Her mother remarried while she was still a child and her name became Stella Saddler. At the age of eight, she performed in children's roles in melodrama. At ten, she had small roles in such melodrama classics as "Rip Van Winkle" and "Uncle Tom's Cabin" with a company that toured Ohio and western Pennsylvania. By the time she was 15, Stella was singing and acting in melodramas and farce-comedy with touring companies.

As a teenager, Stella was tall and thin and was not considered a pretty girl. In fact, a doctor had diagnosed her as being anemic. He advised her to change her surroundings and career aspirations. Stella and her mother moved to Toledo, Ohio, where a friend in the theater business got Stella a job in a small touring company. Her mother was delighted. At first, Stella regarded the acting profession as a cure, but she quickly realized that it offered many opportunities for her.

In 1890, at the age of 16, Stella had her debut in vaudeville when the amusement itself was in its beginnings. She changed her last name to that of her father. Playing with companies wherever she could get a job, Stella was just another singing and dancing member of an ever-changing cast. She quickly adapted to the life of a performer.

In the middle 1890s, Stella traveled to New York, the only place she believed a career in vaudeville could be launched. By this time, she had become quite stout, which restricted the kinds of parts in which she could appear. Her singing talent and delivery were her greatest assets and contributed to a growing reputation in vaudeville. As vaudeville itself became more acceptable and its audiences more sophisticated, Stella's status as a performer improved. By the late 1890s, she was one of the featured performers on bills appearing in the better vaudeville houses.

When coon songs became the new rage, Stella selected these tunes to include in her act. Her physical size, however, relegated her to "mammy" parts. Some managers had her sing in blackface. So well did she perform this role that for five years managers refused to accept her in any other part, despite her obvious talent.

Due to a conflict between actors and the Syndicate in 1900, Stella's career aspirations were interrupted. The Syndicate was a consortium of theater owners and managers that forced actors to join them and pay them a fee for performing. If they refused, no engagements were forthcoming. The White Rats, the actors' union, attempted to fight the Syndicate but was powerless to change the conditions. Many female performers, like Lillian Russell, Marie Dressler, Irene Franklin and Stella, sided with the actors' union. They found that getting work had become very difficult. Frustrated by her inability to play in vaudeville, Stella switched to musicals.

In 1900, Stella's first musical comedy opportunity was in the role of a Black "mammy" in E. D. Stair's production of "Swanee River." The show was a combination melodrama and musical that catered to current audience tastes. It toured for two years, appearing at a variety of theaters across the country, but it never played in New York. Stella's singing talent moved her up the ranks of cast members and she became one of the stars of the show. Still, her songs demanded they be sung by a blackface performer. When Stella stepped out occasionally into vaudeville, she was hired to sing coon songs while dressed and made up as a "mammy" character.

Stella Mayhew (Museum of the City of New York).

"The Show Girl" opened on May 5, 1902, at Wallack's Theater. The story told of a troubled theatrical troupe, which mirrored what was happening to the production itself. A poor plot and mediocre music caused constant changes in the book and in cast members. Stella sang several numbers and was not required to appear in blackface. In fact, her now corpulent size gave her the opportunity for comedy. She used her girth as a self-deprecating foil, as did fellow performers like May Irwin and Marie Dressler. The show ran for two months but freed Stella from the stigma of blackface.

In late 1903, Stella met William "Billee" Taylor, a vaudeville song-and-dance man. Since male-female song and dance acts were in demand, they decided to partner. The partnership turned to marriage in 1904, about the same time Stella was signed to appear in the musical, "The Man from China." The show opened at the Majestic Theater on May 2. Stella sang the show's hit song, "Fifty-Seven Ways to Catch a Man" and appeared in several comic skits. The show lasted through the summer. Stella was suddenly discovered by reviewers, who complimented her on her delivery and interpretations. This served her well as Mayhew and Taylor hit the vaudeville circuit.

The team did well for the next several years, headlining bills except when a top performer was present. In one instance, Eddie Foy was the star of the bill. Both he and Stella lived in New Rochelle, New York. Joking about her size, he introduced Stella as "the other half of New Rochelle."

In 1906, Mayhew and Taylor were signed by Lew Fields, who was a foe of the Syndicate. The team was able to play in all the theaters not under Syndicate control. Fields then selected Stella to appear in his 1910 summer production of "The Jolly Bachelors." Glen MacDonough wrote the book and Ned Wayburn handled stage management. The cast included vaudevillians Joe Welch, John T. Kelly, Emma Carus, Gertrude Vanderbilt and Ed Begley. Problems with the book were immediately raised. MacDonough complained that the performers were ruining it. The performers believed they were saving the show. The show's chorus was the largest ever in a Broadway musical, 48 men and 60 women.

"The Jolly Bachelors" opened on January 6, 1910, at the Broadway Theater. Fields had turned an overstuffed variety show into a cohesive musical. Several performers had quit, so Nora Bayes and Jack Norworth were now the stars and the other vaudevillians were relegated to minor roles. The hit song was Bayes singing "Has Anybody Here Seen Kelly?" Stella sang Irving Berlin's "Stop Dat Rag" to good effect. After a fine run in New York, the show went on extended tour. When J.J. Shubert wanted Stella to appear in another play, Fields refused to let her go because of her crowd appeal.

A year later, Stella was in a Shubert production that premiered at the Winter Garden, destined to become the Shuberts' flagship. "La Belle Paree" opened on March 20, 1911. Newcomer Al Jolson starred in the show and became an overnight sensation. Stella sang all of the ragtime numbers to popular acclaim. The show ran for 104 performances. So popular was Jolson, the Shuberts quickly put together another piece for him.

A three-part production, two parts vaudeville and one part burlesque, "Whirl of Society," a musical, opened at the Winter Garden March 5, 1912, with Jolson in his first blackface role. Stella played the part of a society matron giving a party with Jolson as her servant. Stella again sang several undistinguished ragtime songs. Thanks to Jolson, the show ran for four months. However, Stella was disappointed in the roles given her and the salary she received from the Shuberts and decided to return to vaudeville. She also missed working with her husband.

Between 1909 and 1912, Stella made a number of cylinder recordings for Edison in New

York. They included "That Beautiful Rag" with her husband, "Savannah," and "A Songologue," all songs that she had sung in the musicals in which she appeared.

Mayhew and Taylor toured on the Orpheum circuit. They swore never to separate again. The actress stated: "I don't believe that a stage couple can live happily together when it is necessary for them to be apart most of the theatrical season." They appeared together until 1922, when divorce ended the team. Stella chose to continue in vaudeville with a solo act. Although she performed alone, Stella remained a headliner. The fact that she was nearing 50 years of age bothered some reviewers but her stage presence remained as strong as ever.

The year 1927 proved to be a banner year for Stella. Lew Fields recently prospered by producing a number of hit musicals featuring the music of Rodgers and Hart and books by his son, Herbert. This time, he teamed with Vincent Youmans on a musical called "Hit the Deck." The show opened April 25 at the Belasco Theater, the first time a musical ever played at this venerable house. The show starred Louise Groody, Charles King and Stella. It was an immediate hit but Fields and Youmans had several major disagreements about staging. In what was probably one of his greatest theater mistakes, three days after the opening, Fields sold out his share to Youmans.

As much as Stella enjoyed being the star of a hit show late in her career, her role was an uncomfortable reprise of her early career. She played a mammy, Lavinia, in blackface. To her benefit, she sang the hit tune of the show, "Hallelujah!" a syncopated rag that allowed her to display the best characteristics of her talent. Brooks Atkinson and *Variety* predicted the show "would sail through the summer." It went on to play for 44 weeks.

The show revived Stella's vaudeville status and she performed as a headliner until 1930. In 1928, Stella bought a mansion in Beechhurst, New York, for $84,000, and invested in securities to take care of her retirement years. Then came the stock market crash. All of her investments vanished and she had to sell her home to satisfy creditors. She smiled, told her friends it was part of life, and looked for a job.

The Shuberts helped her out by signing her to appear in "Hello Paris," a musical revue that opened on November 15, 1930, at the Shubert Theater. Stella sang several ragtime songs. Audiences were not attending the theater and the show lasted for only 33 performances. For the next several years, Stella played in vaudeville when she could get an engagement. It was hardly enough to live on.

A subway trip into the city proved to be catastrophic. Stella slipped over a platform and gashed her ankle. Thinking it a trifling wound, she had it bandaged and paid little attention to it. Two weeks later, in great pain, she entered the French Hospital to find that the injury had become infected and she was suffering from blood poisoning. Stella died on May 2, 1934, at the age of 59. She was penniless. The hospital bill and funeral costs were paid by the Actors' Benevolent Association. Burial was in the association's plot at Kensico Cemetery.

Stella was a long-time vaudeville and musical comedy headliner who never quite got the accolades she deserved, given her talent. She began her career when vaudeville was in its infancy. She died when vaudeville itself was in the last throes of its own existence.

Bonnie Thornton

Bonnie Thornton was a vaudeville favorite during the 1890s and early 1900s, a delineator of sentimental and comic songs, what theater people called "serio-comic." She most often appeared as a solo act but sometimes teamed with her husband in a song-and-dance routine. James Thornton wrote songs that Bonnie included in her act, a few of which became hits. Like her contemporaries Lottie Gilson and Stella Mayhew, Bonnie was not good-looking nor did she have a fine voice, but she could put over a song and capture audiences.

Elizabeth Cox was born in May 1872, in New York City. Her parents had come from Ireland and resided in the Irish section of the Bowery. Nearly every block in the neighborhood had a saloon and concert hall that featured entertainment. Elizabeth was influenced by the women performers playing in these venues and wanted to make a career as an entertainer. By the age of 12, she was appearing in local concert halls, singing popular songs of the day.

When Elizabeth was 16 and singing in a concert saloon, James Thornton, variety performer, song writer and alcoholic, was taken with her stage presence and her ability to gain attention from a tough audience made up of hard-drinking and smoking men, the only customers who frequented such places. He proposed that he and Bonnie become a team and tour with one of the available variety companies.

James Thornton was born in December 1861. Like Elizabeth's, his family had come from Ireland, arriving in Boston in 1870. As a child, James was exposed to typical local Irish performers and beer hall venues. His first job was as a singing waiter in Boston. Soon, he had the same job in a New York cafe. It was at this cafe that he discovered Elizabeth.

One of Elizabeth's first vaudeville appearances was in August 1890 at the London Theater. When she teamed with James, she gave up playing in vaudeville companies. While they were performing together, James began writing songs, his first being "Remember Poor Mother at Home," which he sold to a publisher for $2.50. When Elizabeth sang it, the song usually brought tears to the predominantly male audience. James changed Elizabeth's name to Bonnie, a more decidedly Irish name, and to Thornton when they married in 1890. Bonnie was 18, James 29.

James and Bonnie became well known on the concert hall circuit. James dressed in a Prince Albert cutaway coat and appeared dignified and reserved, but once on the stage he told funny monologues, played an excellent piano and was a good dancer. Bonnie also dressed demurely but, when she sang her Irish specialties, audiences whistled and stamped their feet in appreciation. The couple's primary problem, however, was James' drinking.

Bonnie did all she could to keep James sober, at least when he performed, but he claimed he could play better when drunk. It was always a race to see who could get the salary check first. When Bonnie controlled the money, she gave James an allowance and used any excess to buy diamonds, which she did throughout her career. It was once reported that her diamond collection was almost as large as Lillian Russell's. Despite James's behavior due to his alcoholism, they never parted, Bonnie declaring that she loved her husband dearly.

In December 1892, Bonnie appeared at Tony Pastor's Theater, at that time the premier variety house in New York. She was a hit with one of her husband's songs, "My Sweetheart's the Man in the Moon." Over the years, Bonnie served as the inspiration and source of many of James's songs.

Bonnie starred with Lottie Gilson and the Empire City Quartette at the Madison Square Garden roof in June 1894. She sang "She May Have Seen Better Days," a sentimental Irish "mother" song, which were popular at the time. The following year the Thorntons toured the Midwest and East. Each year, Bonnie made an appearance at Pastor's, her favorite venue. She remained one of Pastor's favorite performers. For the next several years, Bonnie put on a solo act and toured the country while James supplied her with songs.

Thornton sold his songs for a price ranging from two to six dollars, not bothering to copyright them or receive royalties from music publishers. His and Bonnie's biggest hit was "When You Were Sweet Sixteen." He sold the song for $15. As a hit, the song made thousands of dollars for the music publisher.

James and Bonnie teamed again in 1910 as part of an "Old Timer's Program" for producer Percy Williams. For the next five years, they continued to play together when James was sober enough to appear on the stage. During this time, he wrote "The Irish Jubilee," "Two Little Girls in Blue," "When Summer Comes Around," and "It Don't Seem Like the Same Old Smile." Bonnie's renditions of these songs helped to make them hits and establish her as a headliner.

After 25 years of performing and almost the same number of years dealing with her husband's drinking, Bonnie retired from the stage. She opened a millinery shop on West 47th Street. Over the next few years, Bonnie would occasionally appear at the end of her husband's act, singing old favorite songs.

In March 1920, Bonnie became so ill that she was removed from her apartment at the Hotel Argonne to Bellevue Hospital. Six days later, on the 13th of March, she died. She was diagnosed as suffering from pneumonia. Bonnie was 48 years old. Her funeral at St. Malachy's Roman Catholic Church was attended by many of the performers she had shared the stage with during her career. She was buried in St. Raymond's Cemetery. Bonnie had left an estate of over $50,000, most of which went to her husband.

Bonnie Thornton

Bonnie was one of the last of the old-time variety and vaudeville performers who began their careers in the smoky beer halls and graduated into high-class theaters. Several of the songs she introduced remain familiar today.

Vesta Victoria

Vesta Victoria, a singing comedienne, was one of the few British performers who became popular in the United States. Each tour of America included new songs and sketch material, making her a continuing box office attraction. Vesta was a hard-working performer who always gave her best.

Victoria Lawrence was born into a theatrical family. Her father, Joseph Lawrence, was a popular music hall comedian and song-and-dance man. His specialties included standing on his head while singing. Her mother, Annie, whose stage name was Marion Nelson, also performed as a singer in music halls. Victoria was born on November 26, 1873, in Leeds, England, the fourth of five children and the only girl. From birth, she was taken on her parents' tours of the "provinces" and quickly learned the life of a child trouper.

At the age of six, using the name "Baby Victoria," she sang songs as part of her parents' act and was well-received by audiences. On October 22, 1883, at the age of ten, Victoria made her debut at the Royal Cambridge Theater, London, singing her mother's songs and performing a clog dance. She was now being advertised as "Little Victoria." By 15, she had matured into a seasoned professional in the music hall circuit, gaining recognition and popularity by performing songs that spoke of her age. To establish her stage identity, she took the name Vesta Victoria. One of the songs that helped to build her following was "Good for Nothing Nan." It would become one of her signature songs.

Vesta Victoria

By the age of 19, Vesta had become a well-known and very popular music hall entertainer. She was known for introducing new songs and routines that kept audiences coming to see her. Her voice, now mature, was low, clear and energetic, "bell-like with a bit of throatiness," according to one critic. She featured tunes that were stories of some misfortune that the singer experienced, but would end well. Audiences loved her renditions and enjoyed the rapport that she established with them.

An act that did not include audience participation was rare. During this period, she introduced a song written especially for her called "Daddy Wouldn't Buy Me a Bow-Wow," which quickly became one of her signature songs. Successive verses were added, with theater patrons singing along.

During the early 1890s, American managers were visiting England and the Continent seeking new performers and plays. Their search brought many comic operas to the United States, initiating a craze that lasted a decade. They also brought back several performers who were stars on local stages. Managers took notice of Vesta's star status in musical halls and believed she would be a popular attraction on the United States vaudeville stage. At age 20, Vesta and her mother came to America to initiate her career in American theaters. After appearing in variety houses on the East Coast, Vesta was engaged by Tony Pastor to headline a bill at his 14th Street Theater. She was so well-received that Pastor kept her for eight weeks, an unprecedented run at his theater. Following that success, she played at Shea's Theater, Buffalo, for three weeks before returning to England. Her successful tour prompted managers and stage door Johnnies to shower her with jewelry. This was the beginning of her interest in collecting jewelry, a hobby that later had the British press claiming she was the richest woman in England.

Between 1893 and 1895, Vesta, now a bona fide vaudeville star, performed in London to full houses and enthusiastic audiences. She and her mother returned to the United States in September 1895 for a full season's tour. Her newest song, "Waiting at the Church," which became another signature tune, was a hit and made her a box office smash. For the next two years, Vesta toured all the major cities in the United States. Each summer she would return to England to rest.

On September 20, 1897, Vesta married Fred McAvoy, a music hall manager. A year later, she had a daughter, Irene. Vesta and Fred were divorced in November 1903, after being separated for several years.

Vesta's act now included songs that reflected common problems and dilemmas that audiences could readily identify with. She mixed satire with broad burlesque. The songs were presented with simplicity, almost bordering on naivete. Vesta expressed sorrow for herself, but audiences knew that everything would be fixed at the end. When audiences sang the last verses with her, it was with a happy-ever-after finality.

From 1899 to 1907, Vesta performed in English music halls, which now presented vaudeville-style bills. As a headliner, she packed theaters and received superlative reviews from even the usually dour critics. She and her colleague Vesta Tilley were the top entertainers in the country. Two women had never before attained that status in England.

In 1907, the Keith organization engaged Vesta to make a brief tour of Eastern cities at a salary of $1,750 a week. For two weeks, Vesta filled theaters with her routines, unique to U.S. audiences. Reviewers marveled at her energy and ability to so quickly gain rapport with audiences. In order to avoid problems with her accent and language, managers passed out song lyrics beforehand to the audience.

Vesta was back in the United States in 1908 for a season's tour on the Keith circuit. On this trip, she came with her brother, also a performer and songwriter. He wrote some material for his sister and remained in the United States to further his career. Vesta again earned a great deal for Keith with her appealing work. He tried to keep Vesta in America, but she wished to return to the English stage, her favorite venue, where audiences understood her every nuance. Many British performers failed in the United States because their brand of entertainment was perceived as "odd" for American audiences. Vesta tailored her act to meet current American tastes and attained great success.

Songs that Vesta introduced included "Just Because They Put Him in Trousers," "He Calls Me His Own Grace Darling" and "It's All Right in the Summertime." For the latter song, she came on stage dressed in pink tights, draped with filmy white gauze. On her head was a white wreath. She carried a lyre. Some of her songs included double entendre lyrics, although she was never accused of performing anything risqué. Such examples included "You Can Do a Lot of Things at the Seaside (That You Can't Do in Town)," "Now I Have to Call Him Father," "The Next Horse I Ride On," and "Some Would Marry Anything With Trousers On."

Vesta toured the United States twice in 1910, arriving in April for a short run and again in December for a tour that closed in May 1911. The press reported that Vesta was earning $3,000 a week, but records suggested it was closer to $2,000. Still, such a large salary for a foreign entertainer was equaled only by the French singer, Yvette Guilbert; very few American women performers earned at this level. Vesta returned to England in 1911 and did not return to the United States for 16 years.

In 1912, Vesta married Herbert Terry but found he had already been married. In spite of this, they stayed together. In 1920, with the death of the other woman, their marriage became official. They were divorced in 1926.

Vesta continued to star in English vaudeville through World War I, coupling theater appearances with entertaining the troops. In 1918, immediately following the war, Vesta retired from the stage. She was 45 years old and had been performing steadily for 35 years.

At the age of 53, in 1926, Vesta was persuaded to come out of retirement to appear at the Victoria Palace, London, on an oldtimers bill. She performed many of her signature songs to delighted audiences. In April 1927, Vesta made her only appearance at the Palace Theater, New York, in an oldtimers bill, singing old favorite songs.

During the 1930s, Vesta's popularity with English audiences remained. In September 1931, she recorded most of her most famous songs. The following year, she toured in an oldtimer's revue, "Stars That Never Failed to Shine." That same year, Vesta was selected to perform at a Royal Command Performance. In 1934, she played in an English movie, "The Broken Rosary," in which she sang.

The Motion Picture Club of New York gave a special luncheon in Vesta's honor. Speakers bemoaned the disappearance of old songs for modern ones. Vesta preferred the old favorites, saying, "I think the songs of today can't compare with the famous ones of the old days. The new tunes are catchy, but the words—'Do-de-oh-doh'- and all that business! Rubbish! It doesn't mean a thing."

In 1937, Vesta played in another movie, "The Schooner Gang," again singing a few of her old favorites. An appearance in 1938 in a revue, "Vaudeville Past and Present," another oldtimers production, kept her name before the public. Vesta's last stage appearance was as part of a bill at a Royal Command Performance, of course, singing her old signature songs.

During her remaining years, she lived in Leeds, her old hometown. She died on April 7, 1951, at the age of 77. Special funeral rites were given in Leeds and London, with thousands of people coming to pay their respects.

Vesta was one of the few vaudeville headliners who continued to perform successfully long after vaudeville disappeared. She entertained a new generation of patrons with her signature material.

Ada Reeve

Another British headliner who toured the United States in vaudeville was Ada Reeve. Unlike her contemporaries, Ada sang comic songs with a sense of dignity. In England, she also starred in musical comedy and, in her later years, in films and television.

Adelaide Mary Reeve was born on March 3, 1874, in London, England. Her father, Charles Reeve, was an undistinguished actor. Her mother was a dancer, Harriet Seaman, billed as Harriet Saunders. Their real name was Isaacs, which was changed to hide their Jewish origin. They were married in 1873. Charles was 30 years of age; Harriet was 19. Harriet retired from the stage after marriage and was said to have borne ten children. Adelaide was the first born.

At the age of four, Adelaide made her debut on the stage in the pantomime "Red Riding Hood" at the Pavilion Theater, Whitechapel, London, on Boxing Day 1878. By the time Adelaide was six, she was known in the music halls as "Little Ada Reeves." For the next several years she toured England, appearing with stock companies that put on melodramas.

In 1882, she starred in "East Lynne" and became the family's primary source of income. Sometime during this period, her name was shortened to Ada Reeve.

Her first appearance in London was at Christmas 1883, when she appeared in "Sinbad the Sailor" at the Pavilion Theater, Mile End. During the next few years, Ada appeared in a number of productions at the same theater, including "The Crimes of Paris" in 1884, "Fairy Kindness" at Christmas of the same year, and "Jack the Giant Killer" in 1885.

After episodes when little Ada stole the show from headliners, she was fired or threatened with lawsuits by other performers angry about being upstaged by a juvenile. However, after some years of perseverance, determination and constant practice, Ada made her first music hall debut in 1886, at 12. Within two years, she had become a familiar name in London music halls due to her singing voice and refined stage demeanor. Her father was now writing all of her material, designed specifically for music hall audiences.

During the next five years, Ada made herself into a formidable music hall entertainer, displaying excellent stage presence, a clear singing voice, versatility and a tasteful acting manner. At the age of 16, she was placed at one of the feature spots on a vaudeville bill, singing three popular songs and encores. As reported by a London newspaper, "Deafening and continued applause brought her back. People were delighted."

Although brought up in poverty, Ada maintained a sense of decorum and strength uncharacteristic for a young woman. Audiences noticed and appreciated her performances.

In 1893, Ada made her first U.S. tour with a performing troupe, starting with an appearance at Koster & Bial's Music Hall in New York. She followed with several weeks at Tony Pastor's, attracting good reviews and additional engagements. Ada was a perfect match for Pastor's family-oriented audiences. She played in Eastern theaters for the next few months before returning to England. The experience was both exhilarating and profitable.

In 1894, Ada married comedian Bert Gilbert (Gilbert J. Hazelwood). A child, Bessie, was born the following year. Ada had signed a contract with impresario George Edwardes to appear in musical comedy as one of his famous Gaiety girls. While pregnant, she starred in "The Shop Girl," but only for five months before she had to retire. This was enough, however, to make her a musical comedy favorite.

Ada appeared next in "All Aboard" in August 1895 at the Criterion Theater and "The Gay Parisienne" in April 1896 at the Duke of York's Theater. She and her husband then went on an extended tour of Australia. While there, Ada filed for divorce due to her husband's cruelty. The situation became so acrimonious that, on their return to England, Ada had to appeal to the ship's captain for protection. Their divorce was finalized in April 1900.

In November 1899, Ada had the lead in the musical, "Floradora," a hit first in England and later in America. For the next decade, Ada alternated between musical comedy and music hall entertainment.

Ada Reeve

Ada married Wilfred Cotton, an actor and manager, in 1902. For the next several years, she appeared in shows produced by her husband. They also toured South Africa in 1906 and 1909.

Ada returned to the United States for the 1911 season with a tour across country on the Keith circuit. The success of the tour persuaded Keith to have Ada return in 1912 for another six months. She did not return to the United States for 13 years.

When Ada played at the Palace Theater, New York, in 1925, popular theater had gone through many changes. Vaudeville was still popular but was now in stiff competition with motion pictures. In fact, many of the high-class vaudeville theaters featured the two media together. Rough Irish and ragtime songs had given way to romantic, melodic ballads. Musical comedy had become quite sophisticated with the introduction of skilled writers and composers. Even the Palace itself was faced with nearby opulent theaters competing with star programs at cheaper prices.

The Palace now featured drama sketches and big bands along with the familiar favorites. Appearing along with Ada were Joe Laurie, a comedian, Marie Dressler, Ina Claire and Fay Bainter, a dramatic actress. This bill followed an oldtimer's week that featured Cissie Loftus, Marie Cahill and May Irwin, vaudeville stalwarts.

Ada made her last appearance in the United States at the Palace again, in January 1928. Her act consisted of a cockney mother talking to her child. Reviewers commented favorably on her acting and singing. But then Ada Reeve disappeared from the minds of American audiences along with the other British stars of the era.

After close to 80 years in theater, Ada retired in 1954. With little money to sustain her, she lived in a modest residential hotel supported by the actors' union. She died on September 25, 1966, at the age of 92. Her obituary in *Variety* consisted of 60 words. Her triumphs in the United States were not mentioned.

Emma Carus

Born in Berlin, Germany, on March 18, 1879, Emma Carus immigrated with her parents to America in 1883. Her father, Carl Carus, was a theatrical agent and her mother, Henrietta Rolland, a noted opera singer, yet they found it hard to earn a living. Emma's mother died after the family settled in New York. A few years later, her father became disabled. Emma lived with relatives during her childhood. With a good singing voice, Emma performed publicly for the first time at the age of six but failed to gain any attention.

At the age of 11, Emma was working at a boardinghouse and caring for two children at the salary of one dollar a week. She often sang the children German lullabies. A music publisher heard her singing and recommended she perform at one of the many dime museums that had opened in the city. A dime museum was usually a converted factory that featured several floors of freaks, oddities and abnormalities of nature. In the basement was a bar and stage with an all-male audience. Performers would appear 20 times a day for $3 a week. At the age of 12, Emma established herself as a singer with the ability to render songs in several languages.

With a strong singing voice, a mature stage presence and a frugal lifestyle, Emma was able to improve her career each year until in 1894, at 15, she made her debut on the vaudeville stage. To do so, Emma had to pursue her own engagements, writing managers to persuade them to book her for a week at their theaters. She gained experience by dealing with managers and agents, and she successfully enhanced her own career. By the time she was 20, Emma was appearing on high-class vaudeville circuits at $1,000 a week and was being singled out as one of the rising vaudeville stars.

In 1900, Emma made a brief appearance in a burlesque, "Nell Go Inn" (a satire of "Nell Gwynn"), at the New York Theater. It was her initial performance in musical comedy, which unfortunately lasted only a few weeks. However, her singing talent gained her a place with the theater's stock company. When acting work in musical comedies was not available, Emma was confident she could easily find work in vaudeville.

"The Giddy Throng" followed two months later. It was called a burlesque with dialogue that included ballet, comedy acts and musical sketches. May Yohe led the cast but was panned by critics for her limited vocal range. Emma, in contrast, was noted for her classical renditions of several popular songs. Emma and newcomer Pat Rooney made up for Yohe's deficiencies, and the show lasted for 164 performances, the fourth longest run of the 1900–01 musical season.

During this time, Emma experienced her first marriage skirmish. Sture Mattson, a Yale graduate, son of the former Minnesota governor and heir to the Swedish royalty, fell in love with Emma. He pursued her with ardor and persuaded her to marry him. Emma, who had already gained a reputation for thrift, now had a husband who spent all his money extolling the virtues of his wife. He often invited large groups of people to see Emma perform at his expense. Mattson seemed too busy spending money to earn it. "No one was ever more devoted to a woman," Emma explained, "but his love for me never drove him to work." Emma divorced Mattson after a few months of marriage. Reviewers debated whether she had made the right decision.

During the next few years, Emma was a member of the New York Theater stock company. She appeared in "The King's Carnival" and "The Defender." "The King's Carnival" was another burlesque revue that united Emma with Marie Dressler, Amelia Summerville and Adele Ritchie. With no plot, the play satirized current popular productions, with some degree of success. In "The Defender," Emma had a good singing role, but Blanche Ring stole the show with her interpolation of "In the Good Old Summer Time."

Emma Carus

Competition for starring roles became no easier for Emma. In "The Wild Rose" she had to compete with Marie Cahill. None of the songs Emma sang in the show reached hit status, although she received good reviews. After appearing in two mediocre musicals, "The Medal and the Maid" (1904) and "Woodland" (1904), Emma returned to the security of the vaudeville stage. Due to her ability to sing in five languages, she billed herself as "The Human Dialect Cocktail." She would often astound audiences by switching from contralto to a deep baritone in the middle of her songs. Amy Leslie, the Chicago theater critic, believed Emma to be the only vaudeville singer with "a cultured and genuine voice."

In 1905, Emma married Harry James Everall, said to be a New York businessman. Like her first husband, he appeared to have trouble finding a job, so she established him as a talent agent. After several separations, they were divorced seven years later.

Emma was at the height of her career when she was tapped for a leading role in a new Ziegfeld production in 1907. The summer show evolved into the first Follies, which featured Emma, Grace La Rue, Helen Broderick and, near the end of the run, Nora Bayes. Other than the fact that she appeared in the first Follies, Emma had little to show for it. Bayes took all the best songs and Ziegfeld made sure audiences had close-up views of the chorus in revealing costumes by marching them into the aisles.

Back to vaudeville went Emma for three seasons, playing to full houses on the Keith circuit at $2,000 a week. Unlike other performers, Emma preferred the stability of working with the Syndicate to operating independently. In fact, she ardently supported Keith when the actors' union attempted to battle the Syndicate. Her position did not seem to offend either her colleagues or audiences.

On July 18, 1910, Emma and Eddie Foy opened in a musical comedy, "Up and Down Broadway," at the Casino Theater. With little plot, the play centered on Foy's jokes and Emma's singing, all of which were favorably received by audiences for more than seven months. Lew Fields persuaded Emma to appear in his summer show, "The Wife Hunters," in 1911. However, he had little time to redo a mediocre plot so he gave over its direction to Ned Wayburn, the show's stage manager. In out-of-town trials, the show appeared to be a success. When the show opened in New York, it suffered from a lack of comedy and the usual Fields novelties. Emma sang a coon song, "Mammy Jinny," which failed to enthuse the audience. A week after the show opened, Wayburn quit. The show lasted 36 performances. Luckily, Emma had vaudeville dates waiting for her.

During the latter part of 1910, Irving Berlin had developed the music for "Alexander" but put it aside without adding lyrics. He promised Emma that, if he could finish the song, she could introduce it in "Up and Down Broadway." However, "Alexander's Ragtime Band" was not published until March 1911. A month later, Emma introduced the song at the American Music Hall in Chicago. It was an immediate hit. Other singers used the song in their acts and it became a familiar tune in a matter of months. Emma continued to plug "Alexander" and it was interpolated in several subsequent plays.

Soon, so many singers were using the song that Emma decided to drop it. She replaced it with "Oh You Beautiful Doll," which was also favorably reviewed. It was only after several years of popular sheet music use and recordings that Emma got the recognition that went with the introduction of "Alexander," one of Berlin's most famous tunes. During the years 1911 to 1917, Emma was heard on many records, but none of the songs were hits. Ironically, Emma never recorded "Alexander."

Prior to World War I, Emma frequently appeared on suffrage bills, openly displaying her support for the movement. Most of these engagements were voluntary. The only movie depicting Emma was an informal affair, the Actor's Fund Day, in 1910, in which she was seen marching and playing baseball with other actors.

Still a headliner in vaudeville during the early 1920s, Emma continued to play the circuits with her good-natured, cheery songs. A 1923 review of Emma's appearance at Keith's Theater described her continuing appeal. "Long an outstanding hit in vaudeville, Miss Carus relied on her usual peppy hits to bring the audience round to her way of thinking." Accompanying her at the piano was J. Walter Leopold. They were soon married, and Leopold remained her pianist until Emma retired from the stage.

In March 1926, while playing in Chicago, Emma was observed to be acting peculiarly.

Her husband took her to Mt. Vernon, New York, to recuperate. She was later moved to a sanitarium in Connecticut, the nature of her illness unknown. Rumors suggested that she was suffering from a mental disease. A friend of Emma's was appointed guardian after she had been declared incompetent in both New York and California courts. Late in 1926, Emma was rushed to Los Angeles by her husband and placed in a sanitarium. The guardian sued, and several court proceedings were unable to resolve the situation.

Emma suffered a severe stroke and died on November 18, 1927. She was 48 years old. Funeral services were held in Venice, California, with burial at Forest Lawn cemetery. Only a few people attended. It was claimed that Emma had left an estate of $200,000 consisting of diamonds and real estate. As Emma had no other family, the estate was finally divided between the guardian and her husband.

Emma had died so suddenly and quietly that no one in the theater business had known of her death. Some time later, an oldtimers week at the Palace Theater honored Emma. Otherwise, the former vaudeville headliner died in obscurity.

Blanche Ring

Blanche Ring possessed a unique, gracious way of delivering a song and getting her audiences to sing along with her. During her vaudeville career, she made several songs famous; her trademark songs remain familiar today. She was an excellent mimic, interpolating both working class people and stage celebrities. Blanche introduced "In the Good Old Summertime" to theatergoers in the early 1900s, and audiences entreated her to include the tune in each performance.

Blanche Ring was born on April 24, 1871, in Boston, Massachusetts, the first of six children. There has been some question about her birth date. Early in her career, she claimed it was 1877, but in the eleventh edition of "Who's Who In the Theater," Blanche said her birth date was 1871. Her father, James F. Ring, was born in 1848 in Boston. He began his career as an actor, but later became an advertising agent. Blanche's mother, Wilhelmina Ross, was born in 1849 in Scotland. James and Wilhelmina were married in Boston in 1870.

Acting was an important legacy for the Ring family. Blanche's great-great-grandfather, Charles Fisher, came to America from England, and took his theatrical caravan on tours as far west as the Mississippi River. Blanche was exposed to the acting profession as a child and, although a girl, was expected to continue the theater lineage. Her training was in drama, but she enjoyed singing popular songs and impersonating celebrities, although this was frowned upon by her father.

At 19, Blanche made her stage debut performing a small part with Richard Mansfield's company in "A Parisian Romance." For the next several years, she appeared in a variety of dramas and melodramas with such well-known actors as Nat C. Goodwin and Chauncey Olcott. In 1895, at the age of 24, Blanche appeared on the vaudeville stage for the first time as a soubrette.

For almost seven years, she played in various traveling companies, learning the business of vaudeville and developing her own acting style. While she performed well on the vaudeville stage, she had a habit of frequently breaking character, engaging in side-talk with the audience and inserting in-jokes. Admonitions by managers did little to change her stage work and she developed a reputation for unwarranted interpolations. The issue would not be resolved until she later appeared in a Lew Fields production.

The 1902–03 theater season opened on July 3 with "The Defender" at the Herald Square Theater. Blanche was a last-minute addition to the cast with only a few lines of dialogue and one song to sing. Although the song, "In the Good Old Summertime" had already been sung on the vaudeville stage, Blanche introduced it in the show and it became an immediate hit, as did Blanche herself. The show had a short life, but it began a run of 15 consecutive productions for Blanche over a span of 12 years. In between these shows, Blanche appeared in vaudeville, often featuring the latest songs she highlighted in the musicals. Because of her versatility and vitality and a repertoire of hit songs, managers often called on Blanche to help rescue a faltering show.

The same season, Blanche played a small role in "Tommy Rot" but sang the show's best song, "The Belle of Avenue A." Her work was well-reviewed. However, the show had a poor plot and a weak cast. It closed quickly, was rewritten, renamed, reopened, but died anyway.

Blanche Ring

Several months later, Blanche had a role in "The Jewel of Asia," which opened February 16, 1903, at the Criterion Theater, New York. While she was given the lead, Blanche did not yet top the name of the show on the marquee. She had no show-stopping song but her dramatic abilities kept the show alive for two months. Another musical was already being prepared for her.

On June 8, 1903, Blanche opened with "The Blonde in Black" at the Knickerbocker Theater. The story had originally revolved around Charles Dana Gibson and the Gibson Girls, but legal action against the production changed the direction of the show. Blanche wore a black wig and had the role of a vaudeville performer who wished to become a great actress. Again, she had no hit song to interpolate but gave an impersonation of "Camille" that amused audiences for 30 performances. (A year later, Eva Tanguay toured the show, under the name of "The Sambo Girl," to greater success.)

Three months later, the musical "The Jersey Lilly" opened at the Victoria Theater, with Blanche's name now above the title of the show on the marquee. The show's plot and songs were no better than Blanche's previous productions, with the exception of "Bedelia" which Blanche interpolated. The song added another to her growing list of hits and sold more than three million copies of sheet music. The show itself lasted for three weeks.

During this time, that Blanche was converting these hit songs into records. With the combination of record and sheet music sales, Blanche's income was substantially enhanced. She continued this activity with each new song she introduced that became a popular hit.

Blanche returned to the vaudeville circuit for six months singing her hit songs and mimicking some well-known celebrities, delighting audiences and filling theaters. Blanche's appearances on Broadway had become so numerous—five shows in a little more than a year—that reviewers had little time or inclination to critique each performance.

A successful English import, "Sergeant Brue," opened April 24, 1905, at the Knickerbocker Theater, featuring Blanche in the leading role. The show lasted several months, highlighted by Blanche's rendition of "My Irish Molly O" delivered with a slight Irish accent. Given the opportunity to interpolate the song any way she wanted, Blanche added impersonations and changed lyrics repeatedly. She stopped the show every night.

Out of the three shows in 1906, only one lasted long enough to make a profit. In March, Blanche starred in "His Majesty" at the Majestic Theater. The story was about members of an opera company who were killed in a railroad disaster and went to Hell. Blanche had no outstanding song to sing and the show disappeared in three weeks. "His Honor the Mayor" opened two months later and lasted close to three months with Blanche interpolating "My Irish Molly O" again to good effect. Although the plot was nonexistent and the acting weak, reviewers called Blanche "indefatigable." Ironically, the hit song of the show, which Blanche did not sing, was "Waltz Me Around Again Willie."

Lew Fields produced his second big musical, "About Town," which opened at the Herald Square Theater on August 30, 1906. The cast was made up of the usual Fields headliners, including Edna Wallace Hopper, Louise Dresser, Jack Norworth, Vernon Castle and Fields himself. The production was a glorified vaudeville bill, each star doing his own specialty. When attendance began to decline, Fields added a long satirical skit, "The Great Decide" (from the hit stage play, "The Great Divide"). He hired Blanche and Peter Dailey to perform in the skit. Another feature of the show was the Gibson Girls, a chorus line that, in one scene, began to rip off their clothing, a very risqué act for a Fields show. Blanche sang no songs, but her vaudeville experience helped the satire score well with audiences. The show ran for 138 performances and then went on tour.

Fields was very much against any performer interpolating, believing that no one had the right to interfere with the flow of the show. When Blanche did it, they argued. She left the show temporarily, but returned and apologized. She never interpolated a song in a musical again.

In late 1908, Blanche played in the revue, "The Great White Way," at the famous but now run-down Casino Theater. Co-starring with the venerable Jefferson De Angelis, Blanche appeared in several comic skits, some of them satires on legitimate shows. Again, the production was made up of a series of vaudeville turns, utilizing Blanche's talents. The revue ran till the end of the year. No sooner did it close than Blanche was recruited by Joe Weber for the "Merry Widow Burlesque" (1908). Lulu Glaser had been the lead but when she retired from the cast, Blanche took over. Her new song, "Yip-I-Addy-I-Ay" became the hit of the show and another addition to her record and music sheet repertoire. The show ran for six months.

Fields hired Blanche for one of his summer shows, "The Midnight Sons" (1909). The show was so successful it ran to 1910. Contributing greatly to the show's success was Blanche's new song "I've Got Rings on My Fingers (And Bells on My Toes)." The song was taken up by other singers, sold millions of music sheets and added another hit to Blanche's series of top tunes. Fields was so pleased with Blanche's performance that he starred her in the show, "The Yankee Girl" (1910). She sang several songs, of which three became profitable to the music publishers: a reintroduction of "I've Got Rings on My Fingers"; "Mrs. Malone"; and "The Glory of the Yankee Navy." The show played for 12 weeks in New York and went on an extended tour.

Another song Blanche introduced, primarily through a record and sheet music, was "Come, Josephine in My Flying Machine." Her rendition made the song famous; it was one of the earliest airplane songs.

Fields had prepared another show for Blanche but money problems forced him to sell the rights. "The Wall Street Girl" opened April 15, 1912, at the Cohan Theater. The cast included Charles Winninger, Blanche's future husband, and Will Rogers, swinging his rope on stage for the first time. Blanche sang another soon-to-be-popular song, "I Want a Regular Man," but the show only lasted seven weeks.

Blanche had tired of the rigors of working with a tight script and repetitive performances. In one of her last musical shows, "When Claudia Smiles" (1914) at the 39th Street Theater, she played a young woman who divorces her husband to build a career as an actress. Real life? a reviewer mused. Along with a few minor songs, Blanche sang several of her former hits to appreciative audiences. The show ran for seven weeks and then went on tour.

The reviewer's comment about the play mirroring life could well have referred to Blanche's marriage adventures. Back in 1897, she had married William McNichols. A son, Gorden Eliot, was born in 1899 from this union. A divorce followed shortly after. Her second husband, James Walker, Jr., a Boston railroad man, lasted until 1906. In 1910 Blanche married Frederick Edward McKay, her theatrical agent during the glory days of the Fields-produced shows. Her co-star in "The Wall Street Girl," Charles Winninger, became her fourth husband in 1912. He was eight years younger than Blanche. They separated in the 1920s but did not officially divorce until 1951. However, Blanche was never at a loss for admirers.

During the war, Blanche continued in vaudeville and also entertained at military camps. In 1921, she appeared in a revue, "The Broadway Whirl," The cast was made up of oldtimers and new performers, singing and dancing familiar and new pieces. Charles Winninger headed the cast and Blanche sang several of her old hits to a nostalgic audience. The show lasted through the summer.

The year 1921 was also when the euphoria of winning the war had dissipated and a general economic recession took its place. Theater attendance declined; fewer shows were produced; and many high-priced performers, including Blanche, found engagements difficult to arrange. It would be three years before Broadway would find new directions with a growing talent base of new composers and scriptwriters. Vaudeville, on the other hand, was already approaching its death throes.

In 1921, Blanche was included on an oldtimers bill at the Palace Theater and was the hit of the show with a reprise of her familiar hits. Her last musical, "Right This Way," played in January 1938. She had a small part and sang "I've Got Rings on My Fingers." Earlier in the 1930s, Blanche played in two serious dramas, "Cradle Snatchers" and "The Great Necker," neither of which were auspicious productions.

Blanche appeared in several movies, both silent and sound. In 1915, she reprised her role in "The Yankee Girl." In 1926, she played a small role in "It's the Old Army Game." Then, between 1940 and 1945, when she was in her late 60s and early 70s, she played dowager roles in four movies: "If I Had My Way" (1940), "Babes on Broadway" (1942), "The Man from Down Under" (1943) and "Having Wonderful Crime" (1945). Reviewers rarely mentioned her; and when they did, they only mentioned her early hit songs. Blanche retired and moved to Hollywood to share a home with her brother.

During the last few years of her life, after suffering a stroke, Blanche lived in a nursing home. She died January 13, 1961, in Hollywood. She was 89 years old. Private funeral and burial services followed. Newspaper obituaries were few; apparently, even the theatrical world had forgotten about Blanche.

A note on a 1920 Victor record catalog summarized Blanche's contribution to the vaudeville stage: "Whether she sings or dances, she is charming and no woman on the stage today can sing a humorous song better than this artist."

Grace La Rue

Actress and vocalist Grace La Rue was a major vaudeville and musical comedy star during the first two decades of the twentieth century. She was equally known for her prima donna exploits on the stage and in her private life.

Stella Parsons was born on April 23, 1880, in Kansas City, Missouri. As a child, she was given voice lessons and sang in church and at social events. Stella began her public career when she was 11 years old singing "The Palms" at the Grand Avenue Church in Kansas City. She made her theatrical debut a year later as a page in Julia Marlowe's traveling company of "As You Like It." Her initial traveling engagement came in 1893, when she was 13, with the Milton Nobles Stock Company, playing boy parts in various melodramas. After only two weeks, she was so homesick that she was promptly sent home to her mother.

Shortly afterward, Stella was sent to a convent and seriously began the study of music. After ten months, she abandoned convent life for the theater.

At the age of 15, Stella debuted in vaudeville, singing the latest ballads with an exceptional soprano voice. She formed a partnership with an actor, a gentleman named Burke, that lasted for more than five years. Stella assumed the name of Grace La Rue for theatrical purposes. A year later, at 16, she married Burke. The duo played in small-time vaudeville houses in the Midwest and East for salaries anywhere from $25 to $50 a week when they could get work. Around 1902, Grace and her husband divorced and she went on alone to further her vaudeville career. By this time, she had been identified as an excellent interpreter of current songs.

But Grace's career seemed stalled in small-time vaudeville. She was just another of many soubrettes on bills featuring dog acts, jugglers, acrobats and comedians. She decided to go to New York, hopefully to improve her chances

Grace La Rue

of "being discovered." During these formative years, Grace had matured as an actress, impersonator and dancer as well as a singer.

In September 1906, at the age of 26, Grace was signed to appear in "The Tourist," playing a snapshot journalist, a role interpolated for the purpose of working in her specialties. She was earning $250 a week. Now recognized by reviewers as a fresh act, she was hired to play in an imported London hit, "The Blue Moon," which opened at the Casino Theater on November 3. The show starred comedian James T. Powers, whose self-importance on and off the stage was legendary. Grace wanted to use the role to feature her special talents. She immediately came into conflict with Powers, who did not allow anybody to upstage him. Grace led the pony ballet and demonstrated her acrobatic prowess. Powers was incensed by her actions. She wanted to add other stunts when she sang. Powers cut out that part of her act, refusing to yield the stage to Grace. She could only repeat a verse of her song. Throughout the show's run, Grace was unable to expand her role. But she learned how to express her independence, particularly as it pertained to actors and managers.

Grace's ongoing row with Powers did not deter Flo Ziegfeld, who was planning the first of his Follies revues. He signed Grace as one of the leads of the show, sharing the stage with star Nora Bayes and the Anna Held Girls. "The Follies of 1907" opened on July 8 on the New York Theater Roof. Reviewers were clearly impressed with the production and lauded Ziegfeld's special touches—beautiful costumes, jewelry, flowers and silk stockings for all the women. Grace sang two songs and was well-received. When Bayes quit the show midway through its run, Grace was given the opportunity to display her talent. Ziegfeld had her back for his 1908 edition.

"The Follies of 1908" opened at the Jardin de Paris on June 15. It again featured Nora Bayes with her husband, Jack Norworth. The song hit of the show, written by the couple, "Shine On Harvest Moon," was an interpolation, overshadowing the score composed by Maurice Levi. While Grace was on the program as a featured singer, her songs left no lasting impressions. The show ran for only 120 performances but Grace let the theater world know that she was on her way to becoming a legend.

Byron D. Chandler had been called the "Million Dollar Kid" because of his financial exploits. Having inherited more than a million dollars, he raced cars, bankrolled numerous businesses and played the ladies' man. In 1902, he married Grace Estelle Stecher. He was sued for $100,000 by an actress for breach of promise and another $30,000 for alienating the affections of another woman. All of this was enthusiastically covered by the press. Grace met him in the fall of 1908. At the time, Chandler was negotiating a divorce.

During the summer, Grace and Chandler traveled together to Europe. When they returned to the United States, rumors spread that they had been secretly married, which the parties did not deny. In early 1909, Chandler was served with divorce papers from his current wife, charging Grace as a co-respondent. A few months later, the final divorce degree was issued. Following the divorce, Grace and Chandler were married in Vermont in late 1909. The press covered the entire episode in lurid style. The publicity made Grace all the more desirable as a headliner.

In 1909, Grace appeared with Sam Bernard in "Nearly a Hero" as part of the touring cast. She sang the songs that Ethel Levey had rendered in the New York company, to good result. The next year, she starred in the musical "Molly May," which opened April 8 at the Hackett Theater. She played the queen of artists' models, but the plot was so mundane that the show closed after 27 performances.

Grace quickly followed with another starring appearance in "Madam Troubadour," which at least ran for ten weeks. The show opened on October 10, 1910, at the Lyric Theater. The plot was a story about a scholar's wife who believes her husband embraces medieval poetry more than her. She decides to flirt with another man to gain her husband's attention. Grace sang no songs but displayed an acting ability that reviewers recognized.

The following year, Grace appeared in what seemed to be her best musical role, in "Betsy." However, while the critics enjoyed the show, ticket sales were anemic. "Betsy" lasted only four weeks. Grace had shown fine acting talent in a complex role, maybe too complex for audiences to understand. Her last two shows failures, Grace returned to vaudeville.

For the next three years, Grace took her act to England. In 1912, she played the vaudeville houses. In 1913, she appeared in a skit, "The Record Breakers," ending up at London's Palace Theater. She captured the audience with a fine display of singing and acting, particularly her introduction to English audiences of the song "You Made Me Love You," Al Jolson's hit of six months previous. Grace followed this success with an appearance in a musical comedy, "The Girl Who Didn't" at the Lyric Theater. She also recorded some songs at London's Gramophone Company. Of course, Chandler accompanied Grace wherever she appeared. They returned to the United States in 1914 to an even greater demand for her services. At the same time, rumors of differences between Grace and her husband were being circulated. When Chandler posted a notice in *The New York Times* that he was withdrawing his wife's authority to pledge his credit, their marital days seemed numbered.

Grace then filed for divorce and demanded $50 a week in alimony until the decree was finalized. The suit dragged on until March 25, 1919. In the meantime, Grace had a future husband standing by.

From 1914 to 1917, Grace was a vaudeville headliner whose successes were recorded by reviewers in every city she played. In August 1914, she made her only appearance at the Palace Theater; her "sweet voice and huge red cartwheel hat" caused audiences to shout for encores. In 1917, Raymond Hitchcock hired Grace to appear in "Hitchy-Koo," his new revue. Starring with Hitchcock were comedian Leon Errol and Irene Bordoni. Grace sang the hit song of the show, "I May Be Gone for a Long, Long Time," but did little else. The show ran for seven months.

Grace again returned to the friendly ways of vaudeville audiences and spent the next four years touring the country. While in St. Paul, Minnesota, she became acquainted with Hale Hamilton, an actor. The two became enamored with one another and Hamilton visited Grace when they happened to be playing nearby. The press took the news and mentioned it in their gossip columns. Hamilton's wife filed a suit against her husband and Grace for stealing his affection. Grace quickly closed out her own divorce from Chandler. The suit against Hamilton revealed that he and Grace were meeting at hotels and that she was sending telegrams to his home threatening to visit and "make a scene." In the summer of 1920, Hamilton was divorced. He and Grace were married soon afterward.

That same year, Hamilton and Grace starred in a movie, "That's Good," which had mediocre success, probably because Grace went under the assumed name of Stella Gray. The reasons for this deception were never revealed. She and Hamilton partnered to perform skits on the vaudeville circuit for the next several years. By 1922, Grace thought of retiring, having been on the stage for more than a quarter of a century. Irving Berlin and Sam Harris changed her mind.

The "Music Box Revue 1922–23" opened on October 23, 1922, at the Music Box Theater. A typical revue, the show was filled with individual acts and lavishly outfitted scenes.

The production starred the new comedy team of MacCullough and Clark, Charlotte Greenwood, tenor John Steel, and Grace. In one scene, called "Diamond Horseshoe," the train of Grace's costume enlarged and covered the stage as she sang "Crinoline Days." An elevator lifted her at the same time her skirt enlarged to fill the stage. Reviewers considered the special effects "superb." By the time the show ended, Grace was in demand again.

Grace and Hamilton toured again for several years, culminating in a successful trip to England in 1924 where they played in a humorous skit, "Dangerous Advice." When they returned to the United States, Grace decided to retire.

Grace returned to acting periodically. In 1928, she appeared in "The Greenwich Village Follies," co-starred with Blossom Seeley and Benny Fields, Bobby Watson and Dr. Rockwell. Grace won applause for the ballad "Every Little Heart That's Lonely" and reviewers remarked how well her voice had held up. The show ran for 155 performances. To do a favor for old friend Mae West, Grace played a cameo role in the 1933 movie, "She Done Him Wrong."

In 1936, Grace was chosen to chair the Republican Women's Club of Santa Monica. Her husband's brother was chairman of the Republican National Committee at the time. In 1940, she made a cameo appearance in a Bing Crosby movie, "If I Had My Way."

When Hamilton died of a cerebral hemorrhage in 1942, Grace moved to Burlingame, California. She died quietly on March 3, 1956, at the age of 75.

Like many contemporaries from the glory days of vaudeville, Grace passed away in obscurity. Her fine singing and acting were almost completely forgotten and her personal affairs of interest only to theater historians.

Yvette Guilbert

She was a masterful singer of impressionistic sketches. Her magnetic stage personality illuminated songs of the common people, their joys and despairs. Yvette Guilbert was France's *star diseuse* (interpretive talker and singer) during the 1890s and early 1900s. Her visits to the United States displayed her vaudeville talents to eager audiences, who were carried away by her expressiveness, vitality and humility although they did not understand the French language. When she changed her career goals to include medieval material, audiences lost interest and her renown gradually declined.

Emma Laure Esther Guilbert was born in Paris to a shopkeeper family attempting to recover from the disasters brought on by the Franco-Prussian War. A shopgirl in Paris, she was discovered by a journalist who persuaded her to go on the stage. Emma quickly found that she was not a good actress but, rather, an expressive and audience-pleasing singer. By the time she was 20 years old, she had become a Parisian headliner. During this time, she changed her first name to enhance her French stage identity. Several tours to Vienna and London solidified her reputation as an interpretive singer, rendering the songs of the humble people of her country. In 1895, Oscar Hammerstein signed Yvette to appear in New York at his Victoria Theater.

On December 16, 1895, Yvette opened her first U.S. appearance at the Victoria Theater. As usual, Hammerstein advertised her coming with grandiose exclamations about her talent and triumphs. Audiences flocked to see the French star perform. She sang seven songs, six in French, and when she left the stage the audience was in an uproar. People in the boxes shouted, "Bravo, Yvette!" Those in the orchestra chanted, "Vive, Guilbert." After seven curtain calls, she received a bouquet of American Beauty roses. Hammerstein had paid Yvette $4,000 a week for a four-week engagement. She played at other New York theaters for another six weeks. By that time, she was the belle of the city, with hostesses fighting to have her at their parties.

The following year, Yvette returned to New York for an engagement at Koster & Bial's Theater, beginning December 14. Her English had improved and she included more American songs in her repertoire. Again, she stayed for several months, playing at various New York theaters. Reporters suggested that theater managers had gotten together to plan her appearances so all of them would reap the benefits of her appeal.

Besides making a resounding hit with reviewers and audiences alike, Yvette met Dr. Max Schiller, a theatrical manager. They married a year later. They remained together until her death.

Although managers frequently tried to persuade Yvette to return to the United States, her next trip took place in 1906. *The New York Times* lauded the immense talent she was bringing to the vaudeville stage: "It is not every 'chanteuse' who returns in ten years with more art and more finesse and in a finer style of performance as she does now."

But Yvette had made some changes in her singing style. She now included songs dating back to the seventeenth and eighteenth centuries and wore appropriate costumes of the period in her presentation. She had begun exploring the collection of old French songs and dropped some of the "songs of the cafe." Reviewers found her selections and renditions "more gracious, more charming and more pleasurable." They wrote about how she conveyed the sentiment of the verses, her variety of gesture, her perfected enunciation and dramatic power.

Yvette toured the country with the English singer Albert Chevalier, under the management of Liebler and Co. At the end of the run, she announced that she was going to abandon vaudeville entertainment for legitimate theater productions. In France, she pursued her goals.

When, in 1909, Yvette returned to appear at the Belasco Theater, she filled the program with old English and French songs. The audiences were polite and appreciative, but not enthusiastic. When she played at the Colonial Theater, members of the audience were noisy and disorderly, almost forcing her to leave the stage. The fact that Yvette was trying to present a serious program seemed too much for the audience. The *Times* reviewer stated that "it has been a long time since such an exhibition of bad taste and ill-breeding has been seen in a New York theater." Unfortunately, Yvette had several similar experiences and she cut the tour short. She had much to say about the bad manners of American audiences.

Yvette came to New York in 1915 to get away from the war. She was engaged for a series of recitals at the Lyceum Theater and then a tour of the country. She performed at dramatic theaters only and her program consisted of medieval songs. Audiences who wished to see her were enthralled by her interpretations. Upon returning to New York, she rented a residence outside the city. She remained in New York until 1922.

During the period from 1916 to 1922, Yvette gave recitals, appeared at private parties and benefits, and participated in old "miracle plays," continuing to promote her interest in medieval composers and writers. She also opened up a voice studio, specializing in medieval studies. Her students frequently performed at recitals at various New York theaters. On February 16, 1922, Yvette gave her last recital at the Town Hall. On the program were French religious pieces, folk songs and poems from the Middle Ages.

When, in 1924, Yvette returned briefly to stage performance, she was singing her old repertoire of vaudeville songs. Audiences welcomed her back with enthusiasm. After an extended engagement at the Empire Theater, Paris, she planned to return to the United States to appear at the Palace Theater. But Yvette was not happy with the situation. A severe illness cancelled the trip. She never played in the United States again, nor did she continue the vaudeville act.

In 1938, Yvette celebrated her seventy-fifth birthday. French theater impresarios gave her a party that spread nationwide. She was no longer performing but continued to teach about the history of French "chanson." France made her a chevalier of the Legion of Honor.

On February 3, 1944, after several years of failing health, Yvette died at her home in Southern France. She was 79 years old. A special memorial service was held and a day of mourning was proclaimed throughout France.

After a ten-year vaudeville career in America as a headliner, Yvette gave her

Yvette Guilbert (Museum of the City of New York).

life to the study and recitation of medieval plays and songs. "I followed a path of noisy glory. It frightened me and I left it. I now have the privilege of choosing my applause."

Nora Bayes

> Has anybody here seen Kelly?
> K-E-Double-L-Y?
> Has anybody here seen Kelly?
> Have you seen him passing by?
> Sure his hair is red, his eyes are blue,
> And he's Irish through and through.
> Has anybody here seen Kelly?
> Kelly with the green necktie?

Nora Bayes made "Kelly" a nationwide hit with a delivery that awed audiences and then converted them into enthusiastic patrons cheering her name. She had a stage charm that was natural and unspoiled. She had a joyous and breezy way of communicating with her audiences. Nora had as much fun singing as the audience did in hearing her. That was the secret of her stage success.

Leonora Goldberg was born October 3, 1880, in Joliet, Illinois. Both her father, Elias, and mother, Rachael (nee Miller), were born in Germany and immigrated to the United

States during the early 1870s. Leonora's parents were devout Orthodox Jews who regarded the theater as evil and acting as mortal sin. As a young teenager, Leonora was allowed to take singing lessons, but she had to convince her parents that her interest in singing was for religious purposes only. Although her teachers encouraged her to study opera, Leonora sought out amateur nights at the neighborhood vaudeville house without her parents' knowledge. Nora recalled that, at age 13, "I had a phenomenal contralto voice."

In 1897, at 17, Leonora ran away to Chicago to seek her career in vaudeville. A quick marriage to Otto Gressing, a barber and stage door Johnny, served to free her from her parents' influence. Small roles in vaudeville choruses followed. Probably her first solo performance was as a singer at the Chicago Opera House. The theater presented melodramas with vaudeville routines between the acts. Leonora was reported to have earned $25 a week for her efforts. The following year she spent as a soubrette with the Fisher Stock Company in San Francisco. It was during this time that she changed her name to Nora Bayes. She had also obtained a divorce from Gressing.

Nora made her Broadway debut in 1901, at 21, in the musical farce, "The Rogers Brothers in Washington," a Keith/Albee production that attempted to copy the success of Weber and Fields. Nora sang two songs in the show but received little attention for her work. While the show toured, however, she received increasing attention from reviewers for her natural, down-to-earth song delivery. Audiences loved to sing with her.

Nora spent the next several years on various vaudeville bills as a soubrette. Her reviewers wrote increasingly about her infectious singing. In 1902, she gained attention with a comic drinking song, "Down Where the Wurzburger Flows." Her popularity as a singer had progressed so quickly that her name was listed on the music sheet cover for "Meet Me in St. Louis, Louis," which she sang at every stage opportunity. Nora now had no problem getting booked on vaudeville programs with several tours on the Keith circuit.

Between 1904 and 1907, Nora visited various cities in Europe appearing on their popular theater bills. She was especially successful in England, touring all the large cities to favorable reviews and crowded houses. Trips to the Continent were not as satisfactory. While audiences enjoyed her stage presence, they had trouble understanding the meaning of her lyrics, possibly because she sang songs with an Irish accent. Nevertheless, Nora made sufficient salary to live comfortably during her extended stay.

Upon her return to the United States, Nora was signed to appear in Flo Ziegfeld's first edition, "The Follies of 1907." She achieved only moderate success in the show. While other singers in the cast belted

Nora Bayes

out coon songs, Nora presented light-hearted sentimental ballads that seemed to get lost in the show's action. She played the role of a soubrette, a flighty girl named Topsy.

In the meantime, she met Jack Norworth, a handsome song-and-dance man, and composer of popular songs like "Shine On Harvest Moon" and "Take Me Out to the Ball Game." They fell in love and teamed to appear in "The Follies of 1908." The show opened on June 15, 1908, to popular acclaim. When the couple introduced "Shine On Harvest Moon," Nora was recognized as a coming headliner. Nora and Jack were married shortly afterward.

Nora and Jack were scheduled to appear in Ziegfeld's "Follies of 1909," and did actually play for the first several weeks. However, a contract dispute with Ziegfeld caused the couple to leave the show. They then played in vaudeville for more than a year, one of the few really successful male-female teams. Percy Williams hired them to appear at his Colonial Theater, New York, for $2,500 a week. He advertised the couple as "The Happiest Married Couple of the Stage," but the program billing said, "Nora Bayes, assisted and admired by Jack Norworth." It was an arrangement that Jack did not appreciate. How equal was the marriage, reviewers wondered?

Their popularity with "Shine On Harvest Moon" gave them an opportunity to make a recording of the song for the Victor Talking Machine Company. It was the first of Nora's many recording sessions, but the song was not issued because other well-known singers had already recorded it. However, three other songs were issued by Victor: "Come Along My Mandy"; "Rosa Rosetta"; and "Turn Off Your Light, Mr. Moon Man." The recording session also produced a single by Nora, "Has Anybody Here Seen Kelly?" which swept the country and made her a national singing star. It was a song that became associated with Nora throughout her career.

In 1910, Nora and Jack were signed by Lew Fields to appear in his summer show, "The Jolly Bachelors," in which "Kelly" made its first stage appearance. The show had been close to being written off, but Fields' selection of the couple saved the production, and it went on tour to good reviews and a profitable box office. Also appearing in the show were Vernon Castle, a dancer in his first comic talking role, and little Helen Hayes, appearing for the first time on any stage. The show was pronounced a success. However, the Bayes-Norworth marriage deteriorated so badly by the end of the tour the couple was not speaking to one another.

Nora and Jack appeared in "Little Miss Fix-It," which opened at the Globe Theater on April 3, 1911. Ironically, they appeared as a courting couple singing "Turn Off Your Light, Mr. Moon Man," which proved to be the highlight of the show. But this show also spelled the end of the couple's relationship.

Between 1910 and 1914, Nora made 17 records for Victor, all solo performances, serving to propel her stardom to even greater heights. From 1911 to 1915, Nora played in vaudeville. She and Norworth were divorced in February 1913. A few weeks after the divorce, Nora married Harry Clarke. Yet, when Nora went to London in the spring of 1914, Clarke did not accompany her. This time her act failed, as did her health. Nora went to Germany to recuperate. Upon her return to the United States, she began a 30-week vaudeville tour, opening at the Palace Theater, New York. She was billed as "The Greatest Single Woman Singing Comedienne in the World." Box office results at the Palace seemed to justify her billing. Her salary for the tour was $2,500 a week.

In 1915, Nora starred in an ill-fated revue, "Maid in America," with "all kinds of music rewritten by Sigmund Romberg" and "words by the actors and their friends." The production flopped, and three of the show's songs Nora cut for Columbia Records were never issued. The next three years were devoted to vaudeville, with successful tours of the country and 16 records, all issued by Victor, which included "Home Sick Blues," the first recording to include "blues" in the title; it was still a novel word to use in popular music. Another song that became identified with Nora was "I Work Eight Hours a Day, I Sleep Eight Hours a Day, That Leaves Eight Hours for Loving!" Reviewers took her to task for the double entendre lyrics but audiences cheered heartily whenever she sang the song.

Because she was having booking problems during 1917, Nora put together her own company and went on tour, limited to some extent by the war. Nora was on stage for most of the show, calling on her vast repertoire of songs. In spite of the war conditions, the tour was quite successful and profitable for Nora. In "The Cohan Revue of 1918," another of a series of revues quickly prepared by George M. Cohan to take advantage of the few number of shows being produced at the time, Nora performed a satire on the knitting vogue; everyone was knitting socks and sweaters for the troops. While she zealously knitted the sweater, her house was burgled and set on fire, which did not prevent her from finishing her task, to the delight of the audience. Several months earlier, Nora helped introduce and promote Cohan's new patriotic song, "Over There." She quickly made the song an integral part of her performances and became identified with it. She also recorded the song, and her picture was on the cover of the sheet music. Nora's salary had now reached headliner heights, $3,500 a week.

The year 1918 was a notable one for Nora. She had a Broadway theater renamed "The Nora Bayes Theater" honoring her contributions to popular entertainment. Her new musical play, "Ladies First," opened at the Broadhurst Theater and was then moved to her own venue. Shifting her alliance from Columbia to Victor, Nora recorded more than a dozen titles through 1923. Some of her big hits included "How Ya Gonna Keep 'em Down on the Farm," "Freckles," "Japanese Sandman," and "Make Believe."

Nora played mostly vaudeville dates during the post-war years, with a weekly salary between $3,500 and $5,000. In 1918, she divorced Harry Clarke. The following year she adopted a boy, Norman. In 1920, she married for the fourth time, this time to Arthur A. Gordoni. Two years later, she divorced him. But that did not prevent her from adopting two additional children, Leonora in 1923 and Peter in 1924. Often, when appearing on stage, she would tell stories about her children. Her fifth marriage, in March 1925, was to Benjamin L. Friedland, a New York financier and garage owner. Their marriage took place on the steamship *Leviathan* on their way to England.

Unfortunately, Nora's health began to deteriorate and it seemed to have some effect on her performance. She had always been a bit egocentric, easily excused because of her stage success, but she displayed increasing symptoms of willfulness directed at managers and other actresses. She had become so disagreeable that E.A. Albee refused to employ her on his vaudeville circuit. Rumors told of backstage conflicts and unfulfilled contracts.

In 1924, Nora went to London to appear at the Palladium at $3,000 a week. Also on stage was Cissie Loftus, a well-loved English entertainer, who happened to be performing an imitation of Nora. The two combined their acts with great success. When they repeated the routine at the Palace, they filled the theater each night. Some time later, again at the Palace, Nora balked at being billed behind Sophie Tucker at a National Vaudeville Artists benefit. This time Nora walked out and received bad press for her action.

Nora performed for Victor in November 1927, making her only electric recordings. The three titles she cut were never released, much to her dismay. In March 1928, Nora asked the manager of the Palace to put up a billboard in front of the theater featuring her picture and announcing her upcoming appearance. After some hesitation and discussion with Albee, the billboard was put up. Nora's salary for this appearance was $5,000. As she drove by the theater, she could enjoy seeing the billboard. A few days later, Nora Bayes was dead.

On March 28, 1928, at age 48, still at the top of her performing career, Nora died of cancer. She had been admitted to Brooklyn's Jewish Hospital some days earlier, her illness a closely guarded secret. She was buried in Woodlawn Cemetery, New York, in a private service. It was Nora's wish that no one view her remains. She wanted to be remembered as she was last seen in life. In spite of many years in which she earned more than $100,000, she left a small estate. High living and generosity toward various charities had claimed most of her earnings.

Nora had risen to fame with an extensive repertoire of songs, from semi-classic to comedy. Her imitations of other performers were flawless. Her direct and unaffected delivery captured the hearts of her audiences. This knack of dramatizing a song combined with a commanding stage presence made Nora a most appealing vaudeville performer for more than a quarter of a century.

Marion Bent

Although a talented and accomplished performer, Marion Bent played her entire vaudeville career in the shadow of her colorful partner, Pat Rooney, Jr. Together, they became one of the most beloved song-and-dance acts on the vaudeville stage. For close to 30 years they were among the most popular of teams.

Arthur Bent, Marion's father, was born in England in 1852. He was one of four brothers who excelled as cornet performers. The family came to the United States in 1872 and the brothers joined the Gilmore Band, one of the country's more familiar orchestra organizations. Alice Lawless, Marion's mother, was born in England in 1853. As a young woman, she was a premier danseuse in Adelina Patti's Opera Company. Arthur and Alice were married in 1877 in New York City. Alice retired from the stage. In 1878 they had a child, Arthur, who died in infancy. Marion was born on December 23, 1879, in New York.

Arthur Bent died of pneumonia in 1885. Alice and her daughter were forced to move from the comfort of a Bronx neighborhood to the tenements of Greenwich Village. A few years later, Alice married a man named Bowen. They had a

Marion Bent

child, William, in 1891. However, Bowen died in the late 1890s, forcing both Alice and Marion to work.

While Marion was raised in a musical environment, the family's trials interfered with any aspirations she may have had to enter the theater. She did learn to sing and dance, but earning a living occupied her time and effort. In her late teens, Marion showed interest in a stage career. For the first several years, she appeared in the chorus of musicals and various vaudeville companies, inauspiciously. In early 1903, when Marion was 23, she was hired to appear in the chorus of "Peggy from Paris," a George Ade show that began its run in Chicago. After several months, the show was deemed ready to appear in New York and opened on September 10 at Wallack's Theater. Unfortunately, it had a very short run.

Near the end of the year, Marion was engaged for the chorus in a holiday show, "Mother Goose." The show was imported from England but had been modified to meet American tastes. "Mother Goose" opened December 2, 1903, at the New Amsterdam Theater, one of the first shows to appear at this new venue. It starred Harry Bulger, veteran Joseph Cawthorne and newcomer Pat Rooney, Jr., son of the late variety headliner. The show played for 105 performances, until the end of February. In the meantime, Marion and Pat had met and were often seen together. Five weeks after the show closed, on April 10, 1904, they were married in Boston. So began a song-and-dance team that lasted for 28 years, longer than any other team in vaudeville.

In the beginning, Marion knew little about partnering. Pat taught her what she needed to know to appear as a team performer. She learned quickly and they were soon signed to tour on the Keith circuit. Their routine consisted of dance, song and a bit of comedy cross talk. Their easy-going and personable demeanor quickly made them popular. Each bit of repartee led into a song, punctuated with dance. Often, Pat would solo. He would shove his hands in his pockets, raise his trouser legs and soft-shoe across the stage. The dance became Pat's trademark throughout his entire career.

Marion and Pat's son, Pat Rooney III, was born in 1909 and traveled with his parents wherever they played. He appeared on stage at an early age, and teamed with his father when Marion retired.

In the summer of 1914, the duo played at the Palace Theater. The press labeled them "beloved characters." They appeared at the Palace again in 1916, their act simply called "Twenty Minutes with Pat and Marion." They filled the theater at every performance. The song and dance that they were best remembered for was "The Daughter of Rosie O'Grady," written in 1918 by Monty Brice and veteran songwriter Walter Donaldson. Audiences still enjoyed Irish songs. Rooney and Bent made "Rosie" a hit, and the song became their own for their career. No performance was complete without including it:

> She's the daughter of Rosie O'Grady,
> A regular old-fashioned girl,
> She isn't crazy for diamond rings
> Silken or satins and fancy things;
> She's just a sweet little lady,
> And when you meet her you'll see;
> Why I'm glad I met her,
> The daughter of Rosie O'Grady.

The nostalgia of the moment, camaraderie with the audience and their ability to put over the song made Rooney and Bent winners every time.

Vaudeville headliners through the war and into the 1920s, Rooney and Bent excelled as crowd pleasers who always captured audiences. In 1921, they bought out the rights to a Sigmund Romberg flop, "Love Birds," rewrote it to feature their talents and toured with the show quite successfully. In May 1925, they appeared at the Palace in a 33-minute act, "Dance of the Hour," which again demonstrated their audience appeal. They toured until the end of vaudeville and remained in demand while other performers dropped out or moved to other media.

In 1932, Marion had to leave the act because of arthritis. Rooney continued to perform. In 1935, Marion joined Pat and Pat III in celebrating their thirty-second anniversary at the Capitol Theater in which they reprised their old hits. At the end of their performance, Marion moved to the front of the stage and said to the audience: "I'm still with my old sweetheart." In 1937, Marion opened a restaurant opposite Carnegie Hall.

In June 1940, Marion was admitted to the French Hospital, reported to be critically ill. She died on July 28 after an illness of two months, following a long period of failing health. Marion was 60 years old. She was buried in Evergreen Cemetery, Brooklyn.

At the height of their career, Rooney and Bent were $4,000-a-week headliners. They were the personification of vaudevillian's dedication to their profession. Pat Rooney was a talented performer and when he teamed with Marion Bent, audiences adored them.

Ethel Levey

Ethel Levey's fame on the stage was assured when she married George M. Cohan. She had starring roles in his first five musical comedies. After their divorce, she became a headliner on her own in vaudeville and musicals in the United States and England. Ethel was a fine singer and comedienne and delighted audiences through the 1920s.

Grace Ethelia Fowler was born on November 22, 1881, in San Francisco, California. Her father, George P. Fowler, was a clerk in an express office. His parents had come from Ireland and settled in San Francisco. Her mother, Martha McGee, was 18 when she married George in 1880. She had come from Kentucky. When Ethelia was four years old, her father died. Martha (Mattie) then married Sol Levey, a newspaperman.

As a child, Ethelia appeared in local amateur theatricals. Discovering her talent singing, dancing and acting, Ethelia aspired to become a serious actress. At the age of eight, she had mastered the elements of stagecraft and was in demand to appear in various melodramas. When actors starring popular melodramas visited San Francisco, local performers were hired to fill the cast. Children were in great demand for these plays, and Ethelia gained experience in such roles. During this time she adopted her stage name, taking the name of Levey from her Jewish stepfather.

During her teens, Ethel continued to mature as an actress, assuming increasingly larger roles in melodramas. She practiced singing and dancing although there was little place for them in the plays in which she appeared. She made her formal debut on the professional stage December 31, 1897, at the age of 16, with a role in the popular melodrama, "A Milk White Flag." Ethel received excellent reviews for her acting.

Believing that New York was the only place for her to advance her career, Ethel moved there and auditioned with various producers. Her singing and dancing abilities, in combination with her performing vitality, got her a spot with a Weber and Fields–managed touring company. This was not the entrance for a performer desiring to be a serious actress, but it was a job that utilized her skills. The Weber and Fields company, one of three that toured the major cities, gave Ethel the opportunity to expand her abilities as a comedienne, since they emphasized comedy over other facets of acting. She toured with them through the 1898 season.

Having acquired some experience on the vaudeville circuit and working with veteran professionals, Ethel obtained an engagement at Koster and Bial's Music Hall, one of the better vaudeville houses in New York. Her act consisted of a combination of singing, dancing and comedy. Reviewers spoke favorably of her skills and predicted a bright future for her.

That bright future was assured when 20-year-old actor, writer and producer George M. Cohan saw Ethel perform at Hyde and Behman's Theater. A courtship followed, mostly by mail as Cohan and his family were on tour. George's parents were not happy about the relationship, but there was no point in arguing when George made up his mind. Ethel seemed to be his equal in temperament, with a strong ego and a desire for stardom. George and Ethel married in 1899. They had a child, Georgette, a year later. Within a few months, the parents opened in their first Broadway musical.

Cohan had expanded on a vaudeville sketch in which the entire family had played successfully while on tour. It was his first attempt at musical comedy. "The Governor's Son" opened at the Savoy Theater on February 25, 1901. The show got poor reviews and had a run of only 32 performances. Ethel played the leading lady, Emerald Green, and had the opportunity to demonstrate her singing and dancing. Reviewers acknowledged Cohan's potential but believed he needed more maturity to put together a more coherent show. Yet, when the show went on tour, it remained a great success for almost two years. The entire Cohan family (father, mother, son, sister and Ethel) performed together, with Georgette taken along wherever the troupe traveled.

On April 27, 1903, Cohan's second musical, "Running for Office," opened at the 14th Street Theater. It was another expanded vaudeville sketch and fared little better than "The Governor's Son," playing for only 48 performances. Again, Cohan took the show on tour for the rest of the season and garnered good profits.

"Little Johnny Jones" premiered on November 7, 1904, at the Liberty Theater, and was Cohan's breakout hit. Once more, Ethel played the heroine whom the hero (Cohan) wins at the end. But Cohan wrote and took all the good songs to sing. Ethel told a few jokes and did some dancing, but she was definitely overshadowed by her husband. The musical ran for only 52 performances, but they were all played before full

Ethel Levey (Harry Ransom Humanities Research Center, the University of Texas at Austin).

houses. Cohan brought the show back six months later for an engagement of four months and in November 1905 for another month. In between, the show was on a very profitable tour.

Cohan's next big musical was an attempt to play on the patriotic theme he used in "Little Johnny Jones." "George Washington, Jr." opened at the Herald Square Theater on February 12, 1906 to rave reviews. The show was Cohan at his flag-waving best. Ethel played George's love but again ceded the spotlight to him as he sang the hit song "You're a Grand Old Flag." She sang "I Was Born in Virginia," which turned into a showstopper, but did little else. The show ran for 90 performances and then embarked on a profitable tour. Ethel felt that her talents were not being fully utilized and she told her husband so. She wished to further her own career. Cohan wished to further his. But they did not have the same goals. Ethel obtained a divorce on February 18, 1907, and took Georgette with her. Shortly after the divorce, the press announced that Ethel was going to marry actor Robert Edeson. When asked, he admitted to the engagement. After an auto accident in which Edeson was driving, Ethel broke the engagement.

After an absence of eight years, with some trepidation, Ethel returned to the vaudeville stage. But her reputation as a musical comedy star immediately got her headliner bookings. Her initial appearance, at the Harlem Opera House in 1907, crowded the theater. She earned excellent reviews and reaffirmed her star status. She sang four songs, all from previous Cohan shows.

Her vaudeville tour was cut short when she was engaged to appear in a Harry B. Smith musical, "Nearly a Hero." The show opened at the old Casino Theater on February 24, 1908. Co-starred with Ethel were Ada Lewis, Zelda Sears and Elizabeth Brice. The show ran for 116 performances and was said to have been profitable. (It usually took 100 performances on Broadway for investors to break even.)

For the next several years, Ethel played with great success on the vaudeville circuit. Now out of the shadow of her former husband, she proved her talent as one of the better singers in the business. Mixing singing with a little dance and comedy, her act reached headliner status.

Ethel had a brief engagement in London in 1909 which made her a star attraction there. But commitments in the United States forced her to return. One commitment was a theater-restaurant revue called "Hell" which opened in April 1911. Ethel starred in a satirical act, actually a series of vaudeville olios for Mr. and Mrs. Devil, who lived "45 seconds from Broadway." The show ran to June. As soon as it closed, Ethel was on a boat for England. In October 1909, she married Pierre Crespins in London. Pierre was a horseman of some note. The marriage lasted only a few years before Ethel divorced him.

Ethel was such a popular entertainer in London that she remained there from 1912 to 1920. During this time, she appeared in a series of musicals: "Hullo Ragtime!" (1912); "Hullo Tango!" (1913); "Follow the Crowd" (1916); "Three Cheers" (1917); and "Oh! Julie" (1920). In between the shows, she toured the provinces and performed for the soldiers during the war.

When London theaters suffered from a poor economy, Ethel decided to return to the United States. But would she be able to maintain her star status after being gone from Broadway for almost a decade?

In December 1916, Ethel married Claude Graham White, an adventurer and aviator. He had been divorced a year earlier. "An American actress" was named in the divorce proceedings. White was said to have been one of the pioneers of British aviation. When Ethel returned to the United States, White accompanied her.

She opened her return to Broadway at the Palace Theater in 1921. She was a big hit, having lost none of her following. The following year, she had a small part in a musical, "Go Easy, Mabel," which opened in May at the Longacre Theater and closed shortly thereafter. Ethel sang a few old songs. With the exception of one movie and several brief appearances in musicals, she remained on the vaudeville stage. The movie, "High Stakes," was released in 1931. When vaudeville lost its appeal, it also lost audiences for its stars. Ethel obtained few engagements during the 1930s.

She and White were divorced in 1939. He returned to England to continue his corporate career in aviation. Ethel moved into a New York hotel, with an uncertain future.

In 1941, Ethel came out of retirement to appear in an Oscar Hammerstein II–Sigmund Romberg show, "Sunny River." She had a non-singing role. The plot and music were mediocre and the show closed after five weeks. Ethel disappeared from public view until 1945 when she had a cameo role in "Marinka," a rehashing of the Mayerling mystery at the turn of the century. Ethel played the role of Madame Sacher, the owner of a Viennese hotel. The show ran for 21 weeks. Her last stage appearance was in a 1950 Chicago production of "Springboard to Nowhere."

Ethel died on February 27, 1955, in the New York hotel room where she had been living for many years. She had suffered a fatal heart attack. Ethel was 74 years old. Obituaries mentioned her marriage to Cohan, but little about her personal triumphs and headliner status in vaudeville.

Louise Dresser

She was one of the highest paid entertainers on the vaudeville stage and later won plaudits for her roles in motion pictures. A celebrated beauty, tall and statuesque, with blue eyes and blonde hair, she had a show business career spanning nearly a half century. Louise Dresser combined a fine singing voice with excellent dramatic acting, allowing her to move easily from vaudeville to musical comedies and film. In 1927, she was the recipient of one of the first Academy Awards.

Louise Josephine Kerlin was born in Evansville, Indiana, on October 5, 1878. William S. Kerlin, her father, was a railroad conductor. When Louise was still a child, he was killed in a railroad accident, leaving the family destitute. Her mother, Ida Shaffer, raised three children, of whom Louise was the first. When Louise and her brother were old enough, they also worked to supplement the family's meager income. Schooling for the children was minimal, but Louise was able to take singing lessons. As a young teenager, she showed a flair for acting.

At the age of 16, Louise appeared in amateur theatricals in Columbus, Ohio, where the Kerlin family had recently moved. She was selected for the cast of a Boston stock company that performed melodramas and musicals. Her natural beauty and fine singing voice were featured with the stock company and the local press often praised her stage work. During the years 1897 and 1898, Louise appeared in a road company of "Peck's Bad Boy," a popular melodrama.

While on the road tour, Louise met Jack Norworth, a young song-and-dance performer and aspiring composer. They fell in love, formed a singing-dancing team and, in 1898, were married. While they were performing in small-time vaudeville in Chicago, they called on a music publisher looking for new material. The publisher introduced them to

Paul Dresser, then one of the most successful songwriters in the country. Recognizing the name Kerlin from his childhood days, Dresser recalled Louise's father protecting him from other boys who tormented him because he was fat. Dresser called a drama editor of the *Chicago Tribune,* told him that his kid sister was in town "and wants to go on the stage." He also called the manager of the Masonic Roof Theater and got Louise and her husband a job. In gratitude, Louise changed her name to Dresser. The change helped launch her career but caused later complications. Louise kept in touch with Dresser and was with him when he died in 1906. People believed she was his sister, but Dresser's brother, Theodore Dreiser, the well-known novelist, insisted the press make the correction. This did nothing to hurt her career.

From 1900 to 1905, Louise, with occasional help from Norworth, built her reputation as a vaudeville headliner. Dresser had written a song especially for Louise, "My Gal Sal," which she introduced and made famous. It was one of his greatest hits and quickly propelled Louise's career. On her vaudeville tours, she was billed together with Lillian Russell and Anna Held.

On the evening of August 30, 1906, the Lew Fields Herald Square Theater opened with "About Town." The production was a revue held together by a slender plot and individual performances. As usual, Fields surrounded himself with talented veterans and promising newcomers. The veterans included Louise Allen Collier and Edna Wallace Hopper. The newcomers were Vernon Castle, Jack Norworth, whom Fields hired away from vaudeville, and his wife, Louise Dresser. Fields quickly discovered that Louise had more talent than her husband. She played the role of a Gibson girl and sang the show's hit song, "I'm Sorry." The show played 138 performances in New York and began a six-month tour of Shubert theaters. Late in the season, Norworth left the show when Louise accused him of adultery with comedienne Trixie Friganza. They were divorced in 1908, and Norworth married Nora Bayes.

In August 1907, Louise began rehearsals for "The Girl Behind the Counter," another lavish Fields production. Starring in the show were Connie Ediss, whom the Shuberts brought from England, George Beban, Vernon Castle and Louise. The show opened at Lew Fields' Herald Square Theater on October 1. Theatergoers welcomed it as the funniest, fastest, and slickest musical comedy of the season. Louise played the daughter of a society matron who planned to have her wed a titled Englishman. Reviewers noted Louise's verve and comic aptitude. Her rendition of "I Want to Be Loved Like a Leading Lady" was the hit of the show.

The show included a barbershop routine between Fields and Castle that became a comic standard. Fields also introduced a song by a German composer called "The Glow Worm" that later became a hit song. But three weeks after the show opened, a new musical by Franz Lehar, "The Merry Widow," swept the country and helped to redefine the American musical. Still, "The Girl Behind the Counter" played for 38 weeks in New York and went on a two-year tour.

In May 1908, the recently formed Friars Club held their first annual benefit performance. Among the stars who volunteered their services were Victor Herbert, Eddie Foy, George M. Cohan and Louise Dresser.

Louise was engaged to appear in De Wolf Hopper's "song play" "A Matinee Idol," which opened at Daly's Theater on April 28, 1910. With a weak plot and mediocre music, the show closed after 68 performances. Louise returned to vaudeville and had no problem filling her time on the Keith and Orpheum circuits for the next few years. She was now reported to be earning $1,750 a week. In the fall of 1914, Louise headlined the bill at the Palace Theater, which also featured Irene Franklin and comedian Tom Lewis. The theater was filled at every performance and Louise had to sing her signature song, "My Gal Sal," at the end of every appearance.

Louise married Jack Gardner in 1910. Gardner was a singer and actor who later became an agent. They remained married until his death 40 years later.

In the fall of 1914, Louise was hired to appear in George M. Cohan's revue, "Hello, Broadway." Cohan co-starred with William Collier to present a fast-paced, breezy production that spoofed the opulence of the Ziegfeld Follies. Louise sang several songs, one of which was "Down By the Erie Canal," backed by a chorus shaking tambourines. The show had a brief run in New York and a tour that lasted to the end of the year.

From 1914 to 1922, Louise continued to play the vaudeville circuits with her usual success. A highlight of the tours during this period was a return to Evansville in 1919 to put on a new sketch written by Jack Lait, a Chicago newsman. The town came out in force, greeted her warmly and cheered her every move during the show's run.

A break from vaudeville occurred in 1917 when Louise starred in the musical, "Have a Heart." The show opened on January 11, at the Liberty Theater. Louise played a shop girl who had become a movie star. Even though the show featured a book by Guy Bolton and P.G. Wodehouse and music by Jerome Kern, it was not a hit and lasted only two months.

In 1922, Louise was recruited by Hollywood to appear in moving pictures. In a period of eight years, she appeared in 36 films, most of them forgettable. Notable among her successes were "The Eagle" (1925) with Rudolph Valentino, Cecil B. DeMille's "A Ship Comes In" (1928), "Mother Knows Best" (1928), and "Madonna of Avenue A" (1928). "Air Circus" (1928) was the first Fox film to contain dialogue sequences and sound synchronization. When studio bosses heard Louise's voice on film, they clamored even more for her services.

Louise starred in "Lightnin'" (1930) with Will Rogers, "Mammy" (1930) with Al Jolson, and three hit movies, "State Fair" (1933), also with Rogers, "David Harum" (1934), and "A Girl of the Limber-

Louise Dresser (Museum of the City of New York).

lost" (1934). She appeared in 13 other films between 1931 and 1937. She retired from pictures in 1943.

Louise and her husband cared for her mother during her last years at their Beverly Hills home. Ida Kerlin died in 1938. After the death of her mother, Louise gave most of her collection of theatrical photographs to the Masquers in Los Angeles. Jack Gardner died in 1950. Shortly afterward, Louise moved into a small apartment in Glendale.

On March 13, 1965, Louise entered the hospital for exploratory surgery. A little over a month later, her condition worsened and she was taken to the Motion Picture Country Hospital. She died there on April 24. Louise was 87 years old. Funeral services and burial were in Forest Lawn Cemetery. Louise had been one of the founders and charter members of the Motion Picture Country Home and Hospital.

Variety reported that the "Louise Dresser Collection" had been placed in the Eppley Theater on the campus of Culver Military Academy, Culver, Indiana. Josh Logan dedicated the building. Louise was one of the few vaudeville stars who made the transition into movies an outstanding success.

Blossom Seeley

Blossom Seeley was a headliner in vaudeville and musicals for almost 50 years. Although pert and tiny, she had a voice that reached audiences in the third gallery. Her ability to interpret coon songs rivaled that of Nora Bayes, Sophie Tucker and Ruth Roye. Her smoldering renditions of ballads and jazz tunes made many of them hits with which her name became associated. Blossom seemed to do her best work when she was teamed with men who complemented her routine. For more than 30 years she appeared with husband Benny Fields in one of the most popular song-and-dance acts of the era.

Minnie Guyer was born in San Francisco, California on July 16, 1886. She later claimed she had been born in 1891.

At an early age, Minnie displayed a talent for singing and dancing. With support from her parents, she appeared in amateur shows at local vaudeville houses. D. J. Grauman (father of Sid, who opened movie palaces in Los Angeles) ran the city's first ten cent vaudeville house and promoted it as a venue for family entertainment. In 1900, at his Unique Theater, one of his popular acts was "The Little Blossom," belting out coon songs (tunes composed by whites using Black dialect). It is likely that Grauman changed Minnie's name for stage purposes at this time. In 1903, Blossom was labeled the "Queen of Grauman's" by a San Francisco newspaper. This suggested that she was much older than she claimed. In fact, in 1904, at the age of 18, Blossom married William P. Curtin in New Haven, Connecticut. Two years later, she had a daughter, Marguerite. If she had been born in 1891, as she claimed, Blossom would have been 13 when she was married.

She played in various vaudeville theaters up and down the West Coast, earning the label "The Queen of Syncopation." Her act consisted of ragtime singing and Negro dialect monologues. In 1908, Blossom starred for an unprecedented 38-week engagement at the Los Angeles Theater. During this time, she was seen by Joe Kane (Cahan), a vaudeville comedian who persuaded her to join him in an act. For the next two years, they played together on the circuits, gradually moving in the direction of New York. When the team appeared in New York, Blossom received favorable attention for her work, one of the reviewers predicting that she would be a hit anywhere she played.

In late 1910, big-time producer and actor Lew Fields was mounting a new show with his usual glittering production values. Called "The Hen Pecks," it opened on February 4, 1911, at the Broadway Theater. Blossom played a minor role in the production, as one of Fields' four daughters. She made the most of a song-and-dance routine that captured the audience. In this scene, she climbed on a table and belted out "Toddlin' the Todalo." Fields had her dance on a table to show off her shapely legs, and she used the platform to launch a dance craze. As an encore, Blossom performed the Texas Tommy, a dance originated by Black dancers in San Francisco. The dances caught the attention of New York society. Soon, the city's night people were doing these fun-producing dances. The show ran until June and then went on tour, compiling excellent box office returns. New York managers wanted Blossom to work for them.

On June 3, 1911, Blossom obtained a divorce from Curtin. He claimed that a theatrical agent had stolen the affections of his wife and named Joe Kane as corespondent. Blossom and Kane married four months later, on October 11, and he became her manager as well.

After the Shuberts opened the Winter Garden, they quickly found that Al Jolson was their best ticket-seller. On March 5, 1912, they premiered a three-part evening, essentially a revue, featuring Jolson in an "operatic melodrama" as Gus, a blackface servant, opposite Stella Mayhew. It was his first appearance in the role he would portray for his stage and film career. Blossom was featured in the first part of the show, repeating "Toddlin' the Todalo" with a chorus backing her. The show ran for four months and reviewers acknowledged her as a sure-fire hit.

Three months later, Blossom appeared in a musical, "The Charity Girl," which opened in Chicago and immediately caused a commotion. The story told of a young heiress who gives up her comfortable life to help the poor. However, the script handled the topic in a flippant manner and proceeded to make fun of poor people and the police. In particular, Blossom's song and dance, "The Ghetto Glide," was considered offensive by critics. Another song, "I'd Rather Be a Chippie Than a Charity Bum," was found especially nasty. The show opened at the Globe Theater, New York, on October 2, 1912, and lasted less than three weeks. Blossom and Kane quickly returned to vaudeville.

At this time, a number of baseball players took advantage of their popularity to enter vaudeville and make good money during their off-season. One of these players was Richard "Rube" Marquard, a star pitcher for the New York Giants. Kane offered him a job appearing with Blossom, which he accepted. Their act was called "Breaking the Record or Nineteen Straight" (referring to Rube's one-year winning record). Blossom sang and danced while Rube pretended to pitch, told jokes and danced. When they played at Hammerstein's Victoria The-

Blossom Seeley

ater, they were favorably reviewed. Within a short time, the press reported more of their off-stage activities than their act.

An irate Kane filed for divorce, named Marquard as co-respondent and sued him for $25,000 for alienating his wife's affections. The press followed Blossom and Marquard to several cities in an attempt to obtain evidence against the pitcher. In Atlantic City, Kane and police officers raided Blossom's apartment. Minutes before, she and Marquard had departed on the fire escape. Accusations were made by both parties and were turned into newspaper headlines. Finally, after three months of court proceedings, the suit was settled with Marquard giving Kane his World Series check for $2,200, which Kane accepted. The divorce was finalized in February 1913, 16 months after Blossom and Kane's marriage. The next month, Blossom and Marquard married in San Francisco in the parsonage of the German Evangelical Lutheran Church with only theatrical friends in attendance.

Later that same year, Blossom, with Marquard, made her first appearance at the Palace Theater. She would often return to the Palace during the next two decades, a welcomed audience favorite.

The team's vaudeville successes were short-lived, however. Marquard had a bad pitching year in 1914 and became less of a crowd attraction. Shortly thereafter, Blossom continued vaudeville touring on her own. They separated in 1916 and were divorced in 1920.

Now appearing on the Keith-Orpheum circuit, Blossom was billed as "The Hottest Girl in Town." Her repertoire included such popular songs as "Somebody Loves Me," "Way Down Yonder in New Orleans," "Jealous," "I Cried for You" and the novelty tune, "Smiles." George Gershwin had written "Somebody Loves Me" especially for Blossom. These songs became identified with Blossom and she used them in her act for the rest of her career.

In 1915, Blossom and the Shuberts tried another musical, "Maid in America," at the Winter Garden. The revue was a patriotic production that took advantage of the audience's attention toward the war. But American flags could not overcome mediocre routines and songs. The show ran for several months. The presence of Nora Bayes as star of the show greatly reduced Blossom's visibility. When Ned Wayburn produced an elaborate revue, "Town Topics," later that same year, he had Blossom leading a ballet on a revolving stage. But Will Rogers eclipsed everyone else that appeared on the stage with his jokes and rope-twirling. The show was unable to compete with other Broadway productions and lasted nine weeks. Blossom returned to vaudeville where she was able to take advantage of her star power.

The following year, Blossom formed an act with Bill Bailey and Lynn Cowan, appropriately called "Seeley's Syncopated Studio." The act played successfully on the Keith circuit for the next two years. When Blossom organized a new trio to back her up, she became particularly interested in one of the young men she hired, Benny Fields. Blossom had him support her in the act with comedy and dancing. Soon, their teamwork was noticed both on and off the stage.

Benny Fields (Benjamin E. Geisenfeld) was born in Milwaukee, Wisconsin, on June 14, 1894. His stage experience consisted of playing in small groups in Midwest vaudeville theaters primarily as a song-and-dance man and secondarily as a comedian. It was at a Chicago nightclub that Blossom saw him perform and asked him to join her. As befitting her star status, Fields would play a supporting role in the act. Shortly after her divorce from Marquard was final, on March 10, 1921, Blossom and Fields married. A civil ceremony had been performed three weeks earlier and the religious ceremony was held in St. Paul, Minnesota.

Seeley and Fields became a featured act during the early 1920s, playing on the major vaudeville circuits to excellent reviews and profitable receipts. Blossom was making $2,000 a week. Fields supplied the comedy and dance; Blossom did the singing. Along with her repertoire of trademark songs, she added "Waiting for the Robert E. Lee" and "A New Kind of Man with a New Kind of Love for Me." Her ability to switch from love ballads to jazz numbers gave audiences all they wanted from her.

In 1925, the duo appeared at the Palace, a great experience for both performers and audiences. A fabulous bill made up of oldtimers opened on April 20. Included on the bill were Weber & Fields (on another of their farewell tours), Marie Cahill, Cissie Loftus (pulled from retirement), Emma Trentini, the opera star, and Seeley and Fields, selected to add a more contemporary note to the bill. The week's business was so good that the performers were booked for a second week. Seeley and Fields received $1,500 a week, less than they normally earned because of the high salary costs for such a star-studded lineup.

At a jazz concert staged in Carnegie Hall at the end of 1925, Blossom and Fields performed in a jazz opera written by George Gershwin, "135th Street," backed by Paul Whiteman and his orchestra. The upscale audience and critics thoroughly enjoyed the unique concert, particularly Gershwin's music. (It was two years after his premiere of "Rhapsody in Blue," with Whiteman's orchestra.) However, the music was rarely played afterward.

In May 1926, Seeley and Fields returned to the Palace, their last stop on a nationwide tour of high-class vaudeville theaters. Included on the bill were Charlotte Greenwood (of high-kicking fame), Jack Norworth and Charles King. But one of the first signs of the diminishing popularity of vaudeville was seen when *Variety* moved their coverage of vaudeville to the back of the paper and replaced it with movies.

March 1927 was noted for two significant events occurring almost simultaneously at New York theaters. The Palace was celebrating vaudeville's one-hundredth anniversary, a fictitious publicity stunt that nevertheless drew large crowds. Seeley and Fields headed an all-star cast that included Elsie Janis, Raymond Hitchcock, Burns and Allen, Ben Bernie and his orchestra and movie star Leo Carrillo. Down the street, S. L. Rothafel opened up the Roxy Theater. It had a huge capacity and was elegantly appointed, with uniformed ushers and a synchronized dance team known as the Roxyettes. Movies dominated along with a few selected vaudeville headliners, all for the price of $1.65, well below the ticket price charged by the Palace.

In September, Palace management had Seeley and Fields open their fall season on a bill that also featured Joe Frisco, Elizabeth Brice, Benny Rubin, Mme. Nazimova and Jack Benny. The bill did well. Yet, that same week in a theater four blocks from the Palace, the Warner, the movie "The Jazz Singer" opened. It was a talkie starring Al Jolson. The entertainment industry was about to change.

Seeley and Fields continued their vaudeville wanderings. Aware that the amusement was losing its appeal and its audiences, they remained headliners. In 1928, they joined the cast of "The Greenwich Follies." It was the eighth edition of a revue produced by the Shuberts and played at the Winter Garden. Blossom sang several of her signature songs, but the show was tepid. When the show closed, it was also the end of the Greenwich Follies.

Blossom and Fields appeared at the Palace in 1929 and 1931, some of the last remaining vaudevillians still working in the theaters. The Palace switched to movies in 1932. In 1936, at the age of 51, Blossom announced her retirement. Fields took a solo act out and was given good reviews.

Blossom appeared in four movies, all produced in 1933. They were "Blood Money,"

"Broadway Through a Keyhole," "Dancing Lady" and "Mr. Broadway." Interestingly, her roles had little to do with singing and dancing.

In 1952, when Paramount released the biopic about Blossom, she came out of retirement to team with Fields again. The movie, "Somebody Loves Me," starred Betty Hutton as Blossom and Ralph Meeker as Fields. The music was great and Hutton did a commendable job putting across the songs. The story was generally true, depicting the life of a couple who stayed together despite the strain of stage careers, but the dialogue was dull.

Blossom recorded several albums of her trademark songs, but her voice lacked the strength and seductiveness of earlier years. Seeley and Fields performed at the Coconut Grove in Los Angeles and at hotels in Las Vegas. During the 1950s, they were regulars on "The Ed Sullivan Show."

On August 16, 1959, Benny Fields died of a heart attack at the New York hotel where the couple lived. He was 65 years old. His body was returned to Milwaukee for burial. Benny once said that the reason stage marriages failed was that "the principals didn't team their careers."

During her last years, Blossom lived in the old actors' home in Englewood, New Jersey, and when it closed moved to the De Witt Nursing Home in New York City. She died April 14, 1974, of old age. The press reported her to be 82 years old; actually she was 89.

Aileen Stanley

Aileen Stanley began her career in vaudeville as a child artist, singing her way into prominence during the first two decades of the twentieth century. In 1920, Aileen made her first recording and quickly swept to fame with her jazz and blues renditions. Introducing Victor recording hits of the day, she was labeled "The Victrola Girl," which helped her reach stardom on the vaudeville stage.

Maude Elsie Aileen Muggeridge was born on March 21, 1893, on a farm near Chicago, Illinois. Robert Sheriff Muggeridge, her father, was born in Surrey, England, in 1854. He was a corn merchant. Maria Capewell, her mother, was born in Derbyshire, England, in 1860. The couple married in 1881 in London and came to the United States in 1888. By that time, they had two children, Elsie, born in 1882, and Howard, born in 1885. They settled on a farm just outside Chicago. Robert Stanley was born in 1890 and Maude three years later. Tragedy struck the family prior to Maude's birth: Both Elsie and Robert, her father, died of a fever within days of one another. Mrs. Muggeridge rented rooms to make a living. Little Howard became a messenger.

Maude and Robert Stanley attended elementary school for a short time. Mrs. Muggeridge encouraged Maude to learn to sing and dance. Often, Maude performed on Saturday nights at the local grange house. When Robert expressed interest in the stage, he, too, learned song and dance. He joined his younger sister performing at the grange. At that time, child teams were the rage in vaudeville and Mrs. Muggeridge obtained an agent to place her children at a local theater. Maude was 11 and Robert was 14.

The duo made their debut at a Chicago suburban vaudeville house where they were billed as "Stanley and Aileen — Singers of Sweet Songs." Their initial attempts at performing were quite amateurish but the agent believed the pair had the talent to succeed. He continued to book them in other Chicago area theaters. After playing for a year, the team took off the summer to build a new act, using what they had learned from others.

In 1905, they achieved greater success and found bookings in other Midwest cities. Their youth undoubtedly helped to put over an otherwise ordinary act. Maude's voice had become quite attractive, demure and earnest, with a bit of sensuality. Reviewers recognized her for her pleasant voice. Within a few years, the team was touring the Midwest and West Coast venues to popular success. Each week, a portion of their earnings was sent home to their mother.

In 1911, Robert Stanley broke up the act by running off with a chorus girl and forming a new routine. Maude had to develop a solo act, which turned out to her advantage. It gave her the opportunity to develop her style and stage persona. At one performance in Chicago, Nora Bayes saw Maude perform. She came backstage to encourage the young girl to continue and suggested she needed a better stage name. By reversing the name of the old act, Stanley and Aileen, Maude became Aileen Stanley.

Aileen joined the Keith circuit in 1912, billed as a "character singer" because of her delineation of blues numbers. She toured on the Keith circuit until 1920. Although she rarely appeared on the program as the headliner, she was always a featured player. Aileen appeared at the Palace Theater in February 1915, listed eighth on the bill of nine acts. Ahead of her were Mme. Emma Calve, the famed opera singer, the Four Marx Brothers, Edward Abeles & Co., in a Shakespearean skit, Webb and Burns (George), and Clara Morton. Aileen received a one-sentence review about her "accomplished singing."

In the summer of 1920, Aileen was hired to appear in a revue, "Silks and Satins," at the Cohan Theater. This revue was no more than a series of vaudeville specialties performed by a variety of actors. Aileen sang several blues- and jazz-oriented songs that got good reviews. The show itself was a failure, lasting only 53 performances. But the Victor recording people were struck by Aileen's renditions and engaged her to record for them. This launched the beginning of a new career for Aileen and helped to increase her popularity.

Her first recordings, issued in November 1920, were "Broadway Blues" and "My Little Bimbo Down on the Bamboo Isle." She also recorded "My Little Bimbo" for Edison the next year, and the song was identified with her in the early 1920s. The lyrics of the song were said to be daring for the period.

Because of her popularity on records, Aileen became known in vaudeville as "The Girl with the Personality" and "The Phonograph Girl." She often appeared on sheet music covers. While appearing on the vaudeville circuit, she had an arrangement to return to New York to record. Her stage popularity soared in the 1920s as she made more recordings. Now with headliner status, Aileen played at the top of the bill at the Palace Theater in October 1920, March 1926, August 1930 and January 1931.

On January 2, 1922, when on tour in Minneapolis, Aileen married Robert Buttenuth, her piano accompanist. They appeared together until May 1927 when she separated from him due to his drunkenness. When Aileen divorced Buttenuth in July 1929, she changed her name legally to Aileen Stanley. They had no children.

In the early 1920s, Aileen recorded blues and songs backed by jazz ensembles. She was promoted as a blues artist and listeners believed they were hearing a Black singer. In 1925, she recorded "When My Sugar Walks Down the Street," which quickly became a national hit. She was paired with Billy Murray, a veteran singer, 16 years older than Aileen, in a series of blues and ballads that included "When the Leaves Come Tumbling Down," "Nobody's Sweetheart" and "It Had to Be You." In the late 1920s, Aileen sang as a torch singer, with songs like "Broken Hearted" and "I'll Get By, As Long As I Have You." By 1930, her popularity had waned and new releases sold poorly. She stopped recording in the United States but made some records in England.

Aileen appeared in a revue by the Shuberts, "Pleasure Bound," which opened February 18, 1929, at the Shubert Theater. She sang several of her favorite songs to admiring audiences. The vaudeville-like show featured Phil Baker and Jack Pearl along with Aileen. The show ran for 17 weeks.

Aileen made frequent trips to England from 1925 to 1937 and appeared in vaudeville theaters there, including the Palladium.

In 1930, Aileen sang in "Artists and Models," another Shubert revue, which opened June 10 at the Majestic Theater. Aileen and Phil Baker headed the cast. The Shuberts dropped the show after seven weeks due to the Depression's effect on theater attendance. At the time, the press reported that Aileen had lost her entire personal estate.

In late 1930, Aileen announced her retirement from the stage. She was a guest on a number of radio

Aileen Stanley (Harry Ransom Humanities Research Center, the University of Texas at Austin).

programs in the 1930s, working with Rudy Vallee and Paul Whiteman. Aileen decided to coach young women singers for the theater, and did this for some years. In 1945, she was asked out of retirement to sing at Carnegie Hall, displaying her old style to an audience of jazz and blues enthusiasts.

After a long illness, Aileen died on March 24, 1982, in Los Angeles. She was 89 years old. In recognition of her radio work, the Pacific Pioneer Broadcasters had awarded her the Diamond Circle plaque a week before she died. Her records from the 1920s are considered collectors' items, her renditions of blues and jazz numbers unique for their era.

Texas Guinan

Texas Guinan began and ended her colorful career on the vaudeville stage. In between, she appeared in musicals and silent films and, during the 1920s, became a brash nightclub hostess, emcee and entertainer. Her wit and unconventionality gained her acclaim in popular theater and ultimately made her the most famous of night club emcees. Her associations with criminals during the Prohibition era made newspaper headlines although she claimed that she never drank or participated in illegal activities.

Mary Louise Cecilia Guinan was born on January 12, 1884, on a small ranch just outside of Waco, Texas. Her father, Michael Guinan, and mother, Bessie Duffy, came from Dublin, Ireland, arriving in America in 1880. They were married in 1881. Michael was running a wholesale grocery business at the time of Mary's birth. She was the second of four children, two boys and two girls.

Mary's parents encouraged their daughter to learn horseback riding and she ultimately became an accomplished rider and roper. Her formal schooling was less successful, for she often disrupted classes while at Catholic school. Mary claimed she had been thrown out of school at the age of 11 but other data indicate she graduated from elementary school. At 14, Mary was sent to study music in Chicago. During her two-year stay there, she developed her singing and dancing skills. Upon her return to Texas, she began performing in amateur theater productions, primarily dramas of the Old West. During her late teens, Mary was also a bronco rider for the circus and a rodeo driver. Due to her birthplace and riding skills, Mary picked up the nickname of Texas, which she would use with enthusiasm throughout her entire career.

At 20, Texas debuted in vaudeville and performed with various touring companies as a soubrette. Both she and the companies were undistinguished. At this time she met John Moynahan, a Denver newspaperman. They were married on December 2, 1904. In two years, the marriage ended.

In 1906, Texas moved to New York believing it offered the best opportunities to succeed in show business. She did an act called "The Gibson Girl" which displayed her figure and her voice. She appeared in the chorus of two short-lived musicals, "The Hoyden" (1907) and "The Gay Musician" (1908).

The year 1909 brought attention and recognition to Texas when she appeared in a 16-minute solo act at the Fifth Avenue Theater. From a basket hanging over the audience, she sang "Pansies Bring Thoughts of You." Reviewers noted her looks and voice, but also the brassiness of her demeanor. Audiences seemed to like her attitude and encouraged her to use it in her routine. That same year, Texas was featured on the cover of the *Dramatic Mirror,* a rare accomplishment considering the newspaper's usually conservative policy.

It took only a year for Texas to become a vaudeville headliner singing in touring companies, although she was rarely booked into high-class theaters. During this time, Texas initiated a campaign of self-promotion, billing herself as "God's Masterpiece," a brash statement but seemingly effective. Her act now added irreverent monologues along with singing and dancing. This act got her into various vaudeville companies but did not propel her career to the extent she would have liked.

She met Julian Johnson, a film critic, and claimed they had been married. No data indicate a marriage ever took place, but the couple was reported to have lived together until 1920.

Texas was recruited to appear in "The Passing Show of 1913," which opened on July 24 at the Winter Garden. The Shubert revue concentrated on satirizing legitimate shows. The group of new performers included Charlotte Greenwood, Charles and Molly King and John Charles Thomas. Texas appeared in the chorus and had one song. The show continued through the summer months, after which she returned to vaudeville. In 1916, Texas joined a company featuring comedy star Billy Gibson. She performed in a skit and sang songs like "Do What Your Mother Did, I'll Do the Same As Your Dad." One of her soon-to-be famous phrases came out of this show: "Give the little girl a big hand." She apparently was referring to herself.

In 1917, Texas was noticed by a scout for the Balboa Amusement Producing Company, a moving picture studio. They offered her a career as a gun-toting Western heroine, a female version of William S. Hart. Her movie career began with a short subject called "The Wildcat." The picture received little attention, being submerged by the country's involvement in the war.

For the next two years, Texas appeared in four movies, all with Western themes. They included "The Fuel of Life" (1917), "The Gun Woman" (1918), "The Love Brokers" (1918) and "The She Wolf" (1919). Texas preferred roles that gave her the opportunity to portray independent women who were real gunslingers. Although her movies were successful, she did not get along with the studios. She began her own company in 1921 and produced two movies, "I Am the Woman" and "The Stampede," before shutting down.

In between movies, Texas entertained the troops in France. She then returned to New York to resume her stage career. Her relationship with Julian Johnson had broken off. In 1920, she was reported to have married George C. Townley, but no records are available to confirm the union. In any case, their relationship lasted only a few years.

In New York, Texas was hired as a singer at a cabaret in the Beaux Arts Hotel. Cabarets had become important entertainment centers thanks to Prohibition and the increased use of risqué material in venues other than the the-

Texas Guinan

ater. The city's amusement seekers filled these venues as they became known as "places to be seen." Performers vied to be engaged because salaries were high and appearances could run for several months.

Texas's outgoing brassy style got her a promotion to master of ceremonies where she could greet patrons and introduce acts. Prior to this time, emcees were men. Texas broke the tradition and took over her new role with zest. Her interaction with audiences was unique. She shared dialogue with patrons and created an atmosphere of casualness and intimacy not otherwise found in such places of entertainment.

In 1924, Texas went to work for Larry Fay, owner of several cabarets and with a reputation that suggested a close friendship with Chicago's gangsters. Their partnership netted considerable money during the time when cabarets offered a wide variety of exciting diversions, from liquor to prostitution. Texas was an inspirational emcee. She was on a friendly, first-name basis with brokers and gangsters, prostitutes and college boys, and they were all treated as equals. When she shouted her famous line, "Hello, sucker!" she meant it. She was open and frank with everyone except the police and judges.

There were interruptions, however. Frequently, police stopped the show to enforce the Prohibition law. Sometimes they arrested prostitutes, although Texas claimed no business was ever conducted on premises. Texas's acquaintanceship with police captains was well-known, and when her show was temporarily shut down, the police always apologized to her.

When Fay's cabaret was closed, Texas moved to another club. After several moves, in 1925 she went to Fay's club in Miami. No matter what the evidence, Texas claimed that no alcohol was sold at her clubs. She was always able to avoid jail time and her activities gained considerable newspaper publicity, which she capitalized on to increase a club's patronage. In 1926, in spite of frequent police raids, it was reported that she earned $700,000.

In 1925, when many clubs and cabarets had been closed, Texas put together a vaudeville act, "Texas Guinan and Her Mob," which opened at the Hippodrome. Included in the act were a jazz sextet, a group of singers called the "Texas Strollers," and a line of pretty and talented showgirls that included future movie stars Ruby Keeler, Joan Crawford and Barbara Stanwyck.

In 1927, her vaudeville tour was temporarily stopped when she was arrested for breaking Prohibition laws at her club on West 54th Street in New York. She protested that she was only the hostess and was acquitted. The trial produced some Guinan quotes that the press used liberally in their coverage of her activities. In court, she addressed the judge, "Hello there, professor. Did you know that Federal Court is my alma mammy?" To the police she bragged, "I am nature's gift to the padlock makers." And to the press, she claimed, "I could walk into the lobby of any apartment building in town and find the name of at least one of my lawyers."

Once free of the court, Texas produced a stage revue which she aptly called "Padlocks of 1927." The press was full of outrageous tales about how she had persuaded the Shuberts to participate in the show. It opened July 5. Many scenes from the show featured Texas's extravagant behavior. Dressed in white chaps, blonde bob, sombrero and overdone rouge, she greeted patrons as they entered the lobby. She rode a horse on stage and she ad-libbed with members of the audience. Appearing in the show were some new faces, Lillian Roth, Jay C. Flippen and a young dancer, George Raft. Billy Rose wrote most of the music. The show ran through the summer.

Texas returned to Hollywood to play herself in two talking movies, "Queen of the Night Clubs" (1929) and "Broadway Through a Keyhole" (1933); neither was a hit. The effects of the Depression and her accumulated reputation with liquor and breaking laws contributed to their failure. Between the two pictures, Texas appeared at New York clubs. She also appeared in a Ziegfeld revue, "Glorifying the American Girl." The show had a short run but was filmed, and years later became a cult classic.

In 1931, with club receipts falling and the end of Prohibition near, Texas took a show to Europe. Her reputation was against her, however. The company was refused entry to each country where they attempted to land. Returning to the United States, Texas turned the company into a revue called "Too Hot for Paris." The revue was successful except in New England towns where it was banned. She attempted to organize other shows but failed. She also wrote a daily column in the ill-fated *New York Graphic* in 1930. Texas soon realized that her particularly colorful career had run its course.

On November 4, 1933, while on a vaudeville tour with her troupe of girls in Vancouver, B.C., Texas collapsed backstage with an intestinal illness. She died the following morning. Texas was 48 years old.

It was reported that more than 12,000 people viewed her body at the Campbell funeral home in New York before she was buried in White Plains. She was later removed to the family plot at Calvary Cemetery in Queens.

In 1929, Texas had moved her parents to New York where they resided in her home on West 8th Street. She had remained devoted to her family and wanted them to leave Waco, which she called a "city of the past." Although she had been quite prosperous during various periods of her career, she died with only a small estate. She left the money to her mother, and the rest of her theater and nightclub artifacts were auctioned off.

Lillian Russell

Lillian Russell achieved fame and fortune as a star in comic opera, but she appeared in vaudeville at various times in her career. Actresses like Lillian were called "in-and-outers" because they played both legitimate and popular theater with equal success. Lillian gained renown in each of these endeavors because of her versatility as a performer and her appeal to a broad range of audiences.

On December 4, 1861, Helen Louise Leonard was born in Clinton, Iowa, the fourth of five daughters. Her mother, Cynthia Van Name Leonard, was an active abolitionist and suffrage supporter. Her father, Charles Leonard, was a newspaperman. The family settled in Clinton so Charles could begin publishing a local paper. Due to the Civil War, the family lived modestly although comfortably. Cynthia was an accomplished musician, and the Leonard home was a center for local singing and musical societies. The five daughters were willing participants in these events.

In 1863, the family moved to Chicago where Charles opened a printing plant. Cynthia expanded her "social reformer" role by joining women's rights groups and actively participating in their activities. The girls were excited about the move to a big city.

Nellie, as her sisters called her, was jealous of the fun her older sisters seemed to be having in school. To placate Nellie, Cynthia taught her to play piano when she was not crusading on behalf of women's rights. Cynthia was so busy that Charles took over raising the children. Not surprisingly, Charles was becoming increasingly displeased with his wife's "reformer" activities.

Nellie was placed in a Catholic elementary school even though the Leonards were Episcopalians. She took music courses and violin lessons, but her singing voice attracted considerable attention from the nuns. At age 11, she gave her first public singing recital. Voice lessons now became mandatory. By 14, Nellie was singing at the famed Chicago Kimball Hall and received favorable comments from the press. Nellie had also become an attractive young woman. The nuns warned Cynthia that Nellie would "turn men's heads." Inspired by the possibility that Nellie could become an opera singer, Cynthia hired a former professional singer as Nellie's voice teacher. At 16, Nellie was singing important roles at Chickering Hall, the city's venue for opera.

Unfortunately, the relationship between Cynthia and Charles had greatly deteriorated. Charles' business had declined; Cynthia was now carrying her

Lillian Russell (Harry Ransom Humanities Research Center, The University of Texas at Austin).

crusades to City Hall. The fire of 1871 burned Charles's printing plant although the Leonard house was untouched. Cynthia decided to move to New York. By this time, the three older girls were quite self-sufficient. Cynthia took Nellie and her younger sister Susan to live in New York City in October 1878.

Cynthia's first act upon arriving in New York was to persuade Dr. Leopold Damrosch to accept Nellie as a pupil. His studio was close to the theater district and Nellie would often visit theaters and, when she could, audition to perform. Her efforts ended in rejection. Managers told her that she had "a nice face, a nice voice, but no personality." Of course, Nellie did not reveal to her mother her forays into the "dreaded" theater.

By chance, Nellie met the son of Col. William Sinn, who owned the Park Theater in Brooklyn. The colonel's wife liked Nellie and persuaded her to audition for E. E. Rice, an old friend and current producer of "Evangeline." Initially, Cynthia was against the audition, but just this once, she allowed Nellie to sing. Rice immediately hired Nellie. She was told to report to Boston's Globe Theater to begin rehearsals. It was her first job and first time away from home.

The orchestra conductor for "Evangeline" was 22-year-old Harry Braham. A tall, lean, handsome man with cheerful eyes, he attracted the young women in the chorus. However, only Nellie was of interest to Harry. After several months of clandestine meetings, Nellie realized she was pregnant. Fearing Cynthia's wrath, the couple were married on November 4, 1879, by a New York justice of the peace. That evening, after the show, they planned to tell Cynthia. The result was not unexpected: First, Cynthia refused to acknowledge the marriage; second, she accused Harry of seducing her daughter; third, she threatened police action; and finally, she refused to communicate with them in any way. Some months later, the family moved to larger quarters where Nellie and Harry had a room of their own. While Cynthia refused to communicate with the couple, she at least tolerated their presence.

"Evangeline" closed; Harry found another job; and Nellie practiced her singing and acting at home. On June 7, 1880, a boy was born, named after his father. Harry got a job to conduct the orchestra at Tony Pastor's theater. Pastor was an astute entrepreneur whose pioneering efforts had popularized and refined vaudeville. Some months later, Harry persuaded Pastor to give his wife an audition. At the time, Pastor was planning to put on a series of Gilbert & Sullivan satires and was looking for singers. Nellie sang three songs for Pastor, afterward holding her breath awaiting his response. "Can you start next week?" asked Pastor. Nellie was to be paid $25 a week.

"But we have to change your name," Pastor suggested. A list was drawn up, pinned on a board, and various combinations were compared. Nellie chose "Lillian Russell" because the name sounded musical. Pastor concurred. On November 22, 1880, Tony Pastor walked on stage to address his audience. He proclaimed Nellie's loveliness and golden voice. "Direct from England," he announced, "I give you Lillian Russell!" Lillian Russell's career was launched.

Pastor taught Lillian stagecraft — how to enter the stage, how to handle the audience and how to deal with encores. He had her learn new songs and change her act frequently. By her third week at Pastor's, Lillian was not only singing but was also acting in short skits. The *New York Clipper* was the first to note her audience appeal.

In contrast to Lillian's immediate success, the Brahams' personal life was suffering. Harry had become jealous of Lillian's success and adoration from male members of the audience. Cynthia complained that both of them were neglecting the child. A maid caring for the baby accidentally stabbed him. A doctor called to assist was unable to stop the bleeding; the baby went into convulsions and died. Recriminations followed. Cynthia continued her censure of Harry; Lillian continued to work because she did not want to give up her career. Not surprisingly, Harry and Lillian separated.

Lillian was selected to play the lead in a number of Gilbert & Sullivan travesties, given as afterpieces on Pastor's bill. Newspapers spoke of her stage success and labeled Lillian "a favorite." Pastor noticed the effect on the 19-year-old Lillian—the repeated encores, long applause, and increasing attention from "stage door Johnnies"—and the difficulty he was having consulting with her.

In the spring of 1881, Pastor assembled his summer touring company. Instead of selecting Lillian for the company, he chose the Irwin twins. Pastor loaned Lillian to Willie Edouin's Company, which would tour the western part of the United States. Although she was disappointed in not being selected by Pastor, she knew the Edouin tour would further educate her. Pastor made the change easier by raising her salary to $50 a week.

Lillian quickly learned the ups and downs of working in a road show and the business of touring. Playing in San Francisco was a revelation to her. The city was open to all sorts of popular theater shows. In one of her skits, Lillian wore tights, and the sight of her walking provocatively across the stage had the audience falling off their chairs. When she appeared at restaurants after the show, Lillian was seen in the company of men smoking. The company played for five weeks in San Francisco to full houses. Lillian's singing and acting made her a local headliner.

When the company arrived in Denver, Edouin discovered he was running out of money. Future dates were cancelled and the company disbanded. Since Edouin had promised Pastor to protect Lillian, he invited her to join his family on their return to New York. Not yet 20, Lillian experienced both the adulation of the audience and the disaster of an empty purse. The New York press reported on Lillian's "engaging" performances and her off-stage activities. Cynthia was outraged at the revelations, but Lillian never denied the charges. As she probably anticipated, the reports got the attention of theater managers who saw an opportunity to capitalize on Lillian's sudden notoriety.

Lillian was quickly hired by a traveling vaudeville company, "The Variety Troupe," to tour through Massachusetts and New Hampshire. She was the company's headliner, received good reviews and filled the houses. When she returned to New York, Pastor believed that Lillian had matured professionally and was ready to further her career. Although he would have liked to retain Lillian, Pastor gave her contract to Col. John A. McCaull, who was preparing a comic opera. Lillian was promised a salary of $75 a week to pay a secondary role in "The Grand Mogul" as Djemma, the snake charmer. The move represented the end of her first vaudeville experiences as she went on to become the queen of comic opera in America.

Dozens of stage successes, two additional husbands, a child, continual battles with impresarios and managers, higher salaries, substantial newspaper coverage, both good and bad, and a unique rapport with both male and female audiences kept Lillian at the forefront of her profession.

But audience tastes change. Comic opera declined; musical comedy was becoming more popular; and vaudeville was on its way to becoming America's top entertainment. Lillian played with Weber and Fields with their Music Hall company as a singer and demonstrated her abilities as a comedienne. When the team separated, Lillian sought new venues. Vaudeville quickly vied for her participation.

Lillian opened at Proctor's 23rd Street Theater October 2, 1905, at $3,000 a week for a ten-week tour. It was the first of her two-a-day performances, sharing the stage with Russian dancers, minstrels, a magician, acrobats and motion pictures. Proctor featured Lillian on a large electric sign outside the theater. Although she sang only four songs, plus encores, each song was accompanied by elaborate changes of scenery. Lillian was quoted as saying she would display 20 new dresses during the tour, each worth several thousand dollars. She added that she would change musical selections each week. Her performances were a tremendous box office success.

Lillian was then signed by Percy Williams, owner and manager of a circuit of first-class vaudeville houses, for a six-week tour at $2,500 a week. She opened at the Colonial Theater, New York, sang four popular songs and encored them upon request. The *New York Herald* reported that "the audience announced its approval and the women gasped with delight." Lillian's stardom in vaudeville continued.

To everyone's surprise, Lillian announced a change in her plans. She believed she had to give up singing roles since the strain of vaudeville appearances had weakened her vocal chords. Instead, she chose to enter dramatic comedy. Five years of mostly successful dramas established Lillian as a force in legitimate theater. But like her other endeavors, she tired of the traveling and the hassle of running a company. Besides, Lillian had just celebrated her fiftieth birthday, and the press implied that she might be at the end of her career, although she was "as beautiful as ever." The Keith circuit was not disturbed by the press reports. They signed Lillian for a tour at $2,500 a week in which she would sing four songs and two encores. Lillian was back in vaudeville!

Werba & Leuscher then booked Lillian for 15 weeks at $2,500 a week. Her performance included four songs, encores, and a succession of beautiful gowns. Crowds were at capacity; reviews were excellent. At the conclusion of her prosperous tour, Weber and Fields asked her to participate in their Jubilee show, with all the old performers from the Music Hall days. Lillian gladly accepted and looked forward to the fun of a tour with a group of old friends and zany comedians. The Jubilee lasted four months and was credited with earning the largest amount of money any touring show had ever made.

Immediately after the Jubilee's final show, Lillian married Alexander Moore, a Pittsburgh newspaper editor and a stalwart of the Republican Party. For the next few years, Lillian's activities were diverse. She appeared in a movie, "Wildfire," an adaptation of her play, co-starring with Lionel Barrymore. She went on a lecture circuit promoting exercise, good eating habits and beauty techniques. She gave demonstrations on "How to Live 100 Years" which appealed to both men and women. She was then persuaded to return to vaudeville on the UBO circuit for a tour of nine weeks and on the Cort circuit for 15 weeks, all at $2,500 a week. Another tour on the UBO circuit for 14 weeks did not pull well. The coming war and her weakening voice signaled she was near the end of her singing career.

World War I found Lillian enthusiastically donating her time and energy, selling Liberty Bonds, entertaining at military camps, and speaking out on behalf of women's suffrage. For her work entertaining the troops, Lillian was made an honorary sergeant in the Marine Corps. When the actors struck against management in 1919, Lillian was one of the negotiators for the Actors Equity organization.

In 1920, Lillian and her husband were Pennsylvania delegates at the Republican Convention where Warren G. Harding was nominated. After Harding's inauguration, Lillian was appointed to be a special commissioner on immigration to study the conditions among people eager to migrate from Europe. After a seven-week tour, Lillian publicly advocated that immigrants be examined by American doctors to "insure against fraud" before they were allowed to sail to the United States. European newspapers found her comments inflammatory.

While in Paris, Lillian became ill and sailed for America. When she arrived in New York, she refused to admit to any personal difficulties. To reporters, she was quoted as saying, "All immigration should be entirely stopped for a period of five years," which set off a fierce debate in Congress. Refusing the advice of her doctor to rest and restore her health, Lillian went to Washington, D.C., to give her report to the House Immigration Committee. Her recommendations about the immigration question set off further debate, some members of Congress accusing Lillian of promoting racism.

Although quite weak, Lillian agreed to tour Eastern cities to speak on conditions abroad. She returned home, barely able to walk.

Doctors were finally able to diagnose Lillian's ailment as diabetes, and the prognosis was not good. On June 4, Lillian complained of pain and members of the family were called to her bedside. Early on the morning of June 6, 1922, Lillian died in her sleep. She was 61 years old. Newspapers across the country announced Lillian's death. She was given two funerals, one in Pittsburgh where she was buried and one in New York, where thousands of fellow actors and admirers honored her. President Harding declared three days of national mourning for Lillian, an honor not bestowed on any theatrical performer before or since.

Florence Mills

Before her untimely death at the age of 32 in 1927, Florence Mills had performed in vaudeville, musical comedy, cabarets and revues. She was an influential figure in the beginnings of the Harlem renaissance, an artistic movement of black artists from all media. She was the first black woman to have her own show on Broadway, the first Black performer to be a headliner at the Palace Theater and the first black star on the London stage.

Both of Florence's parents lived in Virginia and were ex-slaves. Her father, John Winfrey, began as a day laborer and later became a carpenter. Her mother, Nellie Simons, worked in a tobacco factory prior to their marriage in 1880. John was 22 and Nellie was 16 when they married. They had five children, four daughters and a boy. Florence was the fourth child born to the couple, on January 25, 1895, in Washington, D.C. Originally from Lynchburg, Virginia, the family relocated to Washington, D.C., to improve their living conditions prior to Florence's birth. But financial difficulties forced the family to move to a section called Goat Alley, a black slum.

From a very young age Florence demonstrated an unusual singing and dancing talent. At five, she won prizes in amateur contests at local vaudeville houses. At eight, she made her professional debut as the guest star "Baby Florence" in "The Sons of Ham," in a black touring company under the direction of Williams and Walker. She sang "Miss Hannah from Savannah," having learned it from the star of the show, Aida Overton Walker. In 1905, Florence was hired by a vaudeville company headed by Bonita and Hearn in the role of a dancing pickaninny. While the company was led by white performers, they used black children as backup to their dances. Her appearances in New York were terminated by the Gerry Society, an evangelical group whose purpose was to keep young people off the city's stages. She was taken from her family and institutionalized for a short time.

Florence's family moved to New York and, for the next several years, she attended school.

In 1910, Florence and her two older sisters, Maude and Olivia, formed a vaudeville act called "The Mills Sisters." They performed in local black theaters, sometimes playing as far away as Philadelphia and Washington, D.C. They appeared at Coney Island for a season. In 1912, when Florence was 17, she married James Randolph but divorced him shortly afterward.

By 1913, the sisters were performing in black vaudeville theaters in the Midwest and South. Maude then left to team up with a male comedian, leaving "The Mills Sisters" to tour on their own. The following year, Olivia retired and Florence teamed with Kinky Caldwell. For a season, they toured the black vaudeville circuit with some degree of success. When Caldwell withdrew to get married, Florence decided to pursue her career in Chicago, at the time a lively center for black entertainment.

Florence joined with Ada Louise Smith (known as Bricktop for her bright red hair) and Cora Green to form the Panama Trio. They performed at the notorious Panama Cafe for almost two years. The Panama Cafe was noted for its black-and-tan revues, gambling and prostitution and as a place where Blacks and whites danced together, rather scandalous behavior for the time. A shooting incident caused the police to close the club. Undaunted, The Panama Trio continued to perform in local venues until their breakup in 1917.

Florence Mills

Florence's voice had now matured and she was recognized as a very talented singer. Her voice was considered unusual for the time — small, high, sweet and with flexibility. She was likened to a bird or musical instrument. A jazz musician she appeared with, Mezz Mezzrow, thought she sang "like a hummingbird." Her small voice grew as she sang, blending passion and pathos. Moving from mid-stage to the footlights by the end of the song, she had audiences shouting and applauding enthusiastically.

In 1917, an already successful vaudeville troupe, Ralph Dunbar's "Tennessee Ten," signed Florence. Their act included singing, dancing and comedy, all backed by a full jazz band. The dance director was Ulysses "Slow Kid" Thompson who, although a young man, had a background of playing in circuses and saloons. Florence and Thompson soon became lovers.

Throughout 1917 and 1918,

the "Ten" toured the country on the Keith circuit, one of the few black acts found on a normally white route. Nora Bayes hired them to appear in her own show, "The Songs We Love to Sing." The "Ten" were now considered a headliner act and were in great demand by other tour managers. But when Thompson was drafted by the army, Florence left the troupe. The Panama Trio was re-formed with Green and Carolyn Williams replacing Bricktop. Through 1918 and early 1919, the trio had a very successful tour on the Pantages circuit, visiting Canada and western cities. They ended the group in San Francisco when Williams got married. When Thompson returned to the United States, he sought out Florence and together they rejoined "The Tennessee Ten."

In 1919, the "Ten" were hired for an all-star revue, "Folly Town," a summer show. Included in the mixed cast were Bert Lahr and Jack Haley. The show was said to be the first on Broadway to feature black and white performers equally. Florence sang and danced, as did Thompson, but they were just part of the "Ten" company. After "Folly Town" closed its limited run, the "Ten" went out on the Keith-Orpheum vaudeville circuit for a highly successful tour. An increasing number of high-class vaudeville houses in the country (with the exception of the South) now welcomed black performers. Florence also obtained a number of engagements at Harlem's famous Lincoln Theater, considered the best featuring black performers. She was favorably received, reviewers remarking about her unique style of singing. Advertising for the Lincoln called her "Harlem's dainty, sweet singer."

Florence and Thompson's big break occurred in 1921 when they got jobs as replacements for an already successful show, "Shuffle Along." The show was viewed as the best black musical to date and opened up Broadway to black entertainers. The show's replacements, Florence, Adelaide Hall, Josephine Baker and Paul Robeson, were considered better than the original cast. Historians identify "Shuffle Along" as the beginning of the Harlem Renaissance.

For nearly two years, the show played to full houses. Featured songs that became hits were "I'm Just Wild About Harry" and "Love Will Find a Way." When Florence sang "I'm Just Wild About Harry," her rendition stopped the show. She had become a sensation on Broadway. The song's authors were Noble Sissle and Eubie Blake, who went on to become one of Broadway's most notable composing teams. The show played 504 performances in New York. Flush with the success of the show and Florence's ascendancy to stardom, she and Thompson were married.

While "Shuffle Along" was still playing, producer Lew Leslie persuaded Florence to sing at his club, the Plantation Room, atop the Winter Garden. Florence's presence filled the club nightly and reviewers wrote of this new talent as "so rich, so provocative, so saturated with emotion, yet fastidious in its refinement." Managers bid for her services. Ziegfeld tried to get her for the Follies but she refused. Leslie built an entire show around Florence. She became a darling of fashionable society, her name in lights on Broadway.

Leslie had promised to star Florence in a mixed race revue, "From Dover to Dixie," that would premiere in London. Florence was a smash success in both London and Paris. The "Dover" section of the show featured white performers and received tepid reviews while the "Dixie" section was a huge success. When the show returned to the United States, the "Dover" part was dropped and "Dixie to Broadway," a totally Black revue, opened on October 29, 1924, at the Broadhurst Theater. Florence's singing and dancing again stopped the show. After eight weeks of full houses, it went on tour. The hit of the show was Florence's rendition of "I'm a Little Blackbird Looking for a Bluebird," which reviewers believed was a protest against Black inequality. It was to be Florence's last appearance in a Broadway show.

In April 1925, Florence Mills and Company played at the New York Hippodrome with an all-star cast of some of the best black performers available, including Johnny Nit, a headlining tap dancer, and Will Vodery and his orchestra. Two months later, Florence became the first black to headline a bill at the Palace Theater. Late in 1925, a Leslie-produced "Blackbirds" opened to immediate success. The show was being prepared for a tour of England and France where Florence was already recognized as an international star.

An event at the Aeolian Hall on January 24, 1926, became a significant event in the history of the Harlem Renaissance. The International Composer's Guild, a prestigious musical group in New York, presented a concert that featured several important performers and musical compositions. Eugene Goossens, a well-known classical conductor, had his introduction to jazz. Ottorino Respighi made his U.S. debut as a guest conductor and his wife as an operatic singer. And Florence Mills introduced the work, "Levee Land," by the black classical composer William Grant Still. She sang a group of four jazz-based songs. The Mills-Still collaboration was especially singled out by reviewers as a *tour de force* in concertizing. The audience, mostly representing the city's social elite, gave Florence an enthusiastic response. Seen in the audience were Arturo Toscanini, George Gershwin and James W. Johnson. Although Florence had practiced the songs before the concert, she had only a half-hour to rehearse them with Goossens and the orchestra. Goossens was reported to be impressed by her "superb musicianship." Toscanini went backstage to congratulate Florence. Critics raved about her interpretation. "She sang them seriously and lovingly, but she did more, she rolled her eyes here and shrugged her shoulders there and the audience squirmed excitedly and laughed like a good neighbor. It was a pretty jolly evening for a concert hall." Unfortunately, "Levee Land" was not performed again in Still's lifetime.

Late in 1926, Florence reopened with "Blackbirds" at the Alhambra Theater, her farewell performance before leaving for England and France. In Paris, she shared a bill with Maurice Chevalier and at Les Ambassadeurs with Paul Whiteman and his orchestra. In London, she opened in September at the Pavilion. Blackbird parties became the rage with the social elite and the Prince of Wales was a frequent visitor to the theater. In April 1927, "Blackbirds" held its 250th performance to continued acclaim. But people noticed that Florence was visibly tired and possibly ill from the demands of two shows a day and the unending string of parties and special events. Nevertheless, she took the show on a tour of the provinces. Doctors stepped in and recommended that she rest or face the consequences. Reluctantly, she and Thompson went to Baden-Baden, Germany, for a rest cure.

In September 1927, Florence returned to the United States and an array of banquets and awards to honor her accomplishments in Europe. Florence's last performance had been on the ship *Ile de France,* honoring New York mayor Jimmy Walker. On October 25, she entered the hospital, supposedly for an appendectomy. A second emergency operation at New York's Hospital for Joint Diseases found she suffered from an intestinal obstruction with no hope of recovery. Florence died on November 1, 1927.

Newspapers covered Florence's funeral as if it were a royal event. Five thousand mourners attended the service at the Mount Zion Methodist Episcopal Church. It was reported that more than 150,000 people lined the streets for the funeral procession. Many of the performers she had appeared with were among the mourners. Messages of sympathy came from Mayor Walker, producers A.H. Woods, David Belasco, Flo Ziegfeld and Paul Whiteman.

The press called Florence the most popular person in Harlem. They recognized that she had never forgotten her roots and affirmed her heritage. She gave black performers the opportunity to display their talents and reach stardom in the white world of entertainment.

Rae Samuels

Rae Samuels was one of the few singers in vaudeville who specialized in comic rube songs, usually done in dialect. Rubes were coarse characters, ill-dressed, with no manners. Rae sang and acted out these novelty tunes with a zest and vitality that earned her the title "The Blue Streak of Vaudeville." To make her act more humorous, she dressed in elegant gowns while playing the rube. She introduced many songs, but few of them appeared as sheet music because they were so identified with her unique performances.

Rachael May Samuels was born May 3, 1889, in Youngstown, Ohio, the last of ten children. Her parents, Rachael and Philip Samuels, had immigrated from Swansea, Wales, in 1872, settling in Wilkes-Barre, Pennsylvania, where Philip got work in the coal mines. Philip died in 1892, leaving his wife to care for the younger children. A neighbor, called "Aunt Jane" by the children, cared for Rae. She taught Rae to sing and recite poetry and got her to perform at churches and at Sunday night get-togethers. While Rae had no serious intentions to go on the stage, she was persuaded to consider entering vaudeville. Joining her sister or cousin and her husband in an act called the "Musical Hearts," Rae sang several songs. The year was 1905 and Rae was 16 years old. The act was considered mediocre but, since her mother agreed to have her travel, Rae went along. In the process, she learned about touring and theater life. A career on the stage now seemed an appealing choice.

While Rae was playing in San Francisco, a theater manager suggested that she "go out on her own" and offered to book her if she decided to follow his advice. Of course, playing solo meant she would have to learn to manage her career. She needed costumes and songs to build her repertoire. She had to figure out the costs of travel, hotels and food and quickly realized these expenses consumed most of her salary. She visited music publishers to select the latest tunes and diligently practiced them. She obtained an engagement in Oakland at a salary of $50 for the week. Rae performed well and the manager got her additional engagements in California and Arizona. For several years, Rae played in small-time vaudeville houses on the West Coast. A comedy team, Savoy and Savoy, frequently appeared with Rae, and they persuaded her to join them in Chicago.

She had a difficult time finding work in Chicago, and was forced to take low-salary assignments where she could find them. Rae earned $35 a week for eight performances a day and ten on Sunday. As she recalled later in her career, "Nothing I've earned since has given me as much of a thrill as that. I was so sure that $35 was all the money in the world, that it never occurred to me to look for anything better."

All that changed when a music sheet salesman from Leo Feist, a major music publisher, recognized Rae's talent and suggested she augment her singing repertoire with novelty songs, which she did to good effect. Her appearances in Chicago theaters expanded and she soon became known as a fine singer and pleasing entertainer. A newspaperman, Jack Lait of the *Chicago American* (later of *Variety* and editor of the *New York Daily Mirror*), enjoyed Rae's efforts so much that he helped to improve her act and assisted in her business management.

Lait guided her selection of engagements and salary demands. Thanks to his efforts, and Rae's obvious talent, she was signed in 1911 to play on the Orpheum circuit. Included in the arrangement was an accompanist, travel expenses and a salary of $250 a week. Rae was good at matching her act with appropriate songs. She began developing her act by taking rube songs, using dialects to present them and interpreting them in a comedic manner. The Orpheum people asked Rae whether she would be able to begin her tour in two weeks. "Oh yes," she replied enthusiastically. "I have all the songs, the material, but I'll need some new clothes." She got the clothes. Rae was on her way to playing in first-class vaudeville houses.

Initially Rae appeared second on the bill, not a good spot for a novelty singer. However, she distinguished herself quickly by singing rube songs dressed in beautiful gowns and joking with audiences about the apparent incongruity. Patrons immediately took to her offbeat performance and called for encores. Soon she was playing next to closing, a preferable place to entertain audiences. At the end of her first year of touring, she was back in Chicago, this time as a headliner of a bill at the Chicago Palace. One of Flo Ziegfeld's agents saw Rae perform and signed her for the 1912 edition of the Follies.

"The Ziegfeld Follies of 1912" opened at the Moulin Rouge on October 21. The show featured Lillian Lorraine, Leon Errol, Bert Williams and Bernard Granville. Rae sang one of her rube songs with a Jewish accent, so pleasing the audience that they shouted for encores. She also teamed with Granville in another song.

Marty Forkins was a boxing promoter who happened to see Rae perform at the Orpheum Theater in San Francisco. He saw her whenever he could, and a close relationship evolved. In 1912, Forkins switched from boxing promoter to theatrical manager, his first client being Rae. His efforts on her behalf were instrumental in Rae receiving up to $2,000 a week in vaudeville. For almost two years, Forkins pursued Rae. They were married November 16, 1914, in New Orleans, Louisiana. They remained together for 52 years. Forkins was also responsible for signing Bill "Bojangles" Robinson. The dancer became the first Black entertainer to play in high-class vaudeville.

Forkins got Rae a small part in "The Honeymoon Express," which opened at the Winter Garden on February 6, 1913. The show starred Al Jolson, Gaby Deslys, Dixon and Doyle and Ada Lewis. Also in the cast were newcomers Harry Fox and Fanny Brice. Jolson dominated the stage and stopped the show with two hit songs, "You Made Me Love You" and "Who Paid the Rent for Mrs. Rip Van Winkle." Rae sang a character song with an Italian accent. However, she was lost in the theatrical flourishes of Jolson and Deslys and received little attention from reviewers. She was happy to return to vaudeville and another spin on the Orpheum circuit.

In 1914, at the beginning of her fall tour, Rae appeared for the first time at the Palace Theater. She received as many accolades as co-stars Grace La Rue, Bonnie Thornton, Ruth Roye and Valerie Bergere. Her impressive performance at the Palace made the season's tour even more profitable.

From 1914 to 1920, Rae played various vaudeville circuits—Keith, Orpheum, Considine and the Western Wheel—with varying success. It seemed to depend on whether audiences were ready for her dialect character songs. The more diverse nationalities in town, the greater her success at the box office. Forkins then booked Rae in selected cities, those that fully understood and enjoyed her act. One of Rae's most significant contributions to vaudeville occurred in 1918 when she was performing at the Palace. Irving Berlin was at nearby Camp Upton as a soldier. His manager persuaded Rae to introduce Berlin's new song, "Oh, How I Hate to Get Up in the Morning" as part of her act. The theater was filled with soldiers from nearby camps and they cheered, stomped their feet and whistled for encores of the song until the manager pulled Rae off the stage so the program could continue. Berlin was in the audience and, after the show, went backstage to praise Rae for her interpretation.

In May 1919, Rae traveled to London to star in a revue produced by Albert de Courville. The appearance had been negotiated by her husband, who accompanied her. Called the Mr. and Mrs. Micawber of vaudeville, the couple swore they would never travel without one another, and they never did. Just prior to her opening in London, Rae spent several weeks entertaining in camps and hospitals in France.

During the 1920s, Rae continued her career as a vaudeville headliner, always a pleasing act on bills that featured everything from animal acts to opera divas. She appeared again at the Palace in 1923 in the headline spot second to last on the program along with such stars as Bill Robinson, Harland Dixon and Mary Boland. The Palace program identified her as "The Blue Streak of Vaudeville."

Rae Samuels

By the late 1920s, Rae's act had faded along with many vaudeville bills, as movies began to replace live performance in the high-class theaters. Rae continued to find engagements, but salaries had deteriorated and time on stage had increased from two-a-day to four-a-day.

In 1931, even though the Palace had installed sound equipment, it was temporarily still a vaudeville house. Performers who played at the Palace were primarily veteran acts. When Rae last played there, she shared billing with W.C. Fields, Irene Franklin and Jimmy Durante. A year later, a fire at the theater put it out of business for several weeks. A few months later, the glorious Palace, the apex of vaudeville performance, changed its program to an all-movie format.

For the next two years, Rae continued in what remained of vaudeville, but these were tough times. Although she was only 42 years old, she was viewed as an oldtimer with "old" material. She and her husband moved to Los Angeles with the possibility of entering the movies. Unfortunately, no parts were forthcoming. Rae spent the next several years playing in local vaudeville and revue revivals. She retired from the stage in 1935.

Marty Forkins died in 1966. Rae lived to the age of 90. She died on October 24, 1979, at the old actors' home in Mahwah, New Jersey. She had become so obscure that *Variety* did not mention her passing.

Rae's highly successful career in vaudeville ended when vaudeville died. A long-term headliner, she had hosts of admirers who followed Rae to her last curtain.

Alice Lloyd

When Alice Lloyd performed in America, she was at the height of her career and a major drawing power. She was one of the first of the British entertainers to make a hit in America. Alice's career in the United States continued from 1907 to 1928, during which time her singing and acting gained her the title "The Ideal Dainte [sic] Chanteuse."

Marie Lloyd, Alice's older sister, had become famous in England as "The Bernhardt of the Music Halls." The two sisters were opposites. Marie was rough-hewn and her songs had a racy style. Alice was dainty, modest, good-looking and wore beautiful costumes. As popular as Marie was in England, she never was able to score with American audiences. Her visits to the United States failed to obtain audience approval, due likely to her double-entendre songs, some so questionable that censors cut them from her act. Alice sang songs that pleased audiences, her stage persona reminding people of "the girl next door." Reviewers called her songs "unforgettable" and when audiences joined in to sing with her, her popularity was assured. In a period when independent single women were expressing their newfound freedom, Alice presented herself as an innocent and inoffensive soubrette.

Alice Wood was born in London, England, on October 20, 1873. Sister Marie was three years older and sister Grace two years younger. They were born in a slum area of London called Hoxton. Alice's father, Brush Wood, was a waiter. Her mother was a dressmaker. The couple had six daughters and three sons. Alice, Marie, Grace and Daisy became performers.

Marie Lloyd borrowed her name from the *Lloyd's News,* a popular London newspaper, and made her debut on the stage in May 1885. Alice and Grace followed their sister, taking her last name, and making their first appearance on the stage at the Forester's Music Hall, London, on February 20, 1888. Alice was 15 years old and Grace was 13. Calling themselves "The Sisters Lloyd," for five years they sang and danced in music halls until Grace retired to get married. Alice put together a solo act and proved successful, although some of her appeal may have come from Marie, who had already gained headliner status singing risqué songs. In contrast, Alice gained the attention of reviewers by singing pleasing songs like "Never Mind the Rain," "Liza's Wedding" and "Splash Me," a decided audience favorite. Audiences quickly learned the words and sang along.

Alice came to the United States in February 1907. She brought along her husband, Tom McNaughton and brother-in-law Fred McNaughton (a well-known English comedy team), a reputation for singing endearing songs and a contract with the Keith circuit

Alice Lloyd

for a reported $1,500 a week. Alice made her U.S. debut at the Colonial Theater in late February 1907. The McNaughton duo was also on the bill. *Variety* called her act a "dainty, artistic bit of song acting." She was held over for two weeks and then embarked on a long road tour that introduced her to American audiences across the country. They took to her style immediately. After a successful tour, she returned to England to recuperate from the strenuous and demanding trip.

Alice was the first performer to obtain a U.S. copyright on the "business of mirror effects" she used in the act. While singing, she would manipulate a mirror that reflected the spotlight on bald heads in the audience. Other performers were warned not to use this technique or they would be subject to the consequences of arrest and fines. Lottie Gilson, for one, argued that she was the first performer to use mirrors although they were sewn on her dress. Other performers challenged the copyright by using mirrors in other ways while on stage.

In 1908, Alice was a featured headliner on another Keith circuit tour. In June, *Variety* called her act "a knockout." When she played in New York, Alice appeared in two theaters at one time, a rarity in scheduling at the time. She appeared at the Colonial Theater in New York early on the bill, then raced to the Orpheum in Brooklyn where she closed the program. After another successful tour of the country, she returned to England to rest but, instead, was booked to play in music halls for the summer season. When she returned to the United States in 1909, she began a tour of the high-class vaudeville houses, singing her now famous songs, "Stockings on the Line," "Never Introduce Your Bloke to Your Lady Friend" and "Who're You Lookin' At?" all comic tunes that audiences loved to participate in. When *Variety* published a list of performers with the highest weekly salaries in vaudeville, Alice was said to be earning $1,500 a week.

The years 1911 and 1912 brought some changes in actors' performance and touring. Some performers balked at the monopoly held by the Syndicate and opted for movies. Some went into musical comedy. And some went with rival circuits in competition against Keith and Albee. Alice signed with the Pantages circuit, whose theaters were mostly on the West Coast, and prospered anew. When, in 1911, William Morris, the well-known agent and producer, selected his choice of the top vaudeville performers, Alice was one of the names on his list. In 1912, after Nora Bayes had made the musical "Little Miss Fixit" a New York success, Alice took the show on tour and made an equal hit. Well-known to audiences due to her frequent cross-country trips, Alice helped to put over the musical.

When Alice returned to the United States in 1914 after a brief tour of English music halls, she had the distinction of playing opposite her sister Marie in New York. Alice was appearing at the Palace Theater for the first time and Marie was featured at Hammerstein's Victoria. Reviewers believed that Alice's act was better, and attendance at the two theaters confirmed this. When World War I began in August, both sisters returned to England.

Alice and Marie entertained the troops while also appearing at music halls. Alice spent much of her time in charge of the reception committee of the Receiving Hospital to which the wounded were brought back from France. Her husband, Tom McNaughton, was watching for German submarines and mines.

In 1919, Alice returned to the United States to begin another tour of vaudeville houses, starting with an appearance at the Palace Theater, a part of the Keith circuit. Appearing with her were Lew Dockstader, the veteran minstrel man, and newcomers Phil Baker, an accordion player, and Ben Bernie, a violinist. Alice drew more applause than any act and was rewarded with another week, heading the bill. For the next several years, Alice toured successfully, using her popular songs and pleasing manner to capture audiences.

Marie died unexpectedly in October 1922 after ailing for some months. She was 51 years old. Alice returned to England to attend an elaborate funeral. Well over 100 carriages and thousands of mourners followed Marie to her grave. Alice was quite depressed by Marie's death and briefly retired from the stage. When she decided to perform again, she went on a world tour that lasted almost three years.

Alice appeared at the Palace Theater in September 1925, singing to enthusiastic audiences as though she had never left them. Songs like "Naughty But Nice" and "The Older the Fiddle the Sweeter the Tune" entertained theatergoers anew. Judging from the packed houses, she had lost none of her headliner status. Alice was in competition with several opulent movie houses nearby, which also offered live shows, but she was a box office hit.

Alice chose to play the Pantages circuit for the next few years even though she saw that vaudeville was losing its audience appeal. *Variety* reported that she was earning $1,250 a week, which was cheap in their estimation. In early 1928, Alice returned to England, never to appear in the United States again. She played sporadically in music halls for several years, retiring officially in the early 1930s. She had been entertaining audiences in the United States and England for 45 years.

On November 16, 1949, Alice died at her home in Banstead, a suburb of London. She was 75 years old. Unlike the "royal" funeral of Marie, Alice had a private funeral and burial, as was her desire. In an age of solo female acts, many of them "over the top," Alice Lloyd's performance stood out as one of the most appealing on the vaudeville stage. And, unlike her contemporaries, Alice was loyal to vaudeville throughout her career.

Bessie Wynn

With a clear, sparkling, beautiful voice, Bessie Wynn sang her way to vaudeville stardom after building her career in operetta and musical comedy. Called "The Venus with the Velvet Voice" and "The Lady Dainty of Vaudeville," for a quarter of a century she introduced many songs to theater audiences.

Bessie was born in Chicago, Illinois, in June 1876. Little is known of her family background and her childhood except that she was given singing lessons at an early age. The family moved to Philadelphia where Bessie sang for several years in the church choir. At the age of 23, she left home ("ran away," she claimed) and went to New York to enter the theater.

She was hired for the chorus in Anna Held's first musical, "Papa's Wife," in 1899. The following year, Bessie appeared in the chorus of "The Cadet Girls," which opened at the Herald Square Theater on July 25. The show was a Parisian hit, adapted for American audiences by Harry B. Smith and starred Dan Daly, Christie McDonald and Adele Ritchie. The show ran only 48 performances. Bessie returned to Chicago to study voice and played in the chorus of several comic operas that visited the city.

In the fall of 1901, Fred Hamlin, impresario and general manager of the Grand Opera House in Chicago, was seeking a summer show to produce at his theater for 1902. He learned of an operetta taken from a best-selling children's book called *The Wizard of Oz*. During the spring of 1902, Hamlin and stage director Julian Mitchell auditioned performers to fill the singing parts, one of which was a witch and court poet. Bessie was chosen for the role, her first significant part in a major production.

"The Wizard of Oz" opened on June 16, 1902, at the Grand Opera House. Audiences immediately took to the show and reviewers predicted it would last the entire summer. The show starred Anna Laughlin as Dorothy, and Montgomery and Stone as the Tin Man and Scarecrow, respectively. The show ran to the end of the year and was scheduled to open in New York in January. Changes were made in the cast, but Bessie kept her role and was given another song to sing as well.

"Oz" opened at the Majestic Theater on January 20, 1903, quickly winning New York audiences as it had in Chicago. Bessie and Anna Laughlin shared a dressing room that featured large dressing tables, a bath and wardrobe closets. Bessie was taken with the colorful costumes and wished she could be as feminine as Laughlin instead of playing a "trouser" role. It would be several years before she was able to fulfill that desire. In the meantime, she would be viewed by managers as a "trouser" actress. Her next role reinforced the image.

Having worked successfully in "Oz," Bessie was offered a role in Victor Herbert's next operetta, "Babes in Toyland," a Hamlin and Mitchell production. As Tom Tom, Bessie would sing the hit song of the show, "Toyland." She also sang "An Old-Fashioned Rose" at the beginning of the third act.

"Babes in Toyland" opened at the Majestic Theater on October 13, 1903. The show's popularity carried it to June 1904. Several other companies toured the show for years. When "Toyland" closed in New York, Bessie was asked to return to "Oz" as it began its third season on a national tour. She appeared in the same role, but now had three songs to sing. Each season, "Oz" initiated new skits and songs to keep the show fresh.

Because of "Oz"'s continued success, the show ran through 1905. When it closed, Mitchell was sought by Flo Ziegfeld to manage a new revue he was planning to open in 1907. Montgomery and Stone were wooed by Charles Dillingham for a new musical. Bessie was engaged by Herbert for another children's fantasy, "Wonderland," a takeoff on "Alice in Wonderland." The show featured Alice as a street seller of matches who solves the mystery of disappearing princesses. The music was Herbert at his most mediocre and the plot had been hurriedly put together to take advantage of the "Toyland" craze. "Wonderland" opened on October 24, 1905, at the Majestic, now being labeled the house that featured children's fairy tales. Reviewers were not enthused with the production, and the show played only 73 performances. On the road, however, "Wonderland" ran for two seasons with excellent box office receipts. Bessie stayed with the company through 1907. After the show closed, she made her first vaudeville appearance.

As a vaudeville performer, Bessie refused to wear tights. Finally, she was able to realize her ambition to appear feminine, "her greatest asset of stage success," she believed. She designed her own costumes and coiffures with several of them displayed in New York department stores. Her repertoire of songs was considerable and she introduced new songs in her act nearly every week. B.F. Keith was so enamoured with Bessie that he signed her to a multi-year contract for his vaudeville circuit. Her first year quickly vaulted her to headliner status.

Bessie's private life was in the public eye. The press reported various liaisons she had with male cast members. In 1907, she made headlines when she was named a defendant in a divorce case, charged with adultery with a married man. Other rumors circulated periodically every few years, but her popularity was never affected.

Bessie was persuaded to return to musical comedy to appear as the lead in "Miss Nobody from Starland." Playing a chorus girl who gets involved in smuggling and ends up a performer in a Princess Theater show, Bessie did her best to keep the show alive with her distinctive singing. With cast changes, a revision of the script, and some backstage gossip, the show ran for an amazing 15 weeks. The show opened in Chicago January 31, 1910 at the Princess Theater with the hope of a trip to New York. This never materialized. Bessie returned to the safety and comfort of the Keith circuit until she was engaged by Lew Fields to appear in another of his summer shows.

In 1912, Fields began rehearsing his new show, "The Sun Dodgers," to star the unpredictable vaudeville siren, Eva Tanguay. After rehearsals, a poor showing in Philadelphia, and Tanguay's constant tantrums, Fields fired her. After rewriting and recasting, Bessie was given the lead, to sing several new songs by Irving Berlin.

"The Sun Dodgers" opened in New York on November 30, 1912, at the Broadway Theater, featuring Bessie and George Monroe. The show was elegantly staged but the plot, dialogue and comedy were stale. Reviewers were not kind. It closed "for reorganization" after 18 performances. Bessie quickly returned to Keith vaudeville, never again to appear in musical comedy.

Bessie earned $1,500 a week on the Keith circuit and was one of his favorites. He once gave her a bear cub as a present. She took it to her farm where it grew to maturity. In Trenton, Princeton students presented Bessie with a goat along with the note, "You've got our goat." After this, she received many animals as mementos for her performances. After the bear episode, Bessie came out with a new song, "Bessie and Her Little Brown Bear," which began a fad for teddy bears.

Bessie Wynn (Museum of the City of New York).

In 1913, Bessie had the dubious distinction of appearing at the Palace Theater on the same bill as Sarah Bernhardt. At the Union Square Theater the following week, she was showered with bouquets. A rumor suggested that Keith had sent all the flowers to absolve her frustration playing behind Bernhardt.

Bessie played for Keith from 1913 to 1924, continuing as one of the top headliners on his circuit. She introduced such songs as "Tell Me," "Won't You Be My Baby Boy," "All That I Ask Is Love," and "Are You Sincere." This combination of her feminine beauty and fine singing voice earned her the title of "The Lady Dainty of Vaudeville."

By the mid–1920s, Bessie was approaching 50. While she still headlined bills, changing audience tastes positioned her as "old-fashioned," her sentimental songs no longer appealing. She continued to perform, but her admirers gradually disappeared. When vaudeville hit hard times during the Depression, Bessie retired to her farm.

In the late 1920s, Bessie married W. Earlingford Grove, a retired writer and newspaperman. For the next few decades, nothing was heard about Bessie. Like other vaudeville headliners, she had faded into obscurity.

A return to the Palace Theater in 1949 brought up her name again. The Palace had reinstated vaudeville shows to replace movies, and featured many oldtimers on the bill. Bessie was invited back, 36 years since her ill-fated billing with Bernhardt. This time, she was feted as guest of honor. Milton Berle introduced her and gave her a bouquet of 36 red roses. The orchestra played "There's No Business Like Show Business." Everyone in the theater was in tears.

Grove died in September 1956. Bessie lingered 12 more years, dying July 8, 1968, of "old age." She was 92 years old. So forgotten was Bessie that neither the *New York Times* nor *Variety* published her obituary. Only a sharp reader would have found a brief death notice two days later in the *Times* death column. Among Bessie's belongings was a dress worn by the great singer Jenny Lind. It was Bessie's greatest treasure, bringing back old memories of stardom.

Ruth Roye

Billed as the "Princess of Ragtime" during the height of her brief vaudeville career, Ruth Roye brought a fine singing voice and an ingratiating personality to the stage, quickly capturing the affection of audiences. She became famous for introducing such song hits as "Waiting for the Robert E. Lee," "I Love Mountain Music" and "Abba Dabba Honeymoon." She came to prominence in high-class vaudeville and almost as quickly disappeared from the stage.

Rebecca Ruth Becker was born in December 1893 in Philadelphia, Pennsylvania. Jacob Becker, her father, was born in Poland in 1862 and came to the United States in 1881. Esther Becker, her mother, was born in Austria in 1866 and came to the United States in 1874. The couple were married in 1885 and settled in Philadelphia. Jacob was a tailor. They had eight children, four girls, three boys and one child that died at birth. Rebecca was the fourth child. In 1912, the family moved to Brooklyn, New York, where Jacob opened a clothing store. The family was quite religious, holding strongly to the tenets of Judaism. At the same time, Jacob and his sons were committed entrepreneurs.

All of the children received an elementary education. After graduation, the boys helped their father or, like Herman, Ruth's older brother, began their own business. Herman opened a nickelodeon in Brooklyn. Business was not good and Herman fired his employees, a singer and ticket taker. He persuaded Rebecca to assume both jobs. She had a good contralto voice and was paid five dollars a week for her efforts. "I had such a good time singing and I enjoyed it so much that my brother said I shouldn't be paid anything. Like a boob, I agreed with him." The experience, however, launched Rebecca into a stage career.

At the age of 15, Rebecca got engagements in ten-cent vaudeville houses in the New York area. Audiences liked her way of interpreting the new jazz-oriented songs. Within a few years, she was engaged at better theaters, earning a salary of $35 a week. As her act matured, Rebecca laced most of her songs with ragtime syncopation and chose music to complement her style. Her reputation as a jazz singer was building rapidly.

Harry Weber knew show business. As an agent, he handled many headliners and was an astute judge of new talent. He was also known to be a great promoter, even if some of his gimmicks were somewhat dubious. He heard Rebecca sing at one of the vaudeville houses in Manhattan. Convinced of her talent, he booked her into a high-class vaudeville theater and promoted her appearance with an unusual twist. Weber offered a silver cup to the best singer on the bill, to be judged by a reporter attending the show. In between acts, Weber ran to a store to purchase the cup. The reporter was delighted with Rebecca's singing and, when she was finished, he marched down the aisle, went up on the stage and presented her with the cup as the champion jazz singer of America. The press noted the incident and wrote about the discovery of a new talent. Weber also changed Rebecca's name to Ruth Roye.

From that moment on, Ruth packed theaters wherever she performed. She had a fluid, husky voice which, combined with a magnetism that quickly captured audiences, made her an instant hit. Her vitality and jazz-inflected renditions brought down the house.

In order to advertise Ruth's "charged" stage presence, Weber concocted a "secret source" that was responsible for giving her the amazing energy she demonstrated on stage. He put together a room with various electrical devices and invited reporters to see how Ruth was "charged." Then, he got the New York Giants baseball players to come in and be "charged" before an important game. They won the game. Following that event, theaters were unable to hold the crowds to see Ruth perform. In a matter of a few years, Ruth was earning $400 a week and had been given the label of the "Princess of Ragtime."

Ruth's reputation, and Weber's influence, got her an engagement at the Palace Theater in June 1914. She accepted less salary, believing that a long run at the Palace would add to her prestige. She was not mistaken. Ruth played at the Palace for three months, a record that lasted until the late 1920s. During her first week, she played opposite Belle Baker, and the two women competed for audience attention with their similar ragtime renditions. Ruth had been placed second on the bill, when Palace audiences were still arriving. Her reception was so strong, however, that she was placed fourth for the remainder of her stay. While appearing at the Palace, Ruth introduced the novelty song, "Abba Dabba Honeymoon," and scored a great hit.

While Ruth was on tour in 1915, an experience in Cleveland typified her impact on vaudeville audiences who had never seen her perform. According to a reviewer, "people applauded because they liked the way she looked. She beamed a smile across the footlights and the crowd was hers before she did anything." After she sang three songs, "the audience didn't want her to go. She impressed herself upon a new audience in a way that will not be soon forgotten."

Ruth took ordinary songs and

Ruth Roye (Harry Ransom Humanities Research Center, the University of Texas at Austin).

created an excitement with them among audiences, turning the songs into popular hits. One such example was "Waiting for the Robert E. Lee." The song was three years old and had languished because no singer had promoted it. Ruth's delivery was so eruptive that it became her signature song. While rendering the song, she shuffled her feet in time and gave off the sounds of a puffing engine. Audiences loved her interpretation and made her repeat it several times. From that point on, everywhere she played, audiences shouted for "Waiting for the Robert E. Lee."

Ruth returned to the Palace in 1916, this time at full salary, to a crowd that loved every song she sang. Reviewers complimented her on her outstanding talent for "putting over a song." On tour for the next two years, Ruth's successes reaffirmed her headliner status.

In New York in late 1918, Ruth met David Garblik, a manufacturer of cotton goods. They married in 1919 and Ruth abruptly retired from the stage at the age of 26 and at the height of her career. She gave no reasons for her actions. Living quietly as a homemaker, she gave birth to two girls, in 1924 and 1928. No matter how hard managers tried, Ruth could not be persuaded to return to performing, even after her husband filed for bankruptcy in 1932, likely due to the Depression. Shortly afterward, Ruth divorced him.

In 1934, Ruth married Julius Kolleny, a merchant in the clothing trade. By the 1950s, her children raised, Ruth and her husband moved to the Alden Hotel on Central Park West. After a long and debilitating illness, Ruth died on June 12, 1960. She was 66 years old. Both *Variety* and the *New York Times* gave her brief obits, mentioning only that she had appeared at the Palace and was known for her delivery of "Waiting for the Robert E. Lee."

Ruth rose quickly in vaudeville to become a beloved headliner. After reaching these heights, she disappeared from the stage just as quickly.

Sophie Tucker

In the summer of 1906, armed with nothing but the names of a few Tin Pan Alley songwriters, 20-year-old Sophie Tuck arrived at New York's Grand Central Station to seek a career on the popular stage.

Born January 13, 1886, in the *shtetl* of Tulchin in the Ukraine, Russia, Sonya Kalish was the second child of Charles, a tailor, and Jennie, a homemaker. A few months after Sonya's birth, the Kalish family traveled overland to Bremen, Germany, seeking passage to the United States. During their journey, Charles changed the family name to Abuza, probably to protect the family against the rampant anti–Jewish hostility.

After arriving at Castle Garden, the family was assigned to Boston where an apartment was waiting for them in the city's Jewish community. Charles was unable to establish himself as a tailor and obtained a job as a bartender in a local saloon. Jennie took over the care of the household and their two children.

In 1893, the Abuza family moved to Hartford, Connecticut. Two more children had been added: Moses, born in 1889, and Anna, born in 1892. Older brother Philip and Sonya, now called Sophie by her friends, were enrolled in elementary school. Charles obtained a job as a bartender in a saloon on Front Street, the busiest street in the city, next to the docks and wharves lining the Connecticut River and in the midst of the Jewish community. A few years later, Charles and Jennie opened a kosher restaurant, which quickly became a neighborhood fixture. Ten-year-old Sophie helped her mother in the kitchen.

Sophie was soon promoted to waitress. At this time, she showed an interest in music, particularly singing popular songs. Memorizing many of the latest songs, Sophie regaled the restaurant's customers and she earned a few extra pennies. In spite of her parents' opposition, Sophie maintained her interest in singing. She performed so well that at her elementary school graduation, she was encouraged to make a career in vaudeville. She auditioned for a spot on an amateur night bill at the local vaudeville house and was selected, but a juggler won the trophy. Sophie's specialty was coon songs, the latest singing rage.

At 16, Sophie entered high school. She was an attractive girl according to the feminine ideals of the day, more gregarious than her peers, although socially naive. Louis Tuck was 20 years old, good-looking, a sharp dresser, earning $15 a week working for a bottler. He chose Sophie as his girlfriend. Their relationship advanced rapidly, and they soon talked of marriage. When Louis suggested they elope, Sophie agreed, although this was against Jewish traditions. On May 14, 1903, Sophie and Louis were married in Springfield, Massachusetts, by a justice of the peace. When they returned to Hartford to tell Sophie's parents the news, they were confronted by the realities of their deed.

Sophie and Louis were forced to live apart until a formal wedding took place. A year later, Sophie was pregnant. As she grew larger, Louis lost interest in her and in supporting the family. On February 5, 1905, Albert Tuck was born. The situation with Louis had become so difficult that Sophie and the baby moved back with her parents and Sophie returned to help out at the restaurant. Learning the latest songs through purchasing music sheets and visiting the vaudeville house, Sophie quickly regained her joy in singing and desire to perform. With $100 from savings, a set of dresses she believed suitable for stage appearances, and a list of Tin Pan Alley song publishers, Sophie left for New York to launch her show business career. Her parents were shocked and angered at the desertion of her family, her son, and Jewish traditions. It would be years before Sophie was welcomed back into the family.

It took several weeks for Sophie to find her first job in New York, singing at the Metropole Cafe from 5 PM to 3 AM, for $6 a week and meals. Sophie quickly learned that beer gardens were the most likely source for advancement. After an audition, she was hired at the German Village, singing from 4 PM to 2 AM, six days a week for a salary of $15. Sophie visited Tin Pan Alley each day to collect new songs to introduce, and she rented gowns to dress for the role. Sophie practiced the new songs so she could sing them that same evening.

After several months, Sophie was earning nearly $50 a week, $20 in salary and $30 in tips. Half of her money was sent home for her parents and the baby. At the German Village, patrons noticed Sophie's strong voice and articulation. Song pluggers observed that she was learning to "sell" a tune, and audiences expressed their enthusiasm for her renditions.

An agent persuaded Sophie to appear at a ten-cent vaudeville house. Audiences were tough on performers, as ready to jeer someone off the stage as to applaud. Sophie, now using the last name of Tucker, captured the audience with her first song, and they shouted for more. The agent was so pleased with her work that he signed her to appear on the Park circuit, ten-cent vaudeville houses in the New York area, for $20 a week. At her first road date, Sophie was informed that she had to sing in blackface, in order to convey the coon songs she sang and to hide her Jewishness.

After nine months on tour, Sophie returned to New York. She was now a seasoned veteran with a powerful, expressive voice and a large repertoire of songs. She played for a week at Tony Pastor's Theater, a very prestigious billing, and obtained good reviews in the

New York Clipper. The owner of the Hathaway circuit signed her to tour for the summer, to sing her coon songs in blackface and appear in skits as a white. Her salary was $35 a week. Later, Gus Hill, manager of a touring company, "The Gay Masqueraders," hired Sophie to appear in comedy skits and sing in blackface. Sophie's successes got her better positions on the bill and Hill encouraged her to add new songs and routines to her act. Within weeks, Sophie was being billed as the "Queen of Coon Shouters." Sophie's first phonograph record was "Rosie, My Dusky Georgia Rosie," for which she received $25. A few months later, the record company went out of business. Flo Ziegfeld attended a show in Holyoke, Massachusetts, near the end of the "Gay Masqueraders" tour, and suggested to Sophie that she contact him upon her return to New York. Their meeting resulted in an unspecified role in the upcoming "Follies of 1909."

The Follies featured Nora Bayes, her husband Jack Norworth, Lillian Lorraine, Bessie Clayton, Mae Murray, and Gertrude Vanderbilt. Sophie's part was a six-minute song-and-dance called "Moving Day in Jungle Town." The Follies received its usual acclaim; "Jungle Town" was barely mentioned. When Bayes demanded a renegotiation of her contract, Ziegfeld refused. Bayes quit the show and Ziegfeld scurried to find an adequate replacement. He hired the always volatile Eva Tanguay, who after two weeks as the headliner demanded that she assume Sophie's role in "Jungle Town." Sophie was out of a job and very distraught.

Enter William Morris, theater owner and booking agent, who was familiar with Sophie's recent vaudeville successes. Within a week, Sophie was appearing as a headliner in one of Morris's theaters, at $75 a week. Her successive engagements in Newark, Brooklyn, Boston, and Chicago filled the houses and gained excellent reviews. Audiences loved Sophie's songs so much that her act often extended to 25 minutes on stage, rare for any vaudeville performer. Morris raised her salary to $100 and advertised her appearances heavily. Morris also arranged to have Sophie record several popular songs with the Edison Phonograph Company. At this time, Sophie began to include double entendre lyrics in her presentations. Some reviewers scolded her for her stage "behavior," but audiences loved it and shouted for more of the same. A good portion of her salary was sent home for her son Bert and the family restaurant. She promised to buy a home for her parents.

By 1911, Sophie had become a headliner on the vaudeville circuit, now advertised as the "Mary Garden of Ragtime." She appeared in Morris theaters across the country. When she plugged new songs, she got a royalty from the publishers for every music sheet sold. She made records of her popular hits. One of her new songs, "Some of These Days," written by Shelton Brooks, became an immediate hit, so much so that many other singers adopted it. Sophie stopped singing it because she continually sought new material for her performances, but she would not forget its appeal. By 1912, Morris had made Sophie an SRO headliner in New York; the *New York Clipper* described her as standing "in the front rank of coon shouters and rag singers."

That same year, Sophie appeared in her first musical comedy, "Merry Mary." Reviews were negative, and Sophie's songs "not classified as polite." Except for Sophie, the show would have closed in a week. It staggered through six weeks of moderate attendance. Morris convinced a reluctant Sophie to sign for another musical, "Louisiana Lou," at $300 a week. The show was a success, played the entire season and into the next season, with Sophie's salary now at $350. The show's male star, Alex Carr, a "Hebrew delineator," convinced Sophie to use her Jewishness, to interpolate something of her heritage into her songs. This became another successful addition to her act.

While on a Morris-sponsored tour, a piano accompanist, Frank Westphal, joined Sophie. They were soon living together. During a Chicago appearance, Sophie played at her first cabaret. She quickly embraced the performing freedom and audience intimacy offered by this venue. This experience began a career-long friendship with cabarets and their adoring audiences.

In 1913, Sophie returned to Hartford as vaudeville headliner and pride of the ragtime singers. The city was decked out to greet their "hometown girl." Sophie had vowed not to return to Hartford until she was a star. But Sophie wondered how her family and the Jewish community would receive her.

Sophie was met with cheers from the awaiting crowd and hugs and kisses from the family. She had not only been pardoned, but also enjoyed a week of devotion and adulation from family, friends, and nightly audiences. Upon her return to New York, Sophie was featured on the front page of the *New York Clipper* and her bio told the story of her rapid rise to stardom.

Sophie and Frank toured on the prestigious Keith circuit, attracting SRO audiences at every theater. They now included short sketches and humor to go along with Sophie's songs. Whatever the audience, Sophie used her Jewishness with confidence. Her final appearance on the tour was at the Palace Theater, New York, where she scored heavily; it was the first of many starring dates at the country's most famous vaudeville theater.

As she noticed changes in audience tastes, Sophie altered her skits, song selections and lyrics to meet their new desires and demands.

In 1915, while on tour, Sophie received a frantic telegram that her father was dying. She rushed home to care for him during his last days. Sophie was so stricken by his death that she contemplated retiring from the stage. A timely visit by William Morris convinced Sophie to continue her career, with the likelihood of even greater successes and substantial salaries. Sophie played dates in various cities, not yet ready to perform full-time. When she returned to New York, she was greeted with such audience enthusiasm that her time on stage lasted more than a half-hour; it would have gone on longer if the crowd had had its way. She was now labeled "The Empress of Songs." Meanwhile, Frank rebelled at his lack of visibility; he was given a garage to manage. To replace Frank, and in keeping with the updating of her stage presentations, Sophie hired a five-piece band, "Sophie Tucker and Her Five Kings of Syncopation." She began to introduce jazz-style material and songs to her repertoire. For her first tour of the group, Morris paid Sophie $1,000 a week, but she had to pay for musician's salaries, sets, costumes, and travel expenses.

Frank failed at the garage and returned to Sophie, who expressed her love for him. They were married in Chicago on October 13, 1917, after she obtained a divorce from Louis Tuck.

Sophie and her band began a tour by playing at cabarets and on the Orpheum vaudeville circuit. Vaudeville reviewers disapproved of her lyrics, but cabaret audiences loved her. In the meantime, it was reported that Frank had disappeared from the act and was playing in vaudeville in another city. Back in New York, Sophie and the band appeared at a new restaurant-cabaret, Reisenweber's, for a limited engagement. They were instant hits. Instead of a six-week engagement, they played at Reisenweber's for ten months. Sophie was earning more than $2000 a week. However, tension among the band members caused Sophie to fire them and hire new jazz musicians to back her. No matter; Reisenweber's now advertised Sophie as the "Queen of Jazz." Unfortunately, the flu epidemic and the actors' strike prevented Sophie from building the new act and she returned to the vaudeville stage.

A trip to Chicago reaffirmed Sophie's stardom in vaudeville and gave her the opportunity to initiate divorce proceedings against Frank.

Both Reisenweber's and the Orpheum vaudeville circuit wanted Sophie, and she gave herself to both of them. She appeared early in the evening at a vaudeville theater and later at the cabaret. Her act changed again with the addition of dancers and the introduction of Jewish songs to her vast repertoire. When Morris announced that Sophie was going to England, the band quit, forcing Sophie to hire two young pianists to accompany her. One of them, Ted Shapiro, backed Sophie for the remainder of her career, more than 45 years. Sophie expressed her readiness to take on London.

William Morris personally introduced Sophie to London's cabaret patrons. After singing three songs, she became an

Sophie Tucker

overnight sensation. Sophie modified her act to please her English audiences; she found that they enjoyed hearing songs with suggestive lyrics. Sophie's stay in England became a continuous round of publicity affairs. During the day, reporters followed her everywhere. Her evening shows were sellouts, each one reported in detail because she introduced new songs and a new gown at each performance. Orchestras had difficulty following Sophie, so she relied mostly on her pianists. She triumphantly returned to the United States in August 1922.

Sophie's return was heralded by SRO crowds, new songs, and press accolades. "It's Sophie Tucker at her best. What more could one want?" wrote *Variety*. In addition, Sophie admitted to a new love, Al Lackey, a New York merchant, eight years younger than her, but, according to Sophie, "it was love right from the start." Two weeks at the Palace reestablished Sophie as a top vaudeville headliner. Reviewers called her "an entertainment institution that never disappoints."

After several months of successful appearances, and a stint on the West Coast in a musical comedy, "Pepper Box Revue," that ran briefly, Morris got Sophie back on the Orpheum circuit at $2,000 a week. Sophie introduced a new song, "I'm the Last of the Red Hot Mammas," written by Jack Yellin. The song was so well-received that she had to encore it at every show. It would soon become her trademark number, the one audiences wanted to hear at every show for the rest of her career.

For the next several years, Sophie played at various New York theaters and cabarets to record-breaking box office receipts. Playing at the palace in New York, Sophie introduced a new Yellin tune, "Yiddishe Mama"; it gained instant popularity and Sophie was asked to sing it often. Her rendition, in both English and Yiddish, always brought tears to the audience.

In late 1925, Sophie, Ted Shapiro and Al Lackey sailed for London for a tour of English theaters and cabarets. Sophie opened to tremendous ovations wherever she appeared. "Red Hot Mamma" and "Yiddishe Mama" were requested at every show. Unfortunately, Sophie caught a bad cold and was confined to a hospital for several weeks. Upon her return to the stage, her activities still gave newspapers plenty of material to write about. Exclaimed one reviewer, "Sophie was one big party."

A cable from home informed Sophie that her mother had become quite ill. Although deeply concerned, Sophie still had weeks of commitments to fulfill. On December 16, 1925, she received the message she dreaded, "Make first boat home." Sophie cancelled her engagements and prepared to return to Hartford, hoping to arrive before her mother died. She was not on time; but the funeral was held up until Sophie arrived home. After the funeral, William Morris visited Sophie, not to persuade her to return to the stage but rather to discuss future engagements. Still, it was several months before Sophie felt comfortable on stage again.

In the late 1920s, vaudeville, once America's great stage entertainment, was dying. Sophie shifted her attention to cabarets, nightclubs, movies, and frequent trips to England. She retained her headliner status in everything but movies. For 50 years, Sophie had given fully of herself to audiences. During her last years, she received many testimonials, including a command performance before Queen Elizabeth and a fiftieth anniversary celebration that lasted an entire year, wherever she happened to be playing.

On October 25, 1965, Sophie opened at the Latin Quarter, New York. Although quite ill, she performed her entire act. In the dressing room, Sophie collapsed in great distress and was quickly rushed to the hospital. She would never again appear on the stage. Sophie Tucker died on February 9, 1966, at age 80. The causes of death were lung cancer and kidney failure.

During the era in which she lived, Sophie was unique as an artist and distinctive as a person. When she died, an era died with her.

Belle Baker

When vaudeville was at its height, Belle Baker was a standout headliner, a unique song delineator of high caliber. Torch singer deluxe, she shared starring honors with song stylists like Sophie Tucker, Nora Bayes and Rae Samuels. She was reported to have introduced 163 songs by songwriters like Kalman and Ruby, Rodgers and Hart, and her favorite, Irving Berlin.

Bella Becker was born in New York City on December 23, 1893. Her parents had immigrated to the United States two years earlier as part of the large exodus of eastern European Jews escaping from the pogroms of Alexander III. She was one of six children, four daughters and two sons.

After a brief period of schooling, Bella pressed shirtwaists 12 hours a day in a stuffy shop to help support the family. However, she was interested in the stage and worked hard to develop her voice and learn the lyrics of the period's most popular songs. She applied to the owner of a cheap Yiddish theater on Cannon Street. Her audition as a singer got her a tryout opportunity. Both the manager and audience approved of the girl and she was engaged to sing one song each night at three dollars a week. While audiences liked Bella, her parents disapproved strongly that she had taken to the stage and felt the family name had been disgraced. Still, she continued to pursue her career.

Jacob Adler was one of the famous actors of Jewish Theater in New York. In 1906, after seeing her perform, he hired the 13-year-old Bella to play a small role in "The Homeless." Bella won other singing parts and, by 15, was appearing in small-time vaudeville companies in the East.

A meeting with agent and promoter Lew Leslie gave impetus to Bella's career. He changed her name to Belle Baker and taught her how to put across a song and dress the part of a professional soubrette. He booked her in small vaudeville houses in New York in order to get her recognition and reviewer attention. They married in 1909. Belle was 16 years old and Leslie was 23.

Belle made her official high-class vaudeville debut in 1911, with an engagement at Hammerstein's Victoria Theater at a salary of $100 a week. Instead of receiving accolades, she was criticized for the quality of her songs and her costume. C.F. Zittell, a critic, took credit for helping Belle improve her stage presence and supposedly got her a job at a local theater. What Leslie was doing at the time was not mentioned, but he was not one to agree to outside interference. His own efforts to draw the attention of the press to his wife's talents helped make her a vaudeville headliner by the age of 20.

Belle obtained a small part in the Shubert show, "Vera Violetta," which opened at the Winter Garden on November 20, 1911. The show was dominated by Annette Kellerman, the swimmer-performer, and Al Jolson, who as a blackface waiter sang several songs. Jolson's appearance helped to launch his Broadway career. The show played for 112 performances.

Returning to vaudeville, Belle toured on the Keith circuit with good results. She made her first appearance at the Palace Theater at a time when its future existence was in jeopardy. On the bill with her was Sarah Bernhardt, who was the main attraction although performing from a wheelchair. Bernhardt watched Belle introduce an Irving Berlin song, "Put It On, Take It Off, Wrap It Up, and Take It Home," which so enthused the audience that she had to repeat it three times. A year later, Belle returned to the Palace, now viewed as the epitome of vaudeville houses. She introduced two more Berlin songs, "Michigan" and "Cohen Owes Me 97 Dollars," which were greeted with cheers and applause. Belle and Berlin had been friends for several years, and he wrote many songs especially for her to introduce. During this time, Yiddish songs were becoming the rage, and Belle featured them in her act.

Although she was short and chubby even by the standards of the day, Belle's deep, resonant voice, which could move from melancholy to comedy, captured audiences. The *Washington Post* described Belle as a "dynamic personality." The *New York Times* mentioned her "decided spontaneity and radiance." "Her audiences leave the theater impressed," the *Times* reviewer declared, "and she perhaps has a greater number of adherents than any other two-a-day artist." Her rendition of such classic Jewish songs as "Eli, Eli" and "My Yiddishe Mama" helped put over her act. Along with colleague Sophie Tucker, she made these songs popular.

By 1917, Belle was the highest-paid performer on the Keith circuit, earning $2,500 a week. She was spending each season on tour of all the major cities in all the high-class vaudeville houses. Her marriage to Leslie had broken down, each of the parties pursuing their own careers. Belle divorced him in 1919. Shortly afterward, she married Maurice Abrahams (Abrams), a well-known music publisher, 14 years her senior. He helped supply her with new songs, including such hits as "I Cried for You," "What'll I Do" and "All of Me," with thanks to Berlin and Kalman and Ruby for composing them.

A year after the marriage, Belle gave birth to Herbert and briefly retired from the stage. However, when Herbert was six months old, Keith persuaded Belle to appear in his theaters, and she began a highly successful tour that reestablished her as one of vaudeville's finest singers. When she again appeared at the Palace, Prohibition songs were in vogue. But when she sang "I'm a Mother of a Case of Scotch," E.A. Albee, a very straight-laced manager, forced her to drop the song.

For the next several years, Belle toured the country. She was always the featured headliner, no matter what other well-known performer was on the bill. Fifteen years after her first appearance in a musical, in late 1926, Belle was engaged to star in a Ziegfeld production, "Betsy." Even with the music of Rodgers and Hart, the show ran only 39 performances. In the show, Belle interpolated "Blue Skies" by Irving Berlin, much to the consternation of the show's songwriters.

Each vaudeville tour culminated with an engagement at the Palace. In early 1928, Belle was on the bill with Fred Waring and his Pennsylvanians, Donald Brian, and oldtimer Trixie Friganza. By this time, Belle was aware of vaudeville's decline. She sought out other venues to continue her career.

In 1929, she appeared in her first movie, "Song of Love," in which she sang several of her signature songs. She also made an appearance in Ziegfeld's "Midnight Frolics," again singing "Blue Skies," which had now become a hit.

Belle's husband, Maurice Abrahams, died suddenly of a heart attack in 1931. She was so devastated by the loss that she temporarily retired from performing. A year later, Belle appeared on radio, hosting a musical program. A highlight of this engagement was conducting a show from a moving train, the first time this had ever been done. Also in 1932, Belle returned briefly to vaudeville, sharing the bill with movies.

Belle Baker

In early 1934, prior to a trip to London, Belle and old friend Sophie Tucker appeared at a Hartford, Connecticut, fund-raising event for the local synagogue. When the audience shouted for her to sing "Yiddishe Mama," Belle deferred to Tucker, who had introduced the song a decade earlier. When Belle joined in, she encouraged the audience to sing along with her.

The London tour was highly successful. Belle teamed with Beatrice Lillie, and the duo made the rounds of packed music halls. At one show, Belle danced with the Prince of Wales. While in London, Belle played at the Kit Kat Club, a cabaret, and appeared in a British-made movie, "Charing Cross Road." Popular in England, it never made it to the United States.

Belle made her initial appearance in nightclubs with a 1935 engagement at New York's Versailles Club. She played in nightclubs sporadically over the next few years.

In 1937, Belle married Elias Sugerman, the editor of *Billboard* magazine. She divorced him in 1941 on the grounds of three years' separation.

Belle retired from the stage around 1941. In 1947, she was persuaded to appear as the lead in a summer show, "The Vinegar Tree." In 1950, she made her final appearance on stage at an oldtimers show at the Palace Theater. She shared the bill with Pat Rooney, Sr., Smith and Dale and Joe Jackson, Jr. Belle sang a medley of her favorite songs.

In 1955, Belle was honored on Ralph Edwards' "This Is Your Life," a popular television program. On April 29, 1957, she was stricken with a heart attack and died in Cedars of Lebanon Hospital, near her Beverly Hills home. She was 63 years old. Her son, Herbert, a successful Hollywood screenwriter, flew his mother's remains back to New York for funeral and burial services.

A versatile singer, Belle Baker was among the top performers in vaudeville. Her repertoire included both comedy and serious tunes. Her renditions of Jewish melodies made them among the most enjoyable songs on the popular stage.

Olga Petrova

She began her career in England's provincial theaters. With a name and character change, she became a headliner in London's music halls. In the United States, she starred in vaudeville and in Broadway dramas. Her eccentric attire, flamboyant behavior and stage demeanor labeled her a prima donna whose every word and gesture was carefully choreographed. She starred in many silent films assuming the roles of strong and independent women. Her appearances in legitimate theater attracted audiences who specifically came to see her larger-than-life characterizations.

Muriel Harding was born on May 10, 1884, in Manchester, England. Edward Harding, her father, was a druggist-chemist. He and his wife, Leyseur, were married in 1877. They had five children, three sons and two daughters. Muriel was the middle child. Early accounts of her life depict a difficult childhood with a controlling father and Muriel's attempts to break away from the family. In her teens, entering the theater seemed to be the way to assert her independence.

From 1900 to 1904, Muriel appeared in amateur shows and obtained minor roles in various theatrical productions. In 1904, at the age of 20, Muriel went to London to pursue her career, initially in music halls. A booking agent suggested she change her name to fit her looks and temperament. Believing that foreign glamour was more salable to English managers and audiences, she became Olga Petrova, claimed she was from Russia and affected a Russian accent, which she retained throughout her career. Within a few years, Olga was a headliner on the music hall stage. Her singing and dramatic acting had won the hearts of many admirers.

Olga had begun her music hall period playing in cheap music halls for $8 a week. Moving to better theaters, she earned $25 a week. As a headliner, $100 a week was her usual salary. During this time, newspapers reported that Olga may have been married, or at least "intimate," with Boris Petroff, an actor she had known in South Africa.

On April 5, 1911, Olga headlined a bill at the high-class London Pavilion. Her success there anointed her as a star performer and a desirable act for other venues. Jesse Lasky had come to England to find new talent for his theatrical empire. After seeing Olga perform, he signed her to appear in the United States in a new show he was preparing. In association with William Harris, Lasky opened a cabaret-style entertainment called the "Folies Bergere" at the Fulton Theater, New York. What better actress to open his new show than a pretty "Russian" redhead with a dramatic flair?

Vaudeville audiences were unprepared for the sophisticated acts presented. They preferred straight acts with a fast pace. The performers, including Olga, who gave a dramatic sketch, were booed off the stage. The venue closed after a short run. Lasky offered Olga to the Keith circuit. Their management responded with, "She was a failure. What do we want her for?"

For the next two years, Olga played on secondary vaudeville circuits, although usually heading the bill. During this time, her prima donna behavior earned as much of a reputation as her acting.

In 1914, while Olga was appearing at Poli's Theater in New Haven, Connecticut, in a play called "Night of the Party," the Keith people were alerted to her performance. In her act, she sang "My Hero" from "The Chocolate Soldier" in four different voices and gave an imitation of Lena Ashwell in "The Shulamite," bringing the audience to tears. Reviewers considered her performance sensational. Keith hired her to appear in New York. The story of her appearance at Proctor's Fifth Avenue Theater speaks of legend and theater lore.

Olga made an arrangement with the management to appear at Proctor's during the first week with no salary or billing. If she was a success, she would be held over a second week and would receive $125 in salary. Her unqualified success during the first week guaranteed a second week's appearance. Even greater success got her a third week's engagement. This time, she demanded headliner status. An English performer, R.A. Roberts, held the headliner spot. Would he be willing to give it up to Olga? Management persuaded him to relinquish the spot. When he met Olga, he walked out of the show and never played on the American stage again. It was later revealed that early in Olga's English music hall period, Roberts had treated her badly. Olga had obtained her revenge for his slight.

Continuing on the Keith circuit in 1914, Olga played throughout the Midwest. She became ill in Indianapolis and needed a doctor. Dr. John D. Stewart came to her rescue. A romance developed and they were soon married. He would later become a leading physician in New York. There was no mention that Olga had been married before.

In late 1914, the Shuberts hired Olga to appear in two of their dramatic productions, "Panthea" and "The White Picture," at an increased salary. Her success in the dramas attracted silent film producers, and she was signed to appear in a number of films, first for the Solar company and then for the Famous Players–Lasky organization. In 1914, she appeared in "The Tigress." This role, like all the others that followed, portrayed a woman with a strong personality and an independent, authoritative flair. Some critics believed these roles revealed her feelings about women's equality although she never participated in any way with the suffrage movement. Three films were released in 1915, seven in 1916, 12 in 1917 and four in 1918. They included such hits as "The Heart of a Painted Woman" (1915), "The Black Butterfly" (1916), "The Scarlet Woman" (1916), "Exile" (1917), "The Secret of Eve" (1917), "The Undying Flame" (1917) and "The Panther Woman" (1918). By this time, Olga had tired of the movies and it was reported that audiences had tired of her. Olga quit moviemaking and returned to vaudeville.

In 1918, back on the Keith circuit, Olga appeared at the Palace Theater, the venue now considered the greatest variety theater in the world. She was a great success performing essentially the same act she had done at Poli's Theater five years earlier. This began a ten-week tour to a selected number of cities that she had chosen. As part of her contract, she demanded that she be paid more than any other performer who played at that particular theater. If Nora Bayes received $1,500 in Columbus, Ohio, Olga wanted $1,501. In this way, she could claim to have been the highest-paid vaudeville performer in these cities. She attracted full houses using her old act. Upon achieving these goals, Olga announced that she was retiring from vaudeville, instead moving to legitimate theater.

In the early 1920s, Olga appeared in three plays: "The White Peacock" (1921), which she claimed to have written, "Hurricane" and "What Do We Know?" "The White Peacock" was later to cause a lawsuit. The latter two had as their themes birth control and spiritualism.

When Olga played at the Palace Theater, Chicago, in 1923, reviewers believed she had returned to vaudeville for the money. She repeated her familiar act of old songs and recitations. After a successful tour, she highlighted her vaudeville comeback with an appearance at the Hippodrome, New York, in October 1925. In this appearance, she sang songs in French and Spanish and rendered "Carry Me Back to Old Virginny" in three voices. *Variety* noted her unique act and showmanship.

Olga Petrova

The year 1925 also created newspaper headlines when an English author, W.H. Roberts, sued Olga for stealing his play "The Red Wig" and fashioning it into "The White Peacock." Roberts charged that Olga had purchased an option on the play and then rejected it. Two years later, she wrote "The White Peacock," making his play the basis for her plot. The five-day trial ended with Olga having to pay Roberts $7,500 damages.

Shortly afterward, Olga moved to the south of France and lived there until the beginning of World War II. She returned to the United States and settled in Clearwater, Florida. Olga was said to have saved her money and invested wisely while she was earning large sums. When she retired, she said, "I was close to the amount of money I had decided to retire on." She also sold her home in Great Neck, New York, to Walter Chrysler.

Dr. Stewart died in 1938. In his obituary, it was stated that he and Olga were still married. Olga claimed they had been divorced some time before. It is not known when she married third husband Louis Willoughby, a movie actor and director. When he died in 1968, Olga was listed as his wife.

In 1942, Olga wrote an autobiography recounting her life and career. The theme of the book was her early poverty and the desire to excel on the stage and make the money she required to live comfortably. However, dates, places, openings and tribulations were either changed or carefully edited. She remained the prima donna to the end.

Olga died in Clearwater on November 30, 1977. She was 93 years old.

Ethel Waters

Ethel Waters began her childhood in Philadelphia's red light district but, through a combination of determination and sheer talent, achieved a 60-year career in American popular and dramatic theater. Her gifts as a popular singer reached legendary status. She was an actress with extraordinary skills who won critical acclaim on Broadway.

As a black woman in the theater of the early 1900s, Ethel faced formidable barriers to success. She overcame them and gained fame as a performer apart from her race.

Ethel was born on October 31, 1896, in Chester, Pennsylvania, in the home of her great aunt Ida. Her mother Louise Anderson was 12 years old when she was assaulted and impregnated by John Waters. Louise's mother took baby Ethel as soon as she was born and cared for her during her childhood. In her autobiography, "His Eye Is on the Sparrow," Ethel reported that her entire childhood was like "a series of one-night stands. I was shuttled about among relatives, boarded out, continually being moved around to Camden, Chester and Philadelphia homes." Her grandmother boarded near wherever she was working so she could be available if Ethel needed her.

Ethel's childhood was spent in the poverty in slums. At the age of six, Ethel became ill with typhoid fever and pneumonia and was near death. Her grandmother called in a Catholic priest who baptized and anointed the girl. Although she seldom attended church, Ethel remained a religious person for her entire life.

Ethel's schooling consisted of a brief time in a Chester elementary school. When she and her grandmother moved to Philadelphia, Ethel was enrolled in a Catholic school. Ethel had become shy and fearful due to her difficult upbringing but the nuns at the school helped to give her self-confidence. When Ethel was ten years old, she sang and danced at parties. Her friends regarded her as an outstanding "hip shaker" and persuaded her to seek out performance opportunities.

Like her mother, Ethel was assaulted when she was 12 years old. A year later, she reluctantly married Merritt Purnsley, a laborer at a steel company. Purnsley was an abusive and unfaithful husband. Although she wanted to make the marriage work and follow the Catholic teachings, she was unable to take the abuse and, in 1914, left her husband and went to live with her mother. Ethel got a job as a laundress and chambermaid for less than five dollars a week. Her beautiful voice helped to rescue her from this onerous environment.

She won a chance to sing at a local nightclub, Jack's Rathskeller. The challenge was formidable for a very young black girl. There were few opportunities and salaries were slim. In her debut, Ethel sang several blues numbers and aroused considerable attention.

Ethel was 17 when she signed to appear on a Black vaudeville bill. She appeared at Baltimore's Lincoln Theater, earning $9 a week. An agent for black performers signed her to tour northern and southern cities for the Theater Owners Booking Association (T.O.B.A.), also known among blacks as "Tough on Black Artists." She appeared in theaters that were exclusively black, both entertainers and audiences. Within a short time, Ethel was headlining the bill with her singing. Her fans nicknamed her Sweet Mama Stringbean because she was a skinny teenager who danced the shimmy.

While touring in the South, Ethel was nearly killed in an auto accident which left her with an injured leg and body burns. Several hospitals turned her away and the one that accepted her kept her until the entire bill had been paid. Ethel returned home, got work at a cafeteria and sang in a bar. Believing New York offered more opportunities, she moved there and was hired as a singer for a small club called Edmund's Cellar. While the venue was off the main street of better-known nightclubs, it attracted similar patrons. Following the end of the war, the white social elite of the city had discovered the "forbidden" clubs of Harlem. That New York neighborhood had become the locale where Black artists of all kinds could do their work and be recognized. At Edmund's Cellar, Ethel developed into a gifted and innovative singer whose repertoire included blues, Broadway and jazz hits. As she later told columnist Earl Wilson, "I used to work from nine until unconscious. I was just a young girl, and when I tried to sing anything but double-meaning songs, they would say, 'Come on, Ethel. Get hot!'"

Ethel introduced W. C. Handy's "St. Louis Blues" to nightclub and vaudeville audiences. Her rendition generated more night club and vaudeville engagements, but they were still at black theater venues. Of her delivery of "St. Louis Blues," Ethel said, "I sang it out of the depths of private fire in which I was brought up." Audiences were as taken with her rendition as she was singing the song.

During the early 1920s, Ethel starred in black musical revues and toured across the country. Among black audiences, she had become a headliner. Ethel began her recording career in 1921, signing with the Black Swan label and worked with them until 1924. Few records were produced and none reached hit status. In 1925, she replaced Florence Mills at the Plantation Club, New York, and introduced the song "Dinah." Thanks to Ethel's delivery, it became a hit. Columbia Records signed her and she recorded with them for a decade. She was offered an engagement to sing in Paris but turned it down. A young unknown black singer took the assignment instead. Her name was Josephine Baker.

In 1927, a period that theater historians regard as a milestone, Ethel entered white vaudeville with a performance at the Palace Theater. She sang "Shake That Thing," which *Variety* compared to Eva Tanguay's "I Don't Care." That same year, Ethel appeared on Broadway in the all–black musical revue, "Africana," which opened on July 11 at Daly's Theater. The spotlight was on Ethel, who quickly won over audiences with her distinctive voice and dancing. After taking "Africana" on tour, she headlined a vaudeville bill at the Chicago Palace. She sang several songs, from the quiet and proper "I'm Coming Virginia" to some that shocked family audiences. Nevertheless, reviewers credited her with an outstanding ability to put over a song, especially the blues. It was also in 1927 that Ethel married Edward Matthews. They divorced after a few years, Ethel claiming her husband would not work, Matthews complaining about Ethel's drinking and bisexual activities.

For several years, Ethel continued touring in vaudeville, although engagements were dwindling as the amusement was losing favor with audiences. Performers, acutely aware of the changes in audience tastes, sought out new venues like musicals, movies, radio and nightclubs. Racial discrimination remained strong and black entertainers found themselves limited to Black theaters. Ethel had a starring role in Lew Leslie's "Blackbirds of 1930" which opened at the Cotton Club on October 22. It was Leslie's first show to use Black composers exclusively. Although the show purported to "glorify the American Negro," scenes that took place in front of a slave's cabin, a portrait of Aunt Jemima, and black marital and honeymoon comedy mix-ups still catered to white audiences.

In the meantime, Ethel appeared in her first movie, the Warner Bros. production "On with the Show" (1929), which later became the basis for the hit Broadway musical, "42nd Street." Ethel sang two songs that soon gained hit status, "Am I Blue?" and "Birmingham Bertha."

Ethel traveled to London for an extended engagement at the Cafe de Paris. English audiences fell in love with her hit song renditions. She continued to record songs, but they now moved more toward the mainstream of popular music, especially jazz. During the recording sessions of the 1920s and early 1930s, Ethel worked with such fine instrumentalists as Fletcher Henderson, Joe Smith, Coleman Hawkins, James P. Johnson and, later, Benny Carter.

In 1931, she starred in another all–black revue, "Rhapsody in Black," which opened at the Harris Theater May 4. Black shows were slowly finding their way to normally white theaters. The show was a vaudeville-style production produced on a tight budget, the now-common all–black revue for white audiences. In the show, Ethel reprised "St. Louis Blues." Thanks to her, the show ran for ten weeks.

Ethel broke the barrier for blacks in otherwise all-white shows by appearing in "As Thousands Cheer," one of Irving Berlin's greatest musical hits. It was reported that when Berlin heard Ethel sing "Stormy Weather," he hired her for the musical. The show opened at the Music Box Theater on September 30, 1933, and ran for an unprecedented year with a sizable profit, one of the few to accomplish that feat during the Depression. The cast included Clifton Webb, Helen Broderick, Marilyn Miller and Ethel. She sang "Supper Time," "Harlem on My Mind," and the hit of the show, "Heat Wave."

The year 1935 brought additional recognition for Ethel for her appearance in a musical revue with Beatrice Lillie, "At Home Abroad." Also in the show were Eleanor Powell (dancing) and Eddie Foy, Jr. (comedy). The show ran for six months. Ethel sang "Thief in the Night" and "Hottentot Potentate," both with Black-style inflections, but Arthur Schwartz's music produced no hits. Still, critic Brooks Atkinson said of her: "A few words in praise of Ethel Waters, the gleaming tower of dusky regality, who knows how to make a song stand on tiptoe."

During the late 1930s, Ethel mounted her own vaudeville show, "Swing, Harlem, Swing," and took it on tour. At several theaters, racial prejudice against blacks caused audiences to be segregated and blacks charged additional ticket fees. After some months of these episodes, Ethel abandoned the tour. About the same time, Ethel herself was examining her changing career. She was getting older; she had gained considerable weight; and her singing voice had lost some of its verve.

Ethel's next Broadway appearance was in 1939 in her first dramatic role, as Hagar in "Mamba's Daughter." It was the story of a grandmother and mother who contend with a talented daughter. Atkinson's review of Ethel was mixed and the production was short-lived. But Ethel's dramatic abilities were visible enough to propel her into a new theatrical medium at a time when blacks were still being excluded from Broadway's legitimate theater.

A year later, in a musical featuring a black cast, "Cabin in the Sky," Ethel won praise

Ethel Waters

for her acting. The show had a long run and went on a profitable tour. In the show, Ethel introduced the title song, "Takin' a Chance on Love," which became a national hit. Playing opposite the devout Petunia Jackson (Ethel) were Dooley Wilson, Todd Duncan and Rex Ingram, actors who had already proven their worth in drama. The show also included Katherine Dunham and her dancers with the choreography of George Balanchine.

The 1940s saw Ethel appearing in both movies and stage plays. In 1942, she acted in three movies, "Cairo," "Syncopation," and "Tales of Manhattan." The following year, capitalizing on the stage success of "Cabin in the Sky," the show was turned into a movie starring Ethel with support from an all-star black cast of Lena Horne, Louis Armstrong, Eddie (Rochester) Anderson, Rex Ingram and Butterfly McQueen. The movie proved to be even more successful than the play.

Also in 1943, Ethel had a cameo role in "Stage Door Canteen," a war-related movie featuring an array of Hollywood and Broadway stars extolling the virtues of our armed forces. She appeared in two stage musicals, "Laugh Time" (1943) and "Blue Holiday" (1945). "Laugh Time" featured a racially mixed cast, one of the few landing on Broadway, with Ethel, Frank Fay, Bert Wheeler and Buck and Bubbles. "Blue Holiday" was nothing more than a black variety show starring Ethel and featuring Katherine Dunham's dancers and Duke Ellington. The plot was dull, as was the music. The show closed in a week.

Ethel's appearance in the movie "Pinky" helped break the barriers of starring both blacks and whites in a major movie with a controversial story. The movie starred Jeanne Crain as a young black woman who attempted to pass as white. Ethel played her grandmother and won plaudits from critics for her portrayal. She received an Academy Award nomination as Best Supporting Actress. But her battle was constant with producers, managers and with prominent blacks. Producers wanted to put her into "mammy" roles. Prominent blacks wanted her to speak out on behalf of their political agenda. She resisted both. Discovering she had diabetes, she rationed her stamina to meet the rigors of performing.

In spite of the barriers, Ethel achieved her greatest heights in dramatic theater in 1950, playing the role of a maid in a Southern household in "The Member of the Wedding." Co-starred with Ethel was a new actress to Broadway, Julie Harris, and Brandon De Wilde. Brooks Atkinson wrote of Ethel's performance: "Miss Waters gives one of those rich and eloquent performances that lay such a deep spell on any audience that sees her. Although the character has a physical base in Miss Waters' mountainous personality, it has exalted spirit and great warmth of sympathy." The show ran for two years, and won the New York Drama Critics Award for best play of the year.

The play was reprised in a 1952 movie, again featuring Ethel as the maid. Her rendition of the song, "His Eye Is on the Sparrow," brought tears to audiences. The song had a strong spiritual meaning and seemed to represent Ethel's increasing involvement with religion. When asked about what contributed to her stardom, she often credited prayer.

Now ailing, and with little money, Ethel attempted to cut back on her activities. In 1953, she starred in a short-lived television series, "Beulah." The show was the first featuring a black entertainer on television. In early 1957, she had her own Broadway show, "An Evening with Ethel Waters," in which she sang all of her old hits. Nostalgic audiences helped her earn some badly needed money. "The Sound and the Fury" (1959) was her last movie.

In 1957, Ethel joined Billy Graham's Crusades as a gospel singer. She was seeking peace after years of hard living filled with constant battles to remain independent yet keep her black identity. She sang for Graham until her death.

Suffering from a combination of heart disease, kidney problems and diabetes, Ethel died on September 1, 1977, in Chatsworth, California. She was 80 years old.

Ethel Waters had been a leader in a line of Black entertainers who achieved recognition, fame, money and success in show business. She triumphed over almost impossible personal and racial barriers because of her sheer ability, determination and versatility as a singer and actress. For her efforts, she achieved star status in the white world of vaudeville and Broadway theater.

Frederike "Fritzi" Scheff

Opera singers usually lived and died as headliners in their chosen field. Rarely did they ever wander into other entertainment media. Fritzi Scheff was an exception. After establishing a respected reputation in grand opera, she went on the vaudeville stage and continued her long career in other popular theater venues.

Fritzi was born on August 30, 1879, in Vienna, Austria. Her family was part of the city's intellectual and artistic elite. Her father, Dr, Gottfried Scheff, was employed as a royal court physician. Her mother, Hortense Scheff-Jager, was a renowned singer of grand opera. Mrs. Scheff began singing lessons for her daughter at an early age. By five, Fritzi was singing in a church choir.

Fritzi received her musical education at Hoch's Conservatoire, Frankfurt, Germany. At the age of 18, she made her debut singing the leading role in "Martha" at the Nuremburg Opera House on January 10, 1897. For the next two years, she received acclaim for roles in "Romeo and Juliet," "Faust," "La Boheme" and "Mignon." Fritzi was a petite, pretty young woman with long auburn hair, brown eyes and freckles. She displayed a vivacity and piquancy not often seen among opera singers. Her voice was characterized as a light, high soprano and its range was considered one of her greatest assets.

Maurice Grau, director of the Metropolitan Opera House in New York, heard Fritzi sing in Munich in 1900 and immediately engaged her for his company. At the age of 21, she found herself in the midst of a great assemblage of opera artists— Sembrich, Melba, Nordica, Calve, Scotti and Caruso. The environment was exhilarating if not overwhelming at first, but when Fritzi made her debut on December 28, 1900, singing the role of Marcellina in Beethoven's "Fidelio," she was "all business." She received excellent reviews from critics and standing ovations from audiences.

In 1902, Fritzi married Baron Frederick von Bardeleben, said to be a member of the Kaiser's royal family. They honeymooned in Europe, sailing on the maiden voyage of the *Kaiser Wilhelm II.*

During her three years at the Metropolitan, Fritzi sang in "Lohengrin," "Die Walkure," La Boheme," "Don Giovanni," "The Marriage of Figaro" and "The Magic Flute," demonstrating the range and quality of her voice and acting ability. Her knowledge of French, German and English was exemplary.

In 1903, Charles Dillingham, in his first year as a Broadway producer, persuaded Fritzi to go into light opera, alternately called operetta or comic opera, depending on how much critics and reviewers liked the genre. Fritzi's debut was on November 9, 1903, in Washington, D.C., at the National Theater when she starred in Victor Herbert's "Babette." Audiences were on their feet thundering their appreciation. "Babette" opened in New York on November 16, 1903, at the Broadway Theater. Critics called Fritzi a fine actress and superb singer. Herbert composed his music to fit the singer's skill. With Fritzi, he was able to expand his range of composition. He wrote an extended aria for her that gave her the opportunity to show the full range of her virtuosity. But critics gave Harry B. Smith's book a poor evaluation and the show ran for only 59 performances. Dillingham was not disappointed, however, because he had made Fritzi an overnight star.

Fritzi played an unusual role in "The Two Roses," a comic opera that opened November 21, 1904, at the Broadway Theater. She received enthusiastic applause when she interpolated two arias from her operatic repertoire at the end of the show. Still, the show closed in two weeks. Less than a month later, Fritzi began a three-month tour of Eastern cities in a show composed of her repertory of opera.

Fritzi's greatest success in comic opera came in 1905 when she starred in the role of Fifi in Henry Blossom and Victor Herbert's "Mlle. Modiste." The production opened December 25, 1905, at the Knickerbocker Theater. The story centered on the romantic adventures of Fifi, a charming salesgirl who studies to become an opera singer and unites with her love. Herbert wrote several pretty songs for Fritzi but one of them, "Kiss Me Again," not only became a hit but remained identified with her for the remainder of her career. The popular show continued to the end of the season, began again in September and then went on the road for three years. Fritzi never missed a performance during the entire run. One critic summed up the overall praise for her role: "There is no other singer on the American stage today who ranks with her in the field of comic opera."

But like many opera-operetta stars, Fritzi's successes, newfound riches and frequent displays of flamboyant behavior gained her notoriety both on and off-stage. She had her own Pullman car with an attached flat car that carried her Pierce-Arrow. She was said to carry 36 pieces of baggage and an entourage of a pianist, chauffeur, footman and two maids. She demanded that her hotel and dressing rooms be redecorated prior to her arrival. Stories abounded regarding her spending sprees and temperamental outbursts. In April 1908, her husband had become so uncomfortable that he filed for divorce from her. It was more than coincidence that she married John Fox, Jr., eight months later. Fox was an author, already famous for his novels *The Little Shepherd of Kingdom Come* and *The Trail of the Lonesome Pine*. During their marriage, Fox did not publish a single book.

After "Mlle. Modiste" closed, Fritzi was starred in "The Prima Donna." Was this title a joke? critics wondered. The show opened on November 11, 1908, at the Knickerbocker. But this time the combination of Blossom, Herbert and Scheff failed to please reviewers and audiences. With an uninspired book and mediocre music, the show ran for only 72 performances and lost a good deal of money. Rule-of-thumb on Broadway was that a show had to play at least 100 times to earn a profit. Fritzi remained off the stage for more than a year and a half after this failure.

A revival of "The Mikado" on May 30, 1910, starring Fritzi (Yum-Yum), Andrew Mack (Nanki-Poo) and the venerable Jefferson De Angelis (Ko-Ko), lasted several months to mediocre houses. But the show propelled Fritzi to the attention of the public once again.

Victor Herbert's fourth try with Fritzi was a near disaster. "The Duchess" opened October 16, 1911, at the Lyric Theater and played for only 24 performances. The show had been appearing on the road for almost a year, went through numerous changes of name, plot, scenery and songs and still did not come together. Fritzi's stormy behavior on and off the stage did not help the show. She was blamed for its short New York run and Herbert never again wrote for her. The poor returns of the previous two years had used up almost all of Fritzi's earnings, and living on weekly salaries became an uncomfortable reality. Her husband was unable to earn enough to meet Fritzi's needs. She divorced him in late 1912.

Lured by the offer of large salaries, Fritzi turned to vaudeville. Her auspicious debut was at the Palace Theater, New York, on September 1, 1913, at the beginning of their fall season. She was reported to be earning $2,500 a week for singing three songs twice a day. Supporting performers on the bill included Minnie Dupree, a legitimate actress in a one-act play, Horace Golden, a magician, Joe Jackson, a comic cyclist, and Victor Moore and his wife in a comic skit. According to Marian Spitzer, the author of "The Palace," Fritzi's act was not well-received "because Miss Scheff disappointed women in the audience by wearing only one gown throughout." Still, she was held over for a second week. Fritzi then began a tour of the major cities of the country. At about the same time, she married George Anderson, who had managed several of her tours, in New Rochelle, New York.

A break in her vaudeville tour found Fritzi staring in a short-lived musical comedy, "Pretty Mrs. Smith." Stealing the show from her was a newcomer, Charlotte Greenwood, a tall, thin, young girl who displayed some exciting loose-limbed kicking. Greenwood's role earned her the lead in the show's revision and a series of "Letty" comedies, which continued for more than a decade. In 1915, in her only movie appearance, Fritzi reprised her role in "Pretty Mrs. Smith." She quickly retreated to the safer and more lucrative environment of vaudeville.

In July 1918, Fritzi returned to the Palace, billed as "The Brilliant Prima Donna." A month later, she was brought in as a replacement in "Gloriana," a musical comedy on the verge of closing. Her presence extended the show for 96 performances, and she then completed a successful tour that lasted through the spring of 1920.

For the next several years, Fritzi appeared sporadically in vaudeville, always including a stop at the Palace. Touring the provinces had proven to be tiring and had lost its appeal. But Fritzi continued because of the good salary, said to be around $2,000 a week.

In March 1921, Fritzi sought a divorce from Anderson, claiming habitual intemperance and cruelty. She told the court that her husband had frequently struck her, refused to work, and had a liquor bill of $75 a week. It was reported that her friends expressed little surprise at her action. Her third divorce was easily granted.

Fritzi Scheff

In 1927, a new production, "Bye, Bye, Bonnie," was being prepared for Fritzi but she dropped out when the show appeared doomed by its poor script and even poorer music. In 1929, the Shuberts revived "Mlle. Modiste" and got Fritzi to take her old starring role. The show was part of a series of "old" comic operas that the Shuberts were producing to keep the Jolson Theater occupied. It ran for 48 performances. The following year, Fritzi made her next-to-last appearance at the Palace, this time backed by 12 male dancers and singers. She sang three songs, including her trademark, "Kiss Me Again." Reviewers commented on her performance, still "ever glorious" even after so many years. But, as vaudeville declined, Fritzi's circumstances grew desperate. In 1933, Fritzi took a job singing in a 57th Street cocktail room.

While engagements were now rare occasions, Fritzi maintained her figure and voice in the hopes of returning to the stage. She appeared in Billy Rose's Barbary Coast presentation at the New York World's Fair in 1940 and at Rose's Diamond Horseshoe cabaret in 1946. She starred in an Edna Ferber–George S. Kaufman play, "Bravo," in 1948 but it lasted for only 43 performances.

At the age of 71, Fritzi sang at the Cafe Grinzing, a Hungarian restaurant in New York. The engagement got her another, final appearance at the old Palace on a variety bill. During the early 1950s, she made frequent appearances on television and radio. In March 1954, Fritzi was the featured personality on television's "This Is Your Life."

A month later, on April 8, Fritzi was found dead in her home on East 79th Street, in New York. After a cleaning woman had been unable to get into the apartment, a handyman forced the door. The doctor attributed death to "old age and natural causes." Fritzi was 74 years old. She left an estate of only $476.75 along with her old upright piano and bench and a few mementos of her stage glories. The piquant luminary of another era had been active in entertainment until the end. Over the years, she had experienced glory and tragedy, riches and poverty, but she never forgot how to sing.

Irene Bordoni

Her singing voice was not remarkable. She was untrained in music and was an indifferent dancer. But Irene Bordoni was pretty, lively, saucy and charming and her French accent was delightful. A *New York Times* critic summed up Irene's stage personality: "She's everything Americans expect a French girl to be in the theater — and then some."

Irene became a headliner in vaudeville and a star in musical comedy and the movies over a period of 40 years. Audiences in Europe and the United States enthusiastically welcomed the French actress with the big black, roguish eyes, hair bangs, flashing smile and provocative songs.

Irene Bordoni, her real name, was born in Ajaccio, Corsica, on January 16, 1895. Her father, Sauveur Bordoni, was an Italian tailor. Her mother, Marie Lemmonier, was French. Irene was said to have been the great-grandniece of Jean Francois Millet, the Barbizon painter. She was an only child.

Irene was educated in Paris at Lycee de Jeunes Filles, a Catholic girls school, and Conservatoire de Paris, where she decided to major in acting. One day in 1907, 13-year-old Irene had an errand that took her to the Theatre des Varieties, a vaudeville house. On impulse, she auditioned for the manager and obtained a place in the chorus line. For the next few years, Irene's career as an actress and singer gradually moved her up the ranks of performers until she became a headliner in various French revues. However, performing before U.S. audiences was her primary goal.

In 1912, Irene arrived in New York and obtained a job in "The First Affair," a Shubert show at the Winter Garden. She had been hired as a singer but was cast to perform a pantomime dance with a partner. *Variety* did not think much of her performance, but audiences found her a pleasing personality and another Winter Garden appearance followed. On November 20, 1912, 18-year-old Irene appeared in a Shubert revue, "Broad to Paris." The show was built around the exotic dancing of Gertrude Hoffman. Irene played a minor role and was favorably received by audiences. The show ran for a successful ten weeks, but Irene believed her talents had been overwhelmed by Hoffman. She entered vaudeville with a singing routine that featured her rolling eyes, pursed lips, comedic hauteur and voluminous gowns. She quickly became a vaudeville headliner with songs like "Pretty Baby," which she sang in both French and English. She toured the Orpheum circuit for a year.

Irene went to London in 1914 to appear in a musical, "L'Impresario," at the Palace Theater. There she met actor and manager Edgar Becman, and they were married in early 1915. They returned together to the United States. During the fall of 1915, Irene gave birth to a daughter, Raymonde. Two months later, she was engaged to appear in "a comedy with music," entitled "Miss Information," which opened at the Cohan Theater on November 5. Elsie Janis starred in the show with songs by Jerome Kern. Irene had a minor role but gained attention with her rendition of "Two Big Eyes," an interpolation of a song by an almost unknown songwriter, Cole Porter. The show lasted a short time. Irene was happy to return to the familiar surroundings of vaudeville.

Raymond Hitchcock's revue "Hitchy-Koo" opened at the Cohan and Harris Theater on June 7, 1917. Besides Hitchcock, the show co-starred Leon Errol, with his famous drunk act, Grace La Rue and Irene, in her first major role in a musical. Audiences were delighted with the fast-paced and irreverent show, which poked fun at the most respected people in the country. Irene sang several songs and acted in a number of comedy sketches. Most important, however, was her budding relationship with songwriter and producer E. Ray Goetz. The show played for seven months and by its close, Irene and Goetz were lovers. In early 1918, Irene obtained a divorce from Becman, who returned to France. In October of the same year, Irene married Goetz in Chicago, shortly after his own divorce.

The 1918 version of "Hitchy-Koo" opened at the Globe Theater in June. The show again featured Hitchcock, Errol and Irene. This cast was strong enough to overcome a mediocre musical score and book. Irene's singing was a highlight. It ran for nine weeks in New York and then went on a successful tour. Goetz was now Irene's manager and he featured her in his new productions. In late 1918, she starred in "Sleeping Partners," which played only a short time. Her return to vaudeville was welcomed by audiences who had missed her coquettish singing. But Irene now preferred musicals to the rigors of vaudeville touring.

A Goetz production borrowed from the French, "As You Were," opened at the Central Theater January 27, 1920, starring Irene, comic Sam Bernard and Clifton Webb. Bernard is sent back in time to see if any of the earlier beauties were better than his wife. Irene played his wife and all the beauties and Webb all of her lovers. The songs were average, but Irene's acting was singled out as "superb work." The show ran for 143 performances.

In 1922, Goetz produced another show around Irene's saucy acting. However, "The French Doll" drew small audiences and received negative reviews. Later, Goetz combined with George Gershwin to produce "Little Miss Bluebird," which opened at the Lyceum

Theater on August 23, 1923. Gershwin's songs were written especially for Irene and she rendered them with her unique French demeanor. So popular was the show that Goetz and Gershwin decided to take it to London for the 1924–25 season. Irene had crossed the ocean several times during past years and each time her commentary and costumes—daring French gowns and "mad" hats—made headlines. She also claimed to have homes in New York, Paris and Monte Carlo.

In late 1925, Irene returned to the United States to appear in an Avery Hopwood show especially designed for her. "Naughty Cinderella" opened at the Lyceum Theater on November 9, 1925. Irene played a French girl who steals her sweetheart away from a married woman. The show played for a short time in New York and then toured.

Irene Bordoni

This was the first time since her marriage to Goetz that he did not produce her show. The press wanted to know what was happening to their marriage. No one talked.

Sacha Guitry wrote a play for Irene and himself called "Mozart" which had a unique presentation. The show opened at the Music Box Theater on November 22, 1926, with Irene playing the young Mozart in English. A second production, starring Guitry, opened on December 27 and was done in French. The show ran for only five weeks and failed to attract audiences who wanted to see Irene in a male role.

Irene had first appeared at the Palace Theater in 1916. Her songs, French accent and flowing gowns were an immediate hit. On the bill with her were the Three Keatons, young Buster gaining the attention of reviewers with his deadpan comedy antics. Irene returned to the Palace for two appearances in 1927, the first in May, and the second in November. In May, the Palace had just reopened after a near-disastrous fire. Frank Fay and his wife, Barbara Stanwyck, led the bill, which also featured Irene, the Ritz Brothers, Gus Van and Texas Guinan and her troupe. Between May and November, the Palace's new management (E.A. Albee had recently given up his position) made some changes that shocked the popular theater world and its performers. An act featuring near-nude girls was introduced, and was so poorly received that the posters were quickly painted over, covering more of the anatomy, and the girls were more modestly clad. Nothing like that had ever before been seen at the Palace.

Palace management then revealed that they were changing the format from two-a-day to four-a-day shows with lower ticket prices and lower performer salaries. When Irene played the Palace in November, the theater was only half full. Critics claimed there were more homeless people standing outside the theater than audiences inside, due to the new policies. This was one of the first indications that the vaudeville era was beginning to fade.

Irene was back in the headlines with an appearance in Cole Porter's "Paris," her acting and singing as saucy as Porter's lyrics could make it. The show opened at the Music Box Theater on November 8, 1928. Irene played an independent woman who finally nabs a rich husband after many adventures. Her singing of Porter's first big hit, "Let's Do It," was the highlight of the show, which ran for six months. The following year, a film version of the play was also a hit. The movie starred Irene, Jack Buchanan and Zasu Pitts.

The marriage difficulties of Bordoni and Goetz hit the press in 1929 with sensational headlines and copy. Goetz filed for divorce, claiming Irene had deserted him for another man. She filed a countersuit claiming she was never legally married to him, as their 1918 Chicago marriage violated Illinois law specifying that divorces must allow an interval of a year to pass before remarrying. Goetz had divorced his previous wife six months before marrying Irene. Accusations of infidelity came from both parties. Finally, Irene obtained an injunction against Goetz from suing her for divorce. Instead, she obtained an annulment to dissolve their marriage. For some years, the bad publicity affected both of their careers.

For the next several years, Irene toured the United States and England in various musical plays, with indifferent success. The role of French coquette was losing its appeal with a new generation of audiences educated with sound films. Her appearance at the Palace Theater in 1930 was on a bill made up of performers recruited from radio and nightclubs. She was the only veteran recognized by the audience. Her return to musicals in 1938 seemed to rejuvenate her career, although the vehicle in which she appeared quickly folded.

"Great Lady" opened at the Majestic Theater on December 1, 1938. The complicated plot moved back and forth between the United States and France, telling the story of a young woman of dubious reputation who marries the 78-year-old Aaron Burr. Irene did not play the female lead; instead, she was the young woman's mother. She was about to celebrate her forty-fourth birthday. The show lasted 20 performances. When Billy Rose tried to revive live vaudeville, he called on Irene to head a group of former headliners. His experiment failed.

Irene bounced back with the musical comedy hit, "Louisiana Purchase," which opened at the Imperial Theater on May 28, 1940. The book was by Morrie Ryskind and music by Irving Berlin. The show starred veteran Victor Moore, William Gaxton, Vera Zorina and Irene. Playing to type, she portrayed the flirty Madam Bordelaise and sang two of the show's hit songs, "Latins Know How" and "It's a Lovely Day Tomorrow," the latter song causing tears in the audience. The show ran for a full year. In 1941, "Louisiana Purchase" was made into a movie starring Bob Hope. Irene reprised her role as Madam Bordelaise. The film was as successful as the stage production had been.

Irene did not appear on the stage or in movies for ten years, living quietly in her New York City apartment at Central Park South. In 1950, she was asked to take a role in a musical, "The Lady from Paris," but the show did not survive the tryouts. That same year, she was persuaded to return to the Palace Theater on an oldtimer's bill. She sang several of her favorite songs and demonstrated that her voice was still good. In 1951, Irene was selected to play Bloody Mary in the road company of "South Pacific." It seemed an unlikely role, but reviewers praised her work.

The following year, Irene was signed to appear in the road tryout of "Maggie," but she had to withdraw from the cast before it reached New York. The press claimed she left because she was dissatisfied with the part. In reality, she was ill and unable to handle the stress of touring.

On March 19, 1953, Irene died of cancer at Jewish Memorial Hospital in New York. She was 58 years old. A few close friends attended a private funeral and burial. Except for brief obits in *Variety* and *The New York Times,* her passing went unnoticed.

Irene had been at her zenith as a Broadway headliner from 1917 to 1930, starring in vaudeville and musical comedy as the "naughty" French girl of popular theater. Cole Porter so appreciated her talent that his list of superlatives in "You're the Top" included "the eyes of Irene Bordoni."

Isabelle Patricola

As "the scintillating Miss Patricola," she was a vaudeville headliner from the 1920s to the early 1930s. She sang and played the violin with an artistry that captured audiences and reviewers. During the 1920s, she also recorded many popular song hits.

Isabelle was born in Italy in December 1886. Her family came to the United States in 1889 and settled in St. Mary's, a small mining town in north central Pennsylvania. Her father was a day laborer. A brother, Tom, was born in 1891. At an early age, Isabelle showed musical talent and began singing and taking violin lessons.

Isabelle was married at the age of 18. For the next several years she worked at various jobs, but continued to sing and play the violin at amateur theatricals. During World War I, her brother Tom went to New York to seek a career in vaudeville. He was a dancer and played the ukulele. Isabelle's marriage broke up and she obtained a divorce. Meanwhile, Tom had some success in vaudeville and persuaded his sister to join him and find work on the stage.

Isabelle traveled to New York in 1918, at the age of 32. Tom helped her to break into vaudeville, but because of her age managers and agents doubted her chances. In spite of this, she won audiences with her pleasing stage manner and her renditions of popular songs. She was billed as Miss Patricola, to give her act a sense of class. Audiences were taken with her talent and musical skill. Within a few years, Isabelle had established herself as a featured vaudevillian.

Isabelle joined the Keith circuit in 1920 and toured the country. Her combination of skills had made her act unique. Reviewers praised Isabelle for "palpitating the public." The following year, she performed on the Pantages circuit with equal success.

The 1922 craze for anything "sheik" helped to propel Isabelle to headliner status. Valentino had starred in "The Sheik." The song "Sheik of Araby" was a big hit. When Isabelle was asked to make records, her first recording was "Lovin' Sam, the Sheik of Alabam.'" It became a hit and opened up a new medium for Isabelle. Her next hit was a jazz blues number, "An Angel Voice I Hear." The act now consisted of Isabelle singing and playing jazz tunes on the violin.

In 1923, Isabelle was hired by Vocalion Red Records. Their advertising called her "the shining star of vaudeville." She sang "Stingo-Stungo" from "George White's Scandals of 1923" (which, coincidentally, featured her brother Tom) and a blues song, "Oh Sister, Ain't That Hot." At the same time, she was headlining on the Keith circuit. During the summer, Isabelle went to London to perform at the Palladium and made several recordings for a British company. In October, Isabelle appeared at the Palace Theater, New York, heading a bill that included Ann Pennington, William Faversham and the Duncan Sisters. At Thanksgiving, she was selected to be one of the performers to entertain prisoners at Blackwell's Island.

The following year, Isabelle teamed with her brother to record several George Gershwin songs, including "Somebody Loves Me." For the next few years she played at vaudeville houses with great success, highlighted with engagements at the Hippodrome and the Palace. She was on the Loew's circuit for two seasons and played extended engagements at Loew's State Theater and the 81st Street Theater.

The Keith-Orpheum circuit got her back for the 1927 season. During this period, Isabelle continued to record for the Edison Company. Songs like "I Ain't Gonna Be Nobody's Fool," "Mama Loves Papa" and "When You and I Were Young" were big hits in spite of the fact that Edison was close to closing down because they had not kept up with the latest technology.

Isabelle returned to the Palace in 1928 playing opposite George Jessel. During the next few years, vaudeville's decline reduced Isabelle's touring. In 1929, she met Walter Morris, a well-to-do manufacturer. They were married in 1930. Isabelle was 44 years old; Morris was 34. They had two sons.

Isabelle now limited her appearances in vaudeville and relinquished her headliner status. Movies dominated former vaudeville theaters now, with a few of them offering live acts performed by "oldtimers." In 1935, Miss Patricola retired from the stage. Her husband had launched a new business, the Hygienic Phone Service, which sent out people with disinfectants to sterilize telephones. The business was so successful, it enabled Isabelle and her husband to live quite comfortably.

Morris died in 1964. Isabelle suffered a stroke at her Great Neck, Long Island, home and died on May 23, 1965. She was 79 years old. Although she began her career in vaudeville much later than her contemporaries, Isabelle reached stardom quickly with a rare combination of skills and artistry that pleased audiences. Her recording career was equally successful, interpreting the popular hits of the day.

Isabelle Patricola (Museum of the City of New York).

Adelaide Hall

Adelaide Hall was one of the top black singers in vaudeville and musicals. Her career spanned 60 years, from the 1920s to the 1980s. An overlooked and almost forgotten singer, she co-starred with fellow black performers like Bill "Bojangles" Robinson, Ethel Waters, Josephine Baker, Louis Armstrong and Lena Horne. She recorded with such luminaries as Duke Ellington, Fats Waller and Art Tatum.

William Hall, Adelaide's father, was born in New York in 1874. His family had come from Virginia during the Civil War. Elizabeth Gerard, Adelaide's mother, was born in the West Indies in 1877. Her family came to New York in the 1890s. William was educated as a musician and later taught at the Pratt Institute. William and Elizabeth were married in

1898 and settled in an apartment in a middle-class neighborhood in Brooklyn. Adelaide was born on October 20, 1901. Her sister, Evelyn, was born two years later.

William started both daughters in music at an early age. Adelaide preferred singing while Evelyn played the piano. The sisters formed a piano-vocal duet and performed at church and school events. William died in 1915. Elizabeth worked as a maid and rented out to lodgers after the family moved to Manhattan. The family was devastated when Evelyn died during the 1918 influenza epidemic. Adelaide and her mother now had to support themselves.

At the age of 18, Adelaide appeared in New York black vaudeville as a chorus line singer and dancer. In 1921, she first played on Broadway in the musical review, "Shuffle Along," which opened on May 23. She was part of a chorus called the "Jazz Jasmines," who backed up Arthur Porter in "Bandana Days" and Noble Sissel in "Oriental Blues" and appeared in the show's finale. Sissel and Eubie Blake composed the music and lyrics and Flournoy Miller and Aubrey Lyles wrote the libretto. The show began with one-night stands in New Jersey and Pennsylvania, making just enough money to operate. They finally reached New York but were relegated to open in an out-of-the-way, run-down theater on 63rd Street. While reviewers found the plot trite, they raved about the music, particularly the songs "I'm Just Wild About Harry" and "Love Will Find a Way." Blake's music accompanied excellent dancing, with audiences shouting for more. The show was so well-received that it made black musical comedy overall a significant contributor to profitable box office receipts. The show played a total of 504 performances. Included in the chorus were Josephine Baker, Florence Mills and Paul Robeson.

In 1923, Adelaide was selected to appear in the musical revue, "Runnin' Wild," which opened on November 29 at a more prestigious theater, the Colonial. Miller and Lyles were again responsible for the book and James P. Johnson and Cecil Mack did the music and lyrics. Adelaide not only had a speaking part in the show but she sang one song on her own ("Love Bug"), one with partner Ina Duncan ("Old Fashion Love") and one with partner Bob Lee ("Ginger Brown"). She received raves for her singing and was acknowledged for a style that caused audiences to tap their feet in time.

In that era, prejudice against blacks playing in white theaters was still keen. The company began on the road for a tryout run. "Runnin' Wild" nearly floundered at the Howard Theater, Washington, D.C., forcing the cast to accept lower salaries. Soon the show was attracting white audiences, according to *Variety* ("Some performances saw three-fourths of the audience white"). Midnight shows were added and attracted large black audiences who were unable to attend matinees and evening shows. When "Runnin' Wild" moved to Boston, it was greeted with delight, especially the song "Old Fashion Love" as interpreted by Duncan and Hall. The show ran for eight weeks in Boston, which gave it a good financial foundation.

Response to a song by Elizabeth Welch and the chorus, called "Charleston," so moved the audience by its zesty, foot-tapping rhythm that it was repeated several times. The dance song, when published, was called "The Charleston" and quickly became a symbol of the jazz age.

While in town with "Runnin' Wild," Adelaide met Bert Hicks, a merchant seaman from Trinidad. They married in 1923, and Hicks later became her manager. They were together until his death in 1963.

Adelaide was now a headliner and in great demand. She performed at the Club Alabam in New York City, where she worked with the Berry Brothers, Ethel Waters and Josephine

Baker. In 1926, she appeared in "Tan Town Topics," a black revue that featured Fats Waller and his band. That same year, Adelaide starred in the ill-fated "My Magnolia," which was produced by Lew Leslie. The show lasted only a few weeks. Adelaide followed with an appearance in "Desirers of 1927" which opened in late 1926 and closed after four performances. Critics called it a poor black attempt at a white musical. Adelaide then moved to the Cotton Club. At the same time, Leslie wanted her for a new all-black revue he was planning.

Early in 1927, during her six-month engagement at Chicago's Sunset cafe, Adelaide worked with Louis Armstrong, who was leader of the Sunset's resident band. Armstrong was taken with Adelaide's singing style, particularly her scat (no words) singing, and suggested that she incorporate it into her regular song renditions. Adelaide followed his suggestion and found that audiences enjoyed the rhythm and bounce that scat singing added to her repertoire. Many years later, Ella Fitzgerald acknowledged that her "big sister" Adelaide was the impetus for her own singing style.

During late 1927, while she was working in vaudeville on the Keith circuit, Adelaide found herself on the same bill as Duke Ellington and his band. During their engagement, Adelaide discovered a new Ellington song called "Creole Love Call." They recorded it in late October 1927 for the Victor Record Company. The song became a major Ellington hit and Adelaide's signature tune.

Lew Leslie produced "Blackbirds of 1928," an all–black show written by whites, with the music by Jimmy McHugh and the lyrics by Dorothy Fields. The show starred Aida Ward and Bill Robinson. It opened at the Liberty Theater on May 9. Florence Mills had been signed to co-star, but when she unexpectedly died, Adelaide stepped into a role and convinced everyone of her headliner status. The show was a smash, as were the principals. Adelaide introduced "Diga, Diga, Do," "I Can't Give You Anything But Love" and "I Must Have That Man" and was awarded excellent reviews. The show ran for 518 performances.

Adelaide Hall

By this time, Adelaide was earning as much for her recordings as she was from the musicals. She had already made three records before "Creole Love Call" became an overnight hit. She recorded several more in 1932 but then made none until 1957, an original Broadway cast production of "Jamaica."

After the success of "Blackbirds," Adelaide toured in vaudeville on the Keith circuit, earning more than $2,000 a week. The Keith people promoted her as "The Black Madonna" and "The Crooning Blackbird" depending on the city where she was appearing. Encouraged by her husband, Adelaide took up songwriting, working on several of them with Bill Robinson. The song "Lazy Moon" impressed Lew Leslie enough for him to include in a "Blackbirds" production.

Adelaide reached vaudeville heaven with an appearance at the Palace Theater in 1930. Rarely had a black singer received plaudits from both reviewers and audiences at this theater.

"Brown Buddies," a 1930 black revue, starred Bill Robinson and Adelaide. It was the first successful black show since "Blackbirds" after a string of flops. Robinson got credited for one-third of the show with his colorful dancing. Adelaide was given the other two-thirds with her renditions of "Give Me a Man Like That" and "My Blue Melody." The show ran for 111 performances even though it played during the depth of the Depression.

In 1931, Adelaide traveled to England for a two-week engagement at London's Palladium. So well was she received that her trip was extended to include appearances in the provinces. She also signed with the English Decca label, the result being eight new songs that year and numerous others during the next decade.

Back in the United States, Adelaide was on a vaudeville tour when she met Art Tatum. The two performed together as a team, and recorded as well. While Adelaide was a star on Broadway and considered one of the best singers of jazz in America, prejudice against blacks was always close to the surface. She bought a home in Larchmont, New York, for herself, her husband and her mother. The predominantly white community was unable to deal with the situation and, after they failed to force the family out, the house was burned to the ground. Saddened by the episode, Adelaide returned to New York but she was also depressed about continuing to perform in the United States.

In the mid–1930s, Adelaide moved to Paris, where she quickly became a headliner on the popular stage. She did so well that she and her husband opened a cabaret. But when, in 1938, she was threatened with death by a young white man who claimed to be associated with royalty, she quickly moved to London and established a permanent residence. Charles Cockran, a local producer, persuaded Adelaide to star in a musical, "The Sun Never Sets," which proved successful for all parties. She opened two clubs in London, the Floridan and Calypso, and prospered. She also appeared in several English movies, including the 1940 hit, "The Thief of Bagdad." While she had no speaking role, she sang a poignant lullaby that became the hit of the movie.

During World War II, German bombs destroyed Adelaide's clubs. She entertained American soldiers coming to fight in the war. She joined the entertainment corps and performed in combat zones, including Germany before it finally surrendered.

After the war, Adelaide continued performing and making records in England. She switched to musicals, playing in a West End production of Cole Porter's "Kiss Me Kate."

In 1957, Adelaide returned to the United States to appear in a Broadway show, "Jamaica," which starred Lena Horne. The show opened November 31 at the Imperial Theater to rave reviews and ran for more than a year. Horne dominated the show, singing half of the show's 21 songs. Adelaide was given scant attention.

Bert Hicks was ailing and Adelaide temporarily retired to care for him. Several years after his death in 1963, she returned to performing. She was older — 63 — but her voice was as strong and expressive as ever. She appeared in some dramas with Peter O'Toole and

Helen Hayes. Performing in cabarets reinstated her as a headliner, and she also recorded new versions of her old signature songs. Lured back to the United States in 1979, Adelaide appeared in a musical revue, "Black Broadway," which was a nostalgic show reprising the all–black musicals of the 1920s. The show featured oldtimers like John Bubbles, Edith Wilson and Elizabeth Welch and new talent like Bobby Short and Gregory Hines. Adelaide sang "I Can't Give You Anything But Love" to an enthusiastic and appreciative audience. The show rekindled theatergoers' interest in black theater after years of dormancy.

As a result of the movie "The Cotton Club," and renewed interest in the history of Harlem and black musicals, Adelaide found herself in demand. She gave a few performances and interviews, but she was in her eighties and her health was failing.

After several months of illness, Adelaide died on November 7, 1993, in London. She was 91 years old. She was unaware that the Guinness World records archive had honored her for her contributions to music and longevity in the business. Their proclamation read: "Adelaide Hall (USA) is the most durable recording artist having released material over eight consecutive decades. The jazz singer's first record 'Creole Love Call' was recorded with Duke Ellington on 26 October 1927, and her last was made on 16 June 1991 at the Cole Porter Centennial Gala."

What they overlooked was her strong stylistic influence on jazz and pop music and her major contributions to black musical theater.

Ruth Etting

Rising to national radio fame in the 1920s, Ruth Etting began her singing career in Chicago vaudeville and nightclubs. She possessed a sparkling voice and dramatic delivery, making her a featured performer on phonograph records. In the late 1920s and early 1930s, she starred in musicals and in movies. Tragedy accompanied her stardom, forcing her to retire in 1938.

Ruth Etting was born on November 23, 1897, in David City, Nebraska. She was the only child of Alfred and Winifred Kleinham Etting. Alfred was born in May 1871 in Iowa. He was a bookkeeper. Winifred was born in 1875 and came to the United States as a child from Germany. They married in David City in 1896. When Ruth was five years old, her mother became ill and died. Alfred and his daughter moved in with his aged parents so they could help care for Ruth. Shortly after, Alfred remarried, moved away from David City and had scant contact with his daughter.

Ruth's grandfather, George Etting, was owner of a local rolling mill. He was also responsible for building the town's first theater, the David City Opera House. Ruth's experiences at the Opera House stimulated an interest in show business. She learned to sing and dance while performing in the church choir.

Ruth graduated from high school in 1916. She expressed an interest in clothing design and traveled to Chicago to attend the Chicago Academy of Fine Arts. She obtained a job designing costumes at a local nightclub, the Marigold Gardens, one of several nightclubs flourishing in Chicago. Many were owned and operated by gangsters. Rumor suggested that the Marigold Gardens was one of those nightclubs. It was occasionally shut down by police, but opened a few days later with no decrease in its popularity. Singers like Sophie Tucker played at the Marigold Gardens in the late teens.

Ruth got her first opportunity to perform at the Marigold Gardens when a tenor in the cast became ill. She was persuaded to perform because she was the only one who could sing low enough. As a youngster, Ruth admitted to having a "high, squeaky soprano." She discovered a new, lower-pitched voice that was quite compatible with current ballads and blues numbers. Ruth was hired to appear in the chorus, then obtained solo opportunities. By 1918, at the age of 20, she was the Marigold Gardens featured vocalist. She had also matured into a beautiful blond, blue-eyed young woman with attractive stage appeal.

Martin "Moe the Gimp" Snyder, a local gangster, known for the tactics he used to "get things done," saw Ruth perform and fell in love with her. Although she was warned about his character and shady background, Ruth married him on July 17, 1922. After the marriage, Snyder became her agent. In later life, she said she married him "nine-tenths out of fear and one-tenth out of pity."

Ruth Etting (Harry Ransom Humanities Research Center, the University of Texas at Austin.

For several years, Ruth appeared in vaudeville shows and nightclubs in Chicago, some appearances said to have been "fixed" by Snyder. At the same time, her singing talent was recognized and she became a featured headliner in the city. In 1924, after an appearance on a local radio station, she was booked for an extended vaudeville tour throughout the Midwest. In late 1925, Ruth was noticed by an executive of Columbia Records who engaged her for a test recording. It was a success, and her first record was released in March 1926. The songs were "Let's Talk About My Sweetie" and "Nothing Else Will Do." With national exposure, Ruth's record and radio career was launched.

In 1927, Ruth and Martin moved to New York. Her initial appearance was at the Paramount Theater with Paul Whiteman and his Orchestra. Reviews were excellent. She appeared at various New York theaters before being called by Flo Ziegfeld.

After auditioning for Ziegfeld, Ruth was engaged to star in the "Ziegfeld Follies of 1927." The show opened on August 16 at the New Amsterdam Theater. Led by Eddie Cantor and Claire Luce, the show was the usual opulent production featuring beautiful, scantily clad girls and equally ornate sets by Joseph Urban. Irving Berlin wrote most of the music, including one song that Ruth sang, "Shaking My Blues Away." The show closed after a short 167 performances because Cantor complained of fatigue.

Ziegfeld then hired Ruth to appear in "Whoopee." He had reconciled with Cantor, who agreed to head the show. Walter Donaldson, a well-known Tin Pan Alley composer, wrote the music and Urban contributed several lavish sets. Cantor's rendition of "Makin' Whoopee" stopped the show. Ruth also had her moments. She was not an actress; all she did was come on stage and sing, irrespective of the plot, and then leave the stage. Her singing ability was outstanding and she was regarded as Cantor's equal. She sang "Love Me or Leave Me," which was greeted with audience acclaim necessitating many encores at each performance. This became a signature song for the rest of her career.

On February 2, 1930, Ruth starred in the "9:15 Revue" at the Cohan Theater. The show lasted only one week, but Ruth's song, "Get Happy," remained a popular hit for generations.

A week later, Ziegfeld opened "Simple Simon" at his theater, starring Ed Wynn, with songs by Rodgers and Hart and sets by Urban. Ruth's rendition of "Ten Cents a Dance" stopped the show. Ziegfeld then inserted "Love Me or Leave Me" into the show, providing Ruth with two songs that rocked audiences each night.

Ziegfeld had Ruth back for his "Follies of 1931," the last show before he died. The show, which opened on July 1 at the Ziegfeld Theater, was made up of reminiscences and imitations of old performers and their specialties. Ruth impersonated Nora Bayes and sang "Shine On Harvest Moon." Playing a cabaret girl, she sang "Cigarettes, Cigars." The show ran for 165 performances, considered good in the midst of the Depression.

Ruth made her first recording in 1926 and her last in 1937. She recorded a total of more than 200 songs. Prior to the Depression, her most popular hits were "Mean to Me" and "Button Up Your Overcoat." During and after the Depression, hit songs included "Ten Cents a Dance," "Shine On Harvest Moon," "Let Me Call You Sweetheart," "You Made Me Love You," and "Love Me Or Leave Me." In the early 1930s, Ruth appeared on eight different radio programs. She also made several Vitaphone shorts at their studios in New York.

Ruth went to Hollywood in 1928 and sang in short subjects for both Warner Brothers and Paramount. She appeared in six full-length movies, three of which were hits: "Roman Scandals" (1933) with Eddie Cantor, "Gift of Gab" (1934) and "Hips, Hips, Hooray!" (1934).

In November 1937, Ruth announced that she was "through with radio, stage and screen — and matrimony, too." She filed suit for divorce from Snyder, claiming desertion and cruelty. A month later, she was granted the uncontested divorce. She did not ask for alimony.

In August 1938, Ruth married Myrl Alderman, her 30-year-old accompanist and radio music arranger, in a secret ceremony in Tijuana, Mexico. He had received a divorce from Alma Alderman, a radio singer, the previous December, about the same time that Ruth had obtained her final divorce from Snyder.

Two months later, in an incident in which words and recriminations turned to violence, Snyder shot and wounded Alderman. Snyder was arrested for attempted murder. Newspaper headlines told of the event, and the newspapers included pictures of all the involved parties.

Alma Alderman then filed a suit against Ruth for stealing the affections of her husband, asking for $150,000. She charged that Ruth had "induced Alderman to leave her with all the coaxing and every subtle contrivance at her command." She also claimed that Ruth and Alderman were not legally married. This suit generated more sensational headlines.

Midway through Snyder's trial, the press reported that Ruth and Alderman had flown to Nevada to get married. Snyder was convicted of attempted murder and sentenced to 20 years in prison. Newspapers continued to cover the ongoing events.

A year later, Snyder was freed when an Appeals Court reversed his conviction. Alma Alderman, unable to prove that Ruth had stolen the love of her husband, lost her case against Ruth. Snyder was given a new trial in 1940 but was released when Ruth refused to testify again.

In 1938, Ruth and Alderman retired to a small ranch near Colorado Springs and remained in seclusion for almost ten years. In 1947, when Ruth was 50 years old, she attempted a comeback, appearing on Rudy Vallee's radio show and performing at the Copacabana nightclub in New York. Her voice no longer had its appeal and she retired once more.

Ruth died on September 24, 1978, in a Colorado Springs hospital. She was 79 years old. She had been one of the most popular singers in the 1920s and 1930s, alternately called "The Sweetheart of Columbia Records" and "The Queen of All Torch Singers."

In May 1955, MGM released "Love Me or Leave Me," a Hollywoodized and sanitized version of Ruth's life, starring Doris Day and James Cagney. The film received good reviews but attracted average attendance. Audiences did not seem to care about a 1930s singer who was browbeaten by her gangster husband, even if he was portrayed by Cagney.

PART TWO : THE SINGER-COMEDIENNES

Irene Franklin

With flaming waist-length red hair and a personality that quickly won audiences' hearts, Irene Franklin brought sophistication to vaudeville. She was satirical and subtle, witty and beautiful. She possessed talent and stage skills that helped to mature the vaudeville genre, taking it out of its crude slapstick era into a period of more intellectual appeal. Vaudeville was her particular medium; and when the amusement died, Irene's career passed with it. From 1900 to the 1920s, she was one of the finest character singers and mimics in popular theater. In the 1930s, she turned to motion pictures but found them unfulfilling. She died in poverty, bemoaning her lost fame alone.

Irene Franklin was born on June 13, 1876, in St. Louis, Missouri, the first of two daughters of parents who were local stock company performers.

Irene claimed she began her stage career at the age of six months, when her parents carried her on stage during the performance of a melodrama. At three, she was doing a song-and-dance routine between the acts of plays. At six, she was taking children's roles in such melodramas as "Shore Acres," "Editha's Burglar," and "The Fire Patrol." She continued on stage during her childhood and early teen years, touring in Australia and England.

When Irene was 12, she, her sister and her mother traveled to Australia to visit relatives. Her father remained in America and unexpectedly died. A year later, Irene's mother also died, leaving the 13-year-old girl and her younger sister alone. Although they were taken in by relatives, Irene returned to the stage by playing in vaudeville wherever she could be booked. She faced a very difficult situation. She was unknown, very young, and with little experience in popular theater. When she did get work, the most she was able to earn was $25 a week, not nearly enough to support herself. Her act consisted of singing, dancing and monologues as she worked her way around various vaudeville circuits. She put on a reasonably good act but did not attract managers or reviewers.

Tony Pastor often used Irene at his 14th Street Theater but only to fill in if another act was unable to go on. She appeared at other New York vaudeville houses but never as the star attraction on the bill. Irene was confident she had talent but was unsure how best to use it to her advantage. When Pastor introduced her to Burton Green, who had been Pastor's house accompanist, her career began anew.

Green proposed to analyze Irene's act. He suggested she needed more exciting arrangements to take advantage of her style and expressiveness, and new songs to portray her comedic skills. Green volunteered to step in and help her develop a new style of performance. Irene enthusiastically responded to the changes and audiences quickly responded in kind to her new act. The act included songs that she and Green had written together, and the mimicking of women who held commonplace occupations as opposed to those entertainers who preferred to mimic other celebrities. A conversation between a streetcar conductor and a recent immigrant turned into an argument about getting off at Watt Street. "What street?" asked the conductor. (It was a skit taken from a Weber & Fields routine.) She did parodies of hotel maids, waitresses, farm women, schoolteachers and little girls. Since the audience could readily identify with the characterizations, Irene's popularity grew. She found that audiences especially liked her impersonations of little girls. She wrote "kid" songs, wore a romper or short dress and delivered the songs as a little girl might. Audiences shouted for encores and the act became a staple for her.

At the same time, the combination of Green and Franklin grew into a more intimate relationship. But Green was already married to Helen Van Campen, a well-known writer for the *New York Morning Telegraph* and world adventuress. Van Campen had liberal ideas regarding male-female relationships and was an ardent feminist long before such views were popular. When she discovered that her husband had fallen in love with Irene, she granted him a divorce with no financial commitments and gave him custody of their two children. Irene and Green were married in 1905. He became a very important factor in Irene's career. Besides being her accompanist, Green wrote the music to her songs and arranged them. So prominent was he that the theater marquees often featured Franklin and Green together.

The two composed a number of "kid" songs to be featured in Irene's act. They composed the song "Redhead" which described a little girl who complained about the personal attacks by boys who gave her derogatory nicknames due to her red hair. The song became a Franklin trademark for the rest of her career. This song, along with several others, was recorded by Irene, and returned her royalties.

Other "kid" songs they wrote included "I Don't Care What Happens to Me," "I'm Nobody's Baby Now" (which later became a hit song used by other performers), and "Somebody Ought to Put the Old Man Wise." When imitating various characters, rather than changing costumes, Irene would rapidly change the shape and style of her hair to typify the person she mimicked. Audiences loved her brand of comedy and thought she was "irresistible." Her impersonation of a chorus girl entering Broadway theater life was called "a masterpiece of characterization." She performed a song, "Expression," in which she portrayed all the human emotions through her facial features.

By 1910, Irene was at the height of her career, an established headliner in vaudeville earning $2,000 to $2,500 a week in salary. In a 1908 popularity contest, the public was asked to choose the most popular woman vaudeville artist. Irene was selected first, ahead of such headliners as Eva Tanguay and Marie Dressler. This was a period when women performers became more dominant than men in popularity and salaries.

Irene's impersonations did create some criticism that newspapers rushed to publish. A hotel chain complained about her portrayal of a maid; Child's Restaurant did not care for her imitation of a waitress; and, although Irene was in favor of the suffrage movement, they were unhappy with her response when she was asked if a woman's hardest job was getting a man. "No," she replied. "Holding him!" When Irene introduced the song, "What Have You Got on Your Hip? You Don't Seem to Bulge Where a Gentleman Ought To," the Keith/Albee organization tried to ban her use of it, but she refused.

In 1913, Irene and her husband were the first to have published calling cards on the front cover of *Variety*. The ad was made up of nothing more than their names in giant black type. Soon, other performers vied for the opportunity to do likewise.

Irene made her debut in musical comedy in "The Orchid," which opened at the Herald Square Theater on April 8, 1907. Eddie Foy was the star, amply supported by Irene and Trixie Friganza. But Irene had little to do and could not perform her signature routines, so she quickly returned to vaudeville. In 1910, a short stint in a Lew Fields production, "The Summer Widowers," was equally frustrating. She refused musicals for five years, returning to the appreciative patrons of the vaudeville stage. Wherever she appeared on the vaudeville circuit, her songs and impersonations met with full houses and satisfied patrons.

Irene was coaxed back to musicals by Fields, with support from the Shuberts, for the 1915 summer production of "Hands Up." Sigmund Romberg had written a weak score, so Fields turned to a young unknown named Cole Porter and bought several of his songs. Only one, "Esmerelda," appeared in the show. The opening of the show was delayed, several headliners fired, and Fields left the show. The almost totally revamped "Heads Up" opened at the 44th Street Theater on July 22, 1915. It was now a "typical Shubert," plotless revue. Will Rogers was featured. Irene seemed lost in the mixture of various vaudeville-like acts.

Irene was asked to appear in "The Passing Show of 1917," another hurriedly put-together show made up of old and familiar vaudeville acts. The songs were by Sigmund Romberg. The only one that became popular was "Goodbye Broadway, Hello France," which reflected America's involvement in the war. Irene shared honors with De Wolf Hopper, Jefferson De Angelis and Chic Sale. Again, Irene found the experience less than challenging. She just did not seem to be made for musicals.

During World War I, Franklin and Green entertained the troops in both France and America. With post-war theater changes and Irene's age — she was now 44 — that portion of her act dealing with small children no longer resonated with audiences. She had to rely on novelty songs and impersonations, which were still favorites with audiences.

Tragedy struck Irene when, in November 1922, Burton Green died of Bright's Disease. Irene was devastated and contemplated a retirement from the stage. To recover, she took a trip to Australia with her four children, two from her union with Green and two from his previous marriage. But the demands from managers and audiences kept her going although she was now missing an accompanist, composer and arranger. There were few songs to match the old hits she and Green had written together. Audiences sensed that Irene had lost some of her enthusiasm and they, too, lost interest.

A year later, Irene acquired a new accompanist, Jeremiah Jarnagan, an excellent pianist who could keep up with her stage antics. They were married on July 12, 1925. Irene continued in vaudeville although she was aware of its gradual decline in popularity. She starred in bills at the Palace Theater in 1925, 1926, 1929, and 1930 to great audience approval. The reviewers recalled her earlier triumphs. Irene last appeared on stage in the musical, "Sweet Adeline," which opened at the Hammerstein Theater on September 3, 1929. The show was written by Oscar Hammerstein II and Jerome Kern, built for the talents of Helen Morgan. Only one song lasted from the show, "Why Was I Born." The others were songs by Morgan about hope and despair. The production looked like it would run indefinitely but the Depression reduced ticket sales and the show staggered along for eight months.

Irene had the role of Lulu Ward, a Bowery diva, the sort of part she had longed for and played well. The role allowed her to impersonate waitresses, chorus girls and saleslaides and she had the opportunity to poke fun at the great actresses who starred in J.M. Barrie's plays. When asked by a reporter why she though Barrie was so whimsical, Irene answered:

"Because he is usually played by an actress who turns up one corner of her mouth into the mask of Comedy and turns down the other into the mask of Tragedy and talks through the middle with a Scotch accent."

Irene attempted to continue in vaudeville, but with its demise she turned to motion pictures. She had already appeared in one movie, "Wanted for Murder," in 1918. From 1933 to 1939, Irene appeared in 29 movies, all of them in small character parts, none of them featuring her vaudeville talents. In 1934 alone, she was in eight movies. That same year, tragedy struck her again.

One evening, she and her husband were entertaining guests at their home. As the guests were waiting for Jarnagan to come down for dinner, they heard a gunshot. Jarnagan was dead. The event created newspaper headlines regarding what they called "a mysterious death." Irene claimed her husband had been murdered; the coroner declared it to be a suicide. Although she hired private detectives and demanded a new investigation, news of the tragedy disappeared in a few months. Irene now continued to appear in movies because she needed the money.

Irene Franklin (Museum of the City of New York).

In September 1940, Irene reluctantly moved into the Actors Fund Home in Englewood, New Jersey. She was already quite ill, suffering from neuritis. Ironically, she was assigned the room formerly held by the late Fay Templeton. Taken seriously ill on her birthday—doctors reported she had suffered a cerebral hemorrhage—Irene died three days later, on June 16, 1941. She was 65 years old.

Irene's unique skills had been particularly adapted to vaudeville. She acquired huge popularity from appreciative audiences. When vaudeville died, so did Irene's career as well as the public's memories of her stardom.

Fay Templeton

She was one of the most beloved performers on the American stage. Born into a theatrical family, Fay Templeton excelled on the legitimate and vaudeville stages for more than a half a century. As actress, singer and comedienne, Fay's versatility made her a favorite headliner and heroine of popular theater.

Fay was born on December 25, 1865, in Little Rock, Arkansas, where her parents were starring with the Templeton Opera Company. John Templeton, Fay's father, was a well-known Southern manager, comedian and author. He had already spent more than two decades on tour performing many roles and managing various companies. Helen Alice

Vane, Fay's mother, played with her husband and was an artist of fine repute, referred to as the "Star of the South." Another Templeton child died in June 1871, while the family was on tour. If there was any performer who could rightly claim she had been born and raised "on the road," it was Fay.

At the age of three, Fay was dressed as Cupid and sang fairy tale songs between the acts of her father's plays. Gradually, she was incorporated into the productions as a bit player and then, at five, had actual lines to recite. Fay often sang 12 songs (plus encores), danced and played a piano solo during a play's intermission. At eight, Fay played Puck in "A Midsummer Night's Dream" at New York's Grand Opera House. She sang a contemporary tune, "Up in a Balloon," and created a sensation. Appearing in the well-known melodrama "East Lynne," Fay sang so successfully that the audience cheered for encores.

At 15, Fay had a reputation as an accomplished light opera singer. She played in several juvenile versions of Gilbert & Sullivan productions, often as the leading singer. When not performing for other companies, Fay returned to appear in her father's productions. The same year, she eloped with Billy West, a black minstrel performer, but they separated after a honeymoon of six weeks. She divorced him three years later.

Fay's parents did not speak to one another and occupied separate rooms at a hotel. For the past several years, John Templeton had acquired the reputation of working his talented daughter to exhaustion. According to a reviewer, the consequences of such a regimen had affected her to the point that "she must either have a rest or break down." In 1883, Fay chose to go out on her own. Upon her departure, a notice to the company informed them their season would close and the company disbanded. Little is known of John Templeton's career other than his difficulty in finding new engagements.

Alice divorced John shortly after. She married actor Alfred C. Whelan only days after he had been divorced. Fay attended the ceremony in Chicago. The following day, Fay and her mother left for Europe. Whelan stayed at home, supposedly due to prior theater commitments.

On October 7, 1885, Fay had her formal debut in a revival of "Evangeline." For that season, the play had the longest continual run in New York (201 performances). In this show, Fay displayed talent as both a comedienne and a mimic. A slim Fay played Gabriel and a stout Amelia Summerville played Hubert.

After several years on the road playing in various melodramas and musical farces, Fay was given the title role in "Hendrik Hudson," which opened at the 14th Street Theater on August 18, 1890. It was a trouser part, then a popular feature of operettas. Her role was of a faithless husband who goes to Florida with a group of chorus girls. She won accolades singing "The Same Old Thing" but the show itself lasted only 16 performances. A rewritten version of the play was taken on the road with moderate success, but when it returned to New York it closed after two weeks.

Between these shows, in 1887, Fay had married for a second time. Charles J. Osborne was a wealthy broker for Jay Gould, the millionaire. Osborne's mother threatened to cut him off if he married an actress. His own investments more than made up for any such loss. He and Fay lived in England and toured the continent for several years. A highlight of Fay's stay in England was an 1887 appearance in "Monte Cristo, Jr." at the Gaiety Theater. When she sang the song "I Like It, I Do," in a skimpy costume, the English censor complained that her song and dress were indecent. Fay sued the censor and forced the producer, who had dismissed her, to let her appear in the original costume minus only a silk sash. Not surprisingly, the show was a hit and ran for two seasons. Fay's singing and comedy bits were attractive to London audiences. Fay's marriage to Osborne was kept secret until his death in 1895, when it was announced that she was to receive $100,000.

After Fay's return to the American stage in 1890, she formed her own opera company and starred in "Madame Favart" (1893) and other operettas, none of which fared very well financially. In 1895, Fay was the star in E. E. Rice's "Excelsior, Jr.," which opened at Oscar Hammerstein's new Olympic Theater. It was another trouser role for Fay, but reviewers noted her increasing corpulence and questioned her role selection.

In 1896, Weber & Fields bought a Broadway theater and formed a stock company made up of headliners. They initiated a reign of eight years of sparkling productions satirizing legitimate plays. From the time the theater opened, they played to full houses. Fay was one of the headliners selected to appear with this all-star company. She did her best work when parodying famous actresses. Although she was now buxom even by Gay Nineties standards, her comedic versatility, long dark hair, sultry smile and throaty-voiced singing won over audiences. Comedy songs like "Keep Away from Emmaline" and "What? Marry Dat Gal?" by the company's resident composer, John Stromberg, were continually repeated until audiences would sing along with her. Fay thoroughly enjoyed the Weberfieldsian productions and believed her time at the Music Hall to be one of the best of her long career.

During her years with Weber & Fields, Fay displayed a knack for satirizing theatrical pretensions. Her burlesques of grand opera and comic opera divas were reported to be devastating.

Just before the 1899–1900 season began, Fay appeared in summer vaudeville at the New York Roof Garden, which happened to be a Syndicate house. Weber & Fields disliked everything the Syndicate stood for and openly feuded with them for years. Angry at Fay, they decided not to renew her contract. She played in vaudeville during her time away from the Music Hall.

However, the following year Fay was signed because Weber & Fields found that Lillian Russell, now a member of the company, could not replace her in the burlesques. In the 1900 show, Fay introduced Stromberg's "Ma Blushin' Rosie, Ma Posie Sweet." The song was the hit of the show. During rehearsals, a 14-year-old named Al Jolson came into the Music Hall to try out as a chorus boy. He was rejected, but Fay's rendition of "Rosie" so impressed him that he later incorporated it into his repertoire.

In 1901, Fay introduced "I'm a Respectable Working Girl" in the new Music Hall show. It was another winner and she had to encore it several times before the show could continue. During the year, the White Rats actors' union rebelled against the Syndicate and struck Syndicate theaters across the country. Lillian Russell and Fay led the White Rats women's division. Unfortunately, the financial power of the Syndicate crushed the actors' strike and left them powerless for years. Weber & Fields, however, were independents, and they produced and toured their own shows until, in 1904, they separated for personal reasons.

A year after Weber & Fields split, Fay was hired by George M. Cohan to play the lead in his new musical comedy, "Forty-five Minutes from Broadway." The show opened at the New Amsterdam Theater on January 1, 1906. Fay introduced the hit songs "So Long Mary" and "Mary Is a Grand Old Name" and had an abundance of Cohan comedy quips to highlight the show. The production was Cohan at his composing peak; his story, the song lyrics and the dialogue were thoroughly all–American. Interestingly, the show had been tried out in Chicago first and ran for more than three months. In New York, it had only 90 performances. Fay had the role of New Rochelle housemaid Mary Jane Jenkins, who gives up a fortune to marry the impoverished man she loves.

A few months later, Fay married a Pittsburgh industrialist, William Patterson. They were married in August 1906. Patterson was her third husband. She immediately announced her retirement from the stage.

Fay returned to vaudeville in 1911. When Weber & Fields were planning their reunification with a Jubilee touring company featuring all the old Music Hall stars, Fay was one of the first to volunteer. The tour lasted five months and its box office receipts broke all records for touring companies. Fay played some of her old comic bits, like a dead mummy brought to life and Cho-Cho San in a travesty of "Madame Butterfly." She also sang "Rosie" and several novelty numbers, like "Alexander's Bagpipe Band," a travesty of Irving Berlin's hit, that kept the audience in hysterics.

Fay continued in vaudeville with an act that included songs from the Weberfields shows, "Forty-five Minutes from Broadway" and her comic act singing "Poor Little Butterfly" from "Pinafore." She filled theaters and received splendid reviews. She was also perceived as a "great old-time favorite" although she did not care for the implications. In 1913, Fay retired again to become a Pittsburgh society matron like her friend Lillian Russell.

In 1925, Fay came out of retirement to appear in an oldtimers show at the Palace Theater. She worked with Weber & Fields in a comedy skit that featured her being pushed on stage in a roller chair by Joe Weber, since she was even stouter than before. Her performance brought down the house and the show was extended a second week. Only a supremely confident and talented performer would dare to return to the stage in such a self-effacing manner after more than a decade.

Each night when the curtain dropped and performers gave their farewell speeches, Fay cried, unable to talk, and the audience cried with her as they honored this supreme actress. When asked if she would continue to perform, she replied, "It's been great fun but it's a new Broadway and a new theater, and hereafter I'll be content to look on from out front."

Fay Templeton

But Fay returned to the stage again in 1926 to play Buttercup in a Shubert revival of "Pinafore" which ran for 55 performances. It was described as "positively her last appearance on stage." This time she managed to throw kisses to the audience. In 1929, she was lured to Hollywood for a proposed film featuring Weber & Fields and their old colleagues. The movie died with the beginning of the Depression.

Fay's husband, William Patterson, died suddenly in 1931 and Fay found herself in financial difficulties. There was trouble over the will and bequests. Fay felt she had to return to the stage to earn a living. The opportunity came in 1933 with Jerome Kern's "Roberta." The show opened on November 18 at the New Amsterdam Theater. Kern was nearing the end of his Broadway career but his score was as melodic and romantic as ever. Fay played Aunt Minnie, a dress shop owner in Paris. Bob Hope, in his stage debut, handled the comedy. Fay had only one song to sing, "Yesterdays," but it was one of Kern's best. "Roberta" ran for nine months. This show was truly Fay's last on the stage.

That same year, Fay had a cameo role in her only movie. "Broadway to Hollywood" was one of those all-star pictures using a mixture of oldtimers and new talent. The oldtimers played themselves.

Fay found herself again out of funds and was forced to enter the Actors Fund home in Englewood, New Jersey. This gave rise to "sob stories" in the newspapers talking about her poverty and how Broadway had forgotten her. Unhappy with the portrayal, she wrote *The New York Times*: "Let it be clearly understood that I want no benefits. The public owes me nothing. Mentally, morally and almost physically sound, I confess I am financially crippled. So what? I am taking advantage of the comforting hospitality of the Actors Fund Home, but sincerely hope to be again bowing my appreciative thanks to a New York audience I have always found generously loyal to me. Work, not benefits, is what I want." Fay was 71 years old and suffering from arthritis.

In 1937, Fay moved to San Francisco to live with a cousin, Belle Adams. Fay died in obscurity on October 3, 1939, at the age of 74. Few attended her funeral. She was buried in Kensico Cemetery, Valhalla, New York.

Marie Dressler

Though rarely listed as one of the great entertainers of the last century, Marie Dressler had unique stage talent and skills. She was a classic delineator of eccentric comedy. Along with the usual pratfalls, puns, and malapropisms, she excelled as a comedienne whose timing, inflection, body language, and self-deprecation went beyond the realm of slapstick and pedestrian humor. Dressler's comedy showed a deep understanding of human nature. She could be realistic or grotesque, express pathos and arouse sympathy, and sustain laughter, all of this in the midst of a stage routine. A big woman, she quickly learned to use her oversized body to comic advantage, a gambit she used for almost her entire career.

Dressler began her career as a minor player in comic opera, but found a much greater reception as a vaudevillian. For two decades, she mixed vaudeville with revues, burlesque and musical comedy, always returning to vaudeville when money and jobs were in short supply. Brief appearances in silent films set the foundation for her later performances in talkies. During this time, her headliner status was revived and she became one of the most beloved film stars in America.

Leila Marie Koerber was born November 9, 1868, in Cobourg, Canada. Her father, Alexander Rudolph Koerber, had immigrated from Austria in the early 1860s. Her mother, Anna, was a blond Irish-Canadian with an unknown genealogy. While Alexander was an autocratic person who demanded perfection, he was also an accomplished musician who passed his interests to his two daughters, Leila and Bonita. Their mother was the girls' first audience and she supported their interest in the theater. At five, Leila appeared at a church social in the role of Cupid. When she accidentally fell off the stage, the audience laughed heartily. Falling later became an integral part of her comedy routines.

Leila was not a lovely girl; she was large for her age, with green eyes and large cheeks. Bonita, in comparison, was a pretty blond with a shapely figure. Both children were given music lessons by their father, but his abusive behavior so alienated them that the lessons had to be stopped. Alexander's inability to earn a proper living forced Anna to become the primary supporter of the family. Because of Alexander's erratic behavior, the family moved frequently during the girls' childhood years, finally ending in Saginaw, Michigan. At 13, Leila got her first job in a department store. A year later, due to confrontations with her father, Leila decided to pursue a career in the theater. Bonita followed her. Thanks to her mother, Leila chose the name of Marie Dressler, after a deceased aunt.

When Marie was 14, she joined a Nevada stock company, claiming she was 18 and her sister 16. They each earned $6 a week by playing bit parts and singing in the chorus. Bonita was not happy with stage work and returned home. After six months on the stage, Marie was given the role of Cigarette in the perennial melodrama, "Under Two Flags"; the role caused her considerable stage fright. Thus began an education period in which Marie learned the art of acting, playing various roles, and the idiosyncrasies of touring. She also discovered what it was like to be stranded on the road in the middle of winter in a small town.

From 1883 to 1892, Marie appeared in various comic operas in minor singing roles. In 1893, she played opposite Lillian Russell in "Princess Nicotine." The two actresses became close friends. They married at almost the same time, Russell to her co-star, Senor Perugini, and Marie to George E. Huppert, a nice-looking man who aspired to join New York's social elite. Russell and Marie divorced their husbands at almost the same time, in 1896, and Marie lived with Russell for several years as her career opportunities improved.

Marie appeared in five more comic operas. In the last one, "The Lady Slavey" (also reported to be a musical), she starred as a clumsy maid. In this role, her comedic talents were recognized. The show received favorable reviews, as did Marie for her comic antics. The show was so popular that it was revived twice, in 1898 and 1900, both featuring Marie.

In February 1897, Marie appeared in vaudeville for the first time, at Proctor's Pleasure Palace, New York. She starred in the skit "Tess of the D'Urbervilles," a travesty on a legitimate play, featuring the famous Mrs. Fiske. Reviewers noted Marie's droll comedy and imitation of Fiske as highlights of the skit. On the same bill was the Lumiere Cinematograph, Marie's first experience with the fledgling moving picture industry.

A salary and booking disagreement with Syndicate leader Abe Erlanger forced Marie off the stage for a short period of time. The episode was an experience she never forgot. Twenty years later, she would be opposing him again when actors struck against theater managers. Due to her recent record of vaudeville box office successes, Marie was reinstated and sent on another vaudeville tour in a musical farce called "Courted Into Court," in which she sang, danced and displayed her comic talents. Marie gained further attention by singing coon songs and imitating famous actresses. Reviewers now spoke of Marie as "a genuine woman comedienne": She acted with intelligence; she had magnetism; and she was unafraid to be unattractive.

Marie appeared in a number of musical comedies and revues through 1902. Another short run on the vaudeville stage, at $1,000 a week, saw Marie in her first solo act, which was met with enthusiastic audience approval. In 1904, Marie was signed by Joe Weber and Flo Ziegfeld in a typical Weberfields farce. Weber had recently separated from his long-time partner, Lew Fields, and decided to continue the type of entertainment that had made the Weber and Fields Music Hall the best venue on Broadway. The cast featured Anna Held, then Ziegfeld's wife. Marie appeared at Weber's Music hall for two years in various productions, all of them satires on legitimate plays. Weber recalled Marie as an outstanding comedienne. "She loved being a clown. She worked for laughs as nobody else ever did."

In December 1906, Marie reentered vaudeville with a one-woman skit at the Colonial

Theater and later went on tour with the act. Audiences were delighted with her antics, including her propensity to bump into everything—the piano, the scenery, the curtain, even the flowers that had been thrown on stage. This success propelled her into an unusually long engagement, ten weeks at Proctor's 58th Street Theater. Unfortunately, her appearance at Proctor's was marred by frequent illness.

On a train trip from New York to Philadelphia, Marie met Jim Dalton, who purported to have been a millionaire, law school graduate, business executive and partner in a brokerage house, none of which was really true. He was also three years younger than Marie. At the time, Marie was dealing with financial problems and hired Jim to manage her affairs. She soon found out that Dalton was also an alcoholic and gambler. Yet, he became her loyal and obedient servant, not only caring for her personally but also fighting managers and booking agents on her behalf. Marie loved him and they were viewed as partners in her career.

In October 1907, Marie played on a vaudeville program at the Palace Theater, London. Given the opportunity to create her own routine, Marie won London audiences with a combination of song, dance and comedy. She had an unusual and surprising entrance that caused the audience to shout out in appreciation. When

Marie Dressler (Museum of the City of New York).

she came on the stage, she sat down at the piano to begin a song. Putting out her arms, she found that she was too far away to reach the keys. Instead of moving her chair closer, she grabbed the sides of the piano and jerked it toward her. King Edward VII saw her act and invited her as his palace guest. The *New York Telegraph* wrote, "She is hailed as the most delightful comedienne ever sent to London by America." Marie played to full houses until March 1908, ill and tired after an intense vaudeville engagement.

Even before Marie and Jim landed in New York, she was signed by Percy Williams for a month at his Colonial Theater, at $1,500 a week. Although she appeared on stage for only 16 minutes, audience demands on Marie were great. "The strain is terrible," she admitted to a reporter, "and when I am finished, I am played right out."

When Marie talked of marriage to Jim, he revealed that he was already married and that his wife refused to give him a divorce. This problem did not change Marie and Jim's relationship.

Marie's first true stage triumph occurred on May 5, 1910, at Lew Fields' Herald Square Theater. With investment from the Shuberts, Fields produced a play, "Tillie's Nightmare," starring Marie in a role that seemed to fit her size and comedic style. She had signed a three-year contract with Fields, made up of 30-week seasons. Along with a guarantee of $500 a week, Marie would get ten percent of the gross receipts up to $10,000 each week and 15 percent over $10,000. Contracts made during these days often became slippery documents; this one had a hideous history.

Rehearsals for "Tillie's Nightmare" were fraught with numerous problems. Marie walked out several times because of arguments with the Shuberts. When the show opened in Albany, reviewers called it a flop. Marie took over the script and reworked it. Half the cast was fired; Fields fought with the Shuberts to keep the show alive. With constant changes, the show continued on the road. In Chicago there were bad reviews for the show and for Marie as well. The show limped along, with Marie castigating the Shuberts for their penny-pinching and the Shuberts complaining about her frequent tantrums. Then, in Kansas City, the show received a good review. More favorable reviews followed although the tour was almost stopped several times. Only Fields' intervention saved it. When "Tillie's Nightmare" finally opened in New York, it was a big hit, having become entirely Marie's show. She appeared on stage for almost its entire length. After a profitable New York run, the show went on tour for 26 weeks to wide audience acclaim.

Marie was then asked to join the Weber and Fields Jubilee tour in late 1911. Although she was not a member of the original stock company at the old Music Hall, her previous association with Joe Weber and her success in Fields' "Tillie's Nightmare" seemed to qualify her for inclusion. Or possibly, she was the best replacement for Fay Templeton, of similar girth and comedy experience. The tour continued for six months, to June 1912, and was heralded as the most financially successful tour on record.

Marie sang several songs and appeared in many of the company's comic skits. Falling over her feet, or Joe Weber, and bumping into the scenery were frequent slapstick elements to her comedy.

With Lew Fields producing, Marie played the headliner in the "Marie Dressler Players," a vaudeville mixture of songs and comedy skits that was poorly received by audiences. Marie jumped to a vaudeville circuit for a tour of the major cities, which proved more profitable to her. As before, she performed a solo routine. The Shuberts pursued Marie to play another vaudeville tour for them. This one was quite successful and returned good box office receipts for the producers.

When pressed on the issue of women's suffrage, Marie voiced contradictory beliefs. On one hand, she believed that women should be the equal of men. She had frequently confronted managers regarding equality. But she also felt that women should not vote; that political act should be left to men. A woman's place was in the home, she said, except when she had artistic talent, which justified a professional career. A few years later, she came out strongly for women's suffrage, probably influenced by her friend Lillian Russell, who had become a vigorous spokesperson for the women's vote.

To this point in her career, Marie had achieved a number of successes, followed by illnesses that interrupted a tour, legal problems often due to Jim's deals with managers, and then a return to vaudeville to rescue her headliner status. In 1914, Mack Sennett gave her an opportunity to be a moving picture star by offering her a role in a feature he was producing, "Tillie's Punctured Romance," a takeoff from Marie's stage success. Also featured in the film were Mabel Normand and Charlie Chaplin. Initially, Marie was not interested in moving from the stage to the screen. However, a proposed salary of $2,500 a week for 14 weeks of shooting enticed her to travel to Southern California. "Tillie's Punctured Romance" opened November 14, 1914, and was an instantaneous success even though the movie was overly long, worrying theater exhibitors. Critics singled out Marie and her comic capers. "Six thousand feet of undiluted joy," they called it. It was also at this time that Marie and Jim were married in a quiet ceremony.

Marie came back to the stage in a comedy called "A Mix Up," put on by the Shuberts. The show did well on tour. She followed with three more "Tillie" movies, the last two of which she produced. She could not persuade the distributors to feature the films and she lost a good deal of money. Signed to appear in the Ziegfeld-Dillingham revue, "The Century Girl," Marie was unceremoniously dropped after three performances with no explanation. She was nearly 50 years old with no job prospects.

For almost three years, Marie had only a few scattered vaudeville appearances. Instead, during the war, she entertained at military camps and sold Liberty Bonds with the same kind of zest she displayed on stage.

The results of the Actors' Equity strike in September 1919 made her problems more severe. Marie had organized chorus girls to support the actors' demands. Her activities alienated the managers. After the strike was settled, Marie was unable to get an engagement. Jim then confessed that he was still married to his wife and that his marriage to Marie had been faked. He then suffered a stroke and became paralyzed. Nevertheless, Marie tended him until his death in 1921.

Vaudeville saved Marie once again. The Shuberts signed her for a minor role in "Cinderella on Broadway." The show had a short tour. They obtained her services again for a longer role in "The Passing Show of 1921," advertised as a revue but full of individual vaudeville routines. Another Shubert production, "Moments from the Winter Garden," toured the Midwest. Again, Marie played her best comedy routines. In 1923, Marie found work in "The Dancing Girl." Her last vaudeville engagement was at the Palace Theater, New York, in October 1925. In "Old Timer's Week," Marie reprised several of her vaudeville skits. The week was full of nostalgia, audiences seemingly paying farewell to those performers who no longer shared the stage as headliners. Passed up by the changing tastes of audiences, her age and her style of comedy, Marie went into retirement. During this time, she wrote her autobiography, aptly titled, "The Life Story of an Ugly Duckling." The book was the story of her rise to fame on the stage but omitted many pertinent events of her life.

During the 1920s, Marie lived in Hollywood, waiting to be called again to appear in the movies. In 1927, she obtained a small part in "The Joy Girl" and a cameo in "Breakfast at Sunrise." The following year, she got parts in "Bringing Up Father" and "The Patsy." When sound came in, Marie was rediscovered. Her voice and delivery were perfect for talkies, and her comedic touches undiminished. "The Hollywood Revue of 1929" auditioned all of MGM's stock players to see who could make the transition from silents to sound; Marie easily passed the test. During 1929 and 1930, Marie appeared in several films, none of them notable, but they kept her working.

Eugene O'Neill's stage play, "Anna Christie," was reworked into a film, starring Greta Garbo in her American debut. Marie got a good role thanks to her friend and scriptwriter, Frances Marion. The picture was well received and Marie received rave notices for her role. At age 61, she was recognized as an accomplished actress.

Several cheapies followed as the studio took advantage of Marie's new box office appeal. Her starring role in "Min and Bill," opposite Wallace Beery, was an audience winner, and she won the Academy Award for Best Actress in 1931. In 1933, Marie appeared in two pictures that propelled her to national stardom, "Tugboat Annie" and "Dinner at Eight." These roles defined her as one of the most popular and beloved actresses of Hollywood. The comedy that carried her through the tough years of vaudeville greatly contributed to her renewed success. Unfortunately, illness again intervened, this time seriously.

Marie's last movie, "Christopher Bean," was released only six months before she died. She was already in pain. During the last three months of her life, she was being cared for by friends in Montecito, California. On July 28, 1934, at age 65, Marie Dressler died. The cause of her death was a combination of uremia, congestive heart failure and cancer.

Marie had enjoyed several decades of popularity entertaining vaudeville audiences. After some years in obscurity, she received even greater public acclaim by appearing on the screen.

Ina Claire

A versatile actress with a matchless command of the spoken word, Ina Claire began her long stage career in two-a-day vaudeville. Her comedic talents got her engagements in musicals, including appearances in the Ziegfeld Follies. Her determination to become a dramatic actress was fulfilled when she was selected to play the lead at the age of 24. Ina appeared in dramas that extended to the 1950s. Her film career ran from 1915 to 1943.

Ina Fagan was born on October 15, 1893, in Washington, D.C. Her father, Joseph Fagan, a government clerk, had been killed in the collapse of the Ford Theater four months before her birth. He was 37 years old. Her mother, Cara Lieurance, was born in Ohio in 1869. Cara and Joseph were married in 1887. They had two children, Allen, born in 1889, and Ina. Joseph's unexpected death forced Cara to find work to support the family. As a child, Ina attended Holy Cross Academy in Washington, D.C., for a short time, but she had no other formal education.

Nothing is known of her early theatrical training, if any. Yet, at the age of ten, Ina made her vaudeville debut at a local theater as a singing mimic. For the next several years, she appeared in various vaudeville theaters on the East Coast perfecting her imitations of stage celebrities. During this time, her mother and brother accompanied her. Often, Allen shared the stage with Ina as male-female teams, especially young ones, had become a favorite attraction on vaudeville bills. Around this time, Ina changed her last name to Claire. Brother Allen kept the Fagan name because "I thought I would stand a much better chance if I had this name rather than assume her stage name. Some day, I hoped my sister will be proud of me." He went on to play leading roles in stage plays until he died in 1937.

At the age of 15, on March 13, 1909, Ina made her first New York appearance at the American Music Hall. Her act included imitations of many stage stars, but audiences responded most favorably to her imitation of Sir Harry Lauder. Reviewers responded with similar enthusiasm and believed Ina to be a star in the making. For the next two seasons, Ina toured in vaudeville, first with the Orpheum circuit, then with engagements at Keith and Proctor theaters. Along with her imitations, Ina had become a fine comedienne. For the time being, a childhood ambition to be a dramatic actress had to be sidelined.

Ina's vaudeville successes got her a small role in a 1911 musical, "Jumping Jupiter," starring comedian Richard Carle, who also wrote his own libretto for the production. The show opened at the Criterion Theater, New York. Unfortunately, Ina had little chance to impress the reviewers, as the show only lasted three weeks. Ina returned to vaudeville until the fall, when she was engaged as the lead in "The Quaker Girl." The show opened at the Park Theater on November 23. The show was favorably received by critics and audiences, and had a run of 240 performances. There was now no question about Ina's talent and acting skills as she fashioned the starring role to emphasize her assets. Her buoyant one-stage temperament and sense of humor captured theatergoers. Her capricious temperament offstage often gained the attention of the press, but such episodes only improved her appeal.

Since no other engagements immediately came to her, Ina went back to vaudeville. However, her appearance at Hammerstein's Music Hall in July 1913 reminded managers of her abilities and she was signed to appear in London, England, for both vaudeville and musical comedy dates.

Ina made her London debut as the lead in "The Girl from Utah," which opened on October 18, 1913, at the Adelphi Theater. Reviewers especially lauded her acting ability, giving her more recognition than she received from U.S. critics. Charles Frohman brought the show to the United States but, because Ina was already booked in England, gave the leading role to Julia Sanderson. To strengthen the play's musical weakness, Frohman purchased seven songs from an unknown composer, Jerome Kern.

A year later, Ina starred in a musical, "The Belle of Bond Street," also at the Adelphi. Her popularity brought her back to the United States to star in the musical, "Lacy Luxury," which opened at the Casino Theater on December 25, 1914. Even though the beautiful comedienne was given favorable reviews, the show "was a quick, insignificant failure," according to historian Gerald Bordman.

Two months later, Ina appeared at the Palace Theater, New York, as a featured headliner. Sharing the bill with Ina was Alla Nazimova, in a dramatic one-act play, and Nan Halperin. Watching Nazimova convinced Ina that her future career was in dramatic theater. Again, however, she was diverted by an offer from Flo Ziegfeld she could not refuse — a starring role in the Follies.

The Ziegfeld Follies dominated popular theater in New York. When the show opened on June 21, 1915, at the New Amsterdam Theater, audiences witnessed an elaborate revue made up of prominent headliners, beautiful girls and the elegant settings of Joseph Urban. Starring in the revue, besides Ina, were W.C. Fields, Ed Wynn, Bert Williams and Ann Pennington. Ina sang the show's best song, "Hello Frisco!" which took notice of the beginning of transcontinental phone service. Ina was asked to return to next season's edition of the Follies.

The 1916 Follies opened at the New Amsterdam on June 12. As usual, it was filled with stars like Will Rogers, Bert Williams, Fanny Brice, Bernard Granville and Ina. This time, her act included imitations of Geraldine Farrar, Jane Cowl and Irene Castle. She also sang a Kern song, "Have a Heart," judged to best of the show. She toured with the show for the entire season.

Now a recognized star at the age of 24, Ina sought out vehicles for her dramatic aspirations. Her first dramatic role was in "Polly With a Past," which opened at the Belasco Theater on September 6, 1917. Having made the transition from vaudeville and revues, she was immediately identified as a bona fide star of the legitimate stage. During the next 20 years, Ina starred in 17 plays, some short-lived, some playing successfully for two seasons. In all of these productions, Ina was praised for her work.

Ina was married three times. Her first husband was James Whittaker, a Chicago newspaper music critic. They married in July 1919, but kept it a secret for a year. She divorced him in October 1925, charging him with desertion and cruelty. In 1929, she married John Gilbert, the romantic actor. Rumors had suggested that Gilbert was about to marry Greta Garbo. Everyone was surprised when Ina and Gilbert took the train to Las Vegas to get married. Ina had met Gilbert only three weeks before. He was three years younger than Ina and had already been married twice.

Six months later, Ina moved out of their home in Beverly Hills and rented a house of her own. They spoke of separating for only a month but the press noted that both Ina and Gilbert were temperamental people and predicted the marriage would fail. In February 1931, Ina sued for divorce, her "perfect lover" having turned cold to her. She claimed cruelty and neglect. It was a marriage that Ina later described as "my biggest mistake." In March 1939, at the age of 46, Ina married William R. Wallace, Jr., a San Francisco lawyer and member of a prominent Salt Lake City family. They lived together in San Francisco for the remainder of her life.

Ina had a spotty career in motion pictures. Her vaudeville and Follies fame got her roles in two 1915 films, "The Puppet Crown" and "The Wild Goose Chase," neither of which were popular hits. In 1920, she took her stage success of "Polly With a Past" to film. Like the play, the movie was a success. Her next appearance in the movies was in 1929, when she starred in a talkie, "The Awful Truth." After several mediocre films in the early 1930s, she appeared in "Ninotchka" (1939) and "Claudia" (1943) in dowager roles. Ina claimed that "I'm no good in pictures," but no one else believed her. The dramatic roles she assumed were always done with professionalism.

In 1946, Ina starred in "The Fatal Weakness" in New York and toured with the show. Her last appearance was in 1954, at the age of 61, in T.S. Eliot's "The Confidential Clerk." Ina returned to her San Francisco apartment on Nob Hill to pass the time in local social activities.

Ina Claire

Wallace died in 1974. Ina inherited a large sum of money but became a recluse. In 1983, she suffered a stroke and was bedridden. She died February 21, 1985, at the age of 95 from the effects of the stroke. Except for a few brief obituaries in the press, Ina's passing went unnoticed.

During the 1920s and 1930s, Ina had been known as one of the best Broadway actresses, particularly for her high comedy. The vaudeville and revue days seemingly had been forgotten in favor of her dramatic theater ability. That she prospered almost equally on stage and the screen spoke well of her broad appeal and artistic competence.

Trixie Friganza

Few stage personalities enjoyed the esteem of the public and the affection of colleagues as did Trixie Friganza. When she made her first appearance on the stage, she was tall and thin. But it was not long before her figure grew to more generous proportions. The added weight, according to an astute critic, "served to increase the lightness of her comedy and the gaiety of her spirit." By the time her name was flashing on marquees across the country, her performances had become as substantial as her figure.

Cornelius O'Callahan and Margaret J. Friganza were married in Mound City, Illinois, in 1862. Cornelius, born in 1846 in Cork County, Ireland, had come to America in 1860 and fought in the Civil War. Margaret was born in 1846 in Brooklyn, New York. Her mother had immigrated from Spain.

Delia O'Callahan was born on November 29, 1870, in Grenola, Kansas, the first of three girls. When Delia was still a child, the family moved to Cincinnati, Ohio. During her teen years, Delia worked as a salesgirl for $3 a week. She had a good singing voice and, at age 18, decided to make use of it by running off with a dramatic touring company.

In October 1889, "The Pearl of Pekin" was playing in Cincinnati. Delia persuaded the company's manager to hire her for the chorus. As befitting a tall, slim young woman, now a stage actress, Delia changed her name to Trixie Friganza, the last name borrowed from her mother's family. Trixie's mother was upset by her daughter's decision and had the police arrest her. But once the chief of police heard Trixie's story, he told the mother that Trixie's chances for success were much better as an actress than as a salesgirl.

For several years, Trixie played in melodrama companies that toured the country. As her dancing and singing improved, each new part was larger and each new engagement paid a higher salary. In 1892 she appeared in "The Mascot," starring Henry Dixie. Dixie was putting on a number of revivals, which included several Gilbert and Sullivan plays. Trixie was part of Dixie's company during these productions.

Her first substantial role was in "A Christmas Night" in 1894. She got good reviews and quickly found work in other musical farces. By the late 1890s, Trixie had become a leading lady. She was no longer the sylph-like person she had been, having gained considerable weight. During this period, overweight female performers assumed comic roles in the shows where they appeared. As if typed by reviewers and audiences, they poked fun at their larger size as part of their comedy routines.

Trixie obtained a small role in "The Girl from Paris," a musical farce that opened at the Herald Square Theater, New York, on December 8, 1896. With Charles Bigelow and Clara Lipton as co-stars, the show lasted more than six months. Trixie began to demonstrate her versatility, assuming different roles in the show and revealing her singing and comedic skills.

In March 1900, Trixie was signed for a role in "The Belle of Bohemia," starring comic Sam Bernard. A George Lederer production, the show contained all the elements of an operetta, including waltzes and a clog-dancing chorus. Trixie sang several topical songs, danced with the chorus, and participated in a few comic sketches with Bernard, her weight a foil for his jokes. The show ran for only 55 performances in New York but it displayed Trixie's various talents to other producers.

Trixie appeared in "Sally in Our Alley," which opened at the Broadway Theater on August 29, 1902. She sang a few songs and also was star Marie Cahill's understudy. Cahill had a forceful personality, both on and off the stage, and superimposed her talents over the cast. She never missed a performance. Trixie found herself overshadowed by Cahill, but she was still singled out by reviewers for her work.

Her efforts rewarded, she was hired to play a singing and comic relief role in the musical "The Prince of Pilsen." The show opened at the Broadway on March 17, 1903, shortly after "Sally" closed. The show itself was highly praised and contained a number of hit songs. Trixie played with the company until November 1904, when she was called to replace Anna Held.

Flo Ziegfeld and Anna Held had teamed with Joe Weber for "Higgledy-Piggledy" at Weber's Theater. The show opened in October, but a falling-out of the partnership between Weber and Ziegfeld also meant Held would leave the cast. On short notice and with few rehearsals, Weber called Trixie to take Held's role before the show went on tour. However, Marie Dressler was also in the cast and demanded star status now that Held had departed. In fact, she took over the show. She also took over Trixie's song, "A Great Big Girl Like Me," leaving Trixie with a smaller role than she had been promised. There were several women headliners who were overweight and used that fact to their comic advantage. In this case, Dressler outranked Trixie. The situation turned Trixie to vaudeville.

Trixie found the vaudeville metier to her liking. Her audiences enjoyed her brand of singing and comedy. During her initial performance at Hammerstein's in 1906, she did an imitation of Dressler that the reviewers called "payback" for the way she had been treated. Generally, Trixie's routines were a mixture of topical songs and jokes. She added playing various musical instruments to her act. She also introduced dialogue about her weight and size in a funny, self-deprecating way that audiences accepted as humorous and inoffensive. Another part of her act included the singing of songs that suggested she was looking for a man, an audience favorite being "Won't Someone Kindly Stake Me to a Man."

Her vaudeville popularity soared. Reviewers now called her the "champagne girl." Her salary had reached headliner status, upwards of $2,000 a week. A good portion of it was put away for "old age." Trixie's increased following now made her star material for musical comedy. Her return to the musical stage took place in "The Orchid," which starred Eddie Foy. It opened at the Herald Square on April 8, 1907, after three weeks of road tuneups. It was an English import adapted for American audiences with music composed by American authors. The show satisfied audiences for an unprecedented 22 weeks. The show then went on tour for another eight months, but not with Trixie. A disagreement developed between the Shuberts, producers of "The Orchid," and Trixie. She complained about being billed second to Foy instead of being featured as a co-star. While the company was in Chicago, Trixie abruptly left the show because the Shuberts refused to resolve the issue. Irene Franklin, an up-and-coming performer already in the show with a small part, took over Trixie's role.

Trixie Friganza

Trixie then worked for George M. Cohan in his new play, "The American Idea" (1908), a recycled "Little Johnny Jones," according to critics. Typical of a Cohan show, it was filled with snappy dances and songs guaranteed to please the audience. Trixie played "Mrs. Waxtopper," a comic figure, and sang the show's hit song, "F-A-M-E," a spelling song not unlike "Harrigan" from a previous Cohan production. In spite of its similarities, the show ran for eight weeks in New York and then went on extended tour.

The following year, Trixie returned to vaudeville with great success. Her jokes about being fat continued to entertain audiences. In one sketch, where she seemingly was grossly overdressed, she began telling jokes. With each punchline, she discarded a piece of clothing, to the patrons' delight. She talked about her figure being a "perfect 46." And she remarked to audiences that "the way for a fat woman to do the shimmy is to walk fast and stop short."

One of the songs she adapted for herself was the lament "No Wedding Bells for Me." Trixie sang the song until 1912, when she announced her upcoming marriage to Charles A. Goettler, her theatrical agent. They were married in Atlantic City on March 10. Trixie wanted to be married in a Catholic Church, but could not because she admitted having been secretly married once before in a civil ceremony. The husband's name was Dr. W.J.M. Barry. The marriage and divorce dates are unknown. Because of this, Trixie and Charles were married by a justice of the peace. A little more than two years later, Trixie severed her theatrical arrangement with Goettler, and the marriage as well. Trixie divorced Goettler in July 1914. She never married again, although there were rumors about various suitors.

Trixie's vaudeville career reached new heights with her appearance in the "Passing Show of 1912," another Shubert all-star production. The Shuberts, wishing never to be outdone by other producers, wanted to put on a Ziegfeld Follies–like show. The result was a revue made up of specialty turns by various headliners, including Trixie, Jobyna Howland, Willie and Eugene Howard, a comedy team, and newcomer Charlotte Greenwood. The show satirized other productions, featured songs from a variety of composers, including Irving Berlin, and featured a line of beautiful chorus girls. Trixie sang several of her signature tunes and acted as foil to a Howard Brothers act. The show ran for 136 performances and launched an annual Shuberts produced "Passing Show" for 11 years.

Trixie was in the public eye off the stage as well. In 1908, she went with a group of suffragists to see the mayor of New York. She and the other received only jeers from the crowd of onlookers. During World War I, she was stopped for driving her car on a gasless Sunday. Her marriage and divorce produced headlines. In 1930, she was sued by the government for several thousand dollars in back income taxes.

Trixie continued to play on the vaudeville circuit through World War I and into the early 1920s. Throughout this time, she remained a headliner and commanded top salaries. In 1914, she appeared at the Palace Theater, New York. Marion Spitzer, author of "The Palace," called Trixie "a bouncing beauty," likely in respectful jest. Trixie appeared at the Palace in 1920 and again in 1928. In her 1920 appearance, *Variety called* her act "a riotous hit." Trixie called her act "My Little Bag O' Trix." However, in 1928, vaudeville's existence was threatened by the growing popularity of movies. Vaudeville theaters were unfilled unless they also showed movies. Even top performers found it hard to secure vaudeville engagements.

Trixie decided to retire from the vaudeville stage. She was 58 years old and had been performing almost constantly for almost 40 years. She was also beginning to suffer from arthritis. Moving pictures seemed a likely prospect to begin a second career.

From 1923 to 1940, Trixie appeared in 17 films, many of them with small parts in forgettable pictures, but a few where she was a star. In most of the films, she played serious roles, only infrequently expressing her comedic talents. Among all the pictures, she played in two Cecil B. DeMille productions, three pictures for MGM, and three for Universal. In 1928, Trixie starred in the Paramount-Lasky sound production of "Gentlemen Prefer Blondes," written by Anita Loos. She played the mother of the bachelor who finally wins the hand of Lorelei Lee.

In the Selznick production of "A Star Is Born" (1937), Trixie appeared in a small part. She was a wisecracking waitress in a scene where the director takes his new, fresh movie star to lunch. Trixie's last movie, "If I Had My Way" (1940), starred Bing Crosby and Gloria Jean. She appeared in a scene in a vaudeville theater which featured a number of old-time acts. For brief turns, Trixie shared the stage with Blanche Ring, Grace La Rue, Eddie Leonard and Julian Eltinge.

In 1939, Trixie finally retired from the entertainment business, selling her Hollywood home and auctioning off her jewelry and furs. She gave the funds to the Sacred Heart Academy in Flintridge, California. She moved into their convent shortly thereafter, and lived there until her death. During World War II, Trixie frequently left her retreat to perform at veteran's hospitals, despite the ravages of arthritis. During her last years, she was bedridden, but seemed to shine each year on her birthday for photographers.

On February 27, 1955, at the age of 84, Trixie died at the convent where she had resided for 16 years. She was buried in Calvary Cemetery in East Los Angeles.

Trixie's weight did not deter vaudeville audiences from enjoying her talents. She shared the spotlight with Marie Dressler, Stella Mayhew, Emma Carus, May Irwin and Sophie Tucker, all stars of the vaudeville stage. All of these women were comediennes and used their size for comedy. This pattern continues in movies and television today.

Mae West

She was larger than life, the best-known personality ever to have graduated from vaudeville. While other headliners used titillation and double entendres to enliven their acts, Mae West turned sex into a commercial enterprise. Managers and producers squirmed, but audiences loved her show of independence and strutting sensuality. For more than 60 years, Mae was a star of vaudeville, musical comedy, radio, movies, nightclubs and recordings.

Mary Jane West was born in Brooklyn, New York, on August 17, 1893. She was named after her father's mother. John West, her father, was born in Newfoundland in 1865, from Irish stock. During his early years, he was a tough street brawler. When he was married, he was a mechanic; he later became a member of a detective agency and a masseur. Matilda "Tillie" Delker (Doelger) was born in 1870 in a town in Bavaria, Germany. She came to the United States in 1882. Prior to her marriage, Matilda modeled corsets and worked in fashion design. She was known to be as attractive as Lillian Russell. John and Matilda were married January 19, 1889, in Brooklyn. They had four children. Katie, who was born in 1891, died in infancy, which had a profound effect on Matilda. Mary Jane, the next child, was pampered and protected by her mother from birth. Mildred (Beverly) was born in December 1898, and John in February 1900.

At an early age, Mary Jane, nicknamed Mae, was given dancing lessons. Her budding theatrical career was carefully molded and supervised by her mother. At the age of seven, Mary Jane appeared at an amateur night contest at the Royal Theater, Brooklyn, billed as "Baby Mae — Songs and Dances." She won the contest. When Mae was eight, she joined a stock company at the Gotham Theater, New York. She appeared in many melodramas, and gradually grew into speaking parts. Mae was a precocious child, pretty, outgoing, and eager to learn about the theatrical world. Matilda was always at her side, guiding her through the early teen years and minimizing Mae's associations with men, especially stage door Johnnies.

Mae entered vaudeville when she was 13 years old, partnering with a friend and teacher William Hogan in a song-and-dance act. They appeared in secondary vaudeville houses in the New York area. In 1909, at the age of 16, Mae joined 19-year-old Frank Wallace in a song-and-dance act, the kind that usually opened vaudeville bills, called "dumb" acts because they involved no speaking parts. Their act was considered "flashy" which gained them reviews and better bill positions. They went on tour, which prevented Matilda from monitoring her daughter's activities. After living together for a year, Mae and Frank married on April 11, 1911, in Milwaukee, Wisconsin. Matilda was not in attendance. However, at the end of the season, the couple parted and Mae returned home. At the beginning of the next season in September, Frank joined a road company and was effectively out of Mae's life. Mae never married again. After nearly 32 years of separation, Mae divorced Frank in 1943.

The year 1911 found Mae performing a solo act in vaudeville, singing and dancing interspersed with jokes. That year, she was hired for the chorus of the Wayburn show, "Hello Paris." The show opened September 22, 1911, at the Follies Bergere. It lasted only two weeks, but Mae got the attention of reviewers for her rendition of "They Are Irish." Her singing generated several encores. Mae had written extra verses for the song so when she was called back, she surprised the producers by presenting new lyrics. Less than two months later, Mae was hired by the Shuberts to appear in "Very Violetta," which starred Al Jolson and Gaby Deslys. Jolson introduced several songs in blackface, which initiated his career in earnest. The show opened on November 20, 1911, at the Winter Garden, ran for 112 performances and went on tour. Mae sang two songs, neither of which attracted much attention, but it was enough to get another job, this time in a Ziegfeld production.

"A Winsome Widow" was a remake of Hoyt's "A Trip to Chinatown," but was more a vaudeville olio than musical comedy. Performers like the Dolly Sisters, Elizabeth Brice, Charles King, Frank Tinney and Leon Errol presented their specialties. The show opened April 15, 1912, at the Moulin Rouge and played through September. Mae had a limited role singing and dancing and attracted attention from reviewers for her stage mannerisms. A month later, however, she returned to vaudeville which paid higher salaries. *Variety* acknowledged her singing, but considered her eccentric and not yet mature enough to play in high-class houses.

For a short time in 1912, she teamed with Billy O'Neal and Harry Laughlin (the Gerard Brothers) but, by the end of the year, she was again appearing as a solo act. She attracted considerable attention while on a bill at the Model Theater, Philadelphia. An ad describing her act said: "She does a muscle dance in a sitting position. It is all in the way she does it, and her way is all her own." When she played in New Haven, the act caused a riot among Yale students and got her fired from the company. Her unique style was evolving and the "curves in motion" enthused audiences.

The act included a swaying, provocative strut, an almost blasé delivery of lyrics, one hand on her undulating hip and the other on her blond hair, and surprising gestures, like the leg kick that pushed aside the train of her gown. Mae as sex symbol was beginning to emerge. She appeared in many roles and wore many costumes but the same stage behavior remained over time.

In 1916, Mae and her sister Beverly (Mildred) appeared in vaudeville together. Mae sang "I Want to Be Loved the Old Fashioned Way" and "They Call It Dixieland," both hit songs that appealed to audiences. Near the end of her act, she appeared in male attire to sing "Walkin' the Dog" complete with her familiar torso gyrations. *Variety* again questioned her act and her belief that she was ready for the big time. Those comments did not deter her from touring on the Keith circuit for almost two years. Keith managers often complained to E.A. Albee about Mae's stage behavior. But when Mae performed for Albee, she acted the innocent, naive actress who seemingly was not even aware of the words she was singing. Albee told his managers to "clean their minds." Mae continued to entertain audiences with her particular specialty that was becoming a part of her permanent style.

Mae came to prominence by starring in the show "Sometime," opposite Ed Wynn. The show opened October 4, 1918, at the Shubert Theater. The flu epidemic did not prevent the show from being one of the hits of the season. Mae was aptly chosen to play a vamp who demanded "Send me any kind of man." Her every move on stage was greeted with shouts and whistles of approval. She was also credited with introducing the shimmy to the Broadway stage. The shimmy had little movement of the feet, but constant movement of the shoulders, body and pelvis. Mae took full advantage of the opportunity to expand her growing image as a sex symbol. She sang two songs, "Any Kind of Man" and "All I Want Is Just a Little Lovin.'" She would be associated with these kinds of songs for her entire career. Although somewhat hesitant about Mae's antics, reviewers acknowledged that she was near headliner status.

In September 1919, Mae returned to vaudeville as a headliner on the Keith circuit, earning more than $1000 a week. Opening at the Capitol Theater, New York, on October 24, she did her shimmy dance and sang "Oh, What a Moanin' Man" to the audiences' delight. Mae also appeared on the front cover of the *Dramatic Mirror*, a usually conservative newspaper, and was mentioned approvingly. This was a decided victory for her image and career. The following year, Mae opened her season at the Colonial Theater, New York, wearing a tight-fitting black and silver gown and rendering "I Want a Cave Man," "I'm a Night School Teacher" and "The Mannikin." *Variety* finally reported that she was ready for the big time, but she and her audiences already knew that. As the 1920s began, however, Mae found little time for vaudeville.

In 1921, Mae appeared in the "Mimic World of 1921," which opened at the Century Theater on August 15. The revue was one of the few shows that season to receive poor reviews. Its star, James Barton, left the show on opening night. Mae again danced the shimmy but it failed to save the show. To regain her headliner status, Mae teamed with Harry Richman, a pianist, and returned to vaudeville touring. In September 1922, Richman left the act at the same time Mae was hired for an engagement in the "Greenwich Village Follies." The show fea-

Mae West

tured two female impersonators, Julian Eltinge and Bert Savoy, who strove to upstage one another at every performance. Mae's act seemed to get lost in the competition. Ted Lewis and his band helped to bring attention to romantic dance music and launched a fad.

During the mid-1920s Mae devoted her full attention to the use of sex as a personal selling point. She wrote a play called "Sex," about a prostitute, and took the leading role. The show opened at New York City's Daly's Theater on April 26, 1926. It immediately caused a public uproar. The press called the show "daring" and "depraved." The town fathers denounced Mae for her immorality. Yet the show played for 357 performances before the police shut it down. Mae was arrested and, after a jury trial that was covered by the press, she was found guilty of corrupting the morals of youth, fined $500 and sentenced to ten days in jail. It could not have been better publicity. Mae had achieved her goal. She had become a national sex symbol.

In 1927, Mae wrote a play about homosexuals called "The Drag," that was equally panned by the city's moral arbiters. She also wrote and produced "The Wicked Age" that satirized sex. Like "The Drag," it had a short stage life. She did not appear in either play but her persona very much affected its outcome.

Mae's most successful play, "Diamond Lil," opened at the Royal Theater on April 9, 1928, and ran for 323 performances. She wrote and acted as a cabaret performer during the 1890s on the Bowery. It was in this play that she spoke one of her most famous lines, "Come up and see me sometime." The police did not harass her this time but the press continued to question her morality. The show was expanded into a book (1932) and a movie. In later years, Mae revived the play on Broadway and in Hollywood and took it to London.

Mae than shifted her allegiance to Hollywood where her 13 movies portrayed an actress who had become a parody of herself. Audiences continued to enjoy her performances, if not entirely for the sex, for the comedy she brought to the screen. Her first movie was "Pleasure Man" in 1928. "The Constant Sinner" followed in 1931. Others included "She Done Him Wrong" (1933), "I'm No Angel" (1933), "Go West, Young Man" (1936) and "My Little Chickadee" with W.C. Fields in 1940. During these years, she was reported to be making over $300,000 yearly. When she was 77, the durable entertainer, appealing as ever, appeared in "Myra Breckenridge" (1970). Eight years later, she played in the ill-fated "Sextette."

Throughout the years, Mae appeared on the radio, in nightclubs and on recordings, performing the same act she had perfected earlier. Her popularity remained high primarily because she brought back the nostalgia of her times. When she appeared with Edgar Bergen in 1937, she so upset executives with her language that she did not play on radio for 12 years. When, in 1960, she was interviewed on "Person to Person," executives cancelled the show. But the following year, she played with Red Skelton on television.

During her later years, Mae lived in a Hollywood apartment surrounded by furnishings from the 1930s and with the memorabilia she had accumulated during her career. In August 1980 she suffered a stroke that left her speech impaired. On the early morning of November 22, she died in her sleep. Doctors determined the cause of her death as cerebral thrombosis and diabetes that she had contracted 15 year earlier. Her body was shipped back to Brooklyn and buried in Cypress Hills Cemetery next to her father, mother and brother. She had owned much property and jewelry. Much of it was left to Paul Novak, her bodyguard and lover for several decades.

As *Variety* reported after Mae died, "She believed herself forever young, her loveliness unchanging, her talent always growing, and it was almost true." At the age of 80, she looked and acted like the sex symbol of 50 years earlier.

Mae West was ahead of her time with sexual displays and satires on the country's puritanical mores. She contributed a great deal to mainstreaming attitudes about sex. In her eulogy, Kevin Thomas wrote: "Mae West always said that no one was ever to feel sorry for her, and she would not want anyone to start now. Mae West figured that in one way or another she would live forever. And she probably will."

Molly Picon

A long-time star of the Yiddish theater, Molly Picon began her career performing in vaudeville, where she perfected her exceptional stage talents. Her singing and comedy were enjoyed by audiences for more than 60 years. As a headliner, she often returned to vaudeville with appearances at the Palace Theater. Molly's career included world tours, concert hall appearances, musical comedy, radio, the movies and television.

Molly's parents, Louis Picon and Clara Ostrow, came to the United States from Russia as teenagers in the 1870s. They married in 1896. Louis was a shirt maker; Clara was a shirtwaist sewer and, later, a wardrobe mistress. Both spoke Russian and Yiddish and were faithful adherents of Judaism. Molly was born on February 28, 1898, in New York City. After the birth of her sister, Helen, in 1902, the family moved to Philadelphia. Both girls obtained elementary and some high school education. Later, Clara got a job as a seamstress for actresses in local Yiddish theater, which introduced Molly to the acting profession.

At the age of five, Molly won a prize in a children's amateur contest at a vaudeville theater. Within a year, she was appearing as "Baby Margaret" in a vaudeville act that played at Philadelphia theaters. She had learned to play the piano and ukulele, and sang and danced the latest hit songs. Her mother got her a place to play children's roles in a Jewish stock company, in which she appeared for three years. At nine, Molly was working in a nickelodeon where she sang ballads between films for a reported $15 a week. For the next four years, Molly appeared in an English-language company that performed dramatic plays.

From 1912 to 1915, Molly, now a teenager and stage veteran, performed a song-and-dance act in Philadelphia and New Jersey vaudeville theaters. She had a good voice and also demonstrated a comic style that amused audiences when she mimicked current headliners and added humorous touches to otherwise serious ballads. During the summer of 1915, Molly had roles in two musicals, "Broadway Jones" and "Bunty Pulls the Strings," at the Chestnut Street Theater, Philadelphia. Reviewers thought her an up-and-coming singer and comedienne. She remained with this stock company for the next several years, playing increasingly more important roles and gaining a local reputation as a fine actress. These credentials made her an attractive performer for traveling vaudeville companies.

During the 1918–1919 season, Molly toured on the Gus Sun and Ackerman-Harris circuits, both second-tier organizations, with a song-and-dance act called "The Four Seasons." Molly appeared as "Winter" because she was the only cast member who could do a Russian dance. While the circuits were not first-rate, they played in major cities. This worked out well for Molly when their company was stranded in Boston, having run out of money and future engagements. Molly applied for a job at the local Yiddish theater and was hired. Heading the theater was Jacob Kalish. Although a young man, he was already a well-known and respected Jewish writer and producer. A year after they met, Molly and Jacob were married on June 29, 1919.

During 1919 and 1920, Molly appeared in Yiddish repertory with her husband's company at Boston's Grand Opera House. For the next two years, they toured the European capitals with good results. Jacob had written a musical comedy for Molly called "Yankele," in which she played a small boy. Her singing and comedic talents were recognized and the tour produced crowded houses and good reviews. The cities they visited had large Jewish populations and maintained Jewish theater. When the company returned to the United States in 1923, Molly was considered a professional entertainer. She and Jacob settled in New York.

Molly Picon

For the next five years, Molly was a headliner in Yiddish productions at the Second Avenue Theater, New York, mostly written and produced by her husband. Reviewers noted that Jacob's works were primarily musicals, whereas most Yiddish productions of the period were either serious drama or operas. Jacob wrote for Molly's abilities and, in the process, lightened Yiddish theater as well. By the end of the 1920s, Molly had become such a headliner in New York that she was invited to appear at the Palace Theater.

In late 1929, Molly starred at the Palace, at a salary of $2,500 a week. She performed Yiddish songs that had been translated into English and character impersonations. The act also included skits about people at a Jewish wedding and an interview with "Mr. Zeigenfeld," a hilarious takeoff of the impresario that *Variety* called clever and original. Throughout the 1930s, Molly continued to appear at the Palace, with excellent results.

Molly continued to perform in Yiddish musicals at the Second Street Theater, gaining the sobriquet of "The Sweetheart of Second Avenue." In 1931, she embarked on a vaudeville tour of the country starting with an appearance at the Palace. Her comic sketches included "Making Love in Four Nationalities," "The Jewish Wedding" and an imitation of Charlie Chaplin. Given the country's fragile economic condition, the tour barely finished its run.

In 1932, she took her act and the musical "Yankele" to Buenos Aires followed by vaudeville engagements in Paris, France, and Johannesburg, South Africa. During the next few years, Molly performed concert tours in Israel, Poland and Russia as well as New York. In May 1937, Molly headlined a bill at London's Palladium. However, events in Europe had become so combustible, especially for Jews, that Molly curtailed further touring and returned to the United States.

Molly made her debut on Broadway as Becky Felderman in "Morning Star," which opened at the Longacre Theater on April 16, 1940. The show had a short run. On October 12, 1942, the old Jolson Theater, recently called the Venice, was renamed for Molly and she played herself in "Oy Is Dus a Leben," a musical biography. The show recounted her early days in Philadelphia, her rise to stardom in vaudeville and Yiddish theater and her foreign tours. The show ran for 139 performances.

For the next several years, Molly toured the United States and Canada performing at military camps. She also visited displaced persons camps in Europe and did concerts in Africa. Most of these appearances featured many of her old vaudeville routines. For the remainder of the 1940s, Molly played in "For Heaven's Sake, Mother," which opened at the Belasco Theater; performed two Yiddish plays at the Second Avenue Theater; and toured Korea, Japan and Israel for the USO.

Throughout the 1950s and 1960s, Molly appeared, often with her husband, in stock company productions across the country. Still recognized as a star performer, Molly attracted full houses wherever she played. In 1961, Molly had a role in "Milk and Honey," Jerry Herman's first Broadway score. The play ran for a year and a half and, according to historian Gerald Bordman, still lost money. Molly had a comic role of a middle-aged "yenta," looking for and finding a husband for herself. During this period, she performed on radio series and on television in various family comedy series. She continued to perform until 1964 when, at the age of 66, she decided to retire. On occasion, she would appear on special programs at local theaters.

Molly and her husband bought a home in Mahopac, New York. They were among the few remaining actors of Yiddish theater. Jacob died in March 1975. They had been married for 54 years. Molly died on April 6, 1992. She was 94 years old.

With a performance style that pleased audiences for 70 years, Molly was, according to reviewers, the veteran trouper that never grew old. Asked why she continued to perform after so many years on the stage, she said, "If your muscles stay used to it, they don't know they shouldn't just because they're older. I've never been bored a day of my life. I acted because I always felt I was needed."

Marie Cahill

When her career began to falter after two decades of starring in melodramas and musical theater as a singer-comedienne, Marie Cahill turned to vaudeville. As a vaudeville headliner, she was able to maintain her star status until she retired.

Marie was a determined and strong-willed performer. She made each role a personification of her own style no matter what the plot called for, and insisted on interpolating songs quite apart from the story. This resulted in a constant struggle with producers and managers. In vaudeville, there were no such restrictions, and vaudeville audiences loved her performances.

Mary Cahill was born in Brooklyn, New York, on December 20, 1867. Theater historians debated her birth date, but a review of the 1870 census indicates it occurred in 1867. The July 1870 census data listed her as being two years old. Both her father, Richard Cahill, and her mother, Marie Grogan, had been born in Ireland. They were married in 1863. They were considered old for marriage — Richard was 35 and Marie was 33. A son, Richard, was born in 1864. Richard, Sr., was a brushmaker and had established a modest estate by the time of Mary's birth. Marie kept house and supervised the children. The family were strict Roman Catholics.

Although Mary was raised in this rigid religious environment, her parents had allowed her to study voice. Her dress was always in keeping with the religious tenets and she shunned anything that suggested provocative behavior. Mary maintained these characteristics throughout her career.

Mary took her mother's name, Marie, for stage purposes. She had an excellent singing voice, and appeared in local amateur productions. Her first professional engagement was in 1887 as a soubrette in an Irish melodrama, "Kathleen Mavourneen." The following year, Marie made her New York debut at Poole's Eighth Street Theater in the melodrama "C.O.D." Her singing and comedic talents attracted producer Charles Hoyt, and he signed her to take a small part in his renovated musical, "A Tin Soldier." The show opened December 24, 1888, at the 14th Street Theater. Young Marie was favorably reviewed.

Marie left for Europe and spent the next few seasons in Paris and London, appearing in various musicals, including a number of Gilbert & Sullivan operettas. She received good reviews for her work and developed a reputation as an accomplished comedienne as well as singer. These reviews helped when she returned in the United States, as she attracted offers from several sources to appear in musical comedies.

During the next several years, Marie appeared in melodramas and musical productions. "Uperba" was a melodrama and "McKenna's Flirtation" was a musical. Her acting and comedy bits helped to establish her as a leading lady. "Excelsior Jr." opened on November 29, 1895, and became the season's biggest hit. The show appeared at Hammerstein's new Olympia Theater, a house he would soon lose due to his financial difficulties. The music was written by the well-known E. E. Rice, and was the last show he ever wrote before becoming a producer and impresario. New songs were periodically added to the show, contributed by a young composer, A. Baldwin Sloane. Fay Templeton played the title role, supported by Marie and Richard Carle. Templeton was already overweight and had difficulty with the dances. Marie took advantage of Sloane's musical additions by interpolating them into the play. When the show went on tour, Marie assumed the title role.

In 1896 came Marie's appearance in "The Gold Bug," a triumph for her and a failure for composer Victor Herbert, although he was not entirely responsible for the show's short life. Several delays in opening, a shortage of costumes and a seemingly unrehearsed orchestra doomed the show after only one week. Still, Marie was singled out for her performance. She had the role of a young woman seeking the perfect mate even though she had been divorced many times. She sang "When I First Began to Marry" and performed a can-can, stopping the show with her antics. Not mentioned in the program were two actors who would later take their place in American theater history, Bert Williams and George Walker. Although Negro, they were forced to "black up" for their roles.

Augustin Daly signed Marie to appear at his theater, a stint that lasted several years. During this time, Marie had the primary roles in "Sporting Life" (1897), "The Runaway Girl' (1898), and a short-lived (49 performances) production of "Three Little Lambs" (1899). By this time, Marie had become recognized as a star of the popular stage with a reputation for singing humorous songs and for her "ready Irish wit."

In "Star and Garter" (1900), a revue, Marie demonstrated the comedy talents that would later endear her to vaudeville audiences. The show satirized current legitimate productions. Marie appeared in most of the scenes as lead comedienne. Her continued interpolations of songs angered managers but delighted audiences, who had come to expect her to stop the show every time. With singers of popular songs, often a song becomes identified with them. In "The Wild Rose," Marie interpolated a song, "Nancy Brown," which dominated the show, survived through her next comedy and finally gave its name to a new production, entitled "Nancy Brown," that made Marie a New York headliner.

"The Wild Rose" opened on May 5, 1902, starring Eddie Foy, coming into his own as a top Broadway funnyman. Marie was allowed to interpolate "Nancy Brown" into the show. It usually garnered six encores, stopping the flow of the plot. The producers were upset by the intrusion and attempted to persuade Marie to drop the song. She refused and the play continued with its nightly interruption. Marie had won this battle. But other producers were getting exceedingly irritated with interpolations and demanded contracts that forbade them. Marie continued to interpolate until she appeared in a Lew Fields production.

"Sally in Our Alley" followed "The Wild Rose" on August 29, 1902, at the Broadway Theater. Marie's interpolation of "Under the Bamboo Tree" (a song that quickly became a trademark for her) undercut the play's score. Still, the show ran successfully for two months and then went on tour. Audiences continued to enjoy Marie's stage tactics.

A year later, "Nancy Brown" was produced, utilizing Marie's song and turning it into a musical comedy. Marie also reprised "Under the Bamboo Tree" and a new song by Cole and Johnson, "Congo Love Song." The show lasted for 104 performances.

Victor Herbert and Lew Fields put together a show called "It Happened in Nordland," a turning point in the structure of musical comedy. It was one of the first productions to contain a cohesive plot which integrated its songs and dances. Fields wanted Marie to star in the production because she was at the top of her popularity, with a robust charm and a strong voice. Unfortunately, she also wanted to be a grande dame of popular theater. Fields wanted a star and was willing to pay for it, in this case, at the rate of $1,200 a week. Marie insisted on the right to rewrite her part and interpolate the songs of other composers. Herbert normally included a clause in his contract prohibiting interpolations but, for some reason, he had neglected to include it in his contract with Fields.

The show opened on December 5, 1904, at the new Lew Fields Theater. From the beginning, it was clear that Marie intended to interpolate songs into the show. Marie and Fields were already at odds about changing her lines. Herbert refused to be a part of Marie's interpolations, handing over the baton for any interpolated numbers. The behind-the-scenes tension was easily discernable, with some cast members ready to leave the show. In spite of this, the show was an instant hit. What to do about Marie?

Marie Cahill

After four months of almost intolerable relations between Fields, Herbert, and Marie, she struck the final blow. When she interpolated "Any Old Tree," Herbert handed over the baton to the concertmaster. Part way through the song, Marie stopped singing and began to sob. She complained to the audience that the orchestra was sabotaging her song. Then she said: "I will try to sing without the orchestra, it is so intentionally bad." Marie told Fields that she would continue with the show only if he fired Herbert. Fields disliked interpolations and prima donnas. He fired Marie and the show went on successfully.

Undeterred, Marie starred in "Moonshine" (1905), free to interpolate as she liked. In "Marrying Mary" (1906), Marie was lauded for her singing and acting and got the biggest applause for her interpolated songs. Apparently, audiences did not care if a show was interrupted as long as Marie was the interrupter.

Marie was the star in "The Boys and Betty" (1908). For the first time, the songs written for the show were better received than her interpolations. The show played for 17 weeks in New York and went on extended tour. A musical, "Judy Forgot" (1910), did not fare as well. Neither the book nor the music was considered adequate. Still, Marie carried the show for 44 performances. But there were no interpolations. In June 1911, Marie appeared with De Wolf Hopper in a revival of "H.M.S. Pinafore" for a short run. Of course, Marie was forbidden to interpolate in a Gilbert & Sullivan classic.

"The Opera Ball" opened February 2, 1912, at the Liberty Theater and lasted only four weeks. Marie's role seemed wrong for her. Her songs were weak and, with no interpolations, she relied on farce comedy to carry the show. She made up for these deficiencies in her next show, "Ninety in the Shade," with music by a young Jerome Kern. He was not yet powerful enough to prevent Marie's interpolations. She incurred hostility from everyone connected with the show for her interpolations. A few reviewers pointed out that Marie was getting to old for such antics. She was nearing 50.

Marie had married her agent, Daniel V. Arthur, on June 18, 1903. He was responsible for negotiating her contracts, but Marie was intimately involved as well. In 1915, Marie had to claim bankruptcy because of several endorsed notes signed by Arthur. She claimed her assets were exempt, won her case, and was discharged from bankruptcy. They appeared to be a compatible couple and remained married until her death. They had no children.

During World War I, Marie's appeal had declined, due to changes in audience tastes and the maturity of musical comedy productions. A vaudeville debut at the Palace Theater, New York, in 1919, brought her career back to life.

When she entered the stage, Marie was greeted with enthusiasm, her long-time admirers professing their admiration for an old favorite. She treated the audience to a combination of new songs and old comedy routines. Marie concluded her program with audience requests, which were made up of all of her trademark renditions. Several encores followed.

Marie spent the next several years on tour with the U.B.O. circuit earning $2,000–2,500 a week for her work. In fact, Marie earned more money during her vaudeville days than she did during the years playing in musicals. In 1925, Marie played in an oldtimers bill at the Palace co-starring with Cissie Loftus, Emma Trentino, the opera star, and Blossom Seeley. Audiences loved the oldtimers' shows and the gross was high. Marie continued as a featured player in vaudeville until 1930, when she and the medium itself retired.

Her last appearances on the musical stage were in the revue "Merry-Go-Round," which opened at the Klaw Theater on May 31, 1927, and "The New Yorkers" at the Broadway Theater, December 1930. "Merry-Go-Round" included a combination of new stars, Leonard Sillman and Libby Holman, and oldsters Marie and William Collier. Marie appeared in comedy skits and sang her famous songs. The show ran through the summer. "The New Yorkers" was written by Herbert Fields, breaking away from his collaborations with Rodgers and Hart. Marie played the wife of a philandering doctor who was not afraid to talk about her gigolo. This is the closest Marie ever came to using provocative material.

The show seemed to be a hit, but the collapse of the Bank of the United States exacerbated the Depression and spoiled theater attendance and performer salaries. The show staggered on for 20 weeks at a sizable loss. Included in the ill-fated show were Charles King, Ann Pennington, Richard Carle, Jimmy Durante, and Fred Waring and his Pennsylvanians. This was also Marie's last appearance on the stage. She was a tired 63 years of age.

Marie appeared in only one movie, from the stage version of "Judy Forgot," in 1915. She did not like movies because they inhibited her stage performance.

Marie died in New York on August 23, 1933, after several years suffering from heart trouble. She was buried in Holy Cross Cemetery, Brooklyn. Her husband, Daniel, died six years later and was buried next to Marie.

Marie was one of the foremost song interpolators in musical comedy and vaudeville during her career. This tough woman won most of her battles with managers although, according to Bordman, her behavior cost her important roles. Marie entertained audiences with her brand of unique song and comedy for more than 40 years.

Part Three: The Comediennes

May Irwin

May Irwin was a delight and a sensation in the theater in the days of Tony Pastor and Augustin Daly. The swains of the Gay Nineties toasted her in champagne in the lobster palaces of Broadway. The stage door Johnnies of the early 1900s laid their hearts at her feet. *Theater* magazine described May as "the funniest stage woman in America." When Woodrow Wilson was president, he summoned her to Washington for a command performance and offered her the portfolio of Secretary of Laughter.

Her voice was untrained, but beautiful and natural. Enrico Caruso once said May might go far as a real singer if she studied. May laughed. She replied that all the technique she needed was to "take a deep breath and let go." To the theater-going public of her day it was enough.

May believed that humor was spontaneous and could not be analyzed. Either one is born with it or not. It could neither be acquired nor forced. Yet her mysterious comedic talents regaled audiences for more than 40 years.

Robert Campbell and Jane Draper Campbell immigrated from Scotland to Canada just prior to the Civil War in the United States. They settled in the small town of Whitby, Ontario. Their first child, Georgina May, was born June 27, 1862. A second child, Adeline Flora, was born three years later. When Robert died unexpectedly a few years later, the family found itself penniless. They moved to Buffalo, New York, in 1875.

At an early age, both Georgina and Adeline revealed a singing talent and they often performed together at church and school functions. Mrs. Campbell, desperate to stay out of poverty, decided to take advantage of her daughters' talents. In Buffalo, a theater manager got the girls a booking at the Theater Comique, Rochester, where they sang duets dressed in pink stockings and pantalettes. Georgina was 13 and Adeline was ten. For their efforts, they earned $30 for the week. They were so well received that the theater manager booked them in his own theater, the Adelphi, Buffalo, in 1876. The manager also renamed the girls the Irwin Sisters.

For the next year, accompanied by their mother, the girls obtained bookings in various Midwest variety houses singing popular tunes of the day. During the summer of 1877, Tony Pastor and his company were on their annual summer tour with a stop in Detroit. Pastor saw the Irwin Sisters perform and hired them to appear at his theater in New York, beginning the new theater season. Pastor promised Mrs. Campbell that he would take care of the girls while they appeared at his theater, which turned out to be for nearly six years.

Under Pastor's guidance, the girls did a singing sister act and performed in a series of comic skits which satirized current legitimate plays. Pastor was one of the first managers to burlesque Gilbert and Sullivan with skits like "The Pirates of Penn Yan." Such skits usually ended his bill, leaving departing audiences in a happy mood. Much to Gilbert and Sullivan's chagrin, they had neglected to obtain U.S. rights for their play, thus allowing dozens of renditions to be performed. One of the Irwin Sisters' colleagues in these satires was a new Pastor discovery, Lillian Russell. But when Pastor cast his summer touring company, he chose the Irwins over Russell, shipping her out with another company for more stage seasoning. In Pastor's skits, the girls played a variety of roles, from old women to infants, usually dressed in ridiculous costumes to enhance the humor of their parts. Pastor advertised them as "Infantile Actresses, Vocalists and Character Artistes." By the end of their long engagement with Pastor, they were earning $80 a week, and they had learned a great deal about stagecraft.

In 1878, when May was 18, she married Frederick W. Keller, of St. Louis. The marriage was a loving one, unfortunately ending when Keller died in 1886, while May was on tour with the Daly company.

In 1883, May was courted by Augustin Daly to join his company. At the time, it was considered one of the best theater groups in the country. It was also the dream of every performer to appear in a Daly production. With Pastor's blessings, May accepted the job; Adeline, however, retired from the stage. At age 21, May was one of the youngest performers working for Daly. She remained with the Daly company for four years and had the opportunity to appear with such stars as John Drew, Ada Rehan, Otis Skinner, David Belasco and William Gillette.

May's primary parts in Daly plays were as a comedienne and it was here that she developed her comedic skills. She played comic roles, usually as maids or domestics, in such plays as "The Magistrate," "A Night Off," "Nancy and Co." and "The Recruiting Officer."

May Irwin

At first, reviewers regarded May as just another variety actress but she quickly surprised them with her natural talent for comedy and song. The Daly company appeared in London, England, at Toole's Theater for two engagements, and May was singled out for her comic roles.

Four years of working with Daly were inspiring and educational, but the impresario's rigid systems frustrated May. Near the end of 1887, she moved to Charles Frohman's stock company. She admitted that she was not at ease within the confinement of dramatic comedy, preferring instead a freedom to improvise. Frohman tried to give her the opportunity but wondered how long he could keep her satisfied. She survived for three plays, but did not have substantial parts or the opportunity to use her comedic talents. However, in one of the plays, "The Poet and the Puppet," a travesty of Oscar Wilde's

"Lady Windemere's Fan," May popularized Charles K. Harris's "After the Ball," helping make the song an overnight hit.

> After the ball is over —
> After the break of dawn ...

... brought a lump to audience's throats and happened to be one of the few serious ballads May ever sang or recorded.

To obtain the freedom she sought, May started her own company. On September 16, 1895, she starred in "The Widow Jones" at the Bijou Theater. J.J. McNally wrote the farce for her, including a number of coon songs which May interpolated. Critics warned her that she would never be able to handle cast members, and especially women performers. May proved them wrong and went on to produce and star in several more successful farce comedies during the next few years. It was a brave and unprecedented action for a woman of 33 to take.

"The Widow Jones" produced many firsts for May. It made her a Broadway star. She introduced a tune, "The Bully Song," which she sang in a Negro dialect, interpolating what the people called coon songs. Her rendition immediately identified her as a "coon-shouter." But unlike the coon song singers, May never appeared in blackface nor did she restrict her repertoire to this type of song.

"The Widow Jones" created long-term notoriety for May in another way. The play featured a long kiss between May and co-star John Rice. Thomas Edison asked them to pose for the kissing scene, which he filmed. He released the 50-foot-long picture, titling it "The Kiss." "The Kiss" was featured on many bills across the country. Critics, the clergy and moral arbiters objected strongly, and made demands to censor these "soul-destroying pictures." Edison did not drop the film and it placed May at the center of motion picture history.

She followed this success with "Courted Into Court" (December, 1896), a play of similar structure to "Jones." Ironically, her opening followed by one day Lillian Russell's "An American Beauty." Russell had now become a star of comic opera. May could not have been more different from Russell, although they began their careers under similar tutelage.

May continued rendering coon songs, one of which became a hit, "All Coons Look Alike to Me." It soon appeared on records and sheet music. May had the knack of getting across a joke with excellent timing and clear meaning. She often took a daily newspaper on stage and turned some of its stories into humorous episodes. A reviewer called May "the blonde personification of good humor." Another declared, "Laughs were her specialty."

"The Swell Mrs. Fitzwell" opened at the Bijou Theater on November 15, 1897. May played a poor American girl who marries a French count. It was a typical song-filled comedy. "Kate Kip, Buyer" opened in 1898; "Sister Mary" in 1899; and "Madge Smith, Attorney" in 1900. The plots tended to be similar and May's comedy a repeat of some of her best routines. In "Madge Smith," the songs were not mixed with the dialogue. Instead, they were all sung in a single medley led by May and backed with a chorus.

May opened in "Mrs. Black Is Back" (1904) at the Bijou. That same night, George M. Cohan opened in "Little Johnny Jones," heralding the beginning of the era of cohesive musical comedy. May played a widow who lied about her age, pretending that her mature son was a child. While the play contained a serious plot, May found the opportunity to sing songs and inject several comic bits. The show ran for three months, due solely to May's performance.

In 1906, May reentered vaudeville with a skit, "Mrs. Peckham's Carouse," written especially for her by George Ade. The plot was a satire on the morality of the day. May played a dignified lady who imbibes and becomes more drunk as the skit continues. She did this entire act while sitting in a chair. Her comedy had the audience standing and cheering. She used the skit in vaudeville and in several musical farces.

May made her official entry into vaudeville circuits in November 1907, at the Orpheum Theater, New York. It was the beginning of a long tour. When *Variety* wrote that May "looked like a sister act," she came back by beginning each appearance with comments about having become fat, to the delight of the audience. Jokes about her increasing size became a staple part of her routines for the remainder of her career. At about the same time, May married Kurt Eisfeldt, her agent. He was 15 years younger than May. They had two sons, neither of whom went into the theater. The couple remained happily married throughout May's life, a singular circumstance among performers of the era.

May stayed on the lucrative vaudeville circuit for the next 13 years, with brief breaks for four musicals between 1910 and 1915. In vaudeville, May was earning $2,500 a week. She also recorded six songs for Victor in 1907, including the tune "Frog Song:"

> Just lots of folks are like that little frog o' mine,
> Gettin' into trouble just to pass th' time ...

The song was an immediate hit and achieved a broad appeal across a national audience. The song is still sung by folk music entertainers today, particularly for children.

In 1910, May played in the short-lived dramatic musical, "Getting a Polish." The following year, "She Knew No Better" also fared poorly. May had such an excellent vaudeville reputation that poorly done plays had no adverse effect on her stardom. "A Widow by Proxy" (1913) had a short run. "No. 33 Washington Square" gained some longevity thanks to President Wilson. May had written to the president that the government needed a Department of Laughter. She was invited by the president to perform the comedy before his cabinet members and hundreds of members of the National Press Club. Wilson later named May his "Secretary of Laughter."

In 1915, May headed the bill at the Palace Theater, New York, singing two songs, "Kentucky Home" and "Those Were the Happy Days." She recited a story written especially for her by Irving Berlin called "Father's Old Red Beard." She ended the act repeating to audiences that her waistline will never be the same, which always got a laugh as she exited from the stage.

It was also during this time that May, although not an avowed suffragist, strongly supported the movement. She disputed men's comments that a woman's place was in the home. "Woman's sphere is the same as a man's, and that is the world," she declared.

May's 1917 appearance at the Palace was equally successful. Sime Silverman noted in *Variety* that audiences "never fail to recognize an artist." Her 1920 stint at the Palace was as a fill-in for Emma Calve, the renowned opera singer. At the last minute, the Palace manager called May to help him out, as Calve was ill. With no routine ready, May entered the stage and told the audience, "I'm here as a fill-in. I haven't one thing I can do," and then launched into a 30-minute set of comic turns and familiar songs, the audience cheering her every move on stage. The manager was ecstatic at the result and offered May the salary he would have given Calve, but she refused; she had appeared as a favor for an old friend.

May appeared in two musicals, "On the Hiring Line" in 1920, which ran only a few weeks, and "The 49ers" in 1922. "The 49ers," which referred to 49th Street in New York, had been written by members of the Algonquin Round Table, George S. Kaufman, Marc

Connelly, Ring Lardner, and Robert Benchley. It was a satirical revue with old vaudeville turns. The show lasted two weeks. May, then 60 years old, seemed lost in the confused plot.

May made one more brief appearance at the Palace in 1925, on an oldtimers bill. The cast included Cissie Loftus, Marie Cahill, Marie Dressler, Joe Laurie and Weber and Fields. But Weber and Fields walked out because they were billed second to Dressler, who had been their one-time employee. May sang "Bully" and "Frog Song" to enthusiastic patrons. It was her last appearance on any stage.

May made only one other movie, in 1914, a Paramount four-reeler from the stage play, "Mrs. Black Is Back." But "The Kiss" lived on to become one of the treasures of early film.

Actually, May had unofficially retired in 1920, she and her husband moving to their farm in the Thousand Islands, Ontario. She had originally purchased the farm for her sister who was suffering from tuberculosis. May liked farm management, owned a set of prized cattle and supplied milk for the neighborhood. As explained in her obituary, "There, during the long summers, she let life slip by, the advancing years unnoticed. Although she talked fondly of the old times, she hated to be thought an old-timer."

May died on October 22, 1938, of bronchial pneumonia, at the age of 76. She had left the farm ten days earlier to stay in her New York apartment in the Park Crescent Hotel. Her husband and children were at her bedside. When May's will was filed, she had an estate of more than $100,000, including various properties. The estate was split between her husband and children. May had been a frugal performer and carefully planned for her retirement from the stage.

Cissie Loftus

Marie Loftus was one of the best-known stars of the British Music Halls. She was born in Glasgow, Scotland, in 1857 of Irish parents. She lived near the Scotia Music Hall where she often visited. As a young girl, she danced at that hall in amateur night performances. She made her professional debut at Brown's Royal Music Hall in 1874 and in London at the Oxford Theater in 1877. She rose to become a leading music hall star, toured the United States and South Africa, and by the late 1890s was earning $1,500 a week. The press had labeled her "The Sarah Bernhardt of the Music Halls."

Ben Brown, Marie's companion, was himself a music hall headliner. He was part of the comedy, song and dance team of Brown, Newland and Le Clerc, who toured the British Isles.

Their daughter, Marie Cecelia Brown Loftus, was born October 22, 1876, in Glasgow. The Scottish National Archives listed Cecelia's birth as "illegitimate." Only her mother's name was found on the birth certificate.

The young Cecelia was brought up in the stage environment. She learned her mother's routines and observed the routines of many other performers. During her childhood, she served as her mother's maid. Even as a teenager, Cecelia showed a unique talent for mimicking and impersonating stage celebrities, from both the music hall and dramatic theater. Her technique was so pure, according to critics, that she encompassed for the moment the person she was impersonating, convincing audiences that they were not only hearing the celebrities but learning something about them as well.

In her prime, Cissie, as she was nicknamed by critics, was an equal to Elsie Janis, another star impersonator. What made Cissie a headliner was her stage versatility. On one hand, she gained fame in vaudeville with her mimicry act; on the other hand, her dramatic acting abilities got her significant roles with Madame Mojeska, E.H. Southern and Sir Henry Irving. A typical "in and outer," Cissie appeared in vaudeville and legitimate theater alternately throughout her career, with equal success.

During her early teens, Cissie was educated at the Convent of the Holy Child, Blackpool, England. Determined to follow her mother's career, she left the convent and, at the age of 15, persuaded a music hall manager to let her perform a series of imitations. The result was an outstanding success as she impersonated a number of celebrities of the day. She later played at the Alhambra Theater of Varieties, Belfast, to equal success.

In July 1893, after two years of playing at local theaters, Cissie traveled to London where she appeared at the Oxford Music Hall for $25 a week performing her impersonations of male and female stars. Her youth, beauty, and mimic abilities made her an instant success with audiences. She was later a sensation at the Tivoli's Theater, London. She was reported to be earning $1,000 a week, a likely exaggeration since top headliners earned half that amount.

One of Cissie's new admirers was Max Beerbohm, a well-known critic and caricaturist. He wrote to his friends of his new-found love, so enamoured was he of her talent. There is no indication the feeling was reciprocal. It is likely Cissie never met Beerbohm, but his commentary helped to elevate her career. Rumors suggested that Beerbohm had lost interest in his friend Oscar Wilde because of Cissie.

Cissie played at various music halls through 1893 and 1894 to great success. But she also achieved recognition when she appeared at the Gaiety Theater in the dramatic production of "Don Juan." She demonstrated such dramatic talent that producers vied for her services. Instead, she remained with music hall engagements. In 1894, at the age of 18, Cissie eloped with Justin McCarthy, a writer and politician in Edinburgh, Scotland, by a local civil authority. Among the works McCarthy wrote was the classic poem, "If I Were King," which was later turned into a play and, later still, into the operetta "The Vagabond King." As both were Catholics, and the services were civil, a second religious ceremony was necessary. The day before, Cissie was charming music hall audiences with imitations of Sarah Bernhardt and Yvette Guilbert. She sent a note to her manager that she had a severe cold and could not appear. Actually, she was on her way to Edinburgh. The marriage created a sensation. Everybody was pleased except her mother. She threatened to sue McCarthy since he was 15 years older than Cissie.

In 1895, the couple went to New York where Cissie was to make her debut on the vaudeville stage. Cissie appeared on the bill at Koster & Bial's Theater with some degree of success. It was obvious that some of her impersonations were of celebrities unknown to American audiences. In 1897, after a short stint in vaudeville, Cissie played in the musical "The Highwayman" at the West 45th Street Theater. The show turned out to be one of the most successful of the season. She had a minor role but performed in a distinguished way, according to reviewers. The show played for six months. Cissie returned to England and the variety stage where she was in great demand. Her salary was now verified to be about $1,000 a week.

In April 1899, Cissie obtained a divorce from McCarthy, the court decree stating that he had been "unduly intimate" with a woman whose name was not disclosed.

Free of any other commitments, Cissie returned to New York. Her greatest desire was to become known as a dramatic actress, something she believed she could not do in England. Immediately upon her return, she starred in Madame Mojeska's revival of "The Mascot."

The story told of a country girl faithful to the shepherd she loves in the face of abductions and promises of riches. The play had first appeared in the United States in 1881 and had been revived five times. The show received only moderate support. Cissie followed this with roles as Viola in "Twelfth Night" and Hero in "Much Ado About Nothing." She had proved to critics and audiences that she could handle dramatic roles.

Daniel Frohman engaged Cissie for a number of his plays, but none of them gave her the dramatic opportunities she sought and the productions themselves were short-lived. She joined E. E. Southern as his leading lady. Her most famous roles with Southern were Lady Sackverell in "Richard Loveless" (1901) and Katherine in "If I Were King" (1901) from her former husband's poetry.

Cissie returned to England now an attractive and desired dramatic star. Sir Henry Irving employed her to replace Ellen Terry as Marguerite in "Faust" at the Lyceum Theater (1902). The theatrical newspaper *Era wrote*: "Great interest was reported in Miss Cissie Loftus' appearance as Margaret. Miss Loftus has only been known to the London public as a clever imitatress and the

Cissie Loftus

progress she has made since her visit to America astonished and delighted all her well-wishers."

In 1905, Cissie gained considerable acclaim appearing as Peter in Barrie's play, "Peter Pan," at the Trafalgar Theater, London. She and J.M. Barrie had been friends for several years. In 1908, Cissie married Dr. Alonzo Higbee Waterman of Chicago and the following year gave birth to a son, Peter John Barrie, with Barrie as the child's godfather.

When Cissie returned to the United States in 1910, she resumed her headliner status in vaudeville. Her impersonations now included Bert Williams, Nazimova, Enrico Caruso, Harry Lauder, Nora Bayes and Irene Franklin. Once, at a party, she met Caruso. She imitated him and, when she had finished, he poked his finger against her chest and said, "Madonna Mia! My voice — it is in there!"

Cissie made her first movie in 1913, "A Lady of Quality." She did not appear in films again for 17 years, when she made a sound short, composed of some of her impersonations.

During the 1914 season, Cissie toured with William Faversham in "Romeo and Juliet" and other Shakespearean plays. Following the exhaustive tour, she returned to England with her health and marriage in fragile condition. She was already a frail person. A series of operations, a miscarriage and general unhappiness about her relationship with Waterman caused her to become dependent on alcohol and drugs.

In 1915, although not completely healthy, Cissie appeared with Marie Dressler at the Palace Theater. They performed a "sister act" that filled the theater at every performance. A relapse forced Cissie into temporary retirement. During the war, she separated from her husband, living in London with her son while he remained in Chicago. In 1920, they had an acrimonious divorce.

In 1922, newspapers headlined Cissie's arrest for possession of drugs. After one night in jail, she was released on bail and was put on probation for a year. Recovering from a serious illness, she returned to America and the Palace Theater. Her act was scheduled for 20 minutes but the audience did not let her leave and she entertained them for an hour to tremendous ovations. For the next several years, Cissie toured the country giving her now-classic impersonations. In April 1925, she appeared in an oldtimers bill at the Palace. When vaudeville declined in popularity in the late 1920s, Cissie gave up stage appearances.

Beginning in 1931, Cissie appeared in a number of films, making her talking debut in "East Lynne," followed by "Doctor's Wives" and "Young Sinners." Through 1940, Cissie appeared in six films, usually playing elderly relatives. She played in her last movie, "The Black Cat," a mystery, in 1941.

During the middle 1930s, Cissie was engaged to appear in a series of concerts and Sunday performances in New York giving her famous imitations. She continued to receive top billing. Alexander Woollcott declared: "The Loftus mimetic gift seems to have lost nothing by long disuse. As the final curtain rose and fell a dozen times, I hereby toss a bouquet across the footlights and across the years, with love and admiration to Cissie Loftus."

Cissie's last dramatic performances were in Noël Coward's "Tonight at 8:30" (1936). Coward and Gertrude Lawrence were the stars, repeating their London success of the show. Cissie played a minor role. She also had a small role in "Little Dark Horse" (1941), playing a grandmother, and in a touring company of "Arsenic and Old Lace."

Cissie died on July 12, 1943, of a heart attack and the effects of alcoholism. She was 66 years old. She had been staying at the Lincoln Hotel in New York. Her ability to play successfully in both popular and legitimate theater made her one of the most versatile actresses in England and America.

Kate Elinore

She: I'm going on the stage.
He: What are you going to do?
She: I'm going to do a Salome act.
He: Why don't you play Shakespeare?
She: I'd have to buy clothes if I did.

One of the funniest of performers in vaudeville was Kate Elinore. Her spontaneous absurdities seemed to gush from this unassuming, earthy person. Her cheery good humor earned her the name of the "Human Billikin." A member of the audience felt she could call him by his first name, knew his wife and how old the baby was. One of her characteristic actions was to point her finger at the audience as if it were a pistol, sight her eye behind it and click her mouth to make the sound of a shot. Audiences were engulfed in laughter, which encouraged her to even more eccentric actions. She portrayed Irish maids and old maids with humor that destroyed the stereotype of these traditional characters.

Kate Elinore was a loyal vaudeville entertainer for more than a quarter of a century. As a singer and comedienne, she was a perennial headliner. At first teamed with her sister May and later with her husband, Sam Williams, she was considered one of America's foremost Irish comics.

Kate's parents, William and Catharine Savage, were born in Ireland in 1830, married there and immigrated to the United States during the potato famine. They settled in Brooklyn, New York. At first, William worked as a laborer. He later became a policeman. They had two girls, Kate Elinore Savage, born in 1865, and May, born in 1872.

In 1877, William filed a suit against Thomas Farrell, claiming he had made his wife Catharine a drunkard, jeopardizing his marriage and the care of his children. Farrell, in turn, filed suit against Mrs. Savage for assault. The outcome of the suits was ambiguous but revealed a family in turmoil.

The daughters obtained an elementary education and then went out to work. At the usual ages for Irish girls to marry, the Savage sisters remained single. When in their middle twenties, they decided to put together a sister act for the vaudeville stage, since many acts featured Irish performers doing Irish-related skits and singing Irish songs.

In 1894, the Elinore Sisters were appearing in small-time vaudeville houses in New York. Their act consisted of a skit about two Irish women, Kate, who represented the rough, immigrant maid, and May, who represented the more feminine and dignified matron. Kate was the comic and May the straight person, roles that were unique for comedy teams of the era. By 1896, they had perfected their act and were featured on a Tony Pastor bill. Reviewers considered them quite humorous but seemed uneasy because the sisters assumed what would ordinarily be men's roles.

Between 1896 and 1900, the Elinore Sisters, with their Irish skits, had become popular performers on both the Stair and Havlin and Orpheum vaudeville circuits. They toured the country with great success. In 1897, Maurice McLaughlin wrote a skit for them called "Irish 400" which they performed that season. In the skit, Kate embarrasses her daughter May with her bad manners and unfeminine behavior. In turn, May scolds her mother for her insulting attitude. The next year, the sisters had George M. Cohan write a sketch for them, "Mrs. Delaney of Newport." Kate played the immigrant woman who moves into high society through a financial settlement. She displays crude, disruptive behavior offending both men and women. May, her daughter, tries to reform her mother's manners. In these skits, the sisters sang songs such as "The Woman of Red," "If I Were As Rich As Hetty Green" and "Oh, Ireland, Old Ireland." Audiences loved the contrast between the two actresses and laughed even more when Kate played the clown and buffoon by wearing grotesque costumes, saying her lines in a gruff, masculine voice and using eccentric movements.

Ethnic comedy was at its height at the turn of the century and the Elinore Sisters were fine examples of headliners who catered to their immigrant audiences. While Kate was the ideal stereotype of the Irish lower-class woman, the fact that she was the comic with male-comic style clashed with stage convention. She attacked feminine manners and male authority. Some people were convinced that Kate was actually male, since no female could assume such a role. So strong were her female impersonations—usually attributed to male actors in drag—that she disrupted the usual audience perceptions of male-female roles. When, in 1902, "The Dangerous Mrs. Delaney," written by Carroll Flemming and William Jerome,

Kate Elinore, right, with sister Marie (Department of Rare Books and Special Collections, University of Rochester).

was offered, Kate's role had become so identified with her, audiences believed she acted in the same way off stage. Reviewers were quite surprised when they found a pretty, intelligent, well-mannered and fine-speaking young woman.

During the period 1903 to 1906, the sisters were at the peak of their popularity. They toured the United States and England with humorous Irish skits that included "The Adventures of Bridget McGuire," "Troubles of a Flat" by Ed Crissie, and "Double Dealings," by Arthur J. Lamb. Although they were only one act out of nine on a bill, audiences came to the theater specifically to see them perform. They cheered the eccentric antics of Kate's Irish women.

In 1906, Kate met Sam Williams, who was teaching school in Brooklyn during the day and writing songs in the evening. Sam wrote several songs for Kate, their relationship advancing quickly. In 1907, they were married. Shortly after the marriage, Kate decided to break up the sister act and partner with her husband in a comedy song-and-dance act. May was infuriated and accused Kate of ruining her career. Kate and Sam put together their new act and toured on the Keith circuit. May had problems finding work. Over the next several years, the sisters feuded. May blamed Kate for her difficulty in obtaining engagements and claimed that Kate spoke negatively about her to reviewers and theater managers. Further, May asserted that Kate had stolen all of her material. The issues were never entirely resolved.

Kate and Sam had very successful tours on both the Keith and Orpheum circuits as headliners earning $1,500–2,000 a week. Kate's role had changed considerably — no more Irish immigrant or grotesque clown. Still, she remained the comic and Sam the straight man. As audience tastes for ethnic comedy died, Kate changed the act to include husband-wife and male-female comedy, designed to appeal to a more integrated and sophisticated audience. While headliners, they appeared at Hammerstein's Victoria and other high-class vaudeville theaters, but they were never booked into the Palace Theater.

In 1913, Kate was signed by Lew Fields to take over a role played by George Monroe in "All Aboard." Monroe had quit the show before it began its road tour. Monroe was a female impersonator. Kate took over his part. "Someone thought of me," Kate explained. "I stepped into George's part, also into his clothes." She was a hit. The show toured for 16 weeks.

For the next decade, the duo starred in vaudeville, changing their act and songs frequently to keep their routine fresh and topical. Occasionally, Kate would reprise her Irish immigrant role in skits and, each time, she was applauded for her work. However, straight male-female comedy had become the rage after World War I and into the 20s. Kate and Sam adhered to the current comic tastes.

During 1924, Kate and Sam were touring with a skit, "House Hunting," which had been taken from a Music Box revue. In October, Kate became ill with an abdominal problem but continued to perform. In Indianapolis, her situation became critical and she was removed to a hospital. She died the early morning of December 30, 1924, due to complications of abdominal disease. She was 59 years old. Funeral services were held on New Year's Day. Many performers playing nearby made the trip to attend the services. As part of Kate's eulogy, the pastor read from Shakespeare's "As You Like It:"

> "All the world's a stage and all the men and women merely players. They have their exits and their entrances, and one man in his time plays many parts."
>
> The curtain has fallen — the play has ended. Kate Elinore made her exit with the plaudits of her delighted audience. Behind that curtain the tears fall, for the footlights shall know her no more.

Elsie Janis

Performing at two years of age, she was called "Baby Elsie." At five, "Little Elsie" was appearing in melodramas. At eight, she sang, danced, and gave imitations in vaudeville. At 16, Elsie was starring in musical comedies and was advertised as "America's Wonder Child." During World War I, Elsie entertained the troops in France, earning the title of "Sweetheart of the AEF" (American Expeditionary Force). All of this came about through the guidance of her determined mother, whose constant protection and business savvy made her the most famous stage mother in theatrical history.

John Eleazer Bierbower and Jane Elizabeth Cockrell were married on May 1, 1881, in Columbus, Ohio. John was a railroad man and Jane Elizabeth was a milliner. Shortly after the marriage, Jane Elizabeth (Liz, she liked to be called) realized that her union with John had been a foolhardy gesture. To assert her independence, she decided to become an actress. Her pregnancy and the birth of Elsie Bierbower on March 16, 1889, prevented Liz from continuing her career aspirations. Instead, she vowed to devote her entire life to make her daughter a stage star.

Various stories record Elsie's childhood experiences in theater. Some reports suggested she appeared on the stage as early as age two. Another report claims she was acting out scenes from "Romeo and Juliet" at three and had already begun to do imitations. The first verifiable information about this young, talented girl mentions her appearance at a local church function, with songs, dances and imitations. She was reported to have appeared in melodramas with a local stock company, like playing "Little Willie" in the perennial "East Lynne." On December 27, 1897, at the age of seven, Elsie made her professional stage debut in Columbus, Ohio, as Cain in "The Charity Ball." Around this time, both she and her mother changed their last name to Janis.

When Elsie was seven years old, she performed at the White House before President William McKinley. Liz knew McKinley when he was governor of Ohio. Liz took advantage of this engagement to promote her daughter to New York managers. She raised money to move to New York in an effort to further Elsie's career. At eight, Elsie got her first job in vaudeville.

Liz persuaded Mike Shea, a vaudeville manager with theaters in various cities, to put Elsie on the bill. Liz proposed that if Elsie did poorly, she need not be paid. If she did well, she would be paid $125 a week. Her act catapulted Elsie to the top position on the bill. Still only eight, Elsie appeared with the James O'Neill Company, playing boy and girl roles in melodramas. If she did not have a part in the production, Elsie would entertain audiences between acts, singing and doing imitations of famous celebrities.

At ten, Elsie starred for the first time in vaudeville, singing, dancing and mimicking some of the adult stars of the stage, including Eddie Foy, Harry Lauder and George M. Cohan. Elsie's knack for mimicry was outstanding. She captured the substance of the characters along with their speech and body movements. She visited their shows to learn their acting idiosyncrasies and applied this in her act. Audiences applauded her efforts. As she gained experience, her impersonations became more refined and uncannily exacting.

Liz wanted to promote Elsie to headliner status in New York vaudeville. She was prevented from doing so by the Gerry Society, a group of evangelicals, sanctioned by city officials to "protect" children under 16 from appearing on the New York stage. They forbade Elsie to play in New York, so Liz had to take her to other cities to appear on the vaudeville stage. When she was 15, she claimed she was a year older and returned to New York theaters.

Elsie gained headliner status when she performed her imitations on a bill at the New York Theater's roof garden. Along with the familiar mimicry of Foy, Cohan, Lauder, and Ethel Barrymore, she added Fay Templeton, Lillian Russell and Weber and Fields. Enthusiastic audiences begged for more. The following year, while appearing at the Colonial Theater, Elsie impersonated Vesta Victoria, Eva Tanguay and Anna Held as well as her "regulars." *Variety,* not usually complimentary to child performers, said of Elsie's performance, "Miss Janis, taken by herself and considering her youth, pleases any number of people with her impressions."

Also in 1905, Elsie played in the Broadway revue, "When We Were 41." According to reviewers, her impersonations were the high point of the show. Due to this success, she was hired to appear as the lead in "The Vanderbilt Cup." She was considered the youngest woman ever to have had a lead role on Broadway. "The Vanderbilt Cup" was called a musical but was actually a series of vaudeville olios with an inane plot, if one could be understood through all of the various song-and-dance acts. Yet the show ran for two years and made Elsie a star at 16.

Liz dominated and controlled Elsie's life and career. They lived together and traveled together. Liz negotiated contracts, fought with managers, selected Elsie's clothes and what she ate. She comforted Elsie or pushed her, when necessary, and made all of the decisions. Liz protected Elsie from managers, fought for top billing and for the best dressing rooms.

"Ma Janis," as she was called by some managers who had the dubious pleasure of dealing with her, had become an almost fearsome stage mother. Liz once remarked to a reporter, "There are Elsie Janises born every day, but not mothers to give up their whole lives to them." When Elsie performed, Liz was in the wings, cheering for her daughter.

Elsie played in several musicals between 1908 and 1912: "The Fair Co-ed" (1908); "The Slim Princess" (1910); and co-starring with Montgomery and Stone in "The Lady of the Slipper" (1912), a Cinderella story. George Ade provided the book and lyrics for "The Fair Co-ed." One big production number had Elsie and the chorus dressed in naval uniforms. This was a preview of Elsie's appearances before the troops during World War I.

Although Elsie imitated all of the characters in her repertoire, "The Slim Princess," with a slim plot, ran for only three months. "The Lady of the Slipper" had the longest run of any show for the 1912 season. Charles Dillingham, a well-known producer and fan of Elsie, employed Victor Herbert to write the music for the Cinderella story. Montgomery and Stone wore makeup and acted like they had done in "The Wizard of Oz." Elsie was the innocent Cinderella, singing pleasant but undistinguished songs. In her autobiography, Elsie commented that the stars "were the least fitted to sing Victor Herbert's music. Fortunately, we could always go into our dance, and we did!"

In between musicals, Elsie played vaudeville, and was now being called the "Lady of a Million Laughs." The comic songs and dance remained the same, but her imitations took on a new dimension. She continued to mimic other entertainers but now offered idiosyncratic combinations: Cohan singing one of his songs out of the corner of his mouth; Foy doing a clog dance; Ethel Barrymore doing Fanny Brice; and Sarah Bernhardt singing "Swanee." Audiences loved her interpretations and repeatedly encored her to "do one more" at every performance. Elsie was earning $2,500–3,000 a week, equal to the top vaudeville performers of the day.

She appeared in "The Passing Show" (1914), a Shubert production, at the Winter Garden. Elsie had a small role among a bevy of stars the Shuberts loaded into the show to make it more a burlesque than musical. When it was taken to London, Elsie was given a larger role. English audiences responded enthusiastically to her act, especially her impersonations of English performers. A stint in Paris was especially successful. It was during this time that newspapers reported a romance between Elsie and her co-star, Basil Hallam. Liz put a stop to the supposed relationship as she had probably done to any previous love interests.

During this period, Elsie was displaying other aspects of her talent. She had written more than two dozen songs and several scripts for short movies in which she acted: "The Caprices of Kitty" (1915); "T'Was Ever Thus" (1915); "The Imp" (1919). None of these movies were successful because the silents could not demonstrate Elsie at her best, using comic songs and dialogue to perform her imitations.

In between appearances in France and England, Elsie returned to the United States to play in "Miss Information." She played a telephone girl who dons many disguises to win her man. In the Dillingham-Ziegfeld "The Century Girl" (1917), Elsie sang several songs but believed herself underused in this elaborate revue. The production featured songs by Irving Berlin and Victor Herbert, innovative sets by Joseph Urban (including the staircase that became a Ziegfeld trademark) and stars Hazel Dawn, Leon Errol, and Van and Schenck. The show was pleasant enough but lost a considerable amount of money for its producers.

Elsie was in London when World War I began and was one of the first artists to volunteer to entertain the troops. When the United States entered the war, Elsie left the show in which she was appearing and paid her own way to France to entertain the American soldiers. During 1917–18, Elsie gave hundreds of shows, many of them close to the front. Most of the scripts she wrote herself, to raise the spirits of the troops. For her untiring efforts, Elsie was given the title, "Sweetheart of the AEF." Liz was a constant companion and responsible for persuading the French to allow Elsie to perform.

Elsie began each show with "Are We Downhearted?" to which the assembled soldiers answered "No!" Along with entertaining the troops, Elsie visited hospitals and behind-the-lines camps. At age 28, she quickly became America's best-known and best-loved actress. When the war ended, Elsie and her mother returned to the United States. They were greeted in New York as heroes.

Lewis Selznick signed Elsie to a four-picture contract at $5,000 a week, the first being "Everybody's Sweetheart" (1920). Elsie played a society woman who volunteered as a nurse in the war. To capitalize on her public persona, the name of the film was changed to "A Regular Girl," one of her wartime nicknames. Still calling on her war experiences, Elsie returned to Broadway in a show she created, "Elsie Janis and Her Gang," which included performers who had served in the armed forces. The show played only 55 performances in New York but went on tour for more than 800 performances. When Elsie returned to vaudeville, reviewers noticed that her zest for performing had diminished, although she was still earning $3,500 a week.

Elsie Janis

In later years, Elsie revealed the reasons behind her loss of interest in performing. Seeing the war firsthand had affected her outlook on life. "There is no doubt that with the end of the war came the death of something inside me," she related. "Pride? Perhaps, for I have never really felt proud of myself since. I've been pleased with work that I've done and grateful for the success, but the war was my high spot and I think there is only one peak in each life."

Nevertheless, Elsie single-handedly mounted a musical revue, "Puzzles of 1925." She wrote songs for the show and acted as interlocutor for other acts until just before the final curtain. Then she came to the front of the stage to sing many of the songs she had performed for the troops and to imitate Bea Lillie and John Barrymore. Her show ran for 14 weeks.

Elsie's interests turned to the movies. She wrote stories to be filmed instead of appearing in them. In 1928, "Oh, Kay!" a successful stage play, was turned into a movie. She wrote "Close Harmony" (1929), "Paramount on Parade," and the book and lyrics for Cecil B. DeMille's film, "Madam Satan." Elsie also had published two books and a collection of short stories.

In the late 1920s, Liz became ill. Elsie stayed with her until her death in 1930. With the death of her mother, Elsie announced her retirement. She called Liz "her greatest comfort. She gave up her whole life for me. Her only thought was furthering my career." Jokingly, Elsie suggested that her own epitaph might be, "Here lies Elsie Janis, still sleeping alone."

A year after her mother died, Elsie married Gilbert Watson, 26, an unsuccessful actor, 16 years her junior. She said she needed someone to manage her affairs, which happened to include all of her personal and household chores.

"He is a great deal younger than I am, but never having had a husband, and never having had a child, I thought I would combine the two into one." Several times during the interview she was addressed as Mrs. Wilson. She cut in with "Hey, not so heavy on that stuff. It's still Janis speaking."

The couple separated after a few years, but Elsie did not obtain a divorce from Watson until 1948. And, in her will, Watson was given a portion of her estate.

In the 1930s, Elsie was engaged in a variety of activities for both the stage and screen. Retirement had been forgotten. She wrote songs for three movies and provided additional dialogue for DeMille's "The Squaw Man." She wrote a charming autobiography, "So Far, So Good." In 1935, Elsie was hired by NBC to be one of their announcers, the first woman to have such a job. However, listeners complained that they could not accept a woman reading the news and Elsie was dropped. In 1936, Elsie sold her Tarrytown, New York, estate and moved to Beverly Hills, California, supposedly to be close to the movie studios. That same year, she announced that she planned to give most of her estate to charity.

Elsie returned once more to the stage in 1939, putting on a one-woman show at the Music Box Theater, New York, repeating many of her old routines. Critics loved her antics but audiences failed to attend. The show closed in four days, a victim of prevailing tastes. She was asked to appear in "Frank Fay's Vaudeville," an attempt to revive the good old days, but that show, too, failed to amuse audiences. Elsie's last performance of any kind was a small role in a 1940 movie, "Women in War," a cheapie about nurses and wounded soldiers. The movie enjoyed a short life. For the next decade, Elsie got occasional jobs from the studios, but for the most part she lived alone in retirement. She was often seen at celebrity social gatherings in Hollywood, viewed as a "grande dame" of stage entertainment.

Elsie was ill for some time with recurring ulcers and finally had surgery for the problem. She died on February 26, 1956, in Los Angeles, due to complications of the surgery. The only person at her bedside was Mary Pickford, a friend since their vaudeville appearance in 1899 (at the time, Mary was five and Elsie ten). Elsie left instructions that her funeral was to be private with no eulogy or flowers. Elsie was buried next to her mother at Forest Lawn cemetery.

Elsie was a premier headliner in vaudeville at the height of her career. She was one of the first performers to make mimicry a stage feature and many performers followed her lead. She entertained audiences in the United States and England with equal enthusiasm and was a top moneymaker for many years. Elsie was one of the most distinguished of vaudeville entertainers at a time when it was America's most popular amusement.

Florence Moore

"The distinguishing feature of recent musical comedy is provided by a remarkably clever young woman, Miss Florence Moore, who, from being well known in vaudeville, promises to become a habit with musical theater audiences," claimed the *New York Times* reviewer.

Florence Moore began on the vaudeville stage as a chorus girl. When her comedic talents were discovered, she quickly became a headliner. That reputation made her an attractive performer for musicals and revues. She also became the first Mistress of Ceremonies at the Palace Theater, in recognition of her popularity and artistic skills.

Florence Moore (her real name) was born on December 13, 1886, in Philadelphia, Pennsylvania. Her father, Edward Moore, had been a stock clerk in New York. Her mother, Annie T. Miller was a music teacher living in Philadelphia. She had an 11-year-old daughter from a previous marriage and was seven years older than Edward. They were married in 1878 in Philadelphia. The couple had two children, Frank, born in 1880, and Florence. When the children were still young, Edward left the family. At the age of 14, Frank worked as an usher in a theater. At 13, Florence worked as a clerk in a store.

As a child and teenager, Florence sang in church choirs. Frank had entered vaudeville and performed in stock companies. Florence had aspirations to become an opera singer, but her ambition was diverted when her brother, now the manager of a company that featured melodramas, asked her to join the cast. At 14, Florence had begun her theatrical career. The company was small, the demands on the players extensive and the number of killings per tragedy were considerable. Florence quickly learned to double or triple roles in an average evening.

Instead of regarding her roles with seriousness, Florence improvised. She preferred to kill the villain by saying "bang" rather than setting off a false charge. When the mortgage was about to be foreclosed, Florence leaned over the footlights and traded jokes with the orchestra leader. Audiences loved it; her brother was outraged. In a short time, Frank was so upset by his sister's antics that he fired her from the company. "You'll never make an actress," he told her. Instead, she went into vaudeville.

A combination of singing and comic dialogue got her a place on vaudeville bills with reasonable success. When she added impersonations to the routine, audiences laughed all the more. But a woman working alone at the turn of the century was a liability, and Florence sought to overcome this by teaming. For a short time, she worked with Frank as "Florence Moore & Brother," combining comedy repartee with song and dance. Then she discovered William Montgomery, an established vaudeville performer who was looking for a new partner. In 1906, when Florence was 20, they started their own act. In the same year, their partnership became a marriage. Although they had general ideas about dialogue and routines, it was Florence's comic improvisations that drove the act and generated enthusiastic audience response. The inspiration of the moment seemed to carry her, and audiences greatly appreciated this spontaneity. Montgomery played the piano, sang and did a comic dance in an oversize pair of wooden shoes. Within two years, they were playing major theaters and appeared among the top performers on a bill.

In June 1908, Montgomery and Moore were featured at the Alhambra Theater on 128th Street. Promoter C.F. Zittill had seen the team perform and brought them into high-class vaudeville. They played opposite the well-known team of Williams and Walker. By 1909, the team had signed to appear on the Loew's circuit and toured throughout the country. They became one of the best-paid acts on the circuit. Florence remained the big attraction. Her comic routines made the act. Flushed with large salaries, they stayed in the best hotels, gambled heavily and spent all the money they earned.

In 1912, they were tapped for the lead in the New York version of "Hanky Panky," which had originated with Weber & Fields on their Jubilee tour earlier in the year. The show was Montgomery and Moore's introduction to musical comedy, or revue, depending on what reviewers called it. The show opened on August 5 at the Broadway Theater. The cast included Bobby North, Max Rogers, Carter De Haven and Hugh Cameron, all comedians with excellent credentials. But it was Florence who got the attention of reviewers.

"'Hanky Panky' Has a Very Funny Woman," headlined *The New York Times*. "She began being funny as soon as she appeared, and later on she ended by being so excruciatingly funny that she quite dwarfed all of the other performers." The show ran to the end of the year. Florence was quickly signed by Lew Fields for his forthcoming production of "The Pleasure Seekers."

Fields turned "The Pleasure Seekers" into an elaborate and expensive vaudeville show afflicted with gigantism. His partners, the Shuberts, were outraged by his expenditures. "The Pleasure Seekers" opened November 3, 1913, at the Winter Garden, played for eight painful weeks and then spent 12 weeks on the road. The performers were lucky to have been paid in full. Montgomery and Moore's part was limited, the spectacle outshining the plot.

The next two years were both good and bad for the team. They played the top vaudeville houses with great success across the country. But their personal life had become a series of crises. Both had become addicted to drugs and had reached the point where they needed them to perform. Montgomery was unable to break the habit and had to be dropped from the act. Florence took a cure and stayed cured. In 1915, she divorced Will Montgomery. He never recovered, was arrested several times for narcotics possession and died at 43, a trembling, starved-looking derelict.

In contrast, 1916 was a banner year for Florence. She appeared in the Shuberts' "The Passing Show of 1916," which starred Ed Wynn and featured the music of Sigmund Romberg. She married Jules Schwob on January 31, in Atlantic City. Schwob was a watch manufacturer from Germany. And she appeared in her first movie, "The Weakness of Strength," a mediocre film that failed to make use of her comedy. At this time, Florence also made the decision not to return to vaudeville. The years of touring had taken their toll and she did not wish to place herself in such circumstances again.

From 1917 to 1919, Florence starred in the play "Parlor, Bedroom and Bath," a farce that proved to be successful at a time — World War I — when comedy was hard to put across to audiences. The show had an extended stay in New York and then went on tour. In 1917 Florence's second picture, "The Secret of Eve," again found her miscast.

In 1920, Florence starred in another farce-comedy, "Breakfast in Bed," that played a successful long run in New York and then toured. That was followed by two appearances in the Music Box revues, in 1921 and 1923, the brainchild of Irving Berlin. In the 1921 edition, Florence's satire of bedroom farces was considered by some reviewers as the hit of the show even though the cast included such comedians as Sam Bernard, William Collier and Wilda Bennett. In 1923, her act was overshadowed by the work of Robert Benchley and a George Kaufman skit.

One of the last of the Greenwich Village Follies series opened at the Forty-Sixth Street Theater on December 24, 1925. The individual acts were mundane and the music average.

Florence had the burden of producing all the comedy. In spite of its liabilities, the show played for 180 performances. The following year, Florence appeared in the farce-comedy, "She Couldn't Say No!" and carried the show with her comic characterizations.

Back with the Shuberts in the 1927 version of "Artists and Models," Florence played the role of a stiff-upper-lip nurse, quite unlike her usual routines. In the show were Jack Pearl and Ted Lewis and a large chorus of girls who paraded across the stage in see-through costumes. That was likely why the show ran for 19 weeks.

In March of that year, Florence was honored by the Palace Theater by becoming their first mistress of ceremonies, introducing such headliners as Lou Holtz, Sophie Tucker, Van and Schenk, Charlotte Greenwood, George Jessel, Elsie Janis and Burns and Allen. Her comic introductions were well-received by audiences. She returned to the Palace twice in 1928 to perform the same tasks.

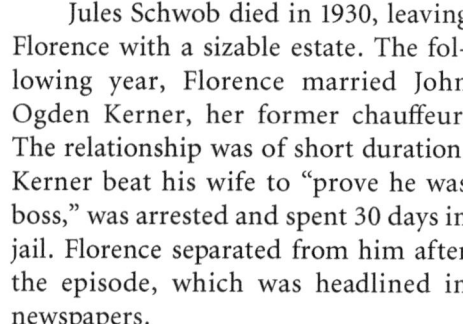

Florence Moore

Florence appeared in two Vitaphone shorts in 1928 that did make use of her comedic talents. Her last stage appearances were the "International Revue" (1930), a revival of "Cradle Snatchers" (1932), and in Cincinnati in "The Passing Show of 1932."

Jules Schwob died in 1930, leaving Florence with a sizable estate. The following year, Florence married John Ogden Kerner, her former chauffeur. The relationship was of short duration. Kerner beat his wife to "prove he was boss," was arrested and spent 30 days in jail. Florence separated from him after the episode, which was headlined in newspapers.

When Florence died of cancer on March 23, 1935, her last name was still Kerner. She died in Darby, Delaware, a suburb of Philadelphia. Interment was in Mount Peace cemetery in Philadelphia. She was 48 years old. In her will, Florence gave her entire estate to a nephew. Kerner disputed the will, claiming she had made another one that did not exclude him. He failed to prove the assertion.

A headliner in vaudeville, Florence became a star comedienne in musical comedy and revues for two decades, one of the few really great women comics of the period.

Nan Halperin

Nan Halperin spent almost her entire career playing in vaudeville. She was a singing comedienne with a gift for characterization and a histrionic ability equal to dramatic stars. Her talent for making a song both dramatic and comedic made her one of the stage's most interesting personalities and one of the best-liked headliners in vaudeville. The rise and decline of her career closely parallels vaudeville's own ascent and descent.

The Halperin family came to the United States from Odessa, Russia, in 1892. Sam Halperin was born in Russia in 1863; Rosa, his wife, was born in 1866. They married in

1881 when Sam was 18 and Rosa was 15. They lived in a Jewish *shtetl,* so the marriage was very likely arranged. The couple had six children, five of whom were born in Russia. Sam was a dry goods merchant. Upon their arrival at Ellis Island, the family was sent to a small town in central Minnesota. In the early 1890s, they moved to Denver, Colorado, where Sam became a jeweler and clothing salesman.

Nancie Halperin was born in May 1890, the fourth consecutive girl in the family. She attended elementary school, and her teachers and parents discovered that she was no ordinary girl. Although she was at the head of her class, she expressed a desire to become an actress. Elocution and singing were her favorite subjects. At the age of 12, Nancie made her first appearance for pay in a small theater in South Dakota. G.J. Prescott was managing a touring company and was seeking an ingenue to fill his cast. He saw Nancie perform and, after he exchanged several telegrams with her parents, she was permitted to join his company for the summer at $30 a week.

Nancie's appetite for acting had been whetted. She was determined to pursue a theater career, and her parents agreed. She joined a stock company that performed a variety of melodramas, from "Ten Nights in a Bar Room" to "Camille." Nancie studied acting with determination and played rehearsals as seriously as the actual performances. The company visited Chicago, where Nancie decided to remain to enter vaudeville. She appeared in small-time houses for several years, perfecting a routine and building a reputation as a character singer, that is, one who imitated other singers and interpreted songs that portrayed the lives of other people.

While performing in Chicago, she met William Friedlander, a music composer, and they were married June 4, 1910. Nancie was 20 years old; Friedlander was 26. Shortly afterward, they moved to New York to pursue their respective careers. Nan shortened her name and obtained work in various local vaudeville houses with success. A critic watched Nan and wrote of her: "Nan Halperin. Write it down in your memory book, you are going to hear a lot about her in the future." M. S. Bentham, an agent, took over Nan's booking and got her contracts to perform for 35 weeks a year during 1913 and 1914. She toured the country, perfecting her comedy act.

Nan was signed to appear in a revue, "Broadway Honeymoon," which debuted in Chicago in September 1913. It opened in New York, but folded in two weeks. Nan did not like the musical format and decided to concentrate her efforts in vaudeville. B.F. Keith hired her to appear on his circuit. Nan made her initial appearance in high-class vaudeville at the Colonial Theater, New York, the week of December 7, 1914. She was listed fourth out of eight acts, the headliner being Ethel Barrymore performing one of her dramatic skits. Nan's character songs were well-received and Keith quickly put her out on the touring circuit for the rest of the season and through the summer of 1915. A stop in Los Angeles was successful; a reviewer called Nan one of vaudeville's up-and-coming stars. Her act, "Just a Little Personality," portrayed in song the lifestyles of average people. Her facial features were particularly noted "because they register more expressions to the minute than one can express in cold type."

Back in New York, Nan played at the Orpheum Theater, with glowing results. She was ecstatic about her success. "When they put my name in electrics, I made my husband walk down Broadway with me every night and I would pretend utter astonishment when he came upon my name blazing away up there."

Nan's newfound popularity brought her to the Palace Theater in April 1916, where she performed a cycle of character songs. She began by presenting a girl's life, in pigtails and calico dress, then a young woman preparing for a dance, one ready for her wedding and, finally, the wife of a soldier waiting for his return. Audiences readily identified with her songs and portrayals. She was held over a second week and was advertised as "vaudeville's new star." She played on a program featuring Irene Bordoni, Helene Lackaye, Lew Brice and Harry Langdon.

The year 1917 found Nan a headliner on the Keith circuit once again, but for this tour, she appeared primarily in New York theaters. By June, she was heading the bill with engagements in Brighton (a summer resort), Brooklyn, Harlem and Newark, as well as several theaters in Manhattan. That same year, she and her husband, now a theatrical producer, formed a company with Nan as business director. They not only sponsored vaudeville performers but Nan also rehearsed the people, designed the costumes and supervised the production numbers. Initially, the business prospered.

Again performing for Keith in 1918, Nan headed each bill with performers that included Kate Elinore, Van & Schenck, and a Charlie Chaplin movie. Her song cycle was the highlight of the program. Throughout the spring and summer, Nan played in New York theaters. She professed not to like touring and preferred staying close to home. When she appeared at the Orpheum in November, Nan was co-starred with Lillian Russell who, at the time, was lecturing about health and nutrition. Lillian used Nan's act as an example of a way to stay fit.

During and after the war, Nan participated in benefits for soldiers, hospitals and women's auxiliaries. She also appeared in suffrage rallies as women sought the opportunity to vote. Throughout her career, she played in events for various Jewish organizations.

In January 1919, Nan headlined at the Palace Theater. The Palace newspaper ad proclaimed: "[S]he deliciously portrays many fetching types of girls and women in her clever character songs. She is an outstanding personality of irresistible charm." Playing on the same bill were Leon Errol, Lew Dockstader and Joe Jackson.

Shortly after this, Nan signed with the Shuberts. For two years, she played entirely in vaudeville, shuttling back and forth among the various Shubert theaters in New York. In the late summer of 1922, the Shuberts announced that Nan, in a new role, would appear in an upcoming musical revue.

"Make It Snappy," starring Eddie Cantor and Nan, opened at the Winter Garden on April 13, 1922. Cantor, hopping around the stage in blackface and white gloves, was "most amusing," according to reviewers. But reviews for Nan were uniformly nega-

Nan Halperin

tive. Her song renditions were criticized and her character delineations were panned as "bad mimickry." The show lasted two months. An unhappy Nan returned to Shubert vaudeville.

In 1923, the Shuberts prevailed on Nan to appear in "Little Jesse James," which opened at the Longacre Theater August 15. She played the lead in a show that was considered mediocre by reviewers. It had only a single set and eight chorus girls. Miriam Hopkins received all of the reviewers' kind words. Nan's "unvarying comedy method" was "tiresome." Yet, the show ran for three months. Nan never again appeared in a musical. She separated from the Shuberts as well.

She was back at the Palace in December, topping a bill that included Kate Elinore, Lou Holtz, Van & Schenck and Anatol Friedland. Her repertoire of character song studies received continual applause and shouts for encores. Again on the Keith route, Nan toured the country through 1924 and 1925. In early 1926, Nan filed for divorce from Friedlander. She accused him of deserting her three years previously. The divorce was finalized April 30. A few months later, Nan married Benjamin Thomson, a clothing manufacturer. She continued to be a headliner for Keith through 1927 and 1928.

Vaudeville was declining in interest and popularity, due to the advent of talking pictures. The medium maintained itself by sharing the theater with a few live acts and a feature film, the latter often advertised above the acts. Performers were aware of the change, with some opting for movie careers, radio, or simply retirement. Nan remained undaunted. She pushed for vaudeville time and continued to perform her familiar routine. She went on the Proctor circuit with some success. An actors' reunion at the Palace in December 1929 did not help Nan. On the bill were stars like Lulu McConnell, Buck and Bubbles and Fred Waring. Reviewers called her act "unimpressive," with "unimportant sketches." Nan played at the Palace again in December 1930, but got a one-line comment only. Her act had become old and tired, as Nan herself was feeling after more than 18 years of almost non-stop performing.

In 1931, Loew's signed Nan to appear at their theaters, but this was a lesser circuit with fewer theaters. He billing prominence had shrunk and, like the remaining vaudeville old-timers, she was fighting the featured movies. In December, Nan was engaged at the Albee Theater in Brooklyn, playing with Boris Karloff's new film "Frankenstein."

Benjamin Thomson died of a heart attack on November 13, 1932. Nan was back on the stage a month later at Loew's Metropolitan Theater, listed below three other performers, including "Fatty" Arbuckle. She remained with Loew's in 1933, getting engagements when she could. Now classified as an "added attraction" to the regular program, Nan continued to perform her familiar characterizations. In August, she married Edgar Gould, a merchant, and she retired from the stage. Her last appearance was at the Club Merry-Go-Round in Atlantic City.

During her later years, Nan participated in charitable events, primarily for Jewish groups. On May 30, 1963, she died at her home in Kew Gardens, New York. She was seventy-three years old.

Nan had made a career of a particular style of delivery and characterization. As vaudeville flourished, so did Nan with repeated visits to the Palace Theater and as a headliner on various vaudeville circuits. When vaudeville declined, Nan's popularity declined as well. When she died, none of the New York newspapers published her obituary.

Fanny Brice

In the first half of the twentieth century, Jewish comedians gained headliner status by enacting Jewish stereotypes and employing a vaudeville style of humor. Fanny Brice's career, from the early days on the vaudeville stage to her final years on radio and TV, illustrates the boundaries and opportunities of being a Jewish comedian. *Variety* called Fanny as "one of the greatest singing comediennes in the history of the American theater."

Fanny Borach was born on October 29, 1891, on Manhattan's Lower East Side, in the Jewish ghetto. Her father, Charles Borach, had been born in Strasbourg, France, in 1861. Her mother, Rose (nee Stern), was born in Hungary in 1867. They married in the United States in 1885. Fanny was the third of four children. Philip was born in 1887; Carolyn in 1889; and Louis in 1893. The family moved to Newark, New Jersey when Fanny was a young child. Charles was a bartender, a gambler and an alcoholic who became a saloonkeeper. According to the children, Rose ran the saloon while Charles drank up the profits. In 1903, when Fanny was twelve, Rose left her husband, sold the saloon, took her four children to Brooklyn, and bought a tenement.

Fanny began her theatrical career singing on neighborhood street corners for a few pennies. When she was thirteen, she entered an amateur contest at Kenney's Theater, Brooklyn, a vaudeville house, where she won a $5 prize. For a year, Fanny appeared in amateur contests in various theaters, sometimes earning $30 a week for her efforts. Her mother encouraged Fanny to pursue a stage career rather than attending school. In between amateur performances, Fanny worked in a stereopticon parlor and as a ticket taker at a nickelodeon.

At age 15, Fanny got a small role in a George M. Cohan musical as a dancer. When Cohen found she could not dance, he fired her. Fanny knew that to get ahead, she had to learn to dance and learn basic stagecraft. From 1907 to 1910, she worked in the chorus, singing and dancing, in a number of touring vaudeville companies. During her third year as a principal singer with Hertig & Seamon's "The College Girls," Fanny took the name of a family friend, Brice. Her change of name may have been due to the desire to mask her ethnic identity.

While playing in "The College Girls," Fanny acquired a song from a young songwriter, Irving Berlin, called "Sadie Salome." She performed the song in a Jewish dialect and parodied Salome's dance. Berlin gave her another song, "The Grizzly Bear," in which she used a similar interpretation. Both songs demanded as much broad physical humor as actual singing. Audiences loved her delivery, and Fanny built her act around physical action, parodies, and a Jewish dialect. At the time, she was earning twenty-five dollars a week.

The year 1910 proved an important year for Fanny. Flo Ziegfeld saw one of her performances and signed her to appear in his Follies of 1910 at seventy-five dollars a week. Appearing with Fanny were Lillian Lorraine, Bert Williams and dozens of glamorous girls. Fanny's act appealed to audiences so well that she was called back for twelve encores. Due to her success, Fanny appeared again in the Follies of 1911, sharing honors with Leon Errol, Bert Williams and the Dolly Sisters.

In 1912, Fanny reentered vaudeville with a four-month tour of New York theaters; mostly she repeated her earlier material. "A Whirl of Society," a musical with individual acts and no plot, followed. Notable among the cast members were Al Jolson, in the role of a butler, and Florence Walton and Maurice, top dancers of the day. Fannie had the role of a maid. It was a typical Shubert production, done on a limited budget and subject to constant cast changes. The show played on the road in Shubert theaters for five months. Another Shubert show, "The Honeymoon Express," appeared at their Winter Garden for three months and featured many of the same performers; Fanny played a domestic. Happily, she returned to vaudeville for the summer months. During this entire period, Fanny's work received few reviews, her career seemingly at a standstill.

During her employment in "The Whirl of Society" (in November, 1912) Fanny met Julius Wilford Arndstein (Nicky Arnstein) and fell in love with the "businessman." He did not reveal to her a former marriage or the nature of his business. Others knew him as a con man and defrauder who had visions of fame and fortune. After a brief trip to London in 1913, where Fanny played several vaudeville theaters with only moderate success, Nicky and Fanny returned to New York and began living together.

Fanny's vaudeville tours, short though they were, established her as a proven entertainer. In February 1914, she opened a fifteen-month vaudeville tour at the Palace Theater, New York. It was her first appearance at this esteemed venue. She was billed as "direct from her eight months at the Palace Music Hall, London," an extreme exaggeration. On the bill, she followed Eddie Foy and the Seven Little Foys, vaudeville's hottest act. Fanny's routine was mostly farce and satire, delivered in a self-deprecatory Jewish accent. Reviewers loved her routine and audiences demanded encores. The tour took her around the country to many places where she had never before performed, giving her status as a superior comedienne.

In 1916, Ziegfeld asked Fanny to return to the Follies, this time as one of the headliners. In the show, Fanny did a hilarious impersonization of Theda Bara; she sang a novelty song, "Nijinsky" (with a Yiddish accept) that featured Bert Williams as the famous dancer; and she gave an uproarious performance in the skit, "The Dying Swan," portraying a fan dancer who had trouble controlling her fans. Fanny was now a Broadway favorite with a reputation and salary to match those of the current vaudeville headliners. Fanny appeared again in the Follies of 1917, co-starring with W.C. Fields, Bert Williams, Will Rogers and, in his Follies debut, Eddie Cantor. The show played from June to the following April 1918. Historians considered Ziegfeld's 1917 version one of the best revues that had ever been produced.

The relationship with Arnstein produced many emotionally charged situations for Fanny. He kept his business deals hidden from her. In 1915, he was indicted and sent to prison for two years. Fanny believed that he had been duped. In 1918, Nicky and Fanny married and later had two children. When, in 1924, Arnstein was again jailed for bond fraud, Fanny paid all of his legal bills. He was released from jail in 1927, but Fanny clearly had had enough of Nicky's activities, particularly his infidelities. After fifteen years of turmoil, she divorced him in 1927.

Nevertheless, this period produced some of Fanny's best stage work. The year 1918 began badly when she starred in a poorly scripted musical comedy, "Why Worry." Reworking did not help it and the show closed after two months. In spite of the show's demise, Fanny received good reviews. She played in Ziegfeld's "Midnight Frolic" in 1918, 1919, and 1920, and then was recruited for the Follies of 1920. She sang several songs in her unique style and appeared in two skits, co-starred with W.C. Fields, Van and Schenck, and Charles Winninger. Fanny's routines had greatly improved, since she had hired comic writers who expertly tailored the comedy material to her talents. She impersonated Theda Bara, Pavlova in her dying swan skit, Ruth St. Denis, Camille ("I've been a bad, bad voman, but awfully good company, nu?") and Martha Graham.

Ziegfeld had Fanny back for the Follies of 1921. It was in this show that she introduced a song, "My Man," that made a sensational hit. It was a torch song about a woman's devotion to a worthless husband that brought tears to the audience. (Observers believed Fanny was speaking of her relationship with Nicky.) The song quickly became her trademark.

The year 1922 found Fanny back on the vaudeville circuit. Her tour of the country ran through July 1923. It was her most successful stage performance and netted enthusiastic audiences and excellent reviews. Then, she returned to Ziegfeld for the Follies of 1923, which played until May 1924, due to its popularity. Fanny sang two songs and played in three skits, enhanced by her Yiddish delivery. A brief stint in vaudeville on the Orpheum circuit presaged an engagement in Irving Berlin's Fourth Annual Music Box Revue, which opened November 24, 1924. Fanny played in two skits and sang four songs. The touring show continued to March 1926.

David Belasco persuaded Fanny to appear in a "melodramatic comedy" written and named after her. While she was flattered by the proposition, Belasco's script was poor. The play lasted three weeks. Rewritten and restaged over the summer, "Fanny" opened again in September and scored a success, at least in the East. This time, the tour ran for four months although Belasco's investment was never recouped.

Never out of work, Fanny was signed to star in the "Hollywood Music Box Revue." Everyone was producing revues in those days with casts of several headliners and beautiful choruses. With great fanfare, the show opened on February 2, 1927, in Hollywood, California. The show lacked new material and was short on preparation. Even Fanny's skit on "Camille," a hit on Broadway, fell flat. The revue closed in nine weeks, a financial loss. Fanny returned to the UBO and Orpheum vaudeville circuits through November 1928.

Fanny felt the need to update her material with new songs and comic sketches. Her current writer, Ballard McDonald, needed a co-worker to handle the assignment. He hired a young songwriter, Billy Rose, who already had a number of song hits. When Fanny met Rose, she disliked him. But when Rose promised to prepare her new act in record time while McDonald was recovering from drinking, they became friends. After polishing the material, Fanny opened at the Palace Theater with one of the best acts of her career. The premier skit in the show was "Mrs. Cohen at the Beach," the first Jewish mother routine given on stage. Its punchline, given to her kids, "Why didn't you do it when you were in the water?" totally brought down the house. So responsive was the audience to her interpretation that this routine became a staple for many years. The vaudeville tour ended in November 1928. It had been a tremendous success for Fanny, featuring glowing accolades from reviewers. And Billy Rose was now identified as Fanny's lover.

Show business was thrown into tumult upon the release of the first talking movie, "The Jazz Singer." The Warner Brothers studio had planned two new talking pictures,

Fanny Brice

another vehicle for Al Jolson and a picture for Fanny, "My Man." Fanny not only played a serious role in the film, she sang seven songs, including "My Man" and "Second Hand Rose," another song closely identified with her, and reprised her stage skit, "Mrs. Cohen at the Beach." Fanny had originally agreed to do the film for $25,000. Rose, flabbergasted at the low salary, renegotiated with Warner Brothers and got her $125,000. Not only was Rose a good comedy writer and songster, but he was also a great businessman.

During the fall of 1928, Fanny was back in vaudeville, playing at the Palace to full houses and about to go on tour. Instead, producer Earl Carroll asked Fanny to appear in "Fioretta," called an operetta but in reality a string of vaudeville acts tied together by beautiful girls and lavish costumes. Leon Errol was also hired, but even the work of the two comedians failed to give the show life. At the same time that the show was in rehearsal, the movie "My Man" was released. The reviews were bad, many of them pointing out that Fanny had been badly miscast. Nor was the stage show well-received when it opened. Yet, thanks to Fanny's efforts, "Fioretta" lasted for five months, four of which were conveniently at Earl Carroll's theater. On February 9, 1929, while "Fioretta" was playing, Fanny and Billy Rose were married. She was eight years older than Rose and four inches taller.

In 1930, Fanny returned to her old standby, vaudeville, even though the entertainment was rapidly dying. She played primarily in New York, where vaudeville audiences were still large. Following were several stage revues in which Fanny sang a few songs closely identified with her and repeated of her most humorous skits. "Sweet and Low" was produced by Billy Rose; the show lasted for seven months. "Crazy Quilt," also staged by Rose, opened in May 1931 and closed in December.

In 1934, the Follies again wished Fanny to take a leading role in the new edition. But Flo Ziegfeld had died two years earlier. The Follies was now being run by committee: E.Y. Harburg, writing the lyrics; Vernon Duke, writing the music; Billy Connolly, doing the staging; and Mrs. Flo Ziegfeld (Billie Burke), acting as producer. The show had its usual complement of beautiful girls and a group of headliners besides Fanny: Willie Howard, Eve Arden, Buddy Ebsen, Jane Froman, and Fred Allen. It opened November 2, 1933, played through all of 1934, and closed March 1935. Considering the effects of the Depression on popular theater, the show did reasonably well in spite of its dated presentation. The Follies of 1936 quickly followed, the entire production now staged by John Murray Anderson. Even with the talents of performers like Fanny, Bob Hope, Eve Arden, and Judy Canova, the show was without vitality, the zest of the Follies having disappeared with its founder. It lasted only four months but portions of it were repeated again in "The New Ziegfeld Follies of 1936–1937." The show ran an astounding eight months on tour, audiences wishing to see it more for nostalgia reasons than for its entertainment. New amusements had made the Follies obsolete.

Participating in the Follies' demise were Fanny, Bobbie Clark, Cass Daley and Gypsy Rose Lee. Fanny sang three songs and appeared in six skits. The show also established Fanny's role as Baby Snooks. She had performed the role in the previous Follies with moderate results. This time, she made the role a part of her comic persona. It was also Fanny's last appearance on Broadway.

Fanny appeared in several additional films, two of them in cameo roles. "Be Yourself" (1930) starred Fanny; she parodied four songs, two of them old routines. She had a small role in "The Great Ziegfeld" (1936) where she played herself and sang two songs, "Yiddle on Your Fiddle" and "My Man." In "Everybody Sing" (1938), one of MGM's cheapies, Fanny played a Russian singer and parodied two songs. MGM released a movie revue, "Ziegfeld Follies," in 1946, made up of cameos depicting many of the former acts seen in the original Follies. Fanny sang one song with Hume Cronyn and William Frawley. It was her last screen appearance.

Fanny's third marriage, to Billy Rose, ended in 1938, due to Rose's infidelity. With vaudeville past and the Follies an ancient stage relic, at forty-five, Fanny sought a new career. She found it in radio as the bratty, mischievous Baby Snooks, resurrected from one of her Follies skits. She appeared as Snooks on NBC's "Good News of 1938," which changed to the "Maxwell House Coffee Hour." It was a half-hour show split equally between Frank Morgan and Fanny. The arrangement lasted five years. For her radio efforts, Fanny was being paid a handsome $6,500 a broadcast.

In 1944, the "Baby Snooks Show" appeared on CBS and remained there until 1948. Fanny then signed with NBC and the show ran until 1951. In 1945, Fanny suffered a heart attack but returned after missing four shows. In 1951, "Baby Snooks" was introduced on television, her character making a successful transition. During these last several years, Fanny's health had been deteriorating with equilibrium problems, a low blood count and severe headaches making performing difficult. She was looking forward to retirement at the conclusion of the 1951 season.

On May 24, 1951, Fanny suffered a cerebral hemorrhage. She was rushed to the hospital. The family gathered. NBC management waited anxiously. The country rooted for her recovery. On May 29, 1951, Fanny died, at age 59.

She was mourned by a national audience who had come to love Fanny and her Baby Snooks character. Fanny as satirist and comedienne had had two theatrical lives: The first was as a headliner in vaudeville and star with the Ziegfeld Follies; the second was as a star impersonator on radio and television. At her death, movie director George Cukor said, "Fanny was one of the great, great clowns of all time."

Winnie Lightner

Winnie Lightner's comic antics delighted vaudeville, revue and movie audiences for nearly twenty years. Her particular brand of humor was loud, rollicking and boisterous. Winnie's facial mugging and a high-pitched voice had audiences laughing no matter what role she played. As she once explained, "I'm an Irish Mick, a natural roughneck and I don't expect anyone to mistake me for a lady." She was like that in her private life as well. Winnie carried her vaudeville persona into the movies, becoming one of the cleverest comediennes in early talking pictures.

She was born Winifred Josephine Reeves on September 17, 1899, in Greenport, Long Island. Her father was born in New York, her mother in Ireland. But for unknown reasons, when Winifred was less than a year old, she had come to live with Andrew and Margaret Hansen in Manhattan. He was a station manager for the railroad. In the 1900 census, the Hansens called her their niece, but there was no real family connection. In later years, Winnie spoke of them as her foster parents. She had two older siblings who did not live with her. Theo, a sister, was ten years older than Winifred. Fred was five years older.

When Winifred was in her teens, the Hansens moved to Buffalo. The backyard of their house was behind a vaudeville theater. When it was closed, Winifred often sneaked into the theater through the back door and did stunts on stage. She wanted to be a serious artist, a dramatic soprano. After hearing her rehearse daily for hours, the Hansen family let her appear her in a local vaudeville theater. Winifred was sixteen years old.

On the night of her debut, Winifred was caught in a rainstorm, her taxi stalled, and she had to make her way to the theater soaked. She arrived just as she was to go on stage. With no time to change, Winifred went on stage to sing her serious songs. Almost immediately, her looks and attire made the audience laugh. When she sang, they laughed even harder. "In a few minutes I had forgotten my fright," she recalled, "and was clowning along with my tragic song as though I had intended it to be a burlesque."

In 1918, Winifred's older sister, Theo, was already in vaudeville, performing in a sister act called the Lightner Sisters. Theo's husband-to-be, Newton Alexander, was appearing with the Exposition Four. When both groups broke up, Theo and Newton teamed as a comedy act and were playing the Orpheum circuit. "Let's put Winnie in the act somewhere and make use of her," Theo proposed. "What can she do?" asked Newton. "She can't do anything but be a mugger but then I guess she'll be a great foil." Debuting with "The Lightner Girls and Newton Alexander," Winnie immediately forgot her lines and resorted to mugging and talking nonsense in a high, squeaky voice. The audience laughed so heartily that the routine became a permanent part of the act.

Winnie Lightner (Harry Ranson Humanities Research Center, the University of Texas at Austin).

In August 1920, the trio played at the Alhambra Theater in a comedy act. Reviewers enjoyed the act, especially Winnie, with her facial gyrations and roughneck behavior. Now costumed for her role, with long, flowing red hair, Winnie played the Irish tough girl with skill. Two months later, the trio appeared at the Palace Theater, although they were not listed at the top of the bill. During the next year, they toured on the Orpheum circuit and received good reviews. On the tour, Winifred met and married Richard Pyle, an actor. Three months later, she divorced him, claiming desertion. A month later, Winnie married William Harold. That marriage was annulled in 1923.

In 1922, the trio was booked to appear in "George White's Scandals," supporting W. C. Fields and Paul Whiteman and his Orchestra. The show opened on August 28 at the Globe Theater. There were no reviews for their act. The show ran for eleven weeks and they were good enough to be asked back by White for his next "Scandals" show. In the meantime, the team played vaudeville dates in New York and surrounding cities.

"George White's Scandals of 1923" opened June 18 at the Globe Theater. Winnie sang several songs in her usual comic fashion. She also teamed with Tom Patricola in a dance routine. Although the show had no outstanding headliners, it ran for twenty-one weeks.

Theo and Newton were also in the show but it would be the last time the trio worked together. Winnie was ready to take her act solo.

She was back with White in 1924. "George White's Scandals" opened June 30 at the Apollo Theater. Winnie sang George Gershwin's "Somebody Loves Me" with an odd staging. As she sang the song, she was pursued by past and current heroes, Mark Antony, Romeo, Harold Lloyd and William S. Hart.

Later in the show, Winnie and Lester Allen parodied "Abie's Irish Rose." The show ran for more than six months.

Next the Shuberts engaged Winnie for their show, "Gay Paree." It opened August 18, 1925, at the Shubert Theater. Winnie was starred opposite Chic Sale. She did a few comedy skits with him and sang in a series of production numbers, backed by a lovely chorus. Reviewers were amazed that the show ran for six months. Winnie had now become a headliner whose comic abilities were recognized and lauded.

In 1926, The Shuberts had Winnie and Chic Sale back for their next edition of "Gay Paree," which opened at the Winter Garden. The show ran for five months, but for Winnie, the primary event was her marriage to George Holtry, a stockbroker. In between shows and vaudeville appearances, Winnie gave birth to a son, Richard. In a short time, she was back to work, appearing at the Palace Theater in June 1927. The *Times* reviewer wrote that her performance had "the usual abundance of gusto." She sang several Tin Pan Alley tunes with her particular style.

Winnie was engaged by Harry Delmar for "Delmar's Revels," a revue also featuring Frank Fay, Patsy Kelly and a newcomer, Bert Lahr. The show opened November 28, 1927, at the Shubert Theater. Each performer acted in a satire, sang songs from a variety of composers and was backed by the precision chorus, the Chester Hale Girls. Winnie sang "I Love a Man in Uniform" and participated in a number of comedy sketches.

The year 1928 was a busy year for Winnie. She appeared in two Vitaphone shorts. She took a European tour, playing in London and Paris. She played at the Palace in September to the usual full houses. She also toured a number of high-class vaudeville houses in Eastern cities. Warner Brothers saw her as an excellent addition to an all-star cast in an upcoming talkie and persuaded her to come to Hollywood.

The film "Show of Shows" was an olio featuring many familiar vaudeville stars. Winnie had one skit that was considered the best in the picture. Parodying "Singing in the Rain," she sang "Singing in the Bath Tub" with all of her zany mugging and comic antics, backed by a male chorus in female attire. Following this starring bit, Warners signed Winnie to another all-star picture, "Gold Diggers of Broadway" (1929), in which she played Mabel, a wild and tough young woman, a role specially written for her. Roy Del Ruth was the director and responsible for guiding Winnie's future in moving pictures.

Winnie starred in eleven films from 1930 to 1934. In most of them, she played the same kind of role that vaudeville audiences found so funny. Del Ruth directed a number of them. Winnie had become Warners' most popular comedienne, one who guaranteed good reviews and excellent box office.

In November 1932, Winnie obtained a divorce from Holtry, citing infidelity. In turn, Holtry countersued her for her activities with Del Ruth, now a well-known Hollywood director.

After her last picture in 1934, Winnie retired from the movies and the stage. She moved to Los Angeles permanently with her son and her sister, Theo. Del Ruth was a constant companion for more than fifteen years. In 1948, they married. He died of a heart attack in 1961.

On March 6, 1971, Winnie died of a heart attack in her home. She was buried next to Del Ruth in the San Fernando Mission Cemetery in Mission Hills, California. At the time of her death, she was known primarily for her movie appearances, her stellar career in vaudeville and revues totally forgotten.

Part Four : The Dancers

La Carmencita

She was a Spanish dancer who blazed across the popular stage for a mere six years. Her flamboyant style and seductive performances made her a headliner not only with vaudeville audiences but also with New York's social elite. Her sensual performances challenged the proprieties of both American and British audiences.

Carmencita Daucet was born in France around 1870. By the time she and her company of Spanish student dancers reached England, via Paris, she was already married to Pablo Echapare, a musician and conductor of the orchestra. Pale, with dark, flowing hair, black brows, and an angular face that highlighted her distinctive Mediterranean appearance, Carmencita costumed herself as the quintessential Spanish dancer. Her whirling dancing style, the "shock" of her sensual body movements and her charismatic effect on men in the audience quickly made her a headliner.

In 1888, Carmencita and her Spanish student dancers appeared in the play "Albion" in London. The show was a great success, due mainly to Carmencita. She introduced fiery Spanish dance to English audiences unfamiliar with the style. A contract with Bolossy Kiralfy, an impresario who worked both in Europe and America, brought "Albion" and Carmencita to the United States.

The show opened at Niblo's Garden on August 17, 1889. American reviewers called it a "ballet extravaganza" and praised Carmencita for her "arresting" performance. But because the show was unusual for America, it ran for only a short time.

A dispute with Kiralfy and a lawsuit ended the arrangement. Carmencita demanded $750 for back pay from Kiralfy, claiming that she had made a contract with him the previous year for $150 a week and a guaranteed engagement for twenty-six weeks. Kiralfy said he had negotiated a new contract with her upon her arrival in the United States. Carmencita denied this. The court ruled in favor of Carmencita but deferred a portion of the money due her. Seeking employment for herself and the company, Carmencita turned to vaudeville.

On February 10, 1890, Carmencita and her dancers opened at Koster & Bial's Theater, New York, to wide acclaim. Theater management retained her for ten weeks due to her almost instant popularity. In a short time, she headlined the bill at the theater. This success led to a tour of the major cities of the East and Midwest. When the company returned to New York in June, Carmencita was feted by the city's social elite at a special benefit.

Carmencita did not perform some of her striking and voluptuous dances for this audience; instead, she chose to present more traditional fare. At first, crowd applause was light and hesitating. Carmencita openly complained about the tepid reception. With a breakout of sustained applause, she danced with renewed energy. Carmencita was later featured at society gatherings.

In the fall of 1892, Carmencita appeared with the play "The Prodigal Father" at the Broadway Theater, dancing after the second act. Reviewers admired her gracefulness and wondered about her obvious gifts. They also remarked on her petulance when the audience did not applaud her quickly enough. One of her dance routines, "Le Pere la Victoire," caused a problem when the audience applauded for too long a time. The show ran to the end of the year.

At the beginning of 1893, Carmencita returned to Koster & Bial's for an extended engagement. In February, she was in court as a co-respondent in a divorce suit. The wife of one of the actors who played on the bill with her was suing for divorce, claiming that Carmencita "usurped the affections" of her husband and that his affections were reciprocated. It became known that Carmencita was married to the conductor of the orchestra at the theater. While she was on tour, the divorce was finalized and Carmencita was removed from the suit.

In the fall of 1893, Carmencita headlined a bill at Koster & Bial's. She spent the remainder of the year and early 1894 on tour, with great success. Audiences loved her Spanish interpretive dancing, although critics mentioned her capricious behavior. Her time in the United States ended in August 1894 with an appearance at the American Theater Roof Garden. She and her husband sailed for England and engagements at a number of London venues.

La Carmencita

Carmencita's fame in America did not carry over to English audiences and critics. They were shocked by her sensational dancing. While critics acknowledged the genius of her dancing, they accused her of "arousing" audiences. Audience response to her act was polite but cold.

Sometime in the fall of 1895, Carmencita died. Few in America recalled her brief fame on the vaudeville stage.

In 1905, Willie Hammerstein, who had a reputation as a "shady" promoter, advertised the farewell appearance of Carmencita at the Victoria Theater. It was actually an obscure chorus girl who had worked at the Belasco Theater several months before. Willie sent her to Europe, advertised her great successes, and brought her back to the United States to headline the Victoria. Audiences were reported to be impressed by the dancer, and her act made headlines although she was not the real Carmencita.

Bessie Clayton

She was considered the greatest acrobatic toe dancer of her time. Lithe, petite, with elfin charm, Bessie Clayton perfected an uncanny combination of classical ballet and the athletic moves from popular stage dances. Bessie was labeled "the American Carmencita." Her professionalism was unique among dancers of her era. She performed on pointe barefoot or in unlined, unreinforced slippers. Bessie was a vaudeville headliner who also appeared successfully in musical comedy, dance concerts and opera.

Bessie was born in June 1878 in Philadelphia, Pennsylvania. Both of her parents were born and raised in New Jersey. Edward Clayton, her father, was born in 1852. He worked as a meter maker for most of his life. Elizabeth "Lizzie" Clayton, Bessie's mother, was born in 1851. The couple married in 1873 and moved to Philadelphia. Bessie was their only child.

As a youngster, Bessie showed an interest in dancing. "In fact," said her mother, "as soon as she could walk she began to dance." To her own enjoyment, Bessie would hop and prance and jump in a fashion all her own. Her parents paid little attention to her proclivities, even though at the age of ten she showed considerable talent. Finally, her reluctant parents sent her to dancing school where Bessie found the opportunity to develop her fondness for dance. At one recital, Bessie discovered she had no ballet shoes and requested them from her mother, to no avail. Instead, Bessie took some old slippers, took off the heels, added laces and began practicing to dance on her toes. Her dancing teacher, amazed at her ingenuity, got her a pair of ballet slippers and began teaching her classical steps.

At the age of eight, Bessie made her first stage appearance in an amateur recital. At ten, she appeared in a formal program, dancing during intermissions. During the next few years, she danced at whatever events she could find, gaining attention as a performer with excellent future prospects. Her conditioning regimen was demanding. She ran miles every day, did flexibility exercises and controlled her diet. Unlike most of her plumper colleagues, Bessie looked like a dancer to modern eyes.

In early 1892, at the age of fourteen, Bessie was hired to play in the chorus of E.J. Nugent's show, "A Knotty Affair," at the Hollis Theater, Boston. Her mother accompanied her, as she did until Bessie's marriage. Bessie was the premier dancer in the chorus.

Hoyt's big hit, "A Trip to Chinatown," had begun its second year of performances. The show's premier dancer was the already acknowledged Loie Fuller, featured in her "butterfly dance." In October 1892, Fuller quit the cast. Who would replace her, critics asked? Who *could* replace her? After auditions, Bessie was selected and performed the "butterfly dance" as well as Fuller, according to reviewers. She captivated audiences with her yellow curls, bright face and slender legs.

Bessie entered vaudeville in 1893 and was an immediate hit. No other dancer in recent history could meld classic moves with popular music. She toured for almost two years, accompanied by her mother.

Julian Mitchell had seen Bessie perform in "A Trip to Chinatown" but showed little interest in her. In early 1894, Mitchell saw Bessie perform again. This time he took *great* interest in her for both business and personal reasons. On May 23, 1894, Julian and Bessie were married. She was not quite sixteen; Mitchell was thirty-two.

Julian Mitchell was born in New York in November 1861. He started his career in the theater as a callboy. At the age of twenty, he produced his first musical and danced in it. By the early 1890s, Mitchell had gained a reputation as one of the best stage directors in the business. He had been previously married to Georgia Lake in 1889. They were divorced in 1893.

Mitchell went on to an illustrious career in stage management, working with such impresarios as Weber & Fields, George M. Cohan, Charles Dillingham, and Flo Ziegfeld. He directed eleven of Victor Herbert's operettas and thirteen of nineteen productions of the Ziegfeld Follies. Mitchell shunned publicity, perhaps because he was partially deaf, a condition that gradually increased as he got older.

At the time of their marriage, both were in the ascendancy of their careers. At eighteen, Bessie was engaged to appear in Charles Hoyt's new production, "A Black Sheep." The show opened at Hoyt's Theater January 6, 1896, and played to full houses for the remainder of the season. Bessie's attractive legs and lively dances were "much admired." At the close of the show, Bessie was signed by a vaudeville company to be their lead dancer. By this time, she was earning $250 a week, a good salary for a solo dancer.

At the beginning of the third year of Weber & Fields' Music Hall, Fields was seeking professionals to write the cast's material and stage the production. Mitchell was hired to put together a chorus, its sets and costumes. Bessie was hired to dance in between acts. The Weberfields show was "Helter Skelter," which opened at their Music Hall on April 6, 1899. It was a hit, presenting satires of straight plays. Mitchell's chorus showed their training and discipline. One reviewer called Bessie's dancing "a terrifying miracle of litheness and agility." Mitchell and Bessie contributed so much to the success of the show that Weber & Fields held them for several years.

Bessie Clayton

Weber & Fields' next show, "Whirl-I-Gig," opened September 21, 1899, and ran at the Music Hall to full houses for thirty-three weeks. Bessie's contribution was to dance between acts, an astounding blend of ballet and acrobatics in "La Dance D'Afrique."

On September 6, 1900, "Fiddle-Dee-Dee" began the Weberfields new season. The show ran for thirty-two weeks. Bessie again entertained with her energetic dancing between acts. In fact, her dancing seemed to belie any form of intermission. In December, she was released to appear in a new musical, "Miss Prinnt," which opened at the Victoria Theater on the 25th. Besides Bessie, the show starred Marie Dressler and Jobyna Howland. However, their combined abilities were unable to prevent the show from closing after one month. By February, Bessie was back with Weber & Fields. Although pregnant, she danced to the end of the season. A daughter, Priscilla, was born August 6, 1901.

"Hoity-Toity," the next Weberfields show, opened September 5, 1901. It was again made up of satires on dramatic shows performed by a stock company of mostly professional comedians that included De Wolf Hopper, Sam Bernard, Lillian Russell, Fay Templeton, Fritz Williams, John T. Kelly and Bessie. The show ran for thirty-three weeks in New York and toured for three more weeks. This time, Bessie had a speaking part to go along with her dancing.

In 1902, Mitchell was hired away by Victor Herbert for his "Babes in Toyland" production. Bessie temporarily retired to care for her daughter. Although the team of Weber and Fields began to dissolve, they played together for two more years. Fields, however, had not forgotten Bessie.

When Fields (alone) put together a new show, with the help of Fred Hamlin (for funding) and Oscar Hammerstein (for the theater), he sought out Mitchell to be stage director and Bessie to play a role. "It Happened in Nordland" opened at the Lew Fields Theater on December 5, 1904, and was an immediate hit. It was one of the first musicals to integrate music and dancing with the plot. This show, and Cohan's "Little Johnny Jones," which had opened a month earlier, ushered in a new era in the development of musical comedy.

Bessie returned to the musical stage in "The Belle of Mayfair," which opened at Daly's Theater on December 3, 1906. The show had a good cast, made up of Irene Bentley, Christie McDonald, Valeska Suratt and Bessie. It ran for four months to good box office receipts. As usual, Bessie's dancing was a feature of the show, according to reviewers.

Joe Weber's new musical, which opened on October 10, 1907, at the refurbished Music Hall, tried to emulate the old Weberfields satires with minimal success. Called "Hip! Hip! Hooray!" it starred Weber, Dick Bernard, Valeska Suratt and Bessie. As Gerald Bordman chronicled, "Miss Clayton's sprightly, high-kicking dancing allowed her to display her still famous, still beautiful legs." But the show ran for only sixty-four performances.

Weber's next musical was an attempt to cash in on the "Merry Widow" craze. "The Merry Widow Burlesque" opened on January 2, 1908, at his theater. Using Lehar's music, with the composer's permission, he engaged several of the Weberfields old stars: Charles J. Ross, Peter F. Dailey, Mabel Fenton and Bessie, plus headliners like Lulu Glaser and, later, Blanche Ring. Bessie performed her familiar dances. The show lasted the remainder of the season.

After several years of appearing in musical comedy, Bessie decided to return to vaudeville. Vaudeville freed up her scheduling and she earned more for less work. For the next three years, she starred on both the Keith and Orpheum circuits, touring the country. On the negative side, spending weeks away from home put a strain on the marriage, a situation heightened when press gossips suggested that Mitchell was seeing women from his chorus. In June 1910, Bessie filed for divorce from Mitchell. They separated, with Bessie's parents taking care of Priscilla while Bessie was touring. However, the divorce was not finalized. The following year, Bessie went to England to perform at various vaudeville houses.

In the fall of 1911, Weber and Fields reconciled. And what better way to show admirers their friendship than to create a show featuring their old skits? Gathering together many of the former stock company members (Lillian Russell, Fay Templeton, William Collier, John T. Kelly and Bessie), the "Weber & Fields 1912 Jubilee" opened at the Broadway Theater February 15. They played to full houses for fourteen weeks in New York and then toured thirty-three cities in one month. The box office receipts of $405,000 were the largest ever achieved for a musical. Bessie did several of the numbers she had performed at the old Music Hall. In the spirit of the event, Bessie and Julian reconciled.

In late 1912, Weber and Fields put together another of their familiar shows, full of satire and comedy. Called "Roly-Poly," the show opened November 12 and ran for eight weeks. It starred Bessie, Marie Dressler, Frank Daniels, Joe and Lew. Crowded houses were the norm.

In 1914, the Weber and Fields All Star Company, featuring many of the same stars, plus Nora Bayes, went on tour but it lasted only three weeks. Bessie was in the cast, but was disappointed when poor theater attendance caused the show to close prematurely. Bessie now had had enough of these revues, and she returned to vaudeville. She never again played in musical comedy.

Bessie appeared at the Palace Theater in 1913, six weeks after the theater opened, and was part of a bill that ultimately made the Palace a renowned venue. Appearing with Bessie were Nat Wills and Ethel Barrymore. In 1915, she headed a bill that included Blanche Walsh and Doyle & Dixon. Bessie was advertised as "The Darling of Terpsichore — America's Premiere Danseuse."

From 1915 to her retirement in 1924, Bessie appeared primarily in vaudeville, with brief stints in concerts and opera, dancing between acts. Touring for the Orpheum and Keith circuits, she continued to be a headliner. No other dancer on the popular stage could outperform Bessie.

In 1923, Bessie filed for divorce, charging Mitchell with desertion. The divorce was granted in December. Bessie's mother died in 1925. Mitchell died of a stomach ailment in June 1926, at the age of seventy-two. Bessie's daughter, Priscilla, was married in July 1926 to Roger Pryor, an actor. At the ceremony, Bessie was accompanied by Bert Cooper, a former actor and current theatrical agent. Bessie retired to a home in Monmouth, New Jersey, a block away from her daughter and son-in-law. In Bessie's divorce agreement with Mitchell, both houses went to Priscilla.

Sometime after 1930, Bessie married Bert Cooper. He died in December 1945, at the age of sixty-three. Bessie died July 16, 1948, at her home in Monmouth. She was seventy years old.

Bessie Clayton made dancing a popular entertainment for vaudeville and musical comedy audiences. Her brand of dancing elevated her to stardom, making her a long-time favorite and headliner.

Ruth St. Denis

Ruth E. Dennis was born on January 20, 1879, in Newark, New Jersey, one month after her parents had signed a marriage by contract, without clergy or license. Thomas L. Dennis, her father, had divorced his first wife in 1878 to marry Ruth Emma Hull.

Thomas L. Dennis was born in England in 1846 and immigrated to the United States prior to the Civil War. During the war, he was a member of the New Jersey cavalry. He began as a saloonkeeper and later became a machinist working at the Brooklyn Navy Yard. Ruth Emma Hull was born in New York in 1844, the youngest of thirteen children. She graduated from the University of Michigan with a medical degree. However, illness prevented her from pursuing medicine. She opened a boardinghouse that catered to a clientele of intellectuals. The couple had a son, called Brother, born in 1885, and Tom brought his son by previous marriage into the family as well.

As a child, Ruth already showed talent for athletics and dance. Mrs. Dennis promoted this talent by having her study social dancing. Excursions to circuses and theatrical extravaganzas, filled with colorful costumes and scenery, were also influential in forming Ruth's interests. Ruth was accepted by a New York dance teacher, but religious relatives forced her to attend the Dwight Moody Seminary for her schooling. Within a short time, Ruth had an argument with Moody regarding her interest in dance. Moody said that making a career on the stage was immoral; Ruth accused Moody of being a narrow-minded old bigot. Ruth returned home to study about health, beauty and religion with her mother, and about the

Delsarte theory of the relationship of motion and anatomy. While Ruth did not understand the theory or its implications for dance, she incorporated much of it into her later dance techniques. Shortly after returning home, Ruth and her parents appeared in a local production of "The Old Homestead." Her first review declared that "Ruthie Dennis was the star of the performance in her skirt dance." Ruth now yearned for a stage career.

In 1894, at the age of fifteen, Ruth appeared at Worth's Family Theater and Museum. Its upper floors contained oddities of nature, historical artifacts (most of them fake), and freaks. The lower floor was a small theater in which Ruth performed a skirt dance doing a collection of splits, jumps and acrobatics. She had to perform eleven times a day for eleven dollars a week. Response to her stage antics was favorable. She continued performing at other vaudeville houses, honing her skills as a dancer. An engagement at the Metropolitan Opera Club attracted the interest of Stanford White. Under her mother's protection, the relationship never matured. At this point, Mrs. Dennis took over Ruth's career, becoming manager, promoter and critic. When her parents separated, Ruth was her mother's sole means of support. There were few dance jobs open, so Ruth worked as a model in a department store, supplementing her income with the infrequent vaudeville appearances.

In 1898, Ruth auditioned for and obtained a role in the ballet chorus of "The Ballet Girl." She quickly learned the primary ballet steps to keep the job and, while performing, ended her bit with an extra flourish, like leaping in the air or falling to her knees and sliding on the floor. Her knees were damaged, so later in her career she covered them with long robes and concentrated on movement above the waist.

Vaudeville dancing at the turn of the century was just beginning to attract attention and to break out of the old staid posing routines. In 1899, Ruth got her chance to dance seriously when she was hired to appear in Augustin Daly's "The Runaway Girl." A year later, she was engaged for the touring company of a David Belasco play, an association that lasted for five years. During that time, she played in the Belasco productions of "Zaza" with Mrs. Leslie Carter, which went to London and was a big success. She had a small role as "Adele." Ruth was frustrated working for Belasco because he was more interested in her acting ability than her dancing. She also appeared in "Madame DuBarry" and "The Auctioneer," shows which taught her about stage lighting, costuming and set design, although she danced infrequently. Belasco decided to change her name to make it more stage-like. He dropped one "n" from her last name and added "Saint" to it, an alteration Ruth embraced. While abroad, Ruth visited Paris and was greatly influenced by the Oriental dancers, displays at the Paris exposition, Art Nouveau design, and the dances of Loie Fuller, already a European sensation. She read many books about Eastern thought and composed her own poetry. Her investigation led her to a study of Christian Science, a religion only twenty-five years old. She later joined the church but, while she readily accepted its mystical harmony of existence, she still used medicines when needed.

In 1904, while on a Belasco tour, she was attracted to a poster advertising Egyptian Deities cigarettes. She was so struck by the designs and colors that she envisioned a dance that incorporated the elements of mystical Egypt. At the end of the tour in San Francisco, she returned to New York and persuaded her mother to help her form a company to perform "Egypta." It was her first dance composition. Quickly, she found that the production would be too costly for her to produce so she abandoned it to a later date. To pay her bills, she was a chorus singer in "Woodland." She danced at social gatherings put on by the city's elite women's clubs, where she was viewed as "charming" and "novel."

Ruth now concentrated on creating Indian dances, reading everything she could about

India. She attempted to sell a dance routine called "Radha" to theater managers, but failed to get their interest. Only one manager, Henry B. Harris, liked the dance and let her appear at one of his matinees. The response to the act was so positive it persuaded him to give her a series of Sunday night concerts, which also proved successful. She then appeared at Proctor's Theater on a vaudeville bill, placed between a boxer and a monkey act. Proctor advertised Ruth as doing the entire dance in her bare feet.

In early 1906, the society ladies of New York sponsored a performance by Ruth in which she danced three of her own compositions, "The Incense," "The Cobras" and "Radha." She was a smashing success and the talk of the social elite. Harris, seeing an opportunity to profit by her innovative dancing, featured her in a series of matinees at his Hudson Theater. Reviews were positive, although the critics were conflicted on whether she was "sensual" or mystical. The debate enhanced her exposure to the theater-going public. She was invited to dance at a society get-together sponsored by Mrs. Jack Gardner, a rich Boston eccentric and suffragette. Ruth's performance caused major headlines in Boston newspapers. Reviewers could not explain her appeal but acknowledged that it was "great." The increasing interest in her innovative dancing techniques initiated a revitalization of dance in the United States.

Ruth St. Denis

In 1906, Harris booked Ruth to appear at matinees at the Aldwych Theater in London. She won critical praise but attracted only small audiences. A Parisian manager saw her and signed her to appear at his theater. Prior to her opening, an imposter using the name of Madame Radha caused the French backers to doubt their decision. However, Ruth's contract was honored and her performances became tremendously successful. Ruth was the toast of Paris and her season ended triumphantly. She was billed as the daughter of an Indian aristocrat and a French officer. Mrs. Dennis accompanied her daughter in London and Paris, to keep interested males away, she said. Ruth's brother helped develop scenic effects. Ruth was immediately signed for a winter tour of Europe at $1,000 a week.

Her first stop was Berlin, where she filled the theater with enthusiastic patrons. The police were called to investigate her act because she wore a costume that bared her legs and midriff. But after they saw her show, they deemed it "mysterious" and not at all sexual. The publicity carried through to all of her future engagements. On the tour, she played in Vienna, Budapest, Brussels, Monte Carlo, and Paris. Interestingly, she had to appear at vaudeville houses or at intermissions at operas because no one could categorize her kind of dancing. She introduced two new dances with a strong Indian motif, "Nautch" and "The Yogi." Much to the dismay of her backup dancers, Ruth often changed costumes and dance steps, improvising on the original dance because she had tired of their formula. The overwhelming success of her European tour made Ruth even more attractive to American audiences.

She returned to the United States in late 1909, now a major stage star. Hudson Theater matinees reintroduced her to New York's social elite. Special evening performances were sold out weeks in advance. She then took a tour of Eastern and Midwestern cities, jamming theaters. Pictures of her in dance costumes were printed in newspapers, and reports of her dances made her act even more provocative. The tour ran through early 1910.

With the money she had earned — Ruth was now getting $2,000 a week — she decided to produce "Egypta," with elaborate sets, lavish costumes, scenic and lighting effects (thanks to Brother) and specially written music. While New Amsterdam Theater audiences thrilled to see her perform these exotic dances, the costs of the show ran far greater than the box office. Still, she continued to present the production on tour, cutting down on the sets and varying the dances for a less sophisticated public. The tour went to Boston, with no complaints about her costume this time, Chicago, Midwestern cities and to the Pacific, many people seeing her for the first time. In Denver March 1911, sitting in the audience was a twenty-year-old dancer, Ted Shawn (Edwin Myers), who fell in love with her work, its meaning and its performer.

Ruth's stage engagements were briefly interrupted when Henry Harris died on the *Titanic* just as she was producing a new dance drama, featuring a Japanese motif. She opened the show on March 11, 1913, to tremendous audience approval but poor box office. Vaudeville remained her bread-and-butter and she returned to that form of entertainment featuring a variety of dances from her repertoire. One-stop performances at concerts and society appearances supplemented her income. The result of this tour permitted her to buy a five-story apartment in Manhattan where she, her mother and Brother could live.

In 1914, about ready to begin a Southern tour, Ruth held auditions for male dancers. Ted Shawn was the last to be seen and so attracted Ruth that she invited him to dinner, during which time they talked continually of dance. The next day, Shawn was hired for the company. As they danced together, they fell in love. For Ruth, it was the first time that she felt sensually aware of her own feelings. Mrs. Dennis tried hard to intervene, attempting to save her daughter's career, she said. She failed, and the couple was married on August 13, 1914. They continued the tour, and finally settled in Los Angeles, without Ruth's mother.

Ruth and Ted opened a school: The Ruth St. Denis School of the Dance and Its Related Arts, or Denishawn, for short, which opened in 1915 with much press fanfare. Shawn organized the school operations and taught classes. Ruth gave demonstrations and philosophical monologues. Martha Graham was a student in 1916, and Doris Humphrey in 1917. During the winter months, the entire troupe toured the vaudeville circuit, making enough money to keep the school in operation. Special performances at the Greek Theater and at the University of California, Berkeley, gained them press coverage that promoted the school as well as the dancing itself. In these special engagements, Ruth used all the students in the school.

World War I forced the school to cut back its activities. Shawn evaded the armed forces until 1918 because he wanted to preserve the school's operations. While Shawn was in the army, Ruth retired from vaudeville to concentrate on her own artistic goals. She had believed that they had been put aside to run the school and perform frequently enough to pay the bills. She formed a small company of the best dancers. Using the music of classical composers, she choreographed new dances characterized by wafting silk scarves and lyrical movement, a repertory of "music visualizations." The costume design for these presentations consisted of a chiffon shift worn over flesh-tone leotards, bare feet and a curly blond wig. There were frequent visits by the police but no show was ever stopped.

Shawn returned to Ruth after the war. He wished to revive Denishawn; Ruth wished to continue her own career. Their marriage was in trouble but, professionally, they needed each other to earn a living. Reluctantly, Ruth went back to Denishawn even though she yearned to be a concert dancer rather than appear on the vaudeville stage. The school's best years were between 1922 and 1925 where the company brought dance to cities and towns across the country. Their act consisted of Shawn's ballets, suites with ethnic and American themes, and Ruth's mystical Oriental works. Dance in America had reached new heights with the popularity of the Castles, large dance bands, cabaret and nightclub shows, and the movies. Dance styles were changing, as the general public participated in this new and exciting entertainment.

In the summer of 1925, the company traveled to Japan and then toured for more than a year through Asian countries, including India. Ruth gathered material to turn into new dance dramas. The tour also created a difficult situation between Ruth and Ted, with arguments all day but sublime performances together in the evening. When they returned to New York, they began construction of Denishawn House, later home of hundreds of students. To make money for the school, Ruth and Ted joined the Ziegfeld Follies for one season. The school survived for five years. The Depression and the demise of vaudeville forced the school to close and ended Ruth and Ted's relationship. They separated but never divorced. In later years, Shawn often called on Ruth to perform on specific occasions or for students at his school.

Ruth and Ted appeared in a movie in 1923, "Look Your Best," the only one in which pictures of the couple dancing together survive. In 1931, she appeared in another picture, "The Cheat," in which she had a minor role but performed one dance.

In the early thirties, Ruth found herself out of work, with overdue bills and a broken marriage. The school was sold for outstanding debts. Shawn went on to form the Jacob's Pillow Dance Festival. Ruth applied for welfare benefits and moved into a small apartment. The thirties were a difficult time for Ruth. She made a living by performing at churches. The Chinese poet Sum Nung Au-Young became an important influence on Ruth. As a mentor, he encouraged her to write and choreograph. They became lovers. In 1938, Ruth got work as director of dance at Adelphi College, an association that continued to the 1960s. In 1939, Ruth published her autobiography, which transformed her public persona. She was now regarded as the mother of American modern dance and was again in demand as a performer. As the "First Lady of American Dance," Ruth prolonged her career for another two decades.

She moved to Hollywood at the beginning of World War II to be near Brother. She opened her own dancing school and occasionally performed. In 1945, after fifteen years, Ruth traveled back to New York for her first joint concert with Ted. Edward Denby, a reviewer, described the performance of the sixty-six-year-old Ruth as still possessing "a wonderfully touching mildness and a striking clarity of movement."

During the 1950s and 1960s, Ruth went back for appearances at Jacob's Pillow. In 1964, she and Shawn celebrated their golden wedding anniversary with a nostalgic dance program. In May 1966, at the age of eighty-seven, Ruth performed the dance "The Incense" at Orange Coast College in Costa Mesa, California. It was her last dance appearance in public. Shortly afterward, she injured herself in a bad fall but returned to give a lecture and dance demonstration at UCLA. Ruth died July 21, 1968, of a heart attack. She was eighty-nine. On her tombstone are lines of one of Ruth's poems: "The Gods have meant/That I should dance? And by the Gods/ I will!" The final line of the poem, somehow omitted from the tombstone, read: "For that is why I dance."

Bessie McCoy

Born Elizabeth Genevieve McAvoy, Bessie McCoy came from five generations of entertainers. She was born "on the road" in 1888. Her maternal grandfather, John Lee, was an English circus manager who came to the United States to bring his brand of circuses to American audiences. Long jumps and the cost of hauling forced him into bankruptcy. Bessie's paternal grandfather, Lawrence McAvoy, was a traveling circus manager in England's provinces. In the United States, he continued to manage circus companies. Bessie's paternal grandmother was a Shakespearean reader.

The song-and-dance team of McCoy and McAvoy was well-known in the circus and on the variety stage. Bessie (called Lizzie in her teens) and her sister Nellie were taught to dance and sing by their father. The children accompanied their parents wherever they played, literally living out of a trunk during their childhood.

McCoy and McAvoy not only played in variety but they also pioneered boat shows on the Mississippi River, traveling from Cairo, Illinois, to Natchez. The girls played small roles in the shows presented. At the age of nine, Bessie and her eleven-year-old sister entered vaudeville.

The act consisted of two women (dressed in bonnets and shawls carrying market baskets) engaging in neighborhood gossip. The girls were demure, polite and charming and executed their routine with the precision of adults. The dialogue led into a music cue and a song about shopping and cooking for the family. The girls made a hit, impressing audiences with their professionalism. They played for five years in vaudeville, mostly touring with their parents.

In 1902, when Bessie was fourteen and Nellie sixteen, the sisters appeared in a farce-comedy, "The Liberty Belles." The tour began in Washington, D.C., and visited Eastern cities. The plot centered on schoolgirls (including Nellie and Bessie) living in a dormitory. Following the tour, the sisters returned to vaudeville, this time without their parents. Their act included dressing as clowns, singing and dancing as they would in a circus.

In May 1905, the sisters played in a skit, "A Yankee Circus on Mars," as part of a larger extravaganza at the Hippodrome Theater. Bessie had suffered from nervousness caused by appearing in the high-class revue, but after two weeks she rejoined the company. *The New York Times* noted her absence and mentioned her return. She was "warmly greeted." Later in the run, Nellie was hospitalized with a nervous breakdown and sent to a sanitarium. Bessie was on her own.

The following year, Bessie was engaged to appear in "The Spring Chicken," a Richard Carle musical. The show opened October 8, 1906, at Daly's Theater. Bessie performed several dances and was a part of the chorus. The show ran for 115 performances. On the basis of her dancing, Bessie was hired to play in a show that would catapult her to stardom.

The Shuberts produced "The Three Twins" which opened June 15, 1908, at the Herald Square Theater. Bessie played a featured role, with several songs written by Otto Hauerbach (later Harbach) and Karl Hoschna. She introduced "The Yamma Yamma Man" dressed as a clown with a cone-shaped hat. It was the hit song of the show and became a signature tune throughout Bessie's career. The show played for 288 performances (36 weeks) even though a fire at the Herald Square forced the company to move and reopen on the road before returning to another venue in New York. In the audience was a reviewer who fell in love with Bessie and her performance. He was Richard Harding Davis, writer, theater critic, adventurer and war correspondent. He wrote a review of the show that generously complimented Bessie and predicted her future success.

Prior to obtaining the "Three Twins" engagement, Bessie and Nellie teamed for a short while. They separated again when Nellie got a job with Lillian Russell. Bessie found employment in the chorus of Fritzi Scheff's operas. The sisters never appeared together again.

In August 1910, Bessie starred in "The Echo," a musical written by Deems Taylor, a young author. She performed a French fandango and a hobble skirt dance, and led the pony chorus in a military routine. According to the *Times,* "it was pretty enough to please and was heartily encored." The show ran until October. Bessie had health problems and spent a few months resting.

Flo Ziegfeld took advantage of Bessie's availability and hired her to appear in the "Follies of 1911." The best-staged Follies to date, it starred Bert Williams, Fanny Brice, Lillian Lorraine, Vera Maxwell, Leon Errol, the Dolly Sisters and Bessie. The production was staged by Ned Wayburn and featured seventy-five beautiful chorus girls. Bessie appeared in two acts and reprised "The Yamma Yamma Man," to the audience's delight. The show played through the summer and went on tour. Throughout this entire run, Bessie was being shadowed by Davis.

At the time, Davis was married but he made no effort to hide his interest in Bessie. He obtained a divorce from his wife, Cecile Clark, daughter of a wealthy Chicago manufacturer, on June 18, 1912. Davis then announced that his marriage to Bessie would take place on July 8 at his Mount Kisco home. Shortly after their marriage, Bessie announced her retirement. Although she was tempted by many offers to return to the stage, she refused, explaining that she was enjoying life on the farm. The couple had a daughter, Hope, in 1913.

That same year, Bessie appeared in her only motion picture, "Popular Players of the Stage," a series by Kinemacolor that included other celebrities like Lillian Russell, Anna Held, Eddie Foy and Weber & Fields.

In late 1915 and early 1916, Davis was a war correspondent covering the war in Belgium. He was forced to return to the United States suffering from angina. On April 11, 1916, Bessie found him dead in the library of their home. He was cremated and buried in the family plot in Levering Cemetery. Bessie did not attend, remaining at home with her daughter. A few months later, she decided to reenter the stage. After five years, critics wondered if she had retained her skills.

Bessie was to costar in the Dillingham and Ziegfeld revue, "Miss 1917." The production featured music by Victor Herbert and Jerome Kern, skits by P.G. Wodehouse, staging by Ned Wayburn and sets by Joseph Urban. Besides Bessie, headliners included Lew Fields, Van and Schenck, Irene Castle, Bert Savoy and Vivienne Segal. With such forces, reported reviewers, the show had to be a success.

"Miss 1917" opened on November 5 at the Century Theater. Initial reviews were excellent. The show had something for everybody — new songs, familiar songs, new routines and old ones that were headliners' specialties. Bessie sang "We Want to Laugh," about modern audiences who "were tired of those strutting leading men/and posing juveniles." The *New York Times* reviewer wrote: "The triumph of 'Miss 1917' was not a matter of doubt from the first scene to the last."

The show closed six weeks later, on January 4, 1918. Since the American entry into the war, theater attendance had dropped off sharply. By December, the show's backers decided it was a losing proposition. The performers were the greatest losers, getting little of the salaries owed them. Bessie decided to retire again.

But the persuasive Ziegfeld got Bessie to appear in "The Nine O'Clock Revue," which also featured Follies favorites Fanny Brice and Lillian Lorraine. The show opened December 9, 1918, but lasted only a few weeks. The war had recently ended but box office receipts had not yet rebounded. Reviewers called her "the old Bessie, a dancer as original and unapproached as Fred Stone." However, Bessie was not convinced that she enjoyed performing as much as before.

Nevertheless, Bessie agreed to appear in John Murray Anderson's first production of "Greenwich Village Follies." It opened on July 15, 1919, at the Greenwich Village Theater. Bessie was considered the star of the show, which received good reviews, enthusiastic audiences and excellent box office receipts. Bessie danced several times, in all-new numbers. First, she appeared as a pansy Jewel, a cabaret type. Next, with strings hanging from the ceiling, Bessie danced like an automated marionette. Finally, she danced elegantly in a skit on Prohibition, "I'm the Hostess of a Bum Cabaret." The show played the entire summer and it appeared that Bessie had renewed her star status.

Morris Gest then had Bessie star in his revue, "Midnight Whirl," opening the end of December 1919 on the Century Roof. The show featured Gershwin music, Bernard Granville comedy and Bessie's dancing.

Bessie McCoy

Bessie repeated her success in the "Greenwich Village Follies of 1920," which opened August 30. The show also starred Bert Savoy and Phil Baker. So popular was the show that it ran for twenty-four weeks and then went on tour. At the close of the run, an exhausted Bessie announced her retirement once again.

In 1921, Bessie last appeared on the stage in a vaudeville act called "Castles in the Air." Her daughter had been sent to France for her education. Bessie followed her and set up a home in Bayonne, where she lived quite comfortably. She had inherited more than $28,000 at her husband's death. Later, Bessie received an additional $136,000 because motion picture companies had purchased many of Davis's stories.

Bessie died of a heart attack on August 16, 1931, in Bayonne, France. She was forty-three years old. Her daughter set up funeral services in Paris. The body was shipped back to the United States and buried in the family plot. Bessie's entire estate was willed to her daughter.

"The Yamma Yamma Girl," as she was affectionately known, had enjoyed a spectacular career as a popular and esteemed dancer in both vaudeville and musical comedy. Reviewers claimed that Bessie's dancing gave each show its alluring and charming moments.

Gertrude Hoffman

From chorus girl to Salome interpreter to choreographer of her own dance troupe, Gertrude Hoffman was an acclaimed dance performer on the vaudeville stage. Hoffman's comic mimickry of other headliners and a unique dancing technique soon made her a popular headliner. Through her dance interpretations, she gained a reputation as one of the "new women" of American popular theater.

Gertrude "Kitty" Hayes was born in San Francisco, California, on May 7, 1885. Little is known of her father, John Hayes, except that he was born in Maine and came to California to open a trades business. Her mother, Catherine Brogan Hayes, was born in Ireland in 1847 and immigrated to San Francisco in 1862, at a time when the Irish dominated both the social and political life of the city. The Hayes family had five children, two boys and three girls. Gertrude was the last child born. When she was eleven years old, her parents divorced.

With her mother's encouragement, Gertrude took dancing lessons. When she was fourteen, again with her mother's support, Gertrude frequently auditioned for local theatrical companies. At the time, a local company managed by Fred Belasco was seeking chorus members. Kitty Hayes, as Gertrude was calling herself, was hired for the chorus and paid twelve dollars a week. She made her vaudeville debut in 1899 at San Francisco's Alcazar Theater. Shortly afterward, Kitty was hired to appear with an operetta company, the Southwell troupe, to sing and dance in their chorus. The manager of the company quickly discovered that Kitty did not have a good voice, and she was fired.

When the vaudeville comedy team of Matthews and Bulger visited San Francisco, they needed dancers to fill their chorus line. Kitty was engaged for her dancing and she toured with the company as it traveled East. In St. Paul, Minnesota, sixteen-year-old Kitty met Max Hoffman, a musical director who had just been signed to conduct the company's orchestra.

Max Hoffman was born in Poland in 1872 and came to the United States at the age of seven. He obtained his musical education in New York and held various jobs in orchestras that toured with vaudeville companies. His job with Matthews and Bulger was his first as a musical conductor. Thirteen years older than Kitty, Max was attracted to this pretty girl whose dancing already encouraged audiences to shout for encores. After several months on the road together, they decided to marry. On April 8, 1901, they were married in Norfolk, Virginia, while appearing at a local theater. They remained married throughout their lives. Gertrude attributed this marital longevity to the fact that they played together during their career, with no separation at any time. Max, Jr., was born on January 1, 1902, in New York. Kitty dropped out of performing for a year to take care of her baby.

For several years, Gertrude — no longer Kitty — Hoffman appeared with various vaudeville companies with some degree of success but little reviewer recognition. During this time she was perfecting her dance routines, picking up ideas from the reigning queens of dance on the American stage, Loie Fuller and Ruth St. Denis. They were the new "modern" dancers and of the "new women" being promoted in popular theater. Gertrude added a bit of her own performing style by mimicking her mentors and other dance headliners like Eva Tanguay, Eddie Foy, George M. Cohan, Anna Held and Nora Bayes. Gertrude was now earning $150 a week, a good salary for a vaudeville entertainer. She also added excitement to her act by wearing more revealing costumes. During this time, Max was musical director for all of Gertrude's engagements and Max, Jr., was carried wherever his parents played.

In the fall of 1906, Gertrude was engaged to appear in an Anna Held-Flo Ziegfeld production, "A Parisian Model." The musical opened on November 27 at the Broadway Theater. Surrounding Held, in typical Ziegfeld fashion, was a large chorus of beautiful girls in gorgeous costumes, dancing to Julian Mitchell's intricate routines. Gertrude led sixteen chorus girls in an exuberant number that featured them lying on a revolving stage kicking their legs in the air and ringing bells tied to their ankles. In another number, Gertrude and Anna danced together. For the first time, Gertrude was singled out for her dancing talents. Max Hoffman had written the score for the show.

The next year, Gertrude and Max returned to vaudeville on the Keith circuit, touring the country. She had not yet reached headliner status, but the nature of her dance routines and her costumes created concern among the Keith management, who had strict rules about appropriate behavior on the stage. On several occasions, local censors complained about Gertrude's "creative" dancing and body-revealing costumes. What bothered them most was her dancing bare-footed.

Between 1907 and 1910, a Salome craze occupied theatergoers, thanks to the stage presentations of Sarah Bernhardt and, in England, the music hall antics of Maud Allen. In the United States, the Salome fad became an important vehicle in vaudeville for women to showcase their female sexuality and independence. Taking advantage of the latest rage, Oscar Hammerstein engaged Gertrude to perform a Salome dance act for his Roof Garden revue. In May 1908, Hammerstein paid for Gertrude to go to London to study Maud Allen and then devise her own version, in as obviously sexual a display as the local censors would allow.

On July 4, 1908, Gertrude opened with "Visions of Salome" at Hammerstein's Roof Garden. Hammerstein had made sure that her appearance was highly publicized and the titillating nature of the act amply displayed. Reviewers spoke of Gertrude's "wild abandon" and her beauty and grace. They were particularly taken with the conclusion of her act, when she

Gertrude Hoffman

writhed to the front of the stage and kissed the decapitated head of John the Baptist. Reviewers also wrote about her brief costume; "the effect is as if she were bare," one critic reported. Gertrude's erotic presentation filled the theater for her entire engagement and quickly made her a desirable and desired headliner.

There was no question that Gertrude enjoyed the performance and the use of coy humor came through strongly with audiences. Hammerstein then signed her to perform the act on a cross-country tour. This proved quite profitable for him at a time when he needed all the money he could obtain to remain solvent. When Gertrude returned to New York for the 1909–10 season, Hammerstein featured her at his Victoria Theater for a record-breaking twenty-two weeks. She received $1,500 a week. When she and Max left for a European vacation in May 1910, she was already committed to appearing on the Keith and Proctor vaudeville circuit.

While attending the theater in Paris, Gertrude became fascinated with the dance productions in such shows as "Cleopatra" and "Scheherazade." She incorporated elements of the dancing techniques into her own act, and explored the possibility of putting together a ballet chorus made up of Russian dancers. When she returned to the United States, Gertrude performed in vaudeville in a program featuring Russian dancers, with great success. She not only managed the troupe but was choreographer and teacher as well. In October 1911, Gertrude brought her company to open at the new Cort Theater, which had replaced the old Alcazar Theater in San Francisco. She was reported to be earning $3,500, but that included the salaries of her company, costumes, travel and housing expenses. Her return to her city of origin as a star made the engagement all the more successful.

Her tour was interrupted in the fall of 1912 when Gertrude was hired by the Shuberts to appear in their all-star revue, "Broadway to Paris." The Shuberts attempted to build the entire show around Gertrude's expressive and erotic dancing and succeeded by virtue of her brief costumes and wiggling torso. The show ran for ten weeks and made Gertrude one of the top entertainers of the day.

For the next few years, Gertrude and her company toured on the vaudeville circuits, to great success. Near the close of 1915, she appeared at the Palace Theater, New York, without her dancers. She was billed as an interpretive dancer, and she did not fail to excite the theater audiences. She received mixed reviews because of her erotic act and revealing costumes. At one point in her act, she retreated to the back of the stage and shed one costume for another, all in the audience's view.

The years 1915 and 1916 heralded in a strong movement by various religious spokespeople and organizations to "clean up" theater, particularly vaudeville. Gertrude and her company were on the list of offenders. New York's "obscenity police" were particularly concerned about Gertrude's latest costume — a gauzy shirt, two cups covering her breasts and a transparent black skirt. After more than 400 performances of Salome and other provocative dances, Gertrude was arrested. She was held on $500 bail, and required to appear at the West Side Police Court to answer the charges against her. She complained that she had been harassed and humiliated by a captain and his lieutenant. "He saw my act from the back of the stage, and as I was going to my dressing room the captain stopped me and said: 'Excuse me, Miss Hoffman, but do you wear tights in your act?'

"Certainly I do,' I replied.

"He then asked me to show them to him and I refused. Then I was arrested."

Her bail was paid and the case dropped when the judge was informed that Gertrude had performed the act in New York for several years with no problems. Still, when her company was on tour, a few cities they visited forbade their performance, claiming the show was obscene.

During the early 1920s, Gertrude and Max continued to appear in vaudeville, taking advantage of the public's increased interest in dancing. Gertrude had formed another dance troupe, called the Gertrude Hoffman Girls, that put on a variety of acts, ranging from Oriental-style to contemporary. Gertrude herself continued to lead the company while Max remained as musical director. In 1926, the Gertrude Hoffman Girls appeared in another Shubert revue, "A Night in Paris," which opened at the Casino de Paris on January 6. As usual, the Shuberts used lower-paid performers or those beginning their careers. Gertrude and the company were dressed as African savages, flowers and gold and silver coins. The show ran for more than five months.

Shortly afterward, Gertrude retired from active participation on the stage. She opened a dance studio in New York and became its chief choreographer. She emphasized the teaching of precision lines, discipline and visual geometry. She supplied groups of Gertrude Hoffman Girls to vaudeville and musical comedies, both on Broadway and Europe.

From 1933 to 1940, Gertrude appeared in thirteen movies, mostly in minor character roles. Several of them, like "Les Miserables" and "Foreign Correspondent," were top films. In none of them did she have a dancing role.

In 1933, Max, Jr., married Helen Kane, the boop-boop-a-doop actress. Their marriage lasted only a few years before she obtained a divorce. In 1945, at the age of forty-three, Max, Jr., unexpectedly died. It was reported that he had died of natural causes, but his devastated parents claimed otherwise. In 1950, Gertrude and Max moved to California. Max, Sr., died in May 1963, at the age of ninety-four. He was buried in Hollywood, California.

During the last fifteen years of her life, Gertrude was retired. She died of a heart attack on October 21, 1966. She was eighty years old. Throughout the years of her greatest popularity, Gertrude had been described as the premier of vaudeville dancers.

Florence Walton

"If the queen asks for a tango," warned the Grand Duchess Anastasia, "be prepared to dance it." When the queen did request the dance, Florence Walton and her dancing partner, Maurice Mouvet, performed it and sixteen others to the queen's satisfaction. The royal performance represented another milestone in Florence's long career as one of the country's most celebrated dancers. She began her dance career in vaudeville, matured to musical theater and, in partnership with talented men, became a headliner in every venue in which she performed.

The Walton family dated back to Revolutionary times, and lived in Wilmington, Delaware, for generations. Alfred Curtis Walton, Florence's father, was born in 1856. He was a master carriage trimmer and later owned an upholstery shop. Mary Maloney, her mother, was also born in Wilmington, where her parents had settled after coming from Ireland due to the potato famine. The couple married in 1881. Mary had ten children, five of whom died at birth or shortly after. Florence was the first living child, born August 31, 1883. She had four siblings, two girls and two boys, born between 1887 and 1898.

Florence graduated from elementary school and attended a parochial high school, graduating at the age of sixteen. There she was introduced to dancing and expressed an interest in the theater. Her first stage appearance was in 1901 as a Quaker girl in a revival of "Miss Bob White" at the Chestnut Street Theater in Philadelphia. As a chorus girl, she earned twelve dollars a week. For the next several years, Florence played in melodramas and musicals in Philadelphia, developing her dancing skills. She entered local vaudeville, her act consisting of imitating the dances of celebrated performers. Florence then moved to New York with hopes of furthering her career.

Lew Fields had hired Julian Mitchell to stage his new musical, "The Girl Behind the Counter." Mitchell put together a chorus line that was considered "the fastest and slickest" in recent history. Florence was hired as a member of the chorus. It was an excellent learning experience for her, because Mitchell was a perfectionist and Fields believed in integrating his chorus into the show's action. The show opened on October 1, 1907, at Lew Fields' Herald Square Theater and ran for thirty-eight weeks in New York.

Florence's next chorus job came in "The Soul Kiss," a January 1908 Ziegfeld production that starred Adelaide Genee, advertised as "the world's greatest dancer." Florence had the opportunity to learn from Genee for sixteen weeks. She also attracted Ziegfeld's eye and was signed for his next show.

"Miss Innocence" opened at the New York Theater on November 30, 1908, and featured Anna Held. Ziegfeld's chorus featured beautiful girls in beautiful costumes. In this show, Florence did several character solos. The show ran for 176 performances. After it closed, Florence spent a year in vaudeville as part of a traveling company. She was beginning to get notices from reviewers.

In the fall of 1910, Florence was hired to appear in "The Bachelor Belles," another vehicle for the aging Adelaide Genee. This offered another opportunity for Florence to learn professional dancing from an expert. The show was mediocre and lasted only a month. A few months later, Florence appeared in "The Pink Lady," a Caryll-McLellen production that starred Hazel Dawn, Alice Dovey and William Elliot. The staging was directed by Julian Mitchell, with further lessons for Florence.

In early 1912, Florence met Maurice Mouvet when Ziegfeld suggested that she partner with him. Mouvet's partner, Joan Sawyer, had eloped with another actor after spurning Mouvet. The team had a dance number in Eddie Foy's show, "Over the River." Florence practiced with Mouvet; they seemed compatible, and that evening they performed in the play. It was the beginning of one of the stage's most elegant dancing partnerships.

Maurice Mouvet was born in March 1889. As a young man, he went to Paris and soon became one of the city's most accomplished popular dancers. American promoters persuaded him to dance in musicals. With a dance partner, his reputation quickly spread as a classy and innovative dancer. Having lost both a love and a dance partner made Mouvet disconsolate until he met Florence. She was not accustomed to ballroom dancing but Mouvet taught her well and she became a worthy successor to Sawyer. She also became his new amour.

Their first show dancing together was "The Rose Maid," which opened at the Globe Theater on April 22, 1912. Although the show was average, the comedy team of Gallagher and Shean and the dancing of Maurice and Walton, as they were billed, kept it alive for twenty-two weeks. Good reviews for the new dancing team were in abundance. They married while the show was running. "We are much in love," Mouvet told reporters. "And it is a good arrangement in other ways. No other man can marry her and obviously she will not act as the dancing partner of a rival of her husband."

The team scored a hit in both musicals and cabaret performances. The ballroom dancing craze made them Vernon and Irene Castle's primary competition. Maurice and Walton appeared at the Palace Theater in late 1913 and again in 1914, to full houses. In June of that year, they danced for the queen of England. In September, they were the headliners at William Morris's Jardin de Dance atop the New York Theater. In October, they opened a restaurant and ballroom.

The Shuberts engaged the team to enliven their revue, "Hands Up," which opened July 22, 1915, at the 44th Street Theater. Sigmund Romberg contributed the music to a vaudeville-like scenario. Will Rogers was featured, but the dancing of Maurice and Walton again stole the show.

In early 1916, Mouvet and Florence left for France, to play at the Casino de Paris and to entertain the troops. Mouvet unexpectedly enlisted in the French army and drove an ambulance. Florence danced for the military. They returned to the United States in July, played at cabarets in New York and left for Europe again in early 1917. Again, while Mouvet was driving an ambulance in Belgium, Florence was giving benefit dances. They returned at the end of the year to play at the Palace Theater. Unfortunately, these separations were taking a toll on their marriage. They went to Europe once more after the war and appeared in Paris, Zurich, Vienna, Berlin, Madrid, London and the fashionable resorts, to great acclaim. When they returned to the United States in May 1919, the press reported on their marital problems.

Florence filed for divorce in November 1919, an "unknown woman" listed as co-respondent. Yet they continued dancing together at the Biltmore Hotel while the press covered the court proceedings. In April 1920, the divorce was finalized and the famous dancing partnership was dissolved. Mouvet went to France; Florence looked for a new partner.

October 1920 found Florence and her new partner, Allan Fagan (Ina Claire's brother), performing at the Palace. In December, Florence purchased a five-story building on East 65th Street, said to cost $100,000. Fagan was now replaced by Leon Leitrim, a twenty-two-year-old from Georgia, Russia. They appeared on the vaudeville circuit for the next few years, including another Palace appearance in September 1923.

Florence and Leon Leitrim were married on December 14, 1922. The press observed that Florence's partners always ended up marrying her. They never mentioned that her partners were always younger than she was. Florence gave her age as thirty-one. She was actually thirty-nine. Leitrim claimed to be twenty-five.

Everything that involved Florence now appeared in the newspapers. While appearing at the 81st Street Theater, she and her husband were robbed of her jewelry as they returned home after a performance. Leitrim pursued the robbers, knocked one down and retrieved the jewelry. When asked by the police why she was carrying jewels of such value — estimated at $150,000 — Florence said that she wore them in her dancing act and considered them safer with her than at her apartment.

When the team was performing in Chicago, Florence was sued for $5,000 for injuring two people in an automobile accident. A few months later, Leitrim was arrested for driving while drunk. In January 1927, Florence announced that she and her husband were leaving for Paris, France, to live there permanently. She was also planning to retire from the theater. She was forty-three years old.

Maurice Mouvet died in June 1927, having suffered from tuberculosis for several years. The press reported that Florence wept when she heard the news. In February 1931, Florence obtained a divorce from Leitrim, claiming his drunkenness had made their marriage "impossible." She had become a modiste with a shop in Paris, and it proved to be a successful business. Leitrim was an automobile salesman. In 1933, he died from a kidney ailment.

Three months after Leitrim's death, the press noted, Florence and Pierre Colombier, a French motion picture director, were married at the city hall in Lardy, France. He was thirteen years younger than Florence. Royalty from both France and Spain attended the wedding.

In 1935, Florence returned to the United States to appear in summer stock in Maine. She rented a cottage with Libby Holman, Fritzi Scheff and Ethel Barrymore, all of whom were performing in summer plays. She decided to remain in the United States, separating from Colombier. They divorced in 1936. The following year, the press reported that Florence and Howard Phillips, a movie actor, were "making an attractive couple." They were married in the late 1930s. Phillips was sixteen years her junior.

Comfortably well off, Florence and her husband lived a quiet life in New York City. Any mention of her earlier career and personal life had disappeared from newspapers and gossip columns. On January 7, 1981, Florence died at the age of ninety-seven. Her last partner, Phillips, seems to have given the grand dame of dance some comfort, and he was by her side when she died.

Florence Walton (with Maurice Mouvet).

Gertrude Vanderbilt

Since she appeared in musical comedies and high-class vaudeville, one might believe that Gertrude Vanderbilt spent her stage career at the heights of popularity. She sang and danced well, headed bills and had the leading roles in plays. But her career was blemished by short-running productions, publicity-driven love affairs and temperamental outbursts. A Ziegfeld beauty who promoted her talents unabashedly, Gertrude never quite achieved the adoration and admiration she so ardently sought.

Gertrude's ancestors were said to be distantly related to the New York Vanderbilts of society fame. However, Gertrude's family was poor, living in the tenements of Brooklyn, New York. Census data confirms she was born in 1889, although some historians claim 1890. During her career, she changed her age and birth date often.

She was raised by a strict mother—no father seemed to be present—who forbade Gertrude to take voice and dancing lessons. In spite of the admonition, Gertrude taught herself to sing and dance. She often told of sneaking out to appear at amateur competitions at local vaudeville houses. When her mother discovered the indiscretion, Gertrude was spanked and sent to bed. At the age of thirteen, she ran away from home to become an actress.

As a teenager with unknown talent, Gertrude still obtained enough jobs in ten-cent vaudeville houses to live a subsistence life. She claimed she was older in order to get engagements. Her mature behavior and appearance helped to prove her claims. In 1905, Gertrude met Joseph Pincus, a booking agent. He assisted her in getting jobs. He also became her husband in 1906. Gertrude was sixteen, Pincus ten years older. For the next two years, Gertrude improved her artistry, helped by Pincus and by other performers who befriended her. Her beauty attracted men and theater managers. Pincus accused her of flirtations and the couple separated in 1908. Gertrude divorced him later that year.

The year 1908 was also when Gertrude made the jump to Broadway. She was hired to appear in the chorus of George M. Cohan's "The American Idea." The show opened on October 5 at the New York Theater. Reviewers panned Cohan for repeating his previous successes with a familiar plot and even more familiar tunes. At the same time, they lauded him for knowing what appealed to audiences. In the cast with Gertrude was Robert Dailey, a handsome young actor. The show played in New York for eight weeks and then went on the road. Gertrude and Robert had an excellent opportunity to get to know one another.

Gertrude's beauty and potential talent was recognized by Flo Ziegfeld as he was casting for the "Follies of 1909." She was hired for the chorus with an opportunity to dance several numbers. The show included Nora Bayes, Jack Norworth, Lillian Lorraine, Mae Murray, Henry Kelly and Sophie Tucker in her first role as a lead singer. Bayes and Ziegfeld fought, with Bayes, and Norworth, her husband, quitting the show shortly after it opened in New York. Ziegfeld brought in Eva Tanguay to replace Bayes. Tanguay had Tucker fired and took over songs from other performers. Gertrude danced well but frequently berated the orchestra for not following her beat. She remained in the cast until the show was ready to go on tour.

Gertrude's year had been tumultuous. On February 6, she had married Dailey. In June, she filed for divorce saying "it is impossible to continue living with Dailey on account of his uncontrollable temper and cruel treatment." Since Gertrude was not yet considered an adult — she said she was nineteen — the court appointed a guardian to prosecute her case. It was several years before the divorce became final. Her behavior while in the Follies cast and her dismissal did not help a situation that threatened her livelihood. Lew Fields came to her rescue.

Fields' new show, "The Jolly Bachelors," opened on January 6, 1910, at the Broadway Theater. An all-star cast included Nora Bayes, Jack Norworth, Stella Mayhew, Josie Sadler, John T. Kelly, Emma Carus and Gertrude in a featured singing and dancing role. A large chorus, led by Robert Dailey, was an attractive addition to the individual performances. Of course, Gertrude and Robert avoided one another. The show ran for twenty-two weeks and went on an extensive tour, but not with Gertrude. She was dropped from the cast, reasons unknown, two months after the show opened.

Another engagement came quickly. Gertrude was engaged as a featured dancer for "A Skylark." The show opened on April 4, 1910, at the New York Theater. The mediocre production did have a beautiful chorus, led by Gertrude, but closed after several weeks.

A few months later, Gertrude was hired for a Caryll and Monckton musical, "Our Miss Gibbs." The show opened on August 29, 1910, at the Knickerbocker Theater and lasted for two months. Gertrude played a shop girl and was given the chance to do several solo song-and-dance numbers. Reviewers said she did a good job in an average show. Once again, Gertrude was looking for another job.

The assignment came in December when "The Happiest Night of His Life," a musical by Junie McCree and Sydney Rosenfeld, began rehearsals. Gertrude was given a good speaking and dancing role, her first real opportunity to demonstrate her talent. Even with Victor Moore as the star, the show ran only three weeks.

Gertrude then teamed with Rosie Green to perform a dance duet in vaudeville. Just as the team was getting good reviews for their work, Gertrude broke up the act to join the cast of a new musical. "The Red Widow," starring Raymond Hitchcock, had played on the road before coming to New York. Gertrude was to appear in the New York cast. The show opened November 6,

Gertrude Vanderbilt

1911, at the Astor Theater. It was a satire on Russian aristocracy, well-handled by Hitchcock and his co-star, Sophie Bernard. Gertrude performed as number of dance numbers in gorgeous, exotic costumes. The show received good reviews and ran for 128 performances. Most important for Gertrude was a reconciliation with her mother, who was seeing her daughter on stage for the first time. Gertrude claimed that she and her mother were going to have a real home. "It's all over now, and we are going to be very happy," she declared to reporters. But census data indicates that they never lived together.

At about the same time, Gertrude filed a suit against Flo Ziegfeld for breach of contract. The suit charged Ziegfeld with canceling Gertrude's role in a proposed musical. After months of testimony, Gertrude won her case, or so it seemed. Ziegfeld had to pay her $1,265. For the next five years, Gertrude was not offered a role in another musical.

During this period, Gertrude teamed with George Moore, playing in a skit called "The Villain Still Pursued Her." The act was a dance parody of a melodrama and was well-received by reviewers and audiences. Equally often, Gertrude appeared in a solo act while touring in vaudeville.

In 1917, Gertrude was engaged to appear in a Sigmund Romberg–Shubert musical, "Maytime." The show featured one of Romberg's best librettos and was the season's hit. It opened at the Shubert Theater August 16 and was immediately hailed for its music and acting. Its stars included Charles Purcell and Peggy Wood. Gertrude had a small part. The success of the show was so pronounced that the Shuberts formed a second company and opened across the street from the original. Gertrude played the lead in the second company. Both companies went on profitable tours that extended into 1918.

Gertrude's work in "Maytime" got her the lead in "Listen Lester," which opened on December 23, 1918, at the Knickerbocker Theater. The show was originally scheduled to open in September, but a flu epidemic closed all New York theaters for almost two months. Nearly all the shows that had fall openings suffered from the closures and never produced to expectations. Gertrude had a speaking role, the singing taken by Ada Lewis and the dancing by Clifton Webb and Ada Mae Weeks. The show played through to early spring with reasonably good reviews for Gertrude.

Gertrude's next show had an equally inauspicious beginning. It was to open in September. Rehearsals had begun in August. But on August 7, Actors' Equity struck against management and closed down all shows and rehearsals. The show "Fifty-Fifty, Ltd." opened belatedly at the Comedy Theater on October 27, 1919. The plot told of a home rented to a variety of boarders, offering every performer a chance to do their specialties. Gertrude did a song-and-dance routine. The show lasted five weeks.

Lew Fields hired Gertrude to appear in his musical, "Poor Little Ritz Girl." During the tryouts, Gertrude began complaining that her role was smaller than she was promised. She quit the show a week before it opened in New York.

In 1922, while playing in vaudeville, Gertrude was selected to replace Ina Claire in Belasco's production of "The Gold Diggers." It was already an established hit, having been on tour for two years. Gertrude continued to carry the show for another year.

It was during this time that Gertrude met William J. Fallon, called "The Great Mouthpiece," one of the most colorful and resourceful New York lawyers of the era. Their relationship turned into a torrid love affair (Fallon was already married). It continued until 1924 when Fallon was indicted for the alleged bribery of a juror. At the trial, Gertrude was forced to testify. The relationship ended, and Fallon died in 1927. In 1929, Gertrude sued the Fallon estate for $25,000, the amount of money she claimed to have lent him. She lost the case. All the publicity tended to erode her stage career.

In 1925, Gertrude had a role in "Oh! Oh! Oh! Nurse," a musical that opened on December 7 at the Cosmopolitan Theater. Reviewers gave the show poor reviews and it closed after thirty-two performances.

Gertrude appeared at the Palace Theater in 1926. While the bill was not filled with old-timers, Gertrude's act was regarded as quite familiar by reviewers and she was upstaged by other performers on the program. She was only thirty-seven years old, but her continual stage and personal encounters made her seen older.

Gertrude retired from the stage in 1929. She attempted to enter the movies but received no offers. In the 1930s, she became a businesswoman and was quite successful in her new enterprise. As part of her work, she gave lectures on etiquette to women's clubs. During the 1950s, Gertrude was a fashion publicist. During this time, she occasionally appeared in summer stock.

On February 19, 1960, Gertrude died at the age of seventy. During her last years, she resided at the Delmonico Hotel on Park Avenue. She was president of the Ziegfeld Alumni Association and was active in work for the Yeshiva Farm Settlement and other charities. As reported in her obituaries, she gained more recognition for her activities in later life than for her stage career.

Adele Astaire

Dancing came early to Adele. While children, she and her younger brother Frederick became a successful dance team in vaudeville. Before she was twenty, Adele had led the duo to headliner status. For the remainder of her stage career, Adele and Frederick shared the limelight in a succession of vaudeville and musical comedy triumphs.

She was born Adele Marie Austerlitz on September 10, 1897, in Omaha, Nebraska. Frederic Austerlitz, her father, had come from Austria in 1895, where he had been in the brewery business. Ann Gelius, her mother, was from Alsace, France. They were married in 1896. Adele's brother, Frederick, was born on May 10, 1899, in Omaha.

At a young age, Adele showed a talent for dancing. Her ambitious mother enrolled her in the Chambers Dancing Academy when she was five years old. Her three-year-old brother accompanied her to the school. In 1904, their mother moved to New York with the children, hoping to further their dancing career. Upon arrival in New York, Adele and Frederick were enrolled in a dance school run by Ned Wayburn, a choreographer and dance director already known for his staging of several Broadway musicals. Wayburn was responsible for making the chorus line professional and elevating the training of chorus girls to a science. He was also the inventor of tap dancing. Adele and Frederick were taught with precision and dramatic effect. Those early years of training laid the foundation for the children's later successes.

In 1905, when Adele was eight, she and her brother made their debut in vaudeville in a small theater in New Jersey. Their mother decided it would be advantageous if the children changed their name to Astaire, taking their uncle's name of L'Astaire, and she had them billed as Fred and Adele Astaire. Mrs. Austerlitz was their educator, manager, chaperone and promoter. In their first act, they danced on top of a giant wedding cake.

The following year, the duo performed on the Keith vaudeville circuit, primarily in the Midwest and West. They were too young to appear on the New York stage.* On tour, the Astaire children did well with their act and began to receive recognition from reviewers. Their act was called "Juvenile artists presenting an electric musical toe dancing novelty."

In October 1908, *Variety* reported on the team when they appeared at the Hudson Theater, New York. The review described their "easy style" and their versatility performing various types of dancing. Fred even sang a song, although his voice was considered average. However, immediately following their appearance, the Gerry Society stepped in and ended their engagement. For the next several years, they toured on the Orpheum circuit, building both their dancing repertoire and their reputation as talented and innovative child performers.

By 1910, they had become featured performers on a vaudeville bill, with Adele considered the better of the two and gaining greater recognition. Their style of dancing had matured, and reviewers labeled them "class dancers," moving with grace and ease. Their dances were termed innovative and witty. For the next six years, Adele and Fred gradually built their vaudeville reputation with outstanding performances and excellent reviews. Mrs. Austerlitz was with them throughout the entire period.

---

*The Gerry Society, an evangelistic group devoted to preventing children under sixteen from appearing in New York theaters, was a force to be taken seriously by managers. Many shows were stopped and managers and performers fined for allowing young people to perform.

The duo's first appearance on Broadway was in a musical comedy. "Over the Top" was a small version of a Winter Garden revue with music by Sigmund Romberg. The show opened on December 1, 1917, at the Forty-Fourth Street Theater. It had a war-doughboy theme and a loose plot. A dance by Adele and Fred grabbed the attention of reviewers and also the attention of the Shuberts, who hired them to appear in "The Passing Show of 1918," which opened at the Winter Garden July 25. The revue featured the music of Romberg and Jean Schwartz and the comedy of Frank Fay. In an opulent number, Adele and Fred sang and danced, dressed as chickens. A positive review by Heywood Broun in the *New York Tribune* singled out Fred's work but also mentioned the dancing team's easy, gliding style. Unfortunately, the show was cut short by the influenza epidemic that struck the public and closed theaters in September.

On October 7 of the following year, delayed a month by the actors' strike, "Apple Blossoms" opened at the Globe Theater. The show was regarded as the season's best by reviewers, with music by Fritz Kreisler and sets by Joseph Urban. The Astaires were singled out for their "vastly entertaining dances." In particular, Fred was mentioned for his "nimble" style, likely the first time he received more attention than did Adele. The team's apparent success also ended their appearances in vaudeville.

In late 1921, the Astaires appeared in "The Love Letter," with both dancing and speaking parts. The Charles Dillingham reworking of an Apple Blossoms–type show failed and it closed quickly. Adele and Fred's fine dancing seemed wasted, but they received good reviews. Four months later, "For Goodness Sake" opened at the Lyric Theater on February 20, 1922, and made the Astaires the talk of reviewers and audiences. Even George Gershwin's music was of secondary importance compared to the Astaires' dancing. In a number called "Upside Down," the duo danced around the stage in ever-widening circles until they had danced off the stage, to the audience's surprise. They stole the show.

In 1923 and 1924, the Astaires shared their dancing style with London audiences. They played for months at the Shaftesbury Theater and the Queen's Theater, to full houses. When they returned to the United States, they were in even greater demand. They and Gershwin combined to make Broadway's biggest hit of the season.

"Lady Be Good" opened December 1, 1924, at the Liberty Theater. Gershwin composed songs like "Fascinating Rhythm," "Oh, Lady, Be Good!" and "The Man I Love." (For some reason, the latter song was dropped from the show.) The Astaires had starring roles and came away with the most applause. The show played for 330 performances in New York and then went on an equally successful tour. The remainder of the country was now learning what made the Astaires headliners.

In 1927, Adele and Fred starred in another Gershwin musical. "Funny Face" opened on November 22 at the newly completed Alvin Theater. The Gershwins supplied "S'Wonderful" and "My One and Only," the latter sung and tap-danced by Fred. The Astaires again had leading roles, although their dancing far outshone their acting abilities. They performed the same circular dance they had used before. But Fred's solo, to "High Hat," stopped the show. He wore a tuxedo and had his hands in his pockets, a style that became a trademark, and captured the audience. The show played the remainder of the season.

Adele's interest in continuing a dance career had gradually declined although, when the opportunity arose, she remained her brother's partner. She seemed to be more drawn to parties and social events and was reported to have had numerous suitors. Fred, on the other hand, became even more obsessed with perfecting his dancing.

When the musical "Smiles" came along in late 1930, the Astaires could not turn it down. Vincent Youmans had written the score, Flo Ziegfeld produced the show, and Joseph Urban contributed his usual elegant settings. The show featured Marilyn Miller along with the Astaires. Yet, "the poor waif adopted by American soldiers and brought home to America" plot had little coherence and mediocre dialogue. The show lasted only eleven weeks, but in the midst of the Depression this was labeled a "miracle." Fred's classic, exuberant dancing brought down the house night after night. Adele played a leading role but her dancing was little noticed.

Five months later, the Astaires starred in "The Band Wagon," which became a seasonal hit. Rather than a plotted musical, the show was a revue, with a score by Schwartz and Dietz and book by Dietz and Kaufman. Audiences were regaled with sparkling individual performances. Fred appeared in various skits, as a French child, a beggar, a suitor, an accordion player and his now familiar tuxedoed dancer to

Adele Astaire (with Fred Astaire).

continual audience applause. The show ran for 260 performances, excellent results considering the economic situation of the country. Adele did a respectable job acting and dancing, but the announcement of her retirement from the stage to get married topped newspaper headlines.

Back in 1929, Adele had begun a relationship with Lord Charles Arthur Francis Cavendish, the second son of the ninth Duke of Devonshire. In May 1932, she quit the stage to marry him. They moved to Ireland to live in Lismore Castle. The couple had three children, a daughter in 1933 and twin boys in 1935, but all of them died soon after birth. Cavendish died in 1942. On April 20, 1947, Adele married Col. Kingman Douglass, an American banker and Air Force Officer, who was also an assistant director of the Central Intelligence Agency. He died in 1971.

In 1981, Adele died of a stroke in Tucson, Arizona. She was eighty-three years old. Adele's career lasted for twenty-eight years. She lived comfortably the remainder of her life. Brother Fred, on his own, went on to become a famous star of movie musicals. He died in 1987.

Mlle. Dazie

Mlle. Dazie was one of the finest delineators of contemporary dance on the vaudeville stage. During a relatively short career, she appeared in the first two Ziegfeld Follies, headlined vaudeville tours across the country and made gala appearances at the Palace Theater.

Daisy Anne Peterkin was born on September 16, 1884, in St. Louis, Missouri. Nothing is known of her parents or ancestry. As a child and adolescent, she took dancing lessons and was interested in the "modern" techniques as expounded by Ruth St. Denis and Isadora Duncan. As a teen, she went to Europe to continue her studies. In 1903, at the age of nineteen, she made her stage debut dancing in a French ballet. She developed an act that featured classical aptitude along with grace of expression. To make her act unique, she dressed in red and wore a red mask. Reviewers identified her as "Le Domino Rouge," her real identity hidden for publicity purposes.

In June 1905, "Le Domino Rouge" arrived in New York to appear as a featured dancer at Wisteria Grove, atop the New York Theater, as part of a summer revue. She received excellent reviews. One of the people who saw her perform was Mark Luescher, then manager of the New Amsterdam Theater under the ownership of Keith and Erlanger. Their relationship resulted in marriage in June 1906. Luescher also took over as her manager. During the summer, they honeymooned in Europe.

In the fall of 1906, Mlle. Dazie, as she was now called, made her first vaudeville tour under the U.B.O. circuit, run by Keith. While performing in New York, she was seen by Flo Ziegfeld, who was in the process of preparing for his first Follies revue.

On July 8, 1907, Ziegfeld's Follies made its debut at the newly named Jardin de Paris on the New York Theater Roof. Nora Bayes was the star of the show, backed by a lavishly dressed chorus of "Anna Held Girls." Unlike later Follies shows, this one changed casts frequently. Mlle. Dazie began with the show and was replaced after playing several months. She was said to have been the first to perform a Salome dance before an American audience. This began the Salome craze that was adopted by several dancers and enthusiastically embraced by audiences across the country. Dazie reportedly opened up a "school for Salomes" which, by 1908, was turning out 150 dancers a month. For her efforts, Mlle. Dazie was hired by Ziegfeld to appear in his 1908 edition of the Follies.

The 1908 Ziegfeld Follies opened on June 15. It again featured Nora Bayes, this time with her new husband, Jack Norworth. Together, they co-wrote and introduced one of the hits of the show, "Shine On Harvest Moon." The theme of the show, Adam and Eve gazing on their progeny in New York, tied together all the production numbers. Dazie performed a solo dance, and later in the show led a chorus attired as taxi cabs whose lights flashed out at the audience. This time she played the entire run of the show.

In June of 1909, Dazie began a tour of the Keith theaters in Boston and followed with appearances in New York, at the Fifth Avenue Theater, and in other Eastern and Midwestern cities. By this time, she had become a headliner and was featured as a leader in contemporary dance. Unlike other dancers of the period, Dazie wore modest costumes and utilized classical ballet technique.

Mlle. Dazie obtained a divorce from Luescher in May 1910, on statutory grounds. Luescher had changed careers, becoming a theatrical producer. Their continual separations due to her touring schedule probably contributed to their problems. Three years later,

Dazie married Cornelius Fellowes, president of the St. Nicholas Hygeia Ice Company and son of a well-known horseman. They remained married until her death in 1952.

When the Shuberts presented their first show, "The Revue of Revues," at the new Winter Garden on September 27, 1911, Mlle. Dazie was one of the featured acts. However, she was obscured by the American debut of a new dancer, Gaby Deslys, who performed an elaborate dance-skit that attracted the complete attention of reviewers. The show was good enough to go on tour.

The Shuberts had Dazie back again for their next Winter Garden revue. "The Passing Show of 1912" was the first of a long series of revues designed to rival Ziegfeld's Follies. The two-part show opened on July 22. The first part was called a "mime-dramatic ballet," and Dazie was one of the primary dancers. The second part was similar to the Weberfields satires coupled with a large chorus of beautiful girls in provocative costumes. The show lasted into the early fall. After its close, Dazie returned to the vaudeville circuit.

In 1914, Mlle. Dazie was the headliner at the Palace Theater. She performed an interpretive dance called "Pantaloon" (after a short story by J.M. Barrie) and was well-received by the audience and reviewers. She again appeared at the Palace in February, 1917, in a dance skit, "The Garden of Puchinello." In between, she played on the vaudeville circuit.

Just after the war, Mlle. Dazie went to London and performed there for a year. She received excellent reviews but few new engagements. Returning to New York, she was hired to appear in Morris Gest's production of "Aphrodite," which opened at the Century Theater, New York, on March 24, 1919. Dazie performed several dances with Michael Fokine, the well-known ballet choreographer. The show played the remainder of the season; when it closed in May 1920, it marked Dazie's last appearance on the stage. Fifteen years of continuous performing and touring had taken its toll on her health.

Mlle. Dazie

Dazie did appear in two movies, "The Secret Dragon" in 1920 and "The Black Panther's Cub" in 1921. She had a dance solo in each movie.

Cornelius Fellowes lost his business in the late 1920s. He and Dazie moved to Miami

Beach, Florida, to set up a new business. But the Depression left them financially destitute. Fellowes ran a business known as Eddie's News and Stuff from 1928 to 1946, with moderate success.

Mlle. Dazie died August 12, 1952, in Miami Beach. She had been out of the limelight for more than thirty years and passed away in obscurity.

Charlotte Greenwood

By the time she was eleven years old, Charlotte Greenwood had reached her adult height of five feet ten inches. She left school because she was the tallest child in class and was awkward. Charlotte overcame the sensitivity about her height when she learned she could make people laugh. "I capitalized on the gawky movements of my long legs," she once explained, "and made a success on the stage." Charlotte went on to become a vaudeville headliner and a star in musical comedy and the movies.

Frances Charlotte Greenwood was born on June 25, 1890, in Philadelphia, Pennsylvania. (Most biographies list her birth as 1893, but the Philadelphia County vital records confirm her birth register and certificate for June 1890.) Her father, Frank Greenwood, was born in England in 1865 and came to the United State in April 1887. He was a barber. Her mother, Annabelle Higgins, was born in 1867 in Wilmington, Delaware. They married in 1889. When Frances Charlotte was one year old, Frank left the family, leaving his wife and child with no means of support. Annabelle went to work in the kitchen of a small hotel. Frances Charlotte was educated in public schools in Boston and Norfolk, Virginia, where her mother worked as a hotel cashier. She and her daughter moved to New York when Colonel Hull Davidson gave Annabelle a management job in a hotel across from Hammerstein's Victoria Theater. When Frances Charlotte was a teenager, Annabelle married James B. Reilly, eight years her junior and a bartender in a cafe. Frances Charlotte lived with them in their West 42nd Street apartment until she was eighteen.

The tall, gangly girl spent an unhappy time at school, so ashamed of being labeled awkward that she left when she was in seventh grade. Her only talent was her voice, a pleasant contralto, and an interest in dancing. Living so close to the Victoria Theater, she got to know several celebrities who encouraged her to follow a career in the theater. She hounded theatrical booking offices until she got a job in the chorus line of "The White Cat," a musical that opened at the New Amsterdam Theater on November 2, 1905. Charlotte — she dropped her first name — was fifteen years old. The show had a very short run, even with the music by Jerome and Schwartz. But Charlotte had her first taste of the stage and she loved it.

She worked in the chorus of small-time vaudeville for almost two years before being hired to appear in the comedy-musical "The Rogers Brothers in Panama" in 1907. In the show, besides dancing, she had her first speaking part. The show played for seventy-one performances before going on an extended tour. In 1908, the company folded when Gus Rogers unexpectedly died.

Charlotte and another member of the cast, Eunice Burnham, decided to form their own vaudeville act. Eunice, short and a little plump, played the piano; tall and lanky Charlotte sang. They billed themselves as "Two Girls and a Piano," which got them jobs in ten-cent vaudeville at twenty-five dollars a week. For the next three years, the team perfected their act, with Charlotte finding her awkwardness a definite comedy asset. The more she experimented with her eccentric gestures, the more laughs she got from audiences. What had embarrassed her as a youth got her laughs and applause on the stage. By 1912, the team was playing in better theaters and Charlotte, in particular, had developed what would become a characteristic dancing routine. She was known for her ability to kick one leg over her head.

Charlotte and Eunice parted. The Shuberts, always on the lookout for young, cheap talent, hired Charlotte to appear in their answer to the Ziegfeld Follies, "The Passing Show of 1912," a revue. The first part of the show was a mime-ballet. The second part was made up of parodies of current Broadway shows. Charlotte sang and danced with partner Sidney Grant. Grant was very short and the height difference made for additional laughter, adding to Charlotte's repertoire as a comedienne. Starring in the show were Willie and Eugene Howard and Trixie Friganza.

Charlotte was asked back for the next edition, "The Passing Show of 1913," in which she sang several songs and had a sketch where her unique dancing was displayed. The revue continued to satirize Broadway shows. In 1914, Charlotte was engaged to appear in a Morosco production of "Pretty Mrs. Smith," which opened at the Casino Theater on September 21. The opera singer turned musical comedy star, Fritzi Scheff, was upstaged by Charlotte's dancing, which included splits and kicks that made the audience gasp with delight. Her role as long, lean, lanky Letty was so well-received that Morosco revised the show and titled it "Long, Legged Letty." With Charlotte as leading lady, the show ran for two years, and more "Letty"s were to follow.

In between musicals, Charlotte returned to vaudeville with an act that soon made her a headliner on the circuit. Her act featured a skit called "The Morning Bath." In it, she was taking a bath when the phone rang, the meter reader appeared and the iceman delivered a large block of ice and left it on the bathroom floor. Getting out of the bath with a towel around her, she attempted to open the icebox and lift the ice up inside it. Suddenly, a burglar leapt through the window and shouted "Stick 'em up." Lights out; end of act. Audiences rolled with laughter at her antics.

In 1915, Charlotte appeared in her first movie, "Jane," a comedy on the order of Chaplin, in which she portrays a woman whose clumsiness gets others into trouble.

The year 1916 brought another Letty show, "So Long, Letty," which opened at the Shubert Theater on November 23. Actually, the show had started its run earlier in California, worked its way East, had a run of ninety-six performances in New York, and went on extended tour through 1917. During this time, the production added new scenes and new music. Every time Charlotte kicked, the audience broke out in cheers and applause.

When Charlotte was playing in Los Angeles at the beginning of the run of "So Long, Letty," she made additional headlines with an announcement of marriage. The *Los Angeles Times* reported: "Revealing a secret romance and her marriage within thirty minutes after she received the proposal, with her maid as her only attendant at the wedding, Charlotte Greenwood announced she was the wife of Cyril Ring, a motion picture actor and brother of Blanche Ring." When she was questioned about the abrupt event, she replied, "Mr. Ring and I met three months ago and were married July 17 [1915]. When Mr. Ring proposed to me, we abolished an engagement by mutual consent, went to the apartment of Rev. Mr. Meyer and were married there."

After "So Long, Letty" closed, Charlotte was back on the vaudeville circuit until Morosco's next installment of the Letty series was being prepared. "Linger Longer Letty" opened at the Fulton Theater on November 20, 1919. Morosco had planned to open the show in September but the flu epidemic closed most theaters and kept audiences home. This version had Letty portraying the family's ugly duckling who finally finds love with the next door neighbor. As usual, Charlotte had a number of eccentric dance numbers in which she kicked high. The show ran for nine weeks and then went on an extended tour across the country. Charlotte found that audiences in the hinterlands appreciated her more than those in New York.

No sooner was the show closed than a new Letty was ready to take off. "Let Em Go, Letty" opened in 1921, but never appeared in New York. Morosco had the show play exclusively on the road for the season because he believed New York theatergoers had tired of Letty. In 1922, Charlotte starred in a musical version of "Maggie Pepper," changing the title to "Letty Pepper." The show opened at the Vanderbilt Theater on April 10, 1922, but received poor reviews. It was quickly sent out of town to greater success but a relatively short run.

A few months later, Charlotte was hired to appear in the second edition of the "Music Box Revue of 1922–23," which opened at the Music Box Theater on November 23, 1922. It featured Charlotte and her high kicking, Grace La Rue, John Steel and comic newcomers Clark and McCullough. Charlotte did a takeoff of Irving Berlin's "Pack Up Your Sins (And Go to the Devil)" in devil's costume, sending jazz musicians to the nether regions. The show ran the remainder of the season, at which time Charlotte played vaudeville at a salary of $2,500 a week. For undisclosed reasons, she obtained a divorce from Cyril Ring at the same time.

Two years later, on December 22, 1924, Charlotte married Martin Broones, an English author and songwriter. He was eleven years younger than Charlotte. They remained together until his death in 1971.

In both 1926 and 1928, Charlotte was on the bill at the Palace Theater, New York. In 1926, she was co-billed with Jack Norworth, Blossom Seeley and Charles King. No Greenwood act would be complete without a high-kicking dance routine and Charlotte never disappointed an audience. In 1928, she starred with Lou Holtz and Florence Moore, the Palace's first female emcee.

Charlotte and veteran Raymond Hitchcock were co-starred in Hassard Short's "Ritz Revue," opening at the Majestic Theater on September 17, 1924. Charlotte reprised her "Morning Bath" routine, which was the best comedy skit in the show. The show was made up of a conglomeration of songs and dances with contributions from ten different songwriters. It ran for 109 performances. Although vaudeville was losing its appeal, Charlotte returned and toured for several years. Stars like Charlotte prolonged vaudeville's popularity and prosperity, but its demise was near.

In 1927, Charlotte was called upon at the last minute to appear in another revue, "Rufus Le Maire's Affairs," which opened at the Majestic Theater on March 28. Martin Broones contributed a near-hit song, "I Can't Get Over a Girl Like You." Charlotte impersonated Lorelei Lee in a satire of "Gentlemen Prefer Blondes" and offered a few high-kicking dances. The show had originated in Chicago and had Sophie Tucker playing Lorelei Lee, which helped to generate full houses for two months. When Sophie decided to double at a local cabaret the same time she was with Le Maire, he was almost angry enough to fire her. Since the show was doing so well on the way to New York, however, he relented. When he found that Tucker was negotiating with William Morris, he fired her on the eve of the show's New York opening. Charlotte, quickly hired, more than adequately replaced Tucker.

Vaudeville was now rapidly declining, suffering badly because most of its former headliners were moving to other, more lucrative media. Charlotte easily moved to the movies, with occasional forays into musical comedy and radio. Between 1931 and 1940, she appeared in ten movies, some of them musical hits, like "Palmy Days" (1931), "Stepping Out" (1931) and "Down Argentine Way" (1940). While she played the lead in lower-budgeted films, she was mainly a supporting performer in the major film musicals, which featured Eddie Cantor, Betty Grable, Carmen Miranda and Esther Williams.

During this decade, she spent a pleasant 1932 season in London, playing in a musical, "Wild Violets," at the Theater Royal, Drury Lane. Another version of Letty, "Leaning on Letty," opened on the road in 1935 and Charlotte appeared in it on and off for several years in between film assignments.

Between 1941 and 1950, she appeared in fifteen movies, all of them in supporting roles. In every musical, she had a high-kicking dance. They included "Moon Over Miami" (1941), "Springtime in the Rockies" (1942), "The Gang's All Here" (1943) and "Oh, You Beautiful Doll" (1949).

Charlotte Greenwood (photography by Edward Thayer Moore, Museum of the City of New York).

Charlotte starred in two radio shows in 1944, "Life With Charlotte" and "The Charlotte Greenwood Show." During 1947 and 1948, she toured in the road company of "I Remember Mama." In 1950, Charlotte renewed her musical comedy affiliation, playing Juno in Cole Porter's "Out of This World," which was predicted by critics to be a surefire hit. According to reviewer-historian Gerald Bordman, "[F]or most theatergoers the triumph of the evening was the joyous cavorting of Charlotte Greenwood. Forty years after her first Broadway appearance, she still retained her regal bearing, the glow in her eyes, and her incredible loose-jointed, high-kicking eccentric dances. She brought down the house nightly singing and dancing a Porter ditty, 'Nobody's Chasing Me.'" Even though the show ran for twenty weeks, business had been so slow, it lost considerable money. Charlotte announced her retirement at the age of sixty-one.

The 1943 musical "Oklahoma" was a major hit that changed the nature of musical theater for decades. The producers had wanted Charlotte to play the role of Aunt Eller but she was unavailable. In 1955, when "Oklahoma!" was made into a movie, Charlotte was called upon to take the role. Reviewers called it a memorable performance. In contrast, her last movie, "The Opposite Sex," was hardly noticed. Charlotte again announced her retirement.

Martin Broones died in August 1971. Charlotte moved to Beverly Hills, California. She died on January 18, 1978, at the age of eighty-seven.

While it was her film career that made her a popular performer, it was her appearances in vaudeville that gave her headliner status. She was one of the few vaudeville stars to transfer her appeal to other amusements and extend a career that entertained audiences for more than forty years.

Janette Hackett

Janette Hackett began her dance career in vaudeville in her teens and later became a Palace Theater standout. She created her own dance acts and costumes, the acts exotic and the costumes scanty. She was a perennial vaudeville performer whose stage career came to an end with vaudeville's decline.

Janette's grandparents came from Ireland. Her father, Morris Hackett, born in New York in 1871, was a railroad conductor. Her mother, Florence Gertrude Spreen, was born in New York in 1880. She and Morris were married in 1897. Florence became an actress, later to appear in silent films. They had three children, Janette, born on July 3, 1898, Albert in 1900 and Raymond in 1903. Both sons became actors. In 1900, the family included Morris and Florence, two children, an aunt and mother-in-law, all living together in New York City. Morris died shortly after Raymond was born, leaving the women of the house to earn a living and care for the children.

Raised in an environment involved with the theater, young Janette wanted to go on the stage. Her primary interest was in dancing. At the age of fifteen, Janette auditioned and obtained a job in the chorus in "The Passing Show of 1913," a Shubert production which attempted to emulate the Ziegfeld Follies. The show starred Charlotte Greenwood, Charles and Molly King and John Charles Thomas. Ned Wayburn was in charge of the staging and dance routines, which came to be the hit of the show. Janette told of meeting fellow chorus member Kitty Doner at the time. Kitty supposedly taught Janette various dancing technique; more likely, the articulate and demanding Wayburn gave Janette the basics she needed to further her career.

The following year, Janette was engaged by Nora Bayes for a touring revue. Janette performed a Hawaiian dance. Another member of the cast, Fay Marbe, did an Oriental dance, which Janette studied carefully. When Marbe left the company, Janette was given her assignment. She now danced exotically and wore body-hugging costumes. Audiences suddenly took notice of this sensual dancer. But after several weeks on the road, Bayes closed the show in Chicago due to illness. Janette was stranded and had to make her way back to New York.

For the next few years, Janette played in secondary vaudeville theaters and nightclubs, doing a solo dance, Oriental-style, with enough success to keep her performing.

In 1919, at the age of twenty-one, Janette got a job with William Seabury, replacing his wife in a dance act. For twenty weeks they toured the Keith circuit, not as headliners but as a featured act. They appeared in the third or fourth position on the program. The salary was satisfactory and, encouraged by her mother and mother-in-law, Janette decided that her dancing career offered substantial opportunities.

When Seabury decided to retire from the stage in early 1919, Janette was forced to look for another dancing partner. While she was appearing in a solo act, she discovered Harry Delmar, a young performer who had already become a vaudeville favorite. They decided to team and Janette created a routine that best suited their respective talents. Delmar was not a good dancer, but practice and actual performance made him a competent partner. Hackett and Delmar made their debut in March 1919, at the 125th Street Theater. They received mixed reviews; Delmar was said to lack the skills of a singer and dancer but Janette "looks big time."

For the next several years, Hackett and Delmar toured, first on the Western Vaudeville Circuit, at secondary theaters, and then on the Orpheum circuit where their act was officially recognized by reviewers and roundly applauded by audiences. Janette and Delmar were married in 1924. Each year, Janette created new dance numbers and costumes. By the mid–1920s, they were considered one of the best vaudeville dance teams. Their act lasted twenty minutes and featured a line of chorus girls supporting Janette, an eccentric number by Delmar, and Janette's skimpy costumes, which often got the eye of reviewers.

In 1926, the team put together a mini-dance revue called "Luxuries" while appearing on the Keith circuit. The highlight of the season was their first appearance at the Palace Theater, New York. "The glittering, ornate and heavily tinseled new dance presentation of Janette Hackett and Harry Delmar contains the usual expert dancing indigenous to vaudeville and it was well received by the audience," said one review of their act. They toured the

Janette Hackett (Harry Ransom Humanities Research Center, the University of Texas at Austin).

country with success. Delmar had become a better dancer, but the marriage was floundering because of his indiscretions. The next year, "Delmar's Revels" was put on, but the title signaled more than just the act. In mid-tour, the couple separated due to Harry's infidelity. Janette finished the season doing a solo act. They were divorced in 1928.

Janette continued her dance act on the Keith circuit supported by various male partners. She was no longer a headliner, instead positioned second or third on the bill. In February 1929, she appeared at the Palace Theater in a dance, "Moments Vitae," supported by three male dancers. James Barton, a musical comedy star, headed the program.

In December, Janette again played at the Palace, this time in a dance number that had a shocking, and unique, ending. A partner dressed in a black cape, hat and mask enticed a girl to dance with him. The dance built in intensity and menace. At the end, the girl pulled off the mask and found the person to be Death. Screaming, the girl ran to the top of some stairs, grabbed a drape and then fell down the flight, with Death trailing her. Audiences "went wild" over the act.

That same year, Janette met John Steel, also on a bill in Cleveland. Steel had introduced "A Pretty Girl Is Like a Melody" in the 1919 Ziegfeld Follies. In a matter of months, they were married. A son, Donn, was born a year later. Janette returned to the stage in December 1930, and played the Riverside Theater behind Buck & Bubbles but ahead of Burns and Allen. She appeared with a company of eight dancers. In February 1931, she returned to the Palace, behind Helen Morgan and Jay C. Flippen. The *New York Times* reviewer wrote of Janette, "Kind words should be found for the elaborate dance turn presented by Janette Hackett."

The Depression and simultaneous demise of vaudeville left Janette with few venues to continue her career. She had infrequent engagements at theaters and nightclubs. One of her last appearances was in May 1933 at Loew's State Theater, where she performed a solo dance. By 1935, Janette had retired from the stage. She spent the following years designing elegant dresses and serving as a hostess on the ocean liner S.S. *France*.

Janette died on August 16, 1979, in New York. She was 81 years old.

Irene Castle

Irene Foote was born April 17, 1893, in New Rochelle, New York. She was the daughter of Herbert Townsend Foote and Annie Elroy Thomas, both of whom came from wealthy families. As a young child, Irene was given all the benefits of the rich. She attended St. Mary's Episcopal Convent in Peekskill, New York, and then a private school for girls, National Park Seminary, near Washington, D.C. At the seminary, Irene appeared in amateur theatricals but showed no great interest in the theater. Instead, she joined the Seminary swim team and claimed to have bobbed her hair at that time, well before it became popular. When she was sixteen, Irene became engaged to a gentleman named Whiting. She dropped out of school and joined her sister Elroy on a trip to see their father.

The following year, Irene broke her engagement with Whiting, which disturbed her parents a good deal and jeopardized her debutante position. During the summer of 1910, she met Vernon Castle at the New Rochelle Rowing Club. Vernon was an aspiring performer in musical comedy and had been signed to appear in Lew Fields' production of "The Summer Widowers." It was his third appearance in a Fields show. Irene's parents were unenthusiastic about her interest in a stage performer, preferring that she marry within her station.

For some months, Vernon had tried to get an audition for Irene, but Fields was reluctant since he wished to have him develop as a comedian. In September 1910, Vernon and Irene finally auditioned for Fields as a dancing team. Irene was given a bit part, with three lines and no dancing. The show was short-lived when the Shuberts abruptly shut it down.

Irene and Vernon's next opportunity came in "The Hen Pecks," another Lew Fields production. The show opened February 4, 1911, at Fields' Broadway Theater after several weeks on the road. In the show, Irene played one of four daughters but again had no dancing assignment. Vernon played opposite Fields and made major contributions to the show's comedy. In the middle of the show's tour, on May 28, 1911, Irene and Vernon married. Irene was eighteen years old. Her parents were very upset that she had married an actor with a dubious career. After the show, they honeymooned in England. While Vernon was a relaxed, happy-go-lucky type, Irene was ambitious and a driven perfectionist. They had many arguments, but when they were on stage, their performances were smooth, exacting and exciting.

In 1912, Irene and Vernon were engaged to appear in Charles Dillingham's "The Lady of the Slipper." The show starred Elsie Janis and Montgomery and Stone. For this show, they were hired to dance. But Irene's rehearsal upset the producer and leading performers, and she was asked to leave the show. Irene had attempted to add sexual titillation into her dancing by wearing a Parisian gown. At certain moments in her dance, her skirt would fly up to her hips. It revealed, as Elsie Janis described it, "the shortest pair of shorts ever glimpsed." Dillingham gasped; Stone turned the other way, embarrassed. Dillingham asked Irene to wear more proper attire. She refused, and Dillingham dropped her from the show. Vernon stayed with the show until after its New York opening.

In March 1912, Irene and Vernon signed to appear in "Elfin-une Revue" at Paris' Olympia Theater. They had their first dancing success in this French production. It was followed with another at the Cafe de Paris. Returning to the United States as popular dancing stars in early 1913, the couple appeared in "The Sunshine Girl," which opened February 3 at the Knickerbocker Theater. They were enthusiastically applauded and encored for their exciting ballroom dancing. Historians point to this appearance as the beginning of the dance craze in America. Capitalizing on it, the Castles co-authored a book, "Modern Dancing," that demonstrated their unique style. It turned out to be a bestseller.

Irene Castle (with Vernon Castle).

Now considered bona fide headliners, Irene and Vernon entered vaudeville in the spring of 1914 with a thirty-two-city tour of the United States. Wherever they visited, they educated audiences about dancing. Women flocked to copy Irene's daring dance clothing, her dance steps and her bobbed hairstyle. The vaudeville tour was a great success and, combined with the proliferation of new dance styles, demand for their performances rapidly grew.

In 1914, the Castles made their first appearance at the Palace Theater, as part of an all-star bill that included Louis Mann, Jack Norworth, Will Rogers, Maggie Cline and Sam Bernard. At the same time, they were appearing at Hammerstein's, backed by a twelve-piece Negro orchestra. Hammerstein refused to allow the Negro orchestra to occupy the pit, so Vernon put them on the stage. When World War I broke out during the summer of 1914, Vernon and Irene were caught in Paris and were delayed in their return to the United States Irving Berlin was waiting for them to appear in his new show, "Watch Your Step."

"Watch Your Step" opened on December 8, 1914, at the New Amsterdam Theater. Berlin was twenty-six and the show was his first musical comedy hit. Since the country was embracing the dance craze, the Castles were the stars. Vernon had several solo numbers, but Irene appeared only as Mrs. Vernon Castle in their own dance numbers. The show was a great success and played for months in New York before going on extended tour.

While the "Watch Your Step" cast was resting, the Castles went on another highly successful vaudeville tour. It was now the height of the dance fad, highlighted by the Castle Walk, the Cakewalk, Walkin' the Dog and the Maxixe. The Castles, too, were at the height of their popularity. The tour ended with another appearance at the Palace, this time opposite a Gilbert and Sullivan company. In 1915, they also appeared in a film, "The Whirl of Life," which featured their dance routines. Next in their ambitious plans was the opening of dance schools.

In New York, they opened Castle House, a dancing school that was immediately filled with students. They opened cabarets in Chicago, New York and Long Beach to take advantage of people's interest in dancing. However, their life changed when Vernon enlisted in the 84th Royal Canadian Flying Corps Squadron. After flight school, in 1916, he was put on active duty in France. The press wondered why he enlisted at a time when he and Irene were at the top of their popularity. In 1917, Vernon was promoted to a flight commander.

In the meantime, Irene continued her career. She toured in "Watch Your Step" (with another dance partner) through 1916. She starred in a fifteen-episode serial, "Patria," in 1917, and made four full-length films for the Astra Film Corporation, Fort Lee, New Jersey. She also appeared in the musical revue, "Miss 1917." The show had all the ingredients for a hit. Dillingham and Ziegfeld were the producers, it had music by Victor Herbert and Jerome Kern, P.G. Wodehouse did the sketches, and the stars were Lew Fields, Van and Schenck, Bert Savoy, Vivienne Segal and Irene. The show initially received good reviews but it was a vaudeville-like revue that, taken all together, did not amuse the audience. The show closed after six weeks to a sizable loss. Irene danced once, in a waltz in a dreamland setting. Her next appearance at the Palace was on film, a serial episode of "Patria," to close the show.

In mid–1917, Vernon was sent to Canada to serve as a flight instructor. Later, he was transferred to Texas where pilots of the Royal Canadian Air Force were training. Vernon was killed in a training accident on February 15, 1918. He was thirty years old.

Irene, at home in New York, received a telephone call but did not believe the news. Vernon had been reported killed before. When she received a telegram from Vernon's fellow officers, she realized it was true and collapsed. "It was a brave man's death, and it is not a woman's part to complain," was all she could say. Funeral services were held at the actors' church, "The Little Church Around the Corner." Two thousand people stood in a cold drizzle until the coffin, draped in British and American flags, passed.

To overcome her sadness and reconstruct her own career, Irene launched herself into a series of movies. Between 1917 and 1919, she played in twelve films, primarily in dramatic roles. In none of them did she dance. Instead, Irene appeared in vaudeville performing a dancing act which audiences found entertaining. The dance craze had passed, and it appeared theatergoers applauded Irene's act out of nostalgia.

In 1919, Irene wrote a book of tribute to Vernon, "My Husband." She continued appearing in films during the early 1920s, again in dramatic roles, except for a cameo in "Broadway After Dark" (1924) where she danced. The same year she wrote about her husband, Irene married a broker's son, Robert Tremain, who had produced several of the movies in which she appeared. The marriage lasted four years; Irene divorced Tremain in 1923. She formed a dance team with Billy Reardon and they played the vaudeville circuit for a year. They had some degree of success but Irene had lost much of her appeal.

In 1923, Irene began a relationship with a much older, wealthy Chicagoan, Frederic McLaughlin, which lasted until his death in 1944. Although they never married, they had two children, Barbara (1925) and William Foote (1929).

Irene became an animal-rights advocate and opened "Orphans of the Storm" in 1928. The program is still in operation. In 1939, RKO released the film "The Story of Vernon and Irene Castle" starring Fred Astaire and Ginger Rogers. The show brought Irene back into the public eye briefly. Lew Fields played himself in the film, thirty years younger and with a toupee that made him look the age he really was. Due to the Astaire-Rogers combination, the movie did well.

Two years after McLaughlin's death, at the age of fifty-three, Irene married a Chicago adman, George Enziger. He died in 1959. Irene moved to Arkansas and it was there she wrote her memoirs, "Castles in the Air."

Irene died January 25, 1969, in Eureka Springs, Arkansas. She was seventy-five years old. She never ceased to recall her glory days with Vernon, although it represented only eight years of her life, as they pioneered the dance craze in the country and made ballroom dancing a respectable and engaging pastime.

Part Five : The Sister Acts

The Cherry Sisters

Audiences loved to demonstrate their opinion of the Cherry Sisters by throwing vegetables and fruit at them at every performance. Their vaudeville appearances earned them the reputation as "the world's worst sister act." Their performance was considered so bad, it caused theatergoer hysteria in New York, yet they played to sold-out houses. They expressed a desire to "clean up" the stage and close theaters on Sunday. They refused to dance, believing it to be immoral. On stage, they only sang moralistic songs and did one-act recitations. They refused to believe that audience reaction was negative; instead, they felt the audience was cheering their efforts. The sisters turned bad reviews and volleys of turnips into a profitable career.

There was always a controversy as to whether the sisters were as awkward and inartistic as they appeared. Some believed that they were smart enough to recognize the gullibility of the public and to take advantage of that to the fullest extent. In the most solemn manner, the sisters professed that their work was of the highest, and that they received a negative audience reaction only because the public did not appreciate the really beautiful. Whatever their artistic merit, their kind of entertainment paid dividends. No one could laugh about that.

Five sisters, Jessie, Ella, Addie, Elizabeth and Effie, and one brother, Isaac Cherry, were born in Wheaton, Illinois, of very religious parents. Their father was born in Rhode Island in 1821, their mother in Vermont in 1831; their marriage took place sometime during the middle 1850s. The family moved to a farm outside the village of Indian Creek, Iowa. The mother died before the 1880 census was taken and the father died shortly after, leaving the children in poverty. The sisters were determined to raise funds to save their homestead. After years of attempting to run the farm, they conceived the idea of going on the stage to entertain and make money. Three of the sisters, Addie, Jessie and Effie, made their stage debut in 1893 on a vaudeville bill at the Marion Opera House. Elizabeth joined them occasionally. Ella took care of the farm. Isaac ran away to Chicago and was never heard from again.

They wanted to visit the Chicago World's Fair but lacked the money. To raise funds, they decided to write, produce and act in a show by themselves. Effie was said to have been the principal author of a melodrama, "The Gypsy's Warning." Their act related in song and gesture the fate in store for a virtuous maiden who ignored the gypsy's warning and was seduced by a Spanish cavalier (played by Addie). They rented a hall in Marion and personally sold tickets to their friends, who came and applauded everything they did. The sisters gave two more profitable performances and then rented Green's Opera House in Cedar Rapids. Here they no longer had an audience made up of friends and well-wishers, and received an entirely different reception. They had not been on the stage more than a few minutes when the audience began to hiss, whistle, stomp their feet and make use of horns left over from the last political campaign.

The sisters, unaware of theater customs, believed the noise was an ovation. Unhampered, they continued, encoring parts of the play that had created the greatest noise, while the audience shouted to drown them out. The theater had been filled and the sisters made a good profit and were convinced of their theatrical success. When the local newspaper published a criticism, the manager found it to his advantage to promote the "world's worst actresses." For three years, they toured the small towns of Kansas, Illinois and Iowa, repeating the same play at every performance and receiving loud jeers and heaps of farm produce in return. Yet they saw the Chicago Fair and paid off the farm's mortgage. So began a tumultuous career on the vaudeville stage.

In October 1896, Oscar Hammerstein read in a theatrical newspaper about an unbelievable troupe of prairie-bred sisters who were entertaining Midwestern audiences with the "worst acting ever witnessed." The seriousness of their performances caused audiences to be overwhelmed with constant laughter. Hammerstein sent his stage manager to Iowa to book the Cherry Sisters for his Olympia Theater. "I've been putting on the best talent and it hasn't gone over," he explained. "I'm going to try the worst." The stage manager signed up the sisters at one hundred dollars a week, plus railroad fare and hotel expenses. To make sure the sisters did not get lost, he took them to New York.

New York theatergoers had read about the act and jammed the Olympia on opening night. A roar greeted the grim-faced "Charming Cherry Sisters," as they were billed. They stumbled out on stage in hand-made red calico dresses and began their act. *The New York Times* reported their act in detail. "They tried a piece in Irish dialect combined with their corn-huskers twang. Addie recited Rosa Hartwick Thorpe's 'Curfew Must Not Ring Tonight,' with stiff gestures. They sang 'Don't You Remember Sweet Alice Ben Bold,' a sad piece to which the audience responded with guffaws."

The next day, the *Times* critic wrote: "They presented a spectacle more pitiable than amusing. Never before did New Yorkers see anything in the least like the Cherry Sisters from Cedar Rapids, Iowa, and it is sincerely to be hoped that nothing like them will ever be seen again." In keeping with the produce missiles the sisters had received in previous performances, Hammerstein had his sons throw vegetables at the performers. Such missiles were thrown at them every night during their six-week engagement. Sidewalk vendors hawking old fruit and vegetables outside the theater made a fortune selling to patrons. Hammerstein rigged a fish net across the footlights to protect the actresses.

The sisters were invited to parties by such celebrities as Lillian Russell, Della Fox, and Diamond Jim Brady. They never accepted, since it was their habit to go to bed immediately after the show and eat only in their own hotel.

During their appearances in New York, the sisters, with dead seriousness, chanted sentimental songs and delivered monologues that sent audiences into almost continuous laughter. It was reported that the sisters loved the hisses and jeers because that meant they were successful. Newspapers published comments that the sisters were "awful," but they were worth seeing for that very reason. They became big hits and the vegetables continued to fly.

In 1898, after the sisters had performed in Odebolt, Iowa, the local critic wrote a scathing review that was picked up by several other newspapers in the state. The sisters sued the newspapers for slander and $15,000 in damages. The next day, the judge and jury saw the act performed. The jury found in favor of the newspapers.

The sisters toured the country for almost ten years, retiring in 1903 to their prairie home after Jessie's death. They were earning a reported $1,000 a week. Their act barely deviated nor did audience reactions to them. Three of the sisters returned to vaudeville during World War I, but the influenza epidemic closed many theaters and they retired once again.

The Cherry Sisters (Museum of the City of New York).

In the early 1920s, two of the sisters made a number of "farewell" tours. They last toured the Midwest in 1934 and made a brief appearance in New York's Gay Nineties Night Club with Addie reciting "A Modern Young Woman," a monologue in which she said, "I sure roast those girls that go around smoking cigarettes."

Twice Effie ran for mayor of Cedar Rapids, in 1924 and 1926, campaigning for longer skirts and against smoking by women and other social reforms. Addie claimed in newspaper interviews that all the publicity generated during their original appearance in New York was untrue. They never owned a farm, Addie explained, and she denied that audiences ever threw anything at them.

Ella died in 1934. Elizabeth died in 1936, at the age of sixty-seven. They were both buried in the "Pauper's Section" of Oak Shade Cemetery, Marion. Addie died in 1942, at eighty-three, and Effie died in 1944, one source giving her age as sixty-five. When she was interviewed a few months before, she replied to the question of her age with "I ain't a-sayin.'" They never married because of their devotion to one another.

The Cherry Sisters' peculiar fame in vaudeville made small fortunes for them. They played their parts straight, regardless of audience reactions. Their legendary career became one of vaudeville's most unique and whimsical stories.

The Dolly Sisters

The Dolly Sisters were the most successful sister act in vaudeville. Small, dark-haired, almond-eyed beauties, they were exotic-looking with a tantalizing quality of glamour and sensuality. Although critics felt the sisters lacked fine singing voices or classy dancing skills, they agreed that their act enthused and excited audiences. The Dollys' flamboyant behavior on the stage made them headliners. Off stage, their capers gave them legendary status.

Their parents, Julius and Margaret Deutsch, were born in Budapest, Hungary. Julius was a commercial artist and sometimes painter. They married in 1892 when Margaret was sixteen. Shortly after their marriage, on October 25, 1892, identical twin girls, Roszika and Yansci, were born. A son, Elbert (Edward), was born in 1898.

The Deutsches immigrated to America in 1904. Unlike most people arriving in this country during that era, they had sufficient funds to reside in a middle-class neighborhood of Far Rockaway, Queens. Margaret enrolled the eleven-year-old twins in ballet school. Julius continued his career in fashion work. While continuing their ballet lessons, the girls also studied voice. Their parents believed the twins were good enough to enter popular theater and attempted to get them engagements.

Seventeen-year-old Roszika and Yansci made their theatrical debut at Keith's Union Square Theater, a vaudeville house, in 1909. Their introduction to audiences were highly successful, not so much for their act, a simple song-and-dance, but rather because of their unique beauty, a novelty among performing women at the time. Their combination of glittering costumes and sensual demeanor sent patrons, especially men, into the delights of whistling and foot-stomping. Reviewers mentioned the twins' beauty and predicted a long career for them.

Two years on the vaudeville circuit made the Dolly Sisters familiar names. Roszika became Rosie and Yansci became Jennie. Dolly came from a friend who mentioned that the twins were as cute as dolls.

Ziegfeld followed the growing reputation of the twins and saw in them a glamour and provocativeness unusual for the stage. They were added to his roster of performers for the "Follies of 1911." What the sisters had not yet generated in the way of a loyal following, Ziegfeld gave to them. The sisters wore identical costumes and hairdos, and matched dance steps. Jennie was portrayed as gregarious, romantic, risk-taking and pleasure-seeking. Rosie was the quiet one and more stable. This may or may not have reflected their personalities, but it gained them attention while they appeared in the Follies. It may even be true that their public personalities followed them in their careers and helped to shape their future behavior, both on and off the stage.

Rosie and Jennie performed a dance routine made up as Siamese twins, with pagoda-styled headdresses, finger cymbals and shiny slit skirts. Their act stopped the show and often forced them into repeating the dance the audience demanded as encores. The act itself proved so popular that the Dollys used it throughout their career. They had begun to develop a degree of popularity in vaudeville; they became stars in the Follies thanks to Ziegfeld.

Their off-stage activities attracted press attention, whether rumor or fact. For example, Diamond Jim Brady was said to escort the twins and their boyfriends to the city's best restaurants. He also reportedly gave them a Rolls-Royce all tied up in a red ribbon. Those stories made good newspaper copy and helped to personify the lives of popular women stage stars. The sisters were identified as fashion-setters; the papers reported their public appearances, wearing body-hugging gowns and considerable jewelry and mingling with New York's elite.

The "Follies of 1911" also included Bert Williams, Leon Errol, Fanny Brice, Lillian Lorraine, Vera Maxwell, Bessie McCoy and a line of seventy-five gorgeous girls still called the "Anna Held Girls," although Anna had already left Ziegfeld. The Dolly Sisters more than held their own with such an array of all-star talent. Still, this was their only appearance in the Follies. The twins wanted to move on to starring roles, higher salaries and more scope for their acting skills. Musical comedy obliged, but not as successfully as the sisters would have liked.

On April 11, 1912, the Dolly Sisters appeared in "A Winsome Widow," a Ziegfeld revision of Charles Hoyt's 1891 classic "A Trip to Chinatown." With little plot, the play was nothing more than a series of vaudeville routines enacted by Leon Errol, Frank Tinney, Charles King and Mae West, attracting attention for the first time. The Dollys sang and danced, but little was said of their performance other than their attractiveness. Still, the show ran for nine months.

Rosie and composer Jean Schwartz were married in 1913. Rosie was twenty-one; Jean was thirty-four. A year later, Jennie married a song-and-dance actor, Harry Fox, and they decided to team as a vaudeville act. For the next several years, the sisters alternately played together in vaudeville and separately in musicals and movies.

In 1914, Rosie appeared alone in "The Whirl of the World," featuring dance more than dialogue. She danced with Lester Sheehan and a *corps de ballet* in "Harlequin and the Bluebird." While the show contained classic dance, it gave Rosie no opportunity for the type of dance now identified with her. A new composer, Sigmund Romberg, wrote the music. The show ran for twenty weeks. In 1915, Rosie appeared in a moving picture, "The Lily and the Rose," directed by D.W. Griffith. The film starred Lillian Gish. Rosie played an exotic dancing woman who stole Lillian's husband. That same year, Jennie appeared in the movie "Call of the Dance." Despite its title, the plot involved murder and white slavery. Prior to this, Jennie and her husband were a dance team on the vaudeville circuit. But wherever the sisters appeared, their reputations always seemed to be tied to their performances.

The sisters were together in "His Bridal Night," which opened at the Republic Theater August 19, 1916. The show had a short run in spite of the Dollys' exotic and sensual dancing. They also appeared in a movie, "Million Dollar Dollies," as themselves, in the role of detectives and with a plot filled with mystics and magic. It was obvious that their name and reputation were being used for publicity purposes no matter the vehicle.

The Dollys frequently played at the Palace Theater, New York, bedecked in beautiful gowns and in an act with several costume changes. They earned $2,000 a week for their efforts. Their singing and dancing may not have improved, according to critics, but their drawing power and popularity continued to grow. In 1918, they appeared in the musical "Oh, Look!" Although they were not the stars, their dancing was considered the feature of the production. The show played only sixty-seven performances in New York, but when it went on tour the Dollys guaranteed full houses and record receipts across the country.

Europe was recovering from the war and entertainment venues put out attractive offers for American performers to play at their theaters. Coincidentally, the sisters were experiencing marital difficulties. Jennie divorced Harry Fox in 1920. Rosie divorced Jean Schwartz the following year. That made them eligible and desirable to the public. Although they had begun their careers a decade earlier, the Dollys represented the 1920s flapper era with ease. They seemed to have taken full advantage of this symbolism.

Their first stop was the London Hippodrome. Successively, they appeared in the musicals "Jig Saw" (1920), "Fun of the Fayre" (1920), "The League of Notions" (1921) and "Babes in the Wood" (1921), all of which were profitable. They were also in demand by London society. In 1922, they starred at the Casino de Paris in the Folies Bergere, where they found their greatest fame. With their bobbed hair, sexy looks, elegant costumes and provocative dances, they were regarded by Parisians as the height of chic decadence.

For the next several years, the Dollys were the toast of two continents, alternating with great success between American vaudeville and European revues.

The Dollys played in the Shubert-produced "Greenwich Village Follies" which opened on September 16, 1924, at the Shubert Theater. The show had only one memorable song, written by Cole Porter, "I'm In Love Again." The sisters appeared in a routine in which their dance movements were mimicked by trained dogs. The show ran for 127 performances in New York and then went on an extensive tour. Others in the production included Moran and Mack and Vincent Lopez and his orchestra. It was the Dollys' last appearance on Broadway.

Rosie married Mortimer Davis, Jr., in 1927 and retired from the stage. Jennie followed her. Once they had established their credentials on the popular stage, they gave it up for society. In turn, society gave them notoriety and wealth. Rumors had it that such luminaries as the Prince of Wales, the Aga Kahn and King Alfonso of Spain were paramours. The sisters amassed a considerable estate from suitors and collected a considerable amount of jewelry to go with homes in England and France. Their next-to-last stage appearance was in a French revue, "Broadway to Paris," in 1928. Audiences refused to let them leave the stage.

Rosie divorced Davis in 1931 and received a substantial endowment. For a short time, the sisters reunited and played the Moulin Rouge with Maurice Chevalier. In 1932, Rosie married Irving Netcher, the heir to a

The Dolly Sisters

Chicago department store. He died in 1953. Jennie was undecided whom to marry: Max Constant, a French aviator, with whom she had a heated relationship made up of passionate love and intense quarrels; and H. Gordon Selfridge, owner of London's famed department store, whose money was very persuasive.

During a motoring trip with Constant, their speeding car crashed and Jennie was severely injured. She spent several months in the hospital undergoing repeated operations to restore her beauty. But her spirit was broken. Rosie brought Jennie home to Chicago and married her off to Bernard Vinissky, a Chicago attorney, in 1935. They separated a few years later. Acute depression drove Jennie to suicide in 1941. She hung herself from a shower rod. She was forty-eight years old.

Rosie continued to enjoy the benefits of a larger-than-life reputation and considerable wealth. Her gambling exploits at Monte Carlo were legendary, full of stories of substantial winnings and losings. While these stories may have had a grain of truth, the casinos and the press used them frequently to create headlines and publicity. Throughout her later years, Rosie remained an elegant dresser and charming socialite. A *Variety* review of her appearance on Edward R. Murrow's "Person to Person" described her as "living like a silken dowager dame in tufted surroundings with abundant memories of riotously rich stage door admirers and also knee-deep in precious gems."

Rosie had broken her hip in 1967, severely curtailing her activities. She died in New York of a heart attack on February 1, 1970. She was seventy-seven. Her ashes were returned to California where she was buried at Forest Lawn Cemetery next to Jennie.

She had lived long enough to see a movie about the Dolly Sisters produced by George Jessel for 20th Century Fox in 1943. June Haver had the role of Rosie; Betty Grable was cast as Jennie. No one claimed it was a biography; instead it portrayed the gaiety of the flapper period. The movie barely covered the sisters' flamboyant life in popular theater and international society.

The Duncan Sisters

Vaudeville featured a number of sister acts but none of them excelled in comedy like the Duncan Sisters, Rosetta and Vivian. They performed a variety of acts in children's roles. Dressed for the part, they wrote routines that exaggerated child behavior for comic effect. When they produced "Topsy and Eva," a travesty on "Uncle Tom's Cabin," they became one-hit entertainers, using the same comedy framework for the remainder of their careers.

The Duncan ancestors came from England during Colonial times and settled in Pennsylvania as farmers. Each generation moved West as the country expanded its borders and land was made available for ownership. Samuel Henry Duncan, the sisters' father, was born in Iowa and began his working life as a farmer. Locke Wheeler, the sisters' mother, was born in Missouri, of farming parents. Both found their way to California and they were married in Los Angeles in 1891. Samuel became a real estate salesman.

The couple had five children, Alexander, born in 1892; Evelyn in 1894; Harold in 1899; Rosetta on November 23, 1900; and Vivian on June 17, 1903. Mrs. Duncan died while giving birth to Vivian. Samuel was able to play several musical instruments. He gave musical lessons to Rosetta and Vivian and had them take vocal lessons as well. The sisters began their performing career by singing at church functions. From the beginning, the girls worked as a team although they were three years apart in age. They dressed as Dutch girls. Rosetta would sing and yodel while Vivian sang and played the piano. When she was twelve, Vivian worked as a pianist in a local movie house for six dollars a week, playing the only tune she knew, "Aloha." The job lasted only as long as she was able to vary the tempo of the piece to match the movie action without the theater manager finding out about her limited repertoire.

Whether due to their differences in personality or to their specific musical skills, the sisters displayed different acting personas. Rosetta was the self-proclaimed leader, considered by critics to have been a "natural-born comedienne." Like many comedians-in-training, she was said to have entertained her schoolmates until sent home for her disruptive behavior. Vivian was quiet and lent support to her sister's antics, a true "second banana" in vaudeville parlance.

As they grew into their teens, the sisters were strongly encouraged by their father to continue performing at church functions and amateur nights at vaudeville houses. They sang and offered comedy bits, with Rosetta highlighting the act with yodeling. In 1914, when Rosetta was fourteen and Vivian twelve, the sisters began their vaudeville career with an appearance at the Pantages Theater in Los Angeles. They were on a bill featuring acrobats, a dog act, sketch artists and comedians. They toured the West on a small-time vaudeville circuit, supervised by their father. When they joined the "Revue de Vogue," a burlesque touring company, the sisters (with their father as guardian) played secondary theaters in Illinois, Iowa and Wisconsin for twenty-five dollars a week.

The Duncan Sisters

Thanks to their sister Evelyn's financial assistance, Rosetta and Vivian traveled to New York. They obtained their first job at Henderson's Music Hall on Coney Island, playing sixteen times a day. They were then hired by Gus Edwards to appear in one of his "kiddie" revues, this one at the Hotel Martinique in New York. They had a small role singing "I'm So Glad My Momma Don't Know Where I'm At." The formation of their children's act began with this engagement.

In May 1917, the Duncan Sisters made their formal New York debut at the Fifth Avenue Theater. They sang several songs dressed as children and speaking in a childish voice. While the audience seemed to like their routine, *Variety's* reviewer was not at all complimentary: "The Duncan Sisters are not ripe as yet for the big time."

However, when the Shuberts were preparing a patriotic revue a few months later, they selected the sisters for the cast. They were probably chosen because they had a novelty presentation and their salary demands were minimal. Featured in the show, which had no plot and was filled with vaudeville turns, were Frank Tinney, Jim Corbett, Ed Wynn, Herman Timberg and Charles Judels. Timberg and Sigmund Romberg provided the music. The revue opened at the Winter Garden on October 18, 1917, and would run until the Shuberts saw a decline in box office receipts. The show played for seventeen weeks, closing the middle of February 1918. During this run, the sisters learned a great deal about what life was like in popular theater.

After the show closed, they were picked up by Charles Dillingham for his new musical comedy, "She's a Good Fellow." The show should have fared well, with Jerome Kern's music and a book by Anne Caldwell, but the actors' strike closed it early in its run and it never recovered. For the first time, the sisters were able to showcase their vaudeville talents. Still, the show struggled along until closure was better than continuing to lose money. Dillingham followed with a musical comedy winner, "Tip Top," featuring the comedy and acrobatic antics of Fred Stone. Opening at the Globe Theater on October 5, 1920, the show played for thirty-nine weeks to full houses, both in New York and on tour. The Duncan Sisters sang and danced, and portrayed the "Terrible Twins" (Bad and Worse) with comedy skits that elicited good reviews.

They returned to vaudeville, often headlining a bill, and now recognized as a top sister act. Their children's routine now consisted of songs they composed and comedy sketches they wrote, with Rosetta the jokester and Vivian the straight person. Many of the songs they performed were comedy numbers, like "I Gotta Code in By Dose," "It Must Be an Old Spanish Custom," and "The Prune Song." After performing "In Sweet Onion Time," they threw onions into the audience. The song "She Fell Down on Her Cadenza" included a dance in which the sisters kicked each other in the posterior, with Rosetta losing the duel and hanging a black crepe on her backside.

In 1922, their child act was well-received by London audiences. After the Prince of Wales saw their act, the sisters became favorites on the party circuit. When the Queen of Spain attended the show, Rosetta went to the side of the stage and, as a child would do, pointed to her skinned knee and said, "I skinned my knee, Princess Mary! Can you see my skinned knee?" It was an improvised joke that brought down the house. Their child routine lent itself easily to new comedy skits and improvisations that kept the act fresh and unpredictable. But when they returned home, they found that vaudeville was now in competition with other entertainment forms. What could they do to freshen their act up for U.S. audiences?

In early 1923, while the sisters were performing in California, they were asked to appear in moving pictures. After exploring the possibilities and not finding an appropriate film script, someone suggested they "black up" (appear in blackface) like such popular performers as Al Jolson and Eddie Cantor. In response to the recommendation, the sisters came up with an idea to do a farce-comedy rendition of "Uncle Tom's Cabin," with Topsy and Eva as the main characters. With the help of writer Catherine Cutting, they wrote the music and lyrics, added comic sketches and changed the roles of all of the main "Tom" characters to comic personalities. Rosetta played the role of "Topsy," in blackface, with comedic eccentricity. Her motto: "I'm mean an' ornery, I is, mean an' ornery. I hate everybody in the world, and I only wish there were more people in the world so I could hate them too." Audiences did not take her role as being racially prejudiced, but critics were equally divided between condemning Rosetta for her portrayal and praising her for turning a tragedy into a comedy for everyone's enjoyment. Vivian, as Eva, in golden curls, was the sweet, innocent heroine, but she, too, added comic touches that added further incongruity to the play.

"Topsy and Eva" opened at the Alcazar Theater, San Francisco, in July 1923, and was an immediate hit. It played for eighteen weeks. The songs included "Moon Am Shinin,'" "The Land of Long Ago," and the hit of the show, "Rememb'ring." The theater in which they were to appear in New York was occupied with a hit show, so they played in Chicago, at the Selwyn Theater. They performed for an unprecedented forty-three weeks to full houses. *Variety* spent more space detailing the sisters' box office earnings, reported to be $179,000 for 1924, than about the quality of their performances. "Topsy and Eva" finally made it to New York, opening at the Harris Theater, December 24, 1924. Comedy skits had been rewritten, songs reworked, and costumes changed, all designed to make the show an even greater travesty on "Tom." Audiences may have had some vague familiarity with the traditional "Tom" but they left the theater with an entirely new and humorous version. The show played for twenty weeks before going on tour. The Duncan Sisters performed almost nothing else for the remainder of their careers.

During the next four years, the sisters traveled throughout the country putting on their hilarious satire. Except for the names of characters, the original play's plot had been entirely replaced. The sisters took the play to England, France and Germany. They also visited South Africa and South America. Some reviewers said that they performed the play in the language of the country.

In 1927, the Duncan Sisters were persuaded to replay "Topsy and Eva" for the movies. Unfortunately, the silent film medium was unable to convey the verbal humor of the play. They appeared in another movie, "Two Flaming Youths," also in 1927. Rosetta appeared alone in "It's a Great Life" (1929), a talking film. "Two Flaming Youths" was a fictional version of their life in the context of a backstage drama. Both were flops. In contrast, they appeared at the Palace Theater with great success repeating their familiar routine. At the time, they popularized such songs as "Bye, Bye, Blackbird" and "Side By Side." The sisters also went on radio doing bits from the play.

The year also found them back in Chicago, for a long run of "Topsy and Eva." Although audiences had seen the play before, they were enthusiastic about seeing it again. An incident with the Cicero police, in which Rosetta received a traffic citation and a broken nose, became the incentive to writing the song, "Mean Cicero Blues," and the incident also was included in the play as a comedy skit. To keep the plot topical, the sisters continually incorporated new material, usually from events that had made the front pages.

Through the late 1920s, the Duncan Sisters alternated playing "Topsy and Eva" and appearing in vaudeville with excerpts of the play. Vaudeville may have been dying, but the sisters continued to survive. They just shifted their act to cabarets and nightclubs.

In 1931, much to the public's surprise, the Duncans filed a voluntary bankruptcy petition. Vivian blamed their losses on Wall Street and too many unsecured notes. A stage version of "Topsy and Eva" was revived, obviously to earn some badly needed money. The show was brought back again in 1934, likely for the same reason.

In 1932, Vivian married Nils Asther, an actor. She divorced him a year later. She later married Frank Herman, a non-professional. Rosetta never married.

The 1930s were generally hard years for the Duncan Sisters. Their best venue, vaudeville, had mostly disappeared. And how many times could they resurrect their well-known play? Sporadic appearances in the United States were supplemented by trips to Europe where they remained popular entertainers. They were brought into the musical "New Faces of 1936" when the show was floundering, performing comic bits from their play. The show lasted for six months. In 1942, the Duncan Sisters formally announced their retirement.

For some reason, rumored to be money, they decided to return to entertaining in 1952 with their old familiar act, mostly in clubs and on television.

On December 1, 1959, Rosetta was badly injured in a car crash outside of Chicago. She lapsed into a coma and died a few days later. Services were held in Chicago and Hollywood, her current home, and burial was in Forest Lawn Cemetery. Rosetta was eulogized as having been "the greatest clown on the American stage." Although Vivian was devastated by the loss of her sister, she continued to perform as a solo act for a few more years.

The Duncan Sisters and their record-breaking travesty on "Tom" rapidly disappeared from audience memory, and their stage exploits are almost unknown today.

Vivian died on September 19, 1986, in Los Angeles. She was eighty-four years old. For some years, she had suffered from Alzheimer's disease and was under constant care in a nursing home.

The Hilton Sisters

Violet and Daisy Hilton were Siamese twins joined at the base of the spine. They spent the first two decades of their life as exhibits in circuses and street carnivals. When they entered vaudeville, they quickly became popular headliners. While they appeared happy, well-adjusted women, their careers were filled with exploitation and prejudice.

The girls were born on February 5, 1908, in Brighton, England. They were pygopagus twins, conjoined at the hips and buttocks. They shared blood circulation but no major organs. Their mother, Kate Skinner, was a young, unwed barmaid. The father was later killed in World War I. Both the mother and father and their parents had been twins. The girls were "adopted" by their mother's boss and midwife, Mary Hilton, then on the second of her six husbands.

At the age of four, Violet and Daisy were being exhibited in circus sideshows and carnivals in England and Europe. For the next three years, they toured Australia with various circuses. They made their first trip to the United States in 1916 to escape the war and work with American circuses. By this time, the girls had had rigorous training in singing and dancing. Mrs. Hilton kept the twins hidden from public view except when they performed. The girls were also taught to play various musical instruments, becoming proficient on clarinet and saxophone. Their education came from private tutors. Mrs. Hilton acted as their guardian, manager and keeper, as the girls were under her entire control.

The family remained in the United States, settling in a mansion in San Antonio, Texas. Mrs. Hilton's successive husbands were said to be physically abusive. One of the girls' biographers spoke of their early lives as a cycle of abuse and exploitation. When Mrs. Hilton died, her husband and daughter took over the sisters' act.

A vaudeville manager, Terry Turner, saw the girls perform and believed they would appeal to vaudeville audiences. After they were rejected by the Keith circuit, Turner persuaded Marcus Loew to book them in his theaters. The Hilton Sisters made their vaudeville debut at Loew's State Theater, Newark, New Jersey, in February 1925. They broke all box office records. The twins earned $2,500 for their weeks of work. They had been transformed from a freak sideshow attraction to vaudeville headliners.

The sisters' act consisted of playing the latest jazz tunes on the clarinet and saxophone, then singing and dancing to some of the latest ballads. They were small, less than five feet in height, and pretty brunettes. Daisy later colored her hair blonde so they could be told apart. Their actions seemed quite natural on the stage. Audi-

The Hilton Sisters (Museum of the City of New York).

ences cheered their obvious talent, but there was always a sense of amazement and discomfort that these human oddities could be so normal. *Variety* reported that the twins could perform on any stage in any city and "the act contains nothing repellant or gruesome."

The sisters toured almost continuously for five years as headliners playing at most of the high-class theaters across the country. However, they were never booked for the Palace Theater in New York. During this time, they earned several thousand dollars a week. Their last recorded appearance was at the Iowa Theater, Waterloo, Iowa, the week of October 5, 1930. Vaudeville was in its dying throes and new bookings had dried up. The sisters returned to San Antonio to fight the Hilton family for their personal freedom. For twenty-three years, they had been under the control of their guardians. Filing a lawsuit against their management, in 1931 they obtained a court order that made them independent entrepreneurs.

In 1932, the twins played themselves in Tod Browning's controversial film, "Freaks." The movie raised the question whether Siamese twins could have a love life. The film answer was yes; in real life, the answer was inconclusive. The twins were refused marriage licenses in twenty-one states. In 1936, Violet married James Walker Moore, a dancer, in Dallas, Texas. He died a few years later. Daisy married Harold Estep, an actor, in Buffalo, New York, in 1941. The marriage lasted two weeks and was annulled.

The sisters gave credit to Harry Houdini for helping them adjust to life and become successful. He had told them: "Character will accomplish anything for you. You must learn to forget your physical link and develop mental independence and you'll get anywhere you want." As Violet explained it, "We learned to get rid of each other mentally. When Daisy had a date, sometimes I quit paying attention and did not know what was going on." Apparently, the system worked well except for marriage.

When the public lost interest in Siamese twins and vaudeville died, the sisters did not want to return to circus life. Instead, they settled in Miami, Florida, and ran a shop called the Hilton Sisters Snack Bar. When the business failed, they traveled to Hollywood. In 1950, they appeared in "Chained for Life," a film that generally followed their lives. The film had poor production values and a limited run. When, in the 1960s, "Freaks" was re-released, it turned into a cult classic. The sisters were recruited to go on a national publicity tour to promote the film. A sequel to "Chained for Life," called "Torn by a Knife," was produced but never released.

In 1960, needing work, the twins got a job in a grocery store in Charlotte, North Carolina. One worked the register, the other bagged. One day when they failed to report to work, they were discovered dead by police in their modest home. They had died on January 6, 1969, of the Hong Kong flu. They were sixty years old.

At one point in their vaudeville career, a reporter asked how they felt about being on display. "We don't mind having people stare at us. We're used to it. We've never known anything else," they replied. Later in life, the twins were reserved, refusing to give interviews or permission to have their pictures taken.

For more than a decade, they had been the most famous Siamese twins in the country, thanks to vaudeville.

Part Six : The Actresses

Valeska Suratt

From Gibson Girl to vamp, Valeska Suratt had a career highlighted by controversial vaudeville acts, passionate melodramas and moving pictures and a penchant for exotic, sensual fashions.

Ralph Surratt, Valeska's father, had been a farm laborer before moving from Virginia to Indiana as a young man. His parents had come from France. Anna Matthews, her mother, was born in Indiana in 1852. Her parents had come from England, having bought land from the government in Owensville, a small town in southern Indiana. Ralph and Anna were married in June 1878. At the time, Ralph was a blacksmith. Anna had been married before and had an eight-year-old daughter.

The couple had four children, two boys and two girls. Valeska was the second child, born on June 28, 1882, in Owensville. When she was seven years old, the family moved to Terre Haute. By the time Valeska graduated from elementary school at the age of fourteen, she wanted to be an actress. To save money for acting lessons, she worked in a photography store. When she was seventeen, Valeska left the family and moved to Indianapolis where she got a job at Block's Department Store. Soon, she had learned about women's fashions and had become a clothing buyer. For the next several years, Valeska saved money in order to travel to New York to seek an acting career. During this time, her actual stage experience was minimal. She appeared in amateur theatricals and sang in the church choir.

In 1902, at the age of twenty, Valeska went to New York. She auditioned for various chorus jobs but was unsuccessful because she lacked experience. Although Valeska was pretty, managers viewed her style of dress and grooming as unconventional. Valeska had learned about fashions while working at the department store, and had attempted to mold her personality through the use of her clothing. Managers were put off by this tall, thin girl with her hair combed straight back and by the cut of her shirtwaist and skirt.

Disappointed by her unsuccessful experiences in New York, Valeska moved to Chicago and she enrolled in an acting school. She made some appearances in second-class vaudeville singing and dancing but went unrecognized, except by vaudevillian Billy Gould. Gould was a comedian from South Africa, currently touring the United States. He had just lost his dancing partner and persuaded Valeska to join him. Gould taught her several exotic dances for their act, including an apache dance that appealed to audience tastes. In 1905, their partnership turned to marriage. The couple then traveled to South Africa and toured for several months. Gould was already well-known in the country and his new partner made the act even more appealing. Valeska had now mastered exotic dancing and matched it with costumes that accentuated her body movements and dance style.

In 1906, the couple returned to the United States and settled in New York. However, finding vaudeville engagements for almost unknown performers was proving to be quite difficult, until Valeska met producer Ernest Edelston.

Edelston was producing a musical import from England, "The Belle of Mayfair," and was casting for a performer that represented the popular Gibson Girl. He saw Valeska at the Savoy Hotel as she was walking down a staircase with some friends. She was wearing a dress she had made: a black velvet sheath gown, covered in front but open to her waist in back. "There," cried Edelston, "there is my Gibson Girl."

Of course, Valeska accepted the assignment. The show opened at Daly's Theater on December 3, 1906. In a cast that included veteran performers Irene Bentley, Christie MacDonald and Bessie Clayton, Valeska distinguished herself with her singing and dramatic acting. The show played into the spring. Vaudeville managers now sought to sign Valeska for their theaters, offering substantial salaries.

Instead, Valeska formed her own vaudeville act and toured on the Keith circuit. Gould was not part of the act but was also on the bill. She was reported to be making $2,000 a week, much more than she had ever earned before. Her act included singing and dancing and wearing revealing costumes of her own design. *Variety* approvingly remarked about her manner of dress although some reviewers thought it was in bad taste.

Valeska Suratt

In 1907, after a highly successful tour, Valeska was signed by Joe Weber to appear in "Hip! Hip! Hooray!" Weber had separated from Fields three years before. The show opened on October 10, 1907, at what had been the old Weber & Fields Music Hall, renamed Weber's Music Hall. Valeska's performance consisted mainly of parading across the stage in large hats and shapely costumes. The show was a poor attempt to resurrect the old Weberfields routines and ran for only sixty-four performances. But Valeska was in great demand.

While playing in Weber's production, Valeska separated from Gould. He unexpectedly died in 1909. For the next several years, she appeared on both the Keith and Orpheum circuits, touring the country. Not only were audiences entranced with her exotic singing and dancing, they were awed by her costumes, each one more elegant and seductive than the last. A fashion magazine called her "one of the best dressed women of the stage." They believed that Valeska was appealing to an audience looking to improve their social class. Audiences sat amazed at her creations. Women attempted to copy her costumes. Alan Dale, the theater critic, called Valeska a "riot of clothes," and alluded to the sexuality she brought to the stage with her fashions. When, in 1909, she put on a skit called "The Belle of the Boulevards," her costume featured bare back exposure, more than had ever been seen before in vaudeville.

Valeska's 1910 skits caused consternation among city officials although audiences were much more accepting. Mayor Gaynor of New York notified the police to stop her performance because it was "salacious." The show was shut down. He also swore that it was his duty to notify his fellow executives throughout the country that her show should not be permitted. Valeska did not do well in a few cities, the town fathers viewing her act as "vulgar." Managers, however, were excited with the publicity because it meant good box office. Valeska's act gave her a unique personal style that separated her from other performers and made for her success in vaudeville. She would never sacrifice these advantages. Being herself meant large salaries and adoring audiences.

In December 1910, Valeska put on her act at Hammerstein's Victoria Theater to full houses. This was the first time she appeared in a specially written skit. For the remainder of her time in vaudeville, she would put on these mini-melodramas, which were built around sultry roles and elaborate costumes. The skit at Hammerstein's, called "Bouffe Variety," had a leading man named Fletcher Norton. Their relationship caused Norton to divorce his wife and, in 1911, he and Valeska were married. Newspapers followed the romance and marriage with their usual gleeful fascination.

In 1911, Valeska appeared in the musical, "The Red Rose," which opened the 1911–12 season in New York on June 22 at the Bijou Theater. Set in Paris, with a comic opera–like story and unimaginative music, the show still managed to last several months. Valeska played the leading role, a concierge's daughter who in reality is a royal's lost child. But it was the show's costumes and sets, all designed by Valeska, that reviewers noticed most. The musical experience was not gratifying to Valeska and she returned to vaudeville.

From 1911 to 1915, Valeska performed skits that featured provocative roles and sexy fashions, to the delight of crowded houses. During this time, the marriage with Norton foundered and Valeska divorced him in 1913, due primarily to their inability to be together for any length of time. At the same time, the success of her skits attracted the attention of Paramount Pictures, who wished to utilize her image as a femme fatale to compete with Theda Bara, then the reigning vamp. In 1915, Valeska starred in "The Immigrant" and "The Soul of Broadway," both successful films that took advantage of her looks and attire. Fox then outbid Paramount for her services and released nine films in two years, promoting her as their improved version of a vamp. The names of the films clearly characterize her roles: "Jealousy" (1916), "The Victim" (1916), "A Rich Man's Plaything" (1917), "She" (1917), "The Siren" (1917), and "Wife Number Two" (1917). But the studio discovered, with all their efforts, that they could not beat Theda Bara. They gave up on Valeska at the same time that she tired of the movie business. She never again appeared in movies.

For the next several years, Valeska took her familiar act on vaudeville routes. She appeared at the Palace Theater in 1920, now being advertised as "The Dynamic Force of Vaudeville." It may have been the peak of her career but it also began a rather dispiriting decline as well.

While she continued to appear on various vaudeville circuits throughout the country, her drawing power declined. Her skits had become too familiar. Her costumes were now less exciting, the Ziegfeld models surpassing even her most imaginative designs, and her singing and acting were overshadowed by a new generation of women entertainers. Valeska would not, or could not, change her routines. Her awareness of this situation often led to frustrating episodes.

She lost her headliner status on some bills and refused to perform. Her salary declined along with box office returns. In 1927, Valeska sued Cecil B. DeMille, accusing him of adapting his movie "The King of Kings" from a book by Mizra Ahmed Schrab, to which she owned the movie rights. DeMille denied the accusation and the suit was thrown out of court, but not before the press made fun of her actions. In 1928, Valeska sued Charles Pyle for $2,000 claiming she entrusted the money to his care. Pyle claimed innocence and won the case. By this time, Valeska had so few engagements that earning money had become a decided problem. During this period she began studying and writing on religious subjects and amassing a sizable library of religious books. Much of whatever money she obtained was given to charities.

During the Depression, Valeska lived in a seedy New York hotel. A benefit was given for her that netted several thousand dollars. She lost most of the money gambling. An attempt to write her autobiography for a New York newspaper was declined when the publisher found that Valeska claimed to be the Virgin Mary. For the next thirty years, Valeska lived in poverty, just another victim of the death of vaudeville.

Valeska died July 2, 1962, in Washington, D.C. She was eighty years old. The body was taken back to Terre Haute, Indiana, and she was buried in Highland Lawn Cemetery. Her glory days on Broadway had been forgotten.

Fannie Ward

Better known for her legitimate stage and movie career than for her time in vaudeville, Fanny Ward was favorably compared to Maude Adams. While in vaudeville, she showed off her dramatic abilities in one-act skits taken from popular plays. She appeared in twenty-four films in five years, playing flapper roles before the flapper era had begun. Fannie never quite reached the top of her profession. She tirelessly devoted herself to appearing perpetually young, an act that made her famous.

Fannie Buchanan was born on February 22, 1872, in St. Louis, Missouri. Her father, John Buchanan, had moved to St. Louis from Pennsylvania after the Civil War and operated a prosperous wholesale dry goods business. Her mother, Eliza Buchanan, was born in Kentucky and came to St. Louis for her schooling. Fannie had an older brother, Benton, who was born in 1869.

Like many star-struck girls, Fannie went to the theater, both legitimate and variety houses, and acted at home what she had seen. Against the wishes of her parents, she decided to become an actress. Fannie appeared in local theatrical companies, playing many different roles. When traveling companies came to St. Louis, she was often selected to play small parts. At the age of seventeen, Fannie went to New York, believing that that city was the only place to make a career of acting.

Because of her ability to learn lines quickly and act with confidence, Fannie got the opportunity to perform small roles in a number of plays. She made her debut on November 26, 1890, in "Pippins," at the Broadway Theater. She played a minor part, but was noticed by impresario Daniel Frohman, who hired her for his stock company. "Pippins" played only a month because its star, Amelia Summerville, was injured in an accident.

Frohman changed Fannie's last name to Ward, easy to remember and different from the Irish names currently found on the variety stage. After several small roles, Fannie played a more demanding part in "Sinbad," which opened June 27, 1892, at the Garden Theater. It was a summer show and was mounted in spectacular fashion. According to reviewers, the sets and costumes outdid the plot. Fanny learned a great deal about stagecraft from the star, Louise Montague, who often challenged Lillian Russell for supremacy of the comic opera stage and men's attention. The show ran for fourteen weeks. Fannie gained notice for her acting and for wearing a costume that critics suggested was daring.

Fannie appeared in ten plays between 1890 and 1894. Frohman's empire extended to London, so Fannie went to London and played the leading role in "The Shop Girl" at the Gaiety Theater. Reviewers acknowledged her acting talent and predicted a promising future. She played starring roles in several plays, among which "The Marriage of William Ashe" was a hit.

In 1898, at the age of twenty-six, Fannie married Joseph "Diamond Joe" Lewis, a wealthy London diamond merchant and owner of Transvaal mines. Fannie retired from the stage and the couple lived in London and Paris, participating in the social whirl of both cities. They had one daughter, Dorthea, born in 1900. During this time, Fannie became obsessed with her personal beauty and the desire to remain as young as possible. She utilized special facial treatments, diets (to keep her weight under 100 pounds), the "proper manipulations of muscles" and the use of a "Siberian snow face mask."

A combination of factors brought Fannie back to the United States. Her marriage was breaking up and she wanted to return to the stage. She entered vaudeville in 1910, performing a scene from the play "Van Allen's Wife" at Percy Williams Colonial Theater. For the week, she received $2,000. The act was quite serious and was not favorably received by vaudeville reviewers and audiences. Fannie followed with a scene from "An Unlucky Star," which reviewers found a refreshing change. Hereafter, her sketches were more lightly drawn with touches of humor. Fannie spent the next several years on the vaudeville circuit giving short skits, mainly taken from plays the audiences likely had already seen. Her use of dramatic gestures and elegant, revealing costumes made her a hit with patrons.

Fannie Ward

In 1913, Fannie caused a highly publicized scandal by divorcing her husband of fifteen years and immediately marrying a man twelve years younger: Jack Dean, an actor in the same traveling company as Fannie. Lewis claimed adultery and named Dean as co-respondent. The publicity did not seem to harm Fannie's career; in fact, her act drew even larger crowds.

In 1915, concerned that at forty-three, she was not advancing her career, Fannie found moving pictures an attractive alternative. At the time, Cecil B. DeMille was seeking a new face to star in a sensational film he was about to produce. Called "The Cheat," it told the story of a wayward wife, her adventures and final demise. Fannie made her screen debut in the role. The film was a tremendous success, and Fannie launched a career that had her appearing in twenty-four movies in five years. Her husband, Jack Dean, appeared in all of her movies. The majority of her roles in these melodramas were women in distress or causing distress. Some of her hits included "A Gutter Magdalene" (1916), "Witchcraft" (1916), "A School for Husbands" (1917), "Innocent" (1918) and "The Yellow Ticket" (1918). By 1917, Fannie was as popular a movie star as her colleagues Mary Pickford, Blanche Sweet, Mabel Normand and Dorothy Gish. She ended her movie career in 1920 although the press contended that she could still pass as an ingenue.

In 1922, Fannie's daughter married Lord Terance Plunket, a friend of the British royal family. It was her second marriage. At the age of seventeen, and against her mother's wishes, Dorthea had married Barney Barnato, a diamond merchant, who died a year later. Fannie thoroughly enjoyed the life of the mother of an aristocrat, especially since she looked no older than her daughter. Fannie and her husband often traveled between America and England, where she occasionally appeared on vaudeville bills.

Fannie returned to vaudeville in the United States in 1926 at the Palace Theater, performing a scene from the play "The Miracle Woman." Critics remarked about her continued youthfulness, noting that she really was somewhere around fifty-four. Fannie kept everyone guessing as to her real age, changing her birth date often when asked by the press. Two years later, Fannie returned to the Palace, this time singing several songs, and wearing costumes that revealed her still shapely legs. She was billed as "the most remarkable looking woman for her age of our age." The snickering comments did nothing to bother her. In fact, she used the publicity of her perennial beauty to open a string of beauty shops. At the time, the Palace was being used by silent movie stars, since the number of old vaudeville stars was decreasing and vaudeville itself was rapidly declining. On her bill were Sessue Hayakawa and Eugene O'Brien, Norma Talmadge's leading man.

In 1931, Fannie made her last appearance on stage, starring in a melodrama, "The Truth Game," and touring with it for the season. Again, she retired from the stage. Tragedy struck when, in 1938, Lord and Lady Plunket died in an airplane crash in California. They had three children, the oldest, age fifteen, who now became heir to the title. Fannie became depressed about the loss of her daughter and declined all offers to return to the stage. Even at the age of sixty-six, she displayed a slim figure and a face without wrinkles.

Jack Dean died in 1950. Two years later, Fannie was found unconscious in her apartment on Park Avenue and was rushed to the hospital. She had suffered a cerebral hemorrhage and lapsed into a coma. She died on January 27, 1952. Fannie was seventy-nine years old but some news people believed she was older. She left an estate of $40,000 but no will. She had a checking account with a balance of $17,000 and jewelry valued at $20,000. She was survived by her three grandsons from the Plunket family.

The "eternal flapper," as she was labeled, popularized serious plays in vaudeville, then used her youthful appearance to star in silent films. In a forty-one-year career, she displayed her acting versatility by appearing in more than fifty plays, movies and vaudeville skits.

Mrs. Patrick Campbell

Although the most successful British actress of her generation, Mrs. Patrick Campbell's eccentric prima-donna demeanor caused difficulties in both her personal and theatrical life. Her off-stage personality revealed an extreme temperament and great wit.

On-stage she was an actress of great talent who worked as hard and as often as any other theatrical figure. She visited the United States quite often, performing various legitimate plays for appreciative critics and audiences. Twice she came to America to appear in vaudeville because "I needed the money."

Beatrice Rose Stella Tanner was born on February 9, 1865, in London, England, to John Tanner, a merchant of the East India Company, and Luigia Romanini Tanner, an Italian actress. Beatrice was raised to appreciate music and the theater. She had enough ability to win a scholarship to further a potential stage career.

In 1884, at the age of nineteen, her drama schooling was left uncompleted when she married Patrick Campbell, a son of the manager of the Bank of India in Hong Kong. A year later, they had a son, Alan, and, the year after, a daughter, Stella. Then, Patrick developed tuberculosis and went to South Africa. He was later killed in the Boer War. Financial difficulties hit the Tanner family, and Beatrice's father and mother immigrated to Texas, leaving their daughter with two young children.

Taking the name of her husband as a stage name, Mrs. Patrick Campbell sought employment in the theater. As a member of the Anomalies Dramatic Club, she made her stage debut at the Alexandra Theater, Liverpool, in 1888.

She then joined the Greet's Company and had opportunities to play several Shakespeare parts. Her London debut was at the Adelphi Theater in 1890. For the next three years, she built a reputation as a fine actress. She came to the critics' attention in 1893 when she starred in "The Second Mrs. Tanqueray" at the St. James Theater. Her starring roles with Beerbohm Tree, John Hare and Forbes-Robertson propelled her to become one of England's most desired actresses.

Mrs. Campbell made her first trip to the United States in December 1901, taking her company to Chicago, Milwaukee and New York. For the one appearance in Milwaukee alone, she received $3,000. The tour was highly successful and she was asked to return. In 1903, Mrs. Campbell came back to play "Magda" in New York. Her reputation as an exceptional actress and temperamental diva generated front-page headlines. She had 42nd Street spread with tanbark because she complained that the noise outside her theater was spoiling the performance. Although smoking for "ladies" was forbidden in the Plaza Hotel, the ruling did not prevent her from lighting up, shocking the management.

In early 1910, after a year in which good plays were in short supply, Mrs. Campbell came to New York looking for work. She was not averse to appearing in vaudeville because "the money was good." E. A. Albee signed her for a ten-week tour at $2,500 a week. He also agreed to her stipulations that she would perform only twice a day with no performance on Sunday and that she would not speak to any other actors on the bill.

Mrs. Campbell appeared in a one-act play, "Expiation!" in which she killed a man and shrieked to the audience about her plight. She complained later that American audiences did not appreciate her dramatic acting. Albee advertised her as the "great tragic actress." *Variety* gave her performance an excellent review and believed seeing her was worth the money. Several months later, while appearing at the Majestic Theater, Chicago, she put on a twenty-four-minute playlet called "The Ambassador's Wife" written by her son Alan. Reviewers felt the story forced the audience to suffer. Throughout the tour, Mrs. Campbell complained about every aspect of the experience and Albee was glad to see her leave the country.

In 1912, Mrs. Campbell suffered a serious illness which temporarily forced her out of theater. During her convalescence, George Bernard Shaw wrote letters to her, some of them quite passionate. Because of their friendship, Shaw starred Mrs. Campbell as Eliza Doolittle in his play "Pygmalion." The year that "Pygmalion" was produced, 1914, she married George Cornwallis-West, within hours after he had been granted a divorce from his first wife, Jennie Jerome, formerly the widow of Lord Randolph Churchill and mother of Winston Churchill.

When Mrs. Campbell brought "Pygmalion" to New York in 1915, she also appeared in vaudeville houses in one-act plays to "pick up some additional change." Actually, she earned more money in vaudeville than all of the sold-out performances of "Pygmalion." Shaw and Campbell disagreed about how the play should end. He wished to leave it ambiguous; she wanted it to have a happy ending and she added a last line to meet her objective. Shaw continued to disagree, but she performed the play with her own last line.

Mrs. Patrick Campbell (Harry Ranson Humanities Research Center, the University of Texas at Austin).

Mrs. Campbell returned to the United States in February 1927 in "The Adventurous Age," which reviewers did not like. Her first motion picture "The Dancers" opened at the Roxy Theater, New York, in November 1930. During the early 1930s, she appeared in several pictures in England and America, the most notable being "Crime and Punishment" in 1935. During the time she was making pictures, Mrs. Campbell also toured on the lecture circuit, speaking on "Diction in Dramatic Art." Some of her stops took her to old vaudeville houses. Her last American visit ended in 1938.

Cornwallis-West died in 1936. During her last years, Mrs. Campbell was unemployed and had to depend upon borrowing from friends and living on credit. She died alone and in poverty on April 9, 1940, in Pau, France, at the age of seventy-five.

Ethel Barrymore

For more than sixty years, she was one of America's greatest dramatic actresses. At her funeral, a *New York Times* editorial commented, "This great actress moved through many roles, playing a leading and unforgettable part in the fascinating drama we may call the life of Ethel Barrymore." Ethel appeared several times at the Palace Theater as a vaudeville headliner, "to pick up some change," as she described it.

Ethel was born in Philadelphia, the daughter of Maurice Barrymore, a well-known and versatile actor, and Georgiana Drew, a comedienne. The Drew family had already built a fine reputation in theater. Ethel attended the Convent of Notre Dame in Philadelphia and, simultaneously, was learning the craft of stage acting. At the age of fourteen, she made her Broadway debut in "The Rivals," which played at Charles Frohman's Empire Theater. Frohman guided her early theater education and, in fact, directed her career until his death in 1915.

In late 1894, at fifteen, Ethel was given a small role in Frohman's "The Bauble Shop," which starred Maude Adams and Ethel's uncle, John Drew. During the play's tour, Ethel and Maude became friends although they were totally different personalities. Maude was shy, serious and committed to the theater. Ethel was a socialite who loved to attend parties and dinners. Frohman likely tolerated Ethel's behavior because it offered a dramatic contrast to Maude's reclusiveness.

The following year, Ethel appeared in an ingenue role in another Drew-Adams play, "That Imprudent Young Couple." The play received mediocre reviews and Frohman quickly replaced it with a past success. Another Frohman production, "Rosemary," gave Ethel a larger role, and gained her more attention from reviewers. Frohman then sent Ethel to England for several years to "learn the trade."

Upon her return to the United States, Ethel got top billing from Frohman as Madame Trentoni in "Captain Jinks of the Horse Marines," which was a success and labeled Ethel as one of the new stars of the dramatic stage. In 1905, J.M. Barrie submitted two plays to Frohman for his stars Ethel and Maude Adams. Who should play Peter Pan, Barrie asked? Frohman chose Maude. "Peter Pan" played for four years and has been revived every few years since. Ethel appeared in "Alice Sit-by-the-Fire," which played less than two years.

For the next seven years, Ethel had substantial roles in a series of Frohman-produced plays. Her dramatic acting was so well-received that critics were calling her the "First Lady of American Theater." However, even the most successful and long-running plays did not offer large salaries, so Ethel sought other ways to enhance her income. Vaudeville paid more to headliners for less work. Ethel decided to try it during the times she was not engaged on the legitimate stage.

Ethel found the transition from dramatic actress to vaudeville entertainer easy. She was already a well-known personality with excellent credentials. Her act consisted of one-act plays, primarily of a dramatic nature, laced with a bit of humor. Her vaudeville appearances were a special treat for audiences who were familiar with her reputation but had never visited, or been able to visit, a legitimate theater.

When the Palace Theater was only six weeks old and still in search of full houses, Ethel appeared on a bill featuring some of the top vaudeville stars, including the Courtney Sisters, Bessie Clayton, an exotic dancer, and Nat Wills, a comedian. Opening April 28, 1913, Ethel performed a one-act play, "Miss Civilization," by Richard Harding Davis, himself a familiar author, journalist and adventurer who had built a unique reputation for risky ventures. For the week Ethel appeared, the theaters were full. She was praised by reviewers and honored by enthusiastic audiences with many curtain calls at each performance.

The following year, Ethel returned to the Palace twice during the summer months. During her appearance in July, she introduced J.M. Barrie's humorous play, "The Twelve Pound Look," with tremendous results. Her act was received so well that she played the Palace again in August, doing the same play. On the bill with her were Robert Edeson, a fellow dramatic actor, W.C. Fields, a juggler-comedian, and Joe Welch, an ethnic song-and-dance man. It was a typical mixture of the serious and comic as represented by a Palace program. During the same year, Ethel appeared in her first movie, "The Nightingale."

Over the next decade, Ethel was seen in various plays, all but one big hits. In 1922, her interpretation of Juliet was panned. Nevertheless, during the 1920s, she starred in some of the best plays of her career, like "The Second Mrs. Tanqueray" and "The Constant Wife."

In 1926, Ethel again visited the Palace, playing "The Twelve Pound Look" and doing what she did best, to audience acclaim. However, she found that vaudeville was no longer the same nor were the salaries as generous.

In 1928, to honor this "First Lady," a theater was named after her. She returned to Hollywood in 1933 and was seen in movies for the next two decades, alternating her screen time with the dramatic stage. During the last years of her life, she appeared on television.

Ethel died of a heart attack at her Beverly Hills, California, apartment in 1959. She was seventy-nine years old. She was buried in a crypt in Calvary Cemetery next to her equally famous brothers, Lionel and John.

Ethel's work was honored by audiences as readily as the comedian or popular singer. She was instrumental in bringing dramatic acting to the vaudeville stage.

Ethel Barrymore

Sarah Bernhardt

At the same time that Sarah Bernhardt was being celebrated by the British for her fifty years on the dramatic stage, she was negotiating a vaudeville contract to tour the United States. Her price was extravagant, but the great actress deserved every dollar. Her appearances brought legitimate theater to the vaudeville stage, encouraged managers to hire other dramatic stars and saved the Palace Theater from closing.

Sarah made her vaudeville debut during the 1912–13 season. Martin Beck, head of the Orpheum circuit, had traveled to Europe to sign up headliners who were willing to perform in vaudeville. He had read that Sarah had scored a triumph playing tragic scenes in French at London's Palladium, not exactly a theater renowned for legitimate drama. If Sarah was willing to perform there, she should be willing to consider popular theater in the United States.

With an impassioned speech that guaranteed she would have the entire country at her feet, Beck convinced Sarah to play in his theaters. She signed for $7,000 a week, the most ever given a performer to appear on the vaudeville stage. Beck then discovered he had neglected to mention Sunday performances to Sarah and feared she would balk at the requirement to play additional time. "Why all the fuss?" she wanted to know. "I'm in the theater all the time, anyway. We play Sundays often in France, too."

Beck was responsible for the construction of the Palace Theater, New York, an opulent edifice destined to become the symbolic epitome of vaudeville achievement. However, after opening March 24, 1913, and even with vaudeville headliners on the bill, the theater lost money. For six weeks, the Palace floundered. Oscar Hammerstein predicted it would close in six months. Beck was seriously contemplating shutting down the theater but things began to change when Ethel Barrymore appeared in a one-act play written by local newspaperman Richard Harding Davis. Sarah's arrival turned the theater into "the place to be."

Sarah's twenty-week tour began at the Majestic Theater in Chicago, Illinois, on December 12, 1912. She performed a one-act play, in French, with her fellow actor and lover, Lou Tellegen, who was less than half her age. Due to a brief bout of illness and some negative reviews, the act nearly stopped in Chicago. Sarah quickly recovered and resumed the tour in a private Pullman car with an entourage of nineteen people. They toured the Midwest, Canada and the West Coast and then returned to New York and the Palace. Sarah had been a sensational success across the country even though few in the audience understood the French language.

Sarah Bernhardt

On May 5, 1913, Sarah opened at the Palace. The "Divine Sarah" scored a major success. Advertising for her appearance had been substantial. Writers and reviewers told stories about her career, her triumphs and disappointments, and her lovers, all designed to bring patrons to the theater. Prices for her appearance were raised from one dollar to three dollars. This did not deter audiences from purchasing tickets, if they could even obtain them.

Sarah played for three and a half weeks, frequently changing her repertoire, which included a play co-authored by her son Maurice, scenes from "Theodora," "Lucrezia Borgia" and "The Lady of the Camellias," the last being the kind that would reduce an audience to tears. Other performers on the same bill were in tears because they *were* on the same bill. Edison Moving-Talking Pictures ended the evening.

The theater grossed $22,000 each week of the engagement. At the end of her stay at the Palace,

New York's top impresarios, Frohman and Belasco, presented her with a gold and silver laurel wreath and exhorted her to return to the United States again soon.

After a dramatic tour of the United States in 1917, Sarah signaled she was ready for another brief appearance in vaudeville (for financial reasons, it was reported). There had been significant changes in her life. Besides more obviously showing her age and the ravages of the war in Europe, she had had a leg amputated. Nevertheless, she continued to mesmerize audiences. She played for three weeks at the Palace, beginning December 17. Her thirty-three-minute renditions of "Lady of the Camellias" and especially "Joan of Arc," with its tragic and highly charged trial scene, sent audiences into emotional ecstasies. She played another week at the Riverside Theater with similar results.

Sarah was seventy-three years old when she acted the eighteen-year-old Joan in two-a-day vaudeville. She had no trouble convincing audiences of her dramatic power and authority on any stage where she chose to appear.

Sarah died on March 26, 1923, at the age of 79.

Fifi D'Orsay

She made her career playing the quintessential Parisian coquette, although she was never in France. Her exaggerated accent gained her headliner status in vaudeville followed by a long movie career. An average singer and dancer, she worked hard to become a colorful entertainer in an era when beauty and stage presence captured the approval of audiences.

Marie-Rose Angelina Yvonne Lussier was born in Montreal, Canada, on April 16, 1904. Her family had a strong theater background. Her aunt, Angeline Lussier, had been called Canada's Sarah Bernhardt. Her mother, Angelina, had appeared in music halls. There is no information available about Yvonne's father. Yvonne did have two siblings, a brother and a sister.

From an early age, Yvonne wanted to be an actress. Her aunt taught her about the theater and encouraged the young woman to pursue her stage aspirations. During her teens, Yvonne appeared in local music halls and dramatic productions. She also worked as a secretary to save enough money to travel to New York. In 1924, at the age of twenty, Yvonne arrived in New York to seek a theater career.

Yvonne's first job in New York was as a fashion model. Her small stature, piquant face, straight black bobbed hair and olive complexion made her an attractive and desirable model. With a French accent, and exuding a hint of seduction, Yvonne was persuaded to seek out theater producers who might be interested in hiring such a unique beauty. It took her ten weeks to see John Murray Anderson, who was casting for the next edition of his "Greenwich Village Follies." Upon hearing her sing "Mr. Gallagher and Mr. Shean" in French, Anderson signed her for the road company of "Follies."

In New York, the "Greenwich Village Follies" starred the ostentatious Dolly Sisters, Moran and Mack in blackface and Vincent Lopez and his Orchestra. The show ran for 127 performances before going on an extended tour. Many cast changes were made for the tour. Anderson had named Yvonne "Fifi" and her billing became "Mademoiselle Fifi." She was to perform an apache dance, but the director quickly discovered that her dancing was average. Instead, she sang the nonsensical song, "Yes, We Have No Bananas," in French. The song was written by Frank Silver and Irving Cohn but took more than a year to gain attention. With the help of the "Follies," the song was published and became a hit.

The road company of the "Follies" was generating only average box office receipts. Cast changes failed to improve the situation until Gallagher and Shean were engaged for the show. That comedy team had been formed in 1910 but split two years later; they were reunited in 1920 and were now at the height of their popularity. When the "Follies" closed in 1925, Gallagher and Shean again separated, having become uncomfortable with one another's success. During the show, Ed Gallagher and Yvonne had become lovers, although he was thirty-seven years older.

In 1926, the comedy team of "Mademoiselle Fifi and Gallagher" quickly found vaudeville bookings. Fifi credited Gallagher with teaching her "everything she learned about show business," which she readily accepted and incorporated into the act. However, Gallagher was an alcoholic, which made their relationship tenuous. After two years together, they separated with Fifi determined to go on her own. Gallagher was already ill and died a year later.

A friend suggested that Fifi see Herman Timberg, a songwriter and agent. Timberg liked Fifi's talents and teamed her with Herman Berrens in a vaudeville routine he had written. "Ten Dollars a Lesson" made the new team a popular hit and they were booked on the Orpheum circuit for two years. In 1929 Fifi, now with the last name of D'Orsay, after the French perfume, was asked to make a screen test for Fox studio. As part of the audition, Fifi sang the songs that gained her attention on the vaudeville circuit. The result was an extended Fox contract. Her first picture was "Hot For Paris" in 1929. She played her now-familiar role as a coquettish French girl. It was her next film, co-starred with Will Rogers, that made her a star. "They Had to See Paris" was released in 1929 and became a hit. Fifi's introduction of the phrase "ou-la-la" became a signature item for the actress and the roles in which she starred.

In 1930, Fifi and Berrens announced their engagement. But several months later, after she had returned from a personal appearance tour of the East, she told the press that it had been broken. "We had been separated so long and our careers will keep us apart so we decided to break our engagement," Fifi stated. Berrens went away brokenhearted while Fifi prepared for her next picture.

During 1930 and 1931, Fifi appeared in six pictures, reprising her role as the French coquette. She played opposite Will Rogers again in 1931 in "Young As You Feel." Seven more films followed between 1932 and 1937. During this time, she was appearing in vaudeville at high-class theaters, such as Palace in 1932. Also in the show were the Mills Brothers and Milton Berle. The bill was held over for three weeks. Press reports suggested that Fifi was earning up to $5,000 a week.

A year after she broke off from Berrens, Fifi announced her engagement to Terrance Ray, the son of an electrical engineer and an aspiring actor. Before the proposed marriage and the beginning of a new picture, Fifi said she was going to visit France for the first time, taking her sister with her. The trip never materialized. Due to a salary disagreement, Fifi left Fox in 1933 and was signed by Warner Bros. After returning from a brief vaudeville tour of the Midwest, Fifi and Ray were to fly to Arizona. A few weeks later, Fifi claimed in a press release that the engagement was "broken by mutual consent," although Ray disputed that version of events.

In September 1933, Fifi revealed a possible betrothal to Maurice Hill, whom she had met in Chicago several months earlier. He was a medical student whose father was a wealthy businessman. After living with Fifi in Hollywood for two months, Hill decided to give up medicine and become a movie actor. Fifi and Hill were married on December 6, 1933. Hill never became a movie actor. In December 1939, Fifi and Hill were divorced because, she claimed, he was unable to support her.

Fifi appeared in nine more films between 1943 and 1968. No longer playing the role of French coquette, she obtained parts as a sophisticated French woman, although with some humor. In 1950, when the Palace Theater revived vaudeville, Fifi returned to give her old familiar but sparkling performance. In television, she had small parts on "Bewitched" and "Perry Mason."

In 1971–72, at the age of sixty-seven, Fifi played "Solange LaFitte" in Sondheim's "Follies." The character was a former Follies headliner, a mirror of Fifi's real life and career. Her song rendition of "Ah, Paris" helped the show to win Tony Awards and Best Musical accolades.

Suffering from cancer during her last years, Fifi died on December 2, 1983, at the Motion Picture and Television Country Hospital in Woodland Hills, California. She was seventy-nine years old. Fifi was buried in Forest Lawn Cemetery.

During her fifty years of performing, Fifi was always on stage, whether in the theater or movies or in her personal life. She assumed a unique role in vaudeville and carried it to stardom in motion pictures where she became known and adored as "The French Bombshell."

Fifi D'Orsay (Museum of the City of New York).

Part Seven: The Male Impersonators

Vesta Tilley

Vesta Tilley was one of England's most popular music hall artists and most renowned as a male impersonator. Already a headliner, she visited the United States five times and was a box office success.

Born Matilda Alice Victoria Powles on May 13, 1864, in Worcester, England, she was the second of thirteen children. William Henry Powles, her father, was originally a china gilder, but in the 1870s he became a music hall comedian and theatrical agent. Later, he managed a music hall in Nottingham. During this time, he changed the family name to Ball. William died in 1888 at the age of forty-six. Matilda Broughton, Vesta's mother, was also born in Worcester. The couple was married in August 1862. Motherhood quickly followed. She had eight children over the next twenty years. Matilda died in April 1901, at the age of fifty-eight.

Due to her father's influence, Matilda became a child performer. She began her stage career at the age of three and, by seven, was appearing in music halls as "The Great Little Tilley." She had assumed the first name of Vesta (meaning virgin) and added Tilley, a family nickname for Matilda. The name was easily recognizable for music hall patrons. At nine, she first appeared in male costume. Vesta worked very closely with her father, a domineering person who controlled her career until she was in her mid–20s. She was the primary source of income for the family.

Vesta's act consisted of dressing like an upper-class gentleman and singing songs that satirized the rich. At the same time, she parodied male dominance in English society. She was likely the first woman to wear men's attire on the English stage. All of this delighted the poorer audiences that attended music halls.

Ten years after her father died, Vesta married Walter De Frece, who wrote her songs and acted as her manager. She became best-known for her renditions of "Strolling Along With Nancy," "The Pet of Rotten Row," "Burlington Bertie" (her most notable signature tune), "Jolly Good Luck to the Girls Who Love a Sailor," and "The Piccadilly Johnny with the Little Glass Eye." During the height of her career, these songs were continually in demand and she was required to include them at every performance. After establishing herself as a male impersonator, she never permitted the publication of her photos in anything but in male costume.

Vesta made her first trip to the United States during the 1894–95 season, appearing at Tony Pastor's Theater on April 16. Her initial performances before American audiences were highly successful although her songs were difficult to understand. She overcame this with a vivacious personality and her striking male mannerisms. She toured theaters in the East for the rest of the season.

Two years later, she was brought back to the United States by Weber & Fields, who wanted her to head up one of their vaudeville touring companies. To Fields, Vesta's act was like a teenage boy trying to act like a man. Her portrayals of various male types, her speech patterns, gestures and costumes were accurate in detail. Fields knew that Vesta's tour would be lucrative.

Outbidding Oscar Hammerstein for her services, Fields got Vesta for an astounding salary of $1,250 a week. In late October 1897, Vesta became the featured attraction at the Weber & Fields Music Hall and remained there for nine weeks. Vaudeville theater managers vied for Vesta's visits, and the Weberfields obliged. On her thirteen-week tour of nine cities, Vesta's company was reported to have netted over $50,000. Accompanying her were the four Cohans, with George able to try out a new farce he wrote, "Money to Burn," and Lew Dockstater, the reigning blackface comedian of the era. Fields' older brother, Max, was put in charge of the touring company.

Vesta Tilley

Vesta returned in 1903, now recognized by American audiences as vaudeville's premier male impersonator and a top headliner. She toured for the season on the Keith circuit, to full houses and box office profitability. When she toured again in 1906, response to her act was less enthusiastic because other top performers were doing male impersonations. Still, she drew good audiences and received excellent reviews.

Vesta's last appearance in the United States was in 1909, and was restricted to Eastern theaters. She was now a familiar act, although still an attractive performer. But English music hall patrons beckoned "The London Idol" to return and she remained there until her retirement in 1920.

During the war, she gained a great deal of popularity with the military singing patriotic songs. Dressed as a Tommy, she sang songs that included "The Army of Today's All Right" and "Luck to the Girl Who Loves a Sailor." She toured camps and hospitals and sold War Bonds. In 1920, at the age of fifty-six, Vesta made her farewell performance at London's Coliseum Theater. She was presented with a volume of signatures from two million admirers.

When Walter De Frece became a member of British Parliament and was knighted in 1919, Vesta became Lady Matilda Alice de Frece. An excellent businesswoman, Vesta had accumulated a fine estate. Her holdings and her husband's income permitted them to live comfortably, devoting their time to charity work. This affluent lifestyle was far removed from Vesta's humble beginnings. De Frece died in 1935. Vesta moved to London and died there on September 16, 1952, at the age of eighty-eight. She was idolized as one of England's greatest musical performers.

Ella Shields

A star attraction in British music halls, Ella Shields actually began her vaudeville career in the United States. In the 1920s, she made several return visits to America, often starring at the Palace Theater. She was one of the most famous male impersonators in music hall history and regaled audiences with her stylish mimicry of male celebrities.

Ella Catherine Buscher was born in Baltimore, Maryland, on September 26, 1879, the oldest of four sisters. Her parents, also born in Baltimore, were descendents of Irish immigrants who came to America due to the potato famine. Ella's father, Edward Buscher, was a janitor. Her mother, Kate, married Edward in 1878 when she was seventeen years old. Little is known of Ella's childhood except that she was interested in singing. As a teenager, she worked at various jobs and participated in amateur theatrical competitions. At the age of eighteen, Ella was hired by the Daniel Kelly Company to appear in their farce-comedy "Outcasts of the City." Ella was a soubrette and earned a good review from an Atlanta newspaper reporter, who wrote: "Miss Ella Shields deserves special mention for the strong work she does and received the approbation of the audience time and again." Ella probably changed her last name at the beginning of her stage career.

In 1898, Ella and her sisters performed in a vaudeville act that appeared in secondary houses in Pennsylvania and New Jersey. Ella gained the reputation as a "coon shouter," an act very popular at the time, and was praised by reviewers for her stylish renditions and friendly stage presence. She was soon appearing in a solo act with a versatile repertoire. That same year, she married Theodore Darwin Middaugh, a newspaper publisher, who was twenty-one years older. They had a daughter, Susan, born in September 1899. The marriage lasted until Ella went to England.

In 1904, an English agent persuaded Ella to come to London to appear in their music halls, the English version of vaudeville. She made an immediate hit with London audiences when she opened at Forester's Music Hall on October 10. She was billed as the "Southern Nightingale." Her accent seemed to match that of British southerners and audiences enjoyed her talent and grace even though she was not British.

During the next several years, Ella established herself as a music hall headliner. She toured the British Isles and Western Europe with success. In 1906, she met William Hargraves, an English writer and song composer. They married that same year. Hargraves often supplied Ella with material for her act.

In 1910, at a party given by music hall performers, Ella was asked to fill in for an actor who was ill. Half of a two-man act, Ella put on male attire to take his place. Response to her routine was so positive that her colleagues suggested she perform male impersonations. It was a turning point in her career. She rarely wore dresses on stage again.

Hargraves wrote a song for Ella, "Burlington Bertie of Bow," that quickly became her signature tune. The song tells the story of a poor Londoner who affects the style and manners of a rich gentleman. While Ella usually dressed in dapper costumes (white tie, top hat and cane), when she sang "Bertie" she wore tattered clothing, an old hat and worn shoes. Following her success in England, Ella toured Western Europe, South Africa, Australia, New Zealand and Canada. In 1914, she returned to tour in the United States.

Bringing her British-style act to American audiences was risky. But Ella prevailed, and the "Bertie" routine was as well-received as it had been in other countries. Overall, her male impersonations were a hit and the tour of vaudeville theaters was a huge success.

Ella returned to England in late 1914 and remained there during the war. Along with numerous appearances in music halls, she played at military camps and hospitals. Always at home with her peers, Ella garnered the title, "The Ideal of Ideals."

At the beginning of 1920, Ella again appeared at high-class vaudeville theaters in the Eastern United States. In January, she headlined at the Riverside Theater, New York, advertised as the "Daughter of America, the Idol of London." Others on the bill included Leon Errol, Bothwell Browne and Joe Cook. The following week, Ella made her first appearance at the Palace Theater in an "engagement extraordinary."

"One of England's greatest girl headliners, on a brief visit to America. A first favorite as a music hall entertainer and true artist. Known to all London as 'The Ideal of Ideals,' and impersonating male types with dash and distinction and convincing fidelity, Miss Shields is incomparable in her exquisitely done specialty," said the newspaper advertisement. Ella filled the theater at every performance. She played on the Keith circuit for several months with equal success.

Ella Shields (Harry Ransom Humanities Research Center, the University of Texas at Austin).

Ella returned to the Palace in 1921. The appearance began a succession of visits to the United States in the 1920s. In 1923, she toured for four months. In 1924, she toured Eastern cities and appeared at the Palace. "Ella Shields is always diverting in her studies of various male characters," the *New York Times* reviewer wrote. Again in 1926 Ella was on the road, culminating in an all–British revue at the Palace.

The following year Ella was back on the Keith circuit. However, the tour was cancelled midway through because of illness. She returned in April 1928, playing New York and bringing out all her old admirers who refused to let her leave the stage until she had sung "Bertie," with several encores. That same year, MGM signed Ella for the movies, but none ever materialized. When she played at the Palace in February 1929, she performed "Bertie" but with a surprising twist. Instead of the tattered costume she normally wore when rendering the tune, she wore a dress. The *New York Times* reviewer said: "One who has seen Ella Shields before on countless occasions can recall no such happening before." It was to be her last appearance in the United States.

Ella had been married to Hargraves for seventeen years when, in 1923, they agreed to a divorce. A year before, the press had reported a "torrid" love affair between Ella and Col.

James Christie. When questioned, Christie claimed they were already married. Ella married again in the early 1930s to a man named Buck, but little is known of their relationship. They divorced several years later.

When vaudeville and the music hall business declined, Ella retired from the stage. She made only periodic appearances on special occasions for some years. In 1947, her career was revived when the British staged a revue, "Thanks For the Memory," allowing Ella to perform male impersonations including "Bertie." The show ran through 1951 and Ella remained in the cast during that time. In August 1952, Ella was singing to an audience of 3,000 at a Lancashire holiday camp concert when she collapsed on stage. She died three days later, on August 5, at Regent's Park, London. Ella was seventy-three years old.

Ella reversed the travels of vaudeville headliners. Born in Baltimore, making her vaudeville debut in U.S. theaters, she became a headliner in London and spent most of her career there. When she did return to America, she arrived as a star performer whose male impersonations and classic songs earned her the heartfelt appreciation of audiences wherever she played.

Kitty Doner

Kitty Doner claimed to have made her first appearance on stage when she was less than a year old. Born to parents who were vaudeville performers, Kitty was a typical "trunk" child. "I never had any real home," she said, "because my father and mother were on the go pretty much of the time."

Kitty went on to appear in musicals, three of them with Al Jolson during the middle and late 1910s. For her vaudeville career, Kitty perfected a male impersonation act. The act was so good that the press compared her to Britishers Vesta Tilley and Ella Shields, two of the best-known male impersonators on the popular theater stage. With this act, Kitty became a headliner, garnering high praise from reviewers and audiences. As the amusement era changed, so did Kitty's career, and she remained active in entertainment to the early 1950s.

Katherine Doner was born in Chicago, Illinois, on September 6, 1895. She was the first of three children. Formal schooling was minimal except for two years in a convent while a teenager. Joe Doner, her father, was born in England in 1864. As a young man, he began a career in show business by dancing in music halls. Nellie Mordeca, her mother, was also born in England, in 1874, and began her stage career as a dancer. Joe and Nellie formed a team and decided to advance their career by going to the United States. At first, they were one of the standby acts at Tony Pastor's theater, but quickly made their way on his bill as dancing comedians. Joe's specialty was dancing on his ear; Nellie performed the soft-shoe. Together, their buck-and-wing dancing had Pastor's audience shouting with delight. The couple married in 1895, shortly before Katherine's birth.

As a child, Katherine appeared in her parents' act, singing and dancing, as did her brother and sister as they became old enough. At the age of ten, taking the nickname Kitty as her stage name, she appeared as a canary in a dance chorus of a children's ballet appearing at the New York Hippodrome. In 1909, at fourteen, Kitty officially made her vaudeville debut in the act Brady's Dancing Dogs, as one of four girls sharing the stage with four dogs.

In 1909, a musical, "The Candy Shop," opened in New York and was well-received. After seven weeks, the show went on a tour that lasted for several years. In 1912, Kitty was chosen as one of the leads in "The Candy Shop," which opened at the Gaiety Theater, San Francisco. She dressed as both male and female and performed so well that reviewers remarked about her versatility. The role began her career as a male impersonator.

When asked how she got started as a male impersonator, Kitty told a story about her father's influence. He had hoped to have a boy. As a child, she often wore male clothes in her parents' act. In her teen years, she was boyish and her dancing mannish. She also was not as pretty as other women performers. The "Candy Shop" experience suggested to her that a career could be made as a male impersonator. But that ambition would have to wait several years, as Kitty was engaged to appear in a number of musicals.

The Shuberts hired Kitty as a dancer to appear in their production of "The Passing Show of 1913." Opening at the Winter Garden on July 24, the revue featured satire of contemporary Broadway hits, which meant that the show was a series of individual olio acts. It starred young performers like Charlotte Greenwood, Charles and Molly King and John Charles Thomas. Ned Wayburn was in charge of the chorus numbers, one of which featured a runway projected into the theater so patrons could be within arm's reach of the chorus girls.

At this point, Kitty's father took over as her manager. Joe's first move was to persuade Flo Ziegfeld to hire Kitty for his Follies. When Ziegfeld cast her in a comic role, complete with pratfalls, after two days of performance, Joe pulled Kitty out of the show. In 1914, Kitty was engaged to play in the musical, "Dancing Around," which starred Al Jolson and Clifton Webb. Kitty performed several dancing numbers with such energy that she was singled out as a featured performer. "That she helps justify the title of the piece is evident to every person who has seen her nimbly tripping about the stage, in every style of dance, from a demure waltz to a neck-breaking acrobatic stunt," reported one reviewer. Her boyish figure was mentioned, as was her man's attire. At this point, Kitty was determined to become a male impersonator. Although the show had few comedic moments and unmemorable music, it ran for 145 performances.

The Shuberts retained Kitty for two more Jolson productions. On February 17, 1916, the revue "Robinson Crusoe, Jr." opened at the Winter Garden. Kitty's dancing was a highlight, but Jolson's interpolations overshadowed Sigmund Romberg's music and everything else.

On February 14, 1918, Jolson's *tour de force*, "Sinbad," opened at the Winter Garden. Kitty's superb dancing was again eclipsed by Jolson's command of the stage and his musical selections, which included "Rock-A-Bye Your Baby to a Dixie Melody," "My Mammy" and "Swanee." The ramp into the audience allowed Jolson, in blackface and white gloves, down on one knee, to reach patrons with an intimacy that made him and his songs famous almost immediately.

In between these shows, Kitty was perfecting her male impersonator act with appearances at vaudeville houses. She was frequently accompanied by her brother and sister. Their act was favorably received by audiences. Even the conservative *Dramatic Mirror* lauded her act, suggesting that she was a dancing star to be emulated. Her act, "A League of Song Steps," got her the title "The Best Dressed Man on the American Stage." Now a headliner with a considerable following, Kitty made seasonal tours of the country, gaining even greater fame. Unlike other impersonators, Kitty restricted her male impersonations to the average man rather than celebrities. This allowed her flexibility and prevented critics and audiences from making comparisons to other impersonators.

A highlight of her career was a month-long engagement at London's Victoria Palace

Theater in 1922. England was known as the home of male impersonators, led by the famous Vesta Tilley, but reviewers thought Kitty's act was as good as Tilley's, if not better. In spite of her obvious appeal, she never visited England again.

For the next decade, Kitty headlined vaudeville circuits. During this period, she also explored other stage media. In December 1924, Fred and Adele Astaire starred in the Gershwin hit, "Lady Be Good." The show ran for 330 performances in New York. When the show went on tour, Kitty and her brother replaced the Astaires with almost equal success.

In May 1926, Kitty took her act to the Palace Theater, New York. She began the act waltzing in an evening dress, then sang a French song, changed to skirts for some high-kicking antics and finally to Scotch kilts for an energetic finale. *Variety* called her "a headliner who offers not only a well known name but some honest-to-John entertainment."

In 1928, Kitty appeared in a Vitaphone short, "A Bit of Scotch," in which she performed a few of her well-known male dance routines. But when she found she was competing with herself, playing down the street from the movie theater, she decided to forgo movies. She continued to play in vaudeville until she saw its rapidly approaching demise.

During the early 1930s, Kitty appeared in a nightclub act, singing and dancing, with Harold Stern and his orchestra. In the 1940s, she was a show director for "Holiday on Ice." In 1950–51, Kitty auditioned talent for "Ted Mack's Amateur Hour," which appeared on television. Afterward, she retired to Los Angeles. She was fifty-six years old but had been in show business for forty-two of those years.

For more than thirty years, Kitty lived a quiet and retiring life, rarely participating in anything having to do with the stage. She died on August 26, 1988, in Los Angeles, at the age of ninety-two. A private funeral and burial and a brief obituary in the press was all that reminded the public of a one-time vaudeville headliner.

Kitty Doner

PART EIGHT: THE NOVELTY ACTS

Anna Eva Fay

For more than half a century, Anna Eva Fay awed vaudeville and variety audiences with her psychic powers. She was the most famous of all mind-reading acts in vaudeville. She introduced spiritualism and psychic manifestations to theater patrons who had never before been exposed to such phenomena. Her work caused a worldwide cult of spiritual theosophists to be founded. Late in her career, she was visited by Harry Houdini, already an outstanding performer; he wished to learn her techniques but she refused to reveal them.

Anna E. Hethman was born in February 1851, in the village of Southampton, Ohio. Her father, Joel Hethman, had been born in Ohio in 1817 after his parents had come from Ireland to Massachusetts and then to promised farmland in Ohio. At the time of Anna's birth, he worked in a boot and shoe store. He later became a shoemaker and continued in this occupation until he retired. Her mother, Eliza Kibler, was Joel's second wife and was twenty-two years younger than he when they married on September 14, 1862. They had six children, four girls and two boys. Anna was the second child.

Little is known of Anna's childhood and teen years. She was said to have belonged to a close family and received the kind of rudimentary education given girls at the time. Anna was small, with gray eyes and flaxen hair. Having been raised in a rural area, she was physically tough. Anna was only seventeen when she married Henry Melville Cummings on August 15, 1868. He was said to be an actor, but actually was a spirit medium of dubious reputation. His theatrical career consisted of playing in second-rate venues. He was thirteen years older than Anna. They had one son, John, born in 1878. Anna's descendents claim that Henry and Anna had a common law relationship and never legally married.

Henry taught Anna everything he had learned about spiritualism and mind reading. The pupil quickly outdid the instructor. So good were her skills that the couple joined the many artists being welcomed by the variety theaters during the early 1880s. They became immediate hits, due to the uniqueness of their act. They had no problem finding engagements throughout the East and Midwest, sometimes as part of a touring company and sometimes on their own. Henry took the last name of Fay to capitalize on Anna's success.

Anna became more than just a mind reader. She perfected the art of physical mediumship, table levitation and dancing handkerchiefs. Her greatest skill, however, was her acute ability to answer questions from the audience that had been written out beforehand and that she supposedly had never seen. Her answers, with details she could not have otherwise known, caused gasps of awe from audiences. Most audiences were convinced she had never seen the questions, let alone knew anything of their private lives. For some members of the audience, the thirty-minute act of exotic mind reading was not enough. They would return to the theater several times to see her perform.

In 1878, shortly after their son, John, was born, Henry died of cancer. By the time John was a teen, he was assisting his mother in the act. Anna married her manager, David H. Pingree, in 1881. She was slightly older than he was, but his theatrical knowledge and intuition had been matured by several years of stage-managing. He sought to make Anna's act more exciting and even more mysterious. Vaudeville was in its early stages of development and Anna's act was decidedly different from anything found on the stage. Her uniqueness quickly made her a vaudeville headliner. With Pingree's help, Anna became a showstopper. Managers chose to close the show with Anna, since nobody else would consider following her.

Anna's act was well-planned and executed. She moved quickly from the wings to the center of the stage where a chair was placed. She wore flowing white or black gowns with a touch of diamonds. Pingree covered her with a large shawl, leaving only her arms visible to the audience. She began answering questions immediately. Her light, quick delivery in a high, clear voice carried throughout the theater. There was never a struggle for an "artistic" impression but rather an attempt to answer as many questions as possible in the allotted time. As Anna noted in a newspaper interview, there were only five subjects that audiences asked about: wealth, health, lost persons, lost articles and the faithfulness of their spouses.

Anna Eva Fay

After about twenty minutes, Pingree would come to his wife's side, lift off the shawl, and catch her as she fainted into his arms, apparently totally exhausted from her efforts. Clutched tightly in her hands, covered by her gown, were her prompter notes. Pingree carried her from the stage as the curtain dropped to overwhelming applause.

Pingree's advance agents planted stories in advance of her appearance that helped make her answers more astounding to audiences. Of course, every show had its doubters, but none seemed to bother Anna or her admirers. She remained a star attraction throughout the 1880s and 1890s. The couple visited Europe several times with great success. The European audiences were just as awed by her act as the Americans. While audiences in large cities may have viewed Anna's act with some skepticism, small-town audiences were awed and impressed.

New, more daring acts were created. A rope-tie routine was presented as a demonstration of physical mediumship. Table levitation always drew gasps from audiences.

Putting her head in a cabinet, securely tied to a post on stage, Anna delivered a monologue while various objects flew over her head unaccountably. She built the Fay name through showmanship and hard work.

Competitors quickly flooded the ranks of vaudeville mind readers. One even took the name of Eva Fay and copied most elements of Anna's act. In fact, Eva Fay grew to be in almost greater demand than Anna due to her colorful stage presentation. She covered her chair with tiger skin; she put incense in two pots astride her chair, the odor wafting over the audience; she blindfolded herself; and the backdrop was a depiction of the inside of an Egyptian temple. Even worse for Anna, her son John joined the Eva Fay forces, causing a mother-son breakup. The bitterness had begun when he married a girl he met in St. Louis and the two women took a dislike to each other.

For a time, Anna withdrew from vaudeville. A reconciliation did not occur until 1908, when Anna became interested in building a school of Theosophy near her home in Melrose Highlands, Massachusetts. Since the Eva Fay company was the only one in vaudeville to feature mind reading, John returned to his mother. Glad of his return, she gave him a house and a substantial amount of money. They contemplated returning to the stage together again.

John liked to play with pistols. He may have feared death but enjoyed the thrill of handling loaded guns. Tragedy struck when, on December 20, 1908, a pistol went off in his face, killing him. Newspapers reported a suicide but the episode was declared an accident. Anna was devastated. She built a large mausoleum for her son. She dropped her plans for the school and returned to the stage. *Billboard* declared that Anna "could go on forever." And she did perform successfully until the early 1920s.

When she injured her wrist following a performance in Milwaukee in 1924—Anna was now seventy-three—she decided to retire. Some months after that, Anna was visited by Harry Houdini, who failed to get Anna to tell him her psychic secrets. Anna died of heart disease on May 12, 1927. She was buried in the mausoleum next to her son.

There was no doubt that Anna had become a shrewd businesswoman who knew how to make her novelty act one of vaudeville's most popular. No matter the magical nature of her presentation, she held an unquestioned reputation. She was the greatest "mental act" in vaudeville.

Carrie Nation

No other performer in vaudeville destroyed her scenery at every performance and had audiences enthusiastically cheering as she accomplished the task. Carrie Nation had created a reputation based on her violent efforts to stop the sale of alcohol. Her activities helped to bring on Prohibition in 1919. Carrie's appearance in vaudeville was viewed by saloon owners as a welcome respite from her destructive crusade.

Carrie Amelia Moore was born on November 25, 1846, in Kentucky. Her father had left the family when Carrie was a child. Her mother died in an insane asylum. Growing up in homes with strong religious convictions about tobacco and the immodesty of women's dress, Carrie came to believe herself on a mission as "the right hand of God." Although she was also a temperance advocate, she married Dr. Herman Gloyd in 1867. She soon discovered he was an alcoholic. He died soon after their marriage. Carrie then taught school and rented rooms. In 1877, she married David Nation, a lawyer and minister. The combination of events in her life made her "savior" feelings even more intense. The Nations moved to Medicine Lodge, Kansas.

On June 6, 1900, Carrie collected a handful of bricks from her backyard. She drove in her carriage to Kiowa, a nearby town, where she smashed the windows of three saloons. In the center of town, she stood up in her carriage and told the crowd that the liquor law had been violated and someone should be punished, either the saloonkeepers or the State. During the next few days, the press spread the word that a new reformer had arisen. Soon she was smashing the saloons themselves with a hatchet. A large, strong woman, she was able to inflict considerable damage. Carrie's husband sued for divorce, claiming he had been deserted.

After being arrested in Wichita three times, in Topeka seven times and once in Kansas City, Carrie took her crusade to New York City. She visited Police Headquarters and John L. Sullivan's saloon. She did no smashing but gained considerable publicity. The enterprising manager of the Eden Musee, a dime museum and variety house, recruited Carrie to appear on his stage. She was an immediate hit with curious audiences.

In her act, the stage set consisted of a saloon complete with bar, tables and chairs, and customers. A special room had been fitted up from photographs of a saloon Carrie had recently destroyed in Topeka. Carrie burst onto the stage, shouted to the audience her beliefs and intentions, scattered the customers and then proceeded to wreck the scenery. She ended the act by preaching about the dangers of alcohol. Of course, the scenery was made up of breakaway material so it could be reused at each performance.

In December 1903, Carrie starred at the Third Avenue Theater in a play, "Ten Nights in a Bar Room." She made up her own lines, destroyed the bar and went into the audience selling miniature hatchets. That same year, she created a disturbance at the White House in Washington, D.C., in an attempt to see President Roosevelt. Rebuffed, she went to the Senate, was arrested and spent thirty days in jail. Her fine was paid by selling hatchets. Returning to New York, Carrie played at the Auditorium Theater where she broke up the bar twice a day and engaged in heated arguments with the audience. In January 1904, she appeared at the Metropolis Theater, a twenty-five cent house, and entertained audiences with her destructive power.

At Hammerstein's Victoria Theater, the features were Carrie and her hatchet and murderess Florence Burns recounting her side of the story. Both were hissed by the audience. Now labeled "The Kansas Reformer" by theater managers, Carrie played many of the small-time vaudeville houses in town with great effect. By 1907, she had visited all of the theaters that were not afraid to feature her act.

In 1908, she began a tour of England, alternating appearances at music halls and local saloons. She was arrested for smashing

Carrie Nation

saloons in Newcastle on Tyne. When she played at London's Canterbury Theater in 1909, she was pelted with eggs. Indignant, she tore up her contract and returned to the United States.

Now a person of notoriety, Carrie returned to Kansas to continue her temperance activities. In all, she was arrested twenty-two times but nothing prevented her from speaking and acting out her crusade. She died at her home in Medicine Lodge in 1911, at the age of sixty-four.

Never before or after did vaudeville witness such a combination of destruction and religious conviction. At first, audiences regarded it as an amusing novelty, but they soon tired of Carrie's relentless diatribes. Hisses and thrown fruit were the final result of her theatrical efforts.

Annette Kellerman

At the turn of the century, two Australian women were well-known in Europe and America: Nellie Melba, the famed opera singer, and performer Annette Kellerman. Melba's reputation lived long after her retirement. Annette was almost entirely forgotten by the general public.

She was a world-class swimmer, speed and marathons her forte; she was a vaudeville headliner; she appeared in silent films; and she wrote books on health, beauty and how to swim. She introduced swimming not only as a competitive sport but also as a commercial business. Her beautiful body made her an attractive performer. Her tight-fitting costumes pushed the boundaries of propriety but were acceptable because she was a swimmer. She invented the one-piece swimsuit and was credited with introducing synchronized swimming.

Annette Kellerman was born on July 6, 1888, in Marrickville, Australia, a small town near Sydney. Her parents were professional musicians. As a young girl, Annette contracted polio and was forced to wear iron braces on her legs. In her early teens, her mother took her to the famous Cavill Baths in Sydney to regain use of her legs. By the age of fifteen, Annette had discarded her braces. Mentored by Freddie Lane, an Olympic champion swimmer, she learned to swim and won several races. In 1902, when she was fourteen, Annette won a 100-yard race in record time. She turned her attention to long distance racing, and swam the mile in a record-breaking time. She was acknowledged as one of the first professional women swimmers.

Annette signed to appear at the Melbourne Aquarium to perform a daily mermaid show, for five pounds a week. She swam in a twenty-meter glass tank that she shared with several varieties of fish. Given the label "The Aqua Queen," Annette traveled to other Australian cities to perform. In 1904, her parents took her to England where her father wanted her to get into show business. They believed that music hall audiences would favorably receive Annette's aquatic talent.

Her father realized that some sort of publicity stunt was necessary. He hired a boat and rowed to the middle of the Thames River, where Annette dived in and swam for a distance of seventeen miles. Dressed in a frock coat and top hat, her father narrated the swim. Crowds flocked to the riverbank to see this young girl perform. The publicity stunt was successful and Annette was inundated with competitive swimming offers.

Lord Northcliffe, a newspaper magnate, signed Annette to swim the English Channel.

While Annette failed in the attempt, she swam further than any man had done. She received sixty pounds for her effort. She tried to swim the Channel two more times but failed. Still, the press called her the greatest distance swimmer in the world.

In 1906, Annette was engaged to appear at the London Hippodrome to display her swimming and diving skills. Her act proved so successful that the newly labeled "Queen of the Mermaids" toured Europe to full houses. It was reported that she was earning $1,000 a week for two shows a day. Not only was Annette viewed as an accomplished diver, but her attractive body helped to make her a popular performer as well.

Annette and her father arrived in America in 1907. Her first engagement was at the White City amusement park in Chicago, where she performed fifty-five shows a week. Her act consisted of diving into an aquatic tank sixty feet high in front of rapt audiences. In the tank, she also performed underwater stunts. At a performance in Boston, Annette attracted press attention. She was playing at Revere Beach where she introduced the first one-piece bathing suit. The city fathers were outraged and demanded Annette be arrested for obscenity.

Annette Kellerman at the Winter Garden (Museum of the City of New York).

The only outcome of their fury was that B.F. Keith hired her to appear in vaudeville for a two-week run on Broadway. The novelty of her act and the publicity created by her new costume made her a headliner. Following the Keith engagement, Annette moved to Proctor's Fifth Avenue Theater, where she regaled audiences for seven weeks. At Keith's theater, E.A. Albee changed the act to take advantage of Annette's bathing suit profile. Albee installed mirrors in strategic positions around the tank so audiences were able to see many views of Annette's body in motion. The usually conservative Albee defended his decision to the Boston press. "Don't you know," he declared, "that what we are selling here is backsides, and that a hundred backsides are better than one."

Following her success in Boston and New York, Annette made a series of vaudeville tours at $2,000 a week. She awed audiences with her aquatic feats and created a public groundswell among women for "modern" swimwear.

In 1910, Annette married her press agent, James Sullivan, in a secret ceremony in Danbury, Connecticut. James then took over as her manager. At the time, James was twenty-three; Annette was twenty-one and already a popular theater star. She was booked for vaudeville tours throughout the United States for the next two years. Now known as the "Diving Venus," Annette was selected as the "perfect woman" for a poster to advertise the 1912 Panama exposition in San Francisco. The poster was so popular that it was stolen from wherever it was installed. It may have exasperated exposition authorities, but the publicity it received increased patronage.

In early 1914, Annette was signed to appear in a number of movies. Shooting was to take place in Bermuda. In an aquatic act at the Bermuda aquarium, the glass tank containing 8,000 gallons of water burst. Annette, pulled out over the edges of broken glass, received severe lacerations on her left side. The episode did not prevent her from starring in her first movie, "Neptune's Daughter" (1914). The movie was a great success. In the picture, Annette set a world high-diving record of eighty-four feet. In another scene, she was hurled off a cliff into the sea while tied hand and foot. In 1916, Annette appeared in "A Daughter of the Gods" in which she staged a spectacular underwater fight with a man. Of course, she won. She also dived again, but this time only fifty-four feet. However, the pool she dived into was filled with alligators. This movie was also highly profitable.

Annette starred in "The Big Show of 1916" at the Hippodrome, New York, after its main attraction, ballerina Anna Pavlova, retired from the cast. The show played for 425 performances and produced one popular song, "Poor Butterfly." Annette performed in a big production number designed just for her. She made a sensational high dive over a waterfall, into a pool with 200 water nymphs. She also introduced elements of water ballet, which would become an integral part of her future vaudeville routine.

During the next two years, Annette appeared in two more movies. "National Red Cross Pageant" (1917) was a patriotic display that featured examples of physical education. "Queen of the Sea" (1918) showed Annette and others in a number of water ballets. In between movies, she continued to appear in vaudeville, with good results.

In January 1918, at the Palace Theater, she opened "Annette Kellerman's Big Show," a forty-minute act that featured her singing and dancing, walking a tightrope, and diving. She enthused audiences with her diving but not the other stage routines. Later in the same year, Annette returned to the Palace but staged aquatic activities only. She then went on an overseas tour that took her to the European capitals and Australia, where she was greeted like royalty.

Annette appeared in two movies after the war. In 1920, she made "What Women Want." It was less a water picture than a love story. In 1924, she appeared in "Venus of the South Seas," a picture that fully utilized her swimming and diving prowess. During the 1920s, Annette also opened a health food shop in Los Angeles and went on the lecture circuit talking about beauty and physical fitness.

Annette appeared at the Hippodrome in 1925. She semi-retired from the stage shortly afterward to assist in rehabilitating crippled children. There were some infrequent vaudeville performances of her diving act until 1930. To keep fit, Annette continued to swim half a mile a day until she was eighty. By the early 1930s, most women were wearing Kellerman-style bathing suits.

In 1961, Annette returned to Australia to live. She died in Southport on November 6, 1975, at the age of eighty-eight.

Billed as the "Diving Venus" and "the form divine," Annette became a headliner on Broadway by combining swimming skills with her shapeliness to be vaudeville's first aquatic glamour girl.

Evelyn Nesbit

Had she not been witness to her husband's shooting of her former lover, Stanford White, Evelyn Nesbit would never have appeared in vaudeville. Although she was a middling performer, her beauty and notoriety gained her immediate headliner status. The remainder of her theatrical life was slow, painful and degrading, the sordid tales of her personal life stalking Evelyn to her death.

Evelyn Florence Nesbit was the first of two children born to lawyer Winfield Scott Nesbit and Florence Evelyn McKensie. Evelyn was born on December 25, 1884, in Tarentum, Pennsylvania, a village near Pittsburgh. Her brother, Howard, was born several years later. Mr. Nesbit was considered a good provider and his income contributed to a comfortable middle-class life style.

Unfortunately, when Evelyn was eight years old, her father died, leaving the family almost destitute. Mrs. Nesbit moved to Pittsburgh with the two young children and attempted to make a living by running boardinghouses. When that failed, she took in washing and sewing. To avoid paying rent, she frequently moved the family from place to place. The children's education ended early.

Evelyn was a beautiful young girl. When she was thirteen years old, a portrait painter from Philadelphia painted her. A photographer saw the picture and asked Evelyn to sit for various studies. The photographs were printed in an art magazine and quickly attracted attention. Evelyn found herself being pursued by artists and photographers. Soon the money that she was earning as a model, said to be seventeen dollars a week, became the primary support for the family. Her mother, realizing the commercial value of her daughter, moved them to New York to take advantage of the modeling opportunities there. At the age of fifteen, Evelyn modeled for artists like Charles Dana Gibson. Aware that fashion modeling was more lucrative than portraiture, Evelyn appeared on the fashion pages of the *Sunday World* and *Sunday American*. When a theatrical magazine published her photo, managers were at her door, hoping to sign her for their shows.

A musical from London, "Floradora," was about to open in New York. One of its primary features was a chorus of young men and women. Evelyn was engaged to appear in the chorus. She would learn to sing and dance while performing. The show opened at the Casino Theater on November 12, 1900. It floundered until a new manager stepped in to revise the production. A double sextette of six chorus men and six chorus women sang the soon-to-be-popular song, "Tell Me Pretty Maiden, Are There Any More At Home Like You?" The show resurrected, audiences filled the theater. After 505 performances, the show finally closed, only the second musical to have passed the 500 mark.

The chorus became the primary focus of the show. Stories abounded about its young women being fervently pursued by stage door Johnnies, many of them rich men. Some girls did marry and became the symbols of the opportunity for upward mobility afforded by being on the stage.

At the age of sixteen, Evelyn was one of the beauties of the chorus. Through a colleague she met Stanford White, a rich, married man who already had a checkered reputation with young women. The splendor of his living style and suave masculinity seduced Evelyn, and she became his mistress.

Another man whom friends warned her against was millionaire Henry K. Thaw, fifteen years older than Evelyn. In 1902, she began to receive anonymous gifts. Later, at a party, Thaw introduced himself as the gift-giver and initiated a campaign to woo her. A conflict developed between Thaw and White. In the meantime, Evelyn and young John Barrymore became good friends. White interceded and sent Evelyn to the DeMille School for girls in New Jersey. (Mrs. DeMille was the mother of film magnate, Cecil B.) Seven months later, Evelyn was hospitalized with what the press speculated was appendicitis. Thaw visited Evelyn often, lavishing her with gifts, getting Mrs. DeMille and Evelyn's mother to like him and dominating her life at the same time that White's interest in her was waning.

In 1904, Thaw, Evelyn and her mother went on a European tour. During the trip, Evelyn revealed to Thaw her story of relations with White, which infuriated him. Henry Thaw and Evelyn Nesbit were married on April 4, 1905, in a private ceremony in Pittsburgh. Only family members attended.

In 1906, during a two-week trip to New York, Thaw and Evelyn went to the opening of a musical, "Mamzelle Champagne." White was in attendance. On their way out of the theater, Thaw took out a gun and shot White three times at close range. White died and "The Trial of the Century," as newspapers called it, began. It created a sensation and lasted several years.

Theater managers vied with one another to get Evelyn to appear on their stages. At first, she refused, but when money was getting short, she agreed. Her act consisted of simple dancing and singing hits of the day. From 1910 to 1912, Evelyn was a headliner on the Keith circuit, thanks to her beauty and reputation. Her appearances in vaudeville also caused considerable debate about her and the amusement itself. Some critics declared she was the symbol of illegitimate stardom. Others saw her act as a sign of vaudeville's deterioration. Thaw's mother objected to Evelyn's "immoral dancing" and cut off her allowance. On the other hand, managers reaped considerable profit from Evelyn's appearances at their theaters.

Her career was interrupted when she gave birth to a son, Russell, in 1912. Thaw denied paternity. A promised payment by mother Thaw to assist Evelyn never materialized.

Willie Hammerstein, Oscar's brother and booking agent for the Victoria Theater, still saw opportunities to exploit the Thaw-White-Nesbit affair. In 1913, he signed Evelyn to play in England in a musical, "Hello Ragtime," in which she sang and danced. For the show, she was teamed with Jack Clifford (Virgil Montani), who helped to improve her dancing style. When she and Clifford returned to the United States, Willie Hammerstein booked them into the Victoria for four weeks. His effort to sell the act to the public was enhanced when Thaw escaped from the insane asylum where he had been placed after being found guilty of killing White. The publicity could not have been better timed. Evelyn and Clifford, playing to full houses at advanced prices, made $1,750 a week. Management earned $100,000, the most that any performer had supplied the box office in any vaudeville theater.

For the remainder of 1913, the duo played on the Comstock and Gest circuit for a reported $3,250 a week. In 1915, they appeared at the Palace Theater to a week of sellouts. Reviewers attributed this to Evelyn's notoriety.

Evelyn obtained a divorce from Henry Thaw in 1916. Shortly afterward, on May 24, she and Clifford were married. Less than a year later, the couple separated, and in 1918, they were divorced. Evelyn claimed that Clifford had lived on her money the entire time they were married. She took on another dancing partner, Bobby O'Neill, but managers and audiences were tiring of her act.

Evelyn Nesbit

Evelyn had begun her movie career in 1909 by appearing in a picture about the White affair, called "The Great Thaw Trial." In 1915, she played in "The Threads of Destiny," which featured her son and Clifford. When, in 1917, she appeared in a film titled "Redemption," she had the role of a young mother forced to confess to her son a past indiscretion. Publicity from the film got her a contract from the Fox studio. They released seven pictures starring Evelyn, all of them indirectly alluding to her personal history. "Her Mistake" in 1918, with her son, was, indeed, a mistake. "I Want to Forget" (1918), "The Woman Who Gave" (1918), "A Fallen Idol" (1919), "Thou Shalt Not" (1919) and "Woman, Woman!" (1919) were mediocre movies, but they kept Evelyn's name in the news. Another film, "The Hidden Woman, with son Russell, had been made earlier and was finally released in 1922.

From 1919, Evelyn's career declined. The Thaw affair had receded in the public's memory, and Evelyn was no longer a young innocent. She tried acting in "Open Book," a show that closed after a few weeks. She opened a tearoom in 1921, but it lasted only a few months. She attempted suicide by poison when she was evicted for nonpayment of rent in 1922. Two years later, she turned up, inexplicably, in a Yiddish drama in Atlantic City. In 1926, she drank a disinfectant in an unsuccessful attempt to take her life.

In 1937, Evelyn endeavored to make a comeback. She published the first of her memoirs for a New York newspaper. Over the years, her stories changed, becoming even more sensational, or pathetic, depending on the reader's point of view. An act that combined torch songs, swing numbers and comedy ballads took her through a number of second-rate cabarets in New York and New Jersey.

In 1955, Hollywood hired Evelyn as a consultant for "The Girl in the Red Velvet Swing," a movie that supposedly was based on her life. She received $30,000 for permission to tell the latest version of her story.

For the last two decades of her life, Evelyn lived a quiet existence in a downtown Los Angeles hotel. In 1965, she moved to a convalescent home in Santa Monica. She died there on January 17, 1967, at the age of eighty-two. A Requiem Mass was said for her at a church in Brentwood and burial was at Holy Cross Cemetery in Inglewood. Only a few people attended the funeral. The rest of the world had forgotten her.

Evelyn once said, "Stanny White was killed but my fate was worse. I lived." A reluctant headliner on the stage, Evelyn was never able to escape her beauty or her notoriety.

Helen Keller

Unique in the history of vaudeville was the presence of Helen Keller on the stage of its first-class houses. Her act consisted of telling rapt audiences about how she conquered her physical handicaps. Vaudeville was ready to accept any performer who demonstrated special skills. Helen gave audiences no songs or dances or comedy; instead, she gave them reasons to be a happy participant of life.

Helen Adams Keller was born in 1880. At the age of eighteen months, a serious illness destroyed her sight and hearing. For the first five years of her life, she was a wild and unruly child. Her parents visited Alexander Graham Bell who, besides inventing the telephone, was an authority on teaching speech to the deaf. On Bell's recommendation, the Kellers consulted with the Perkins Institution, which recommended twenty-year-old Anne Mansfield Sullivan, partially blind herself, to teach the seven-year-old Helen.

After several months devoted to establishing rapport and confidence in the new relationship with Anne Sullivan, Helen displayed a hunger to learn. She was taught to read using printed words in raised letters. A year later, she learned to read Braille. By 1890, she was learning to speak. Her impressive progress was noted by the press, and Helen was besieged with offers to appear at popular events, like the World's Fair in 1893. At the age of fourteen, Helen began her formal schooling. In 1904, she graduated from Radcliffe College with honors in German and English. While still at Radcliffe, Helen began a writing career and had several articles about her rehabilitation appear in ladies' magazines. Her reputation had built to the point where she and Sullivan went on the lecture circuit raising funds for organizations for the blind.

Lectures paid little. In 1913, when Helen needed to make money, she turned to vaudeville. Managers were happy to book a person who was already a headliner, if not in theater. She opened her career in vaudeville with an appearance at the 48th Street Theater on March 30, 1913. Response to her act was immense and launched a series of tours across the country.

In the Keller-Sullivan act, the rising curtain showed a drawing room with a garden seen through French windows. To the music of Mendelsohn's "Spring Song," Sullivan came on stage and told of Helen's life. Then Helen opened a curtain, came on stage and conversed with Sullivan for several minutes. When she appeared at the Palace Theater, a *New York Times* reviewer wrote: "Helen Keller has conquered again, and the Monday afternoon audience at the Palace, one of the most critical and cynical in the world, was hers." Helen was reported to be earning $1,000 a week.

There had been some trepidation about booking Helen at the Palace, but she mesmerized audiences with her feats of speech and intelligence. So well was she received that she was held over for a second week. Co-star Sophie Tucker was taken with Helen and helped her put on makeup before each performance.

Helen appeared in vaudeville nearly every season from 1913 to 1924, except during the war years, when she visited hospitals visiting soldiers who had lost their sight. Between 1920 and 1924, promoters Harry and Herman Weber presented Helen in a twenty-minute act that toured the country. Although some people were reported to be scandalized by her commercialism, Helen loved the stage. She argued that her vaudeville appearances helped the cause of the blind. Her final tour, in 1924, visited New England's high-class houses with great success.

Moving to Forest Hills, Queens, New York, in 1924 with Sullivan and her husband, Helen used her new home as a base for fund-raising tours on behalf of the American Foundation of the Blind. She collected considerable funds and sought to alleviate the living and working conditions of the blind. During the years before World War II, Helen toured the world on behalf of the blind and deaf, visiting twenty-five countries on five continents. When Sullivan died in 1936, Helen moved to Westport, Connecticut, her home for the remainder of her life. During the 1950s and 1960s, she was honored by institutions throughout the world for her work. Helen died in 1968 at the age of eighty-eight.

Helen's philanthropic activities and many books gained her great distinction in her later years. It was on the vaudeville stage, however, that Helen brought her message to the notice of audiences across the country.

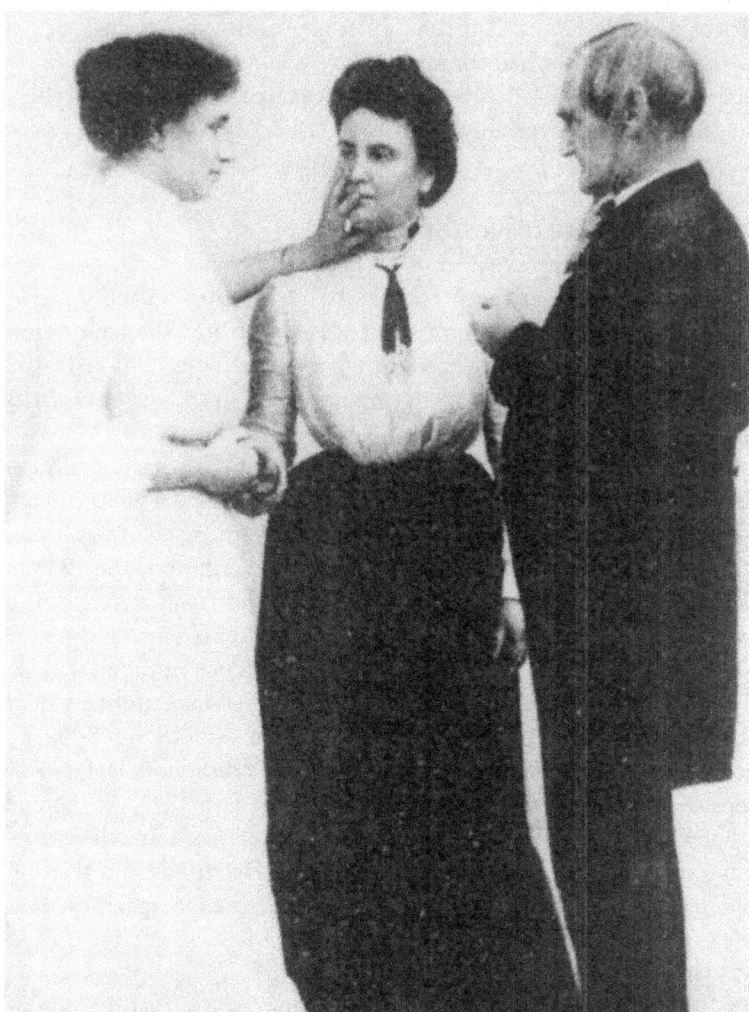

Helen Keller (left, with Ann Sullivan and Joseph Jefferson).

Part Nine: Headliners' Heritage

It was the opening of Weber & Fields' Jubilee show in February 1912. The partners had recently reunited. To star in the show, they brought back all the old performers from the Music Hall days.

Among them was John T. Kelly, the jovial Irishman, who began the second act singing a song especially written for him by Jean Schwartz, "If It Wasn't For the Irish and the Jews":

> I really heard Belasco say,
>   You couldn't stage a play today,
>   If it wasn't for the Irish and the Jews.

The song was greeted with cheers and applause. While the lyrics were meant to humorous, there was also a great deal of truth to them.

In this study of eighty women vaudeville headliners, more than one-third were of Irish or Jewish origins. During the early days of vaudeville, most performers were Irish. As vaudeville matured, other ethnicities entered the medium. Still, almost one-quarter of all headliners surveyed here had an Irish heritage, spanning the years from 1873 to 1919.

Considering they represented a much smaller population, we found that 13 percent of the women were raised in Jewish households. Two others could possibly qualify: Anna Held had a Jewish father but later converted to Catholicism; Gertrude Vanderbilt had a mother who forbade her to enter the theater, married a Jewish man and later in her life gave generous contributions to Jewish organizations. While Jewish women performers entered vaudeville later than the Irish did, all but one, Molly Picon, began their vaudeville careers between 1893 and 1908.

During this era, New York was the center of vaudeville, from its entry levels at ten-cent houses to its opulent presentations at the Palace Theater. A large number of Irish and Jewish women came from the New York area. Many managers and agents were also Irish or Jewish, which helped performers with the potential to enter the business.

Theater historians estimated that more than 25,000 women attempted to pursue careers in vaudeville. Only a few thousand of them were deemed good enough to reach secondary theaters. Only several hundred ever appeared at high-class vaudeville theaters. Among these select few, some had short-lived careers due to factors other than their talent, like illness, marriage, or family tragedy. Some were unable to handle the physical and psychological stress associated with demands of performance. Others were satisfied to play minor roles or support headliners.

The women who made headliner status were bold and courageous, with unswerving ambition and a desire to entertain audiences no matter what the obstacles. Of course, these women had talent, but it was what they did with that talent that made them successful. They were a hearty group, carving a niche out for themselves in a highly male-dominated competitive environment.

There were personal similarities among the eighty women studied here that contributed to their stage success, such as family background, education, early stage experiences, and the comportment of their adult lives. If one phrase could identify these women, it would be that they represented a *marginal group* of people in our society. A review of their lives tells a compelling story.

More than half of these women were born into and experienced poverty during their childhood. Both parents, if they were available, had to work to support the family. Children worked on the streets by the time they were six or seven. Most had large families, an average of four living siblings. Infant and childhood deaths were frequent.

Most forebears of these women were already living in the United States prior to marriage and children. Few had any kind of education or occupational skills. Men tended to work at service-oriented jobs like bartenders, wagon drivers, and street cleaners. Women tended to the household chores, raised the children and, when they could, took in washing and sewing.

Those who came to the United States in the late nineteenth century tended to be better off, at least in terms of education and work skills. These families had fewer children and the children were given some elementary education. They also were more stable or had better support services when needed.

Whether these families lived in poverty or not, many suffered some form of breakdown of the family structure. For example, a parent died while the children were young; a parent was severely injured; there was a divorce, desertion or abuse. Often, one parent was unable to raise children and work, so children were sent to other homes. Four out of ten of these families suffered a breakdown so severe that it caused a significant disruption in the children's lives. Another four out of ten retained some family ties but the children were, nevertheless, forced into work at an early age and had little parental guidance.

Among headliners, one-fifth had no formal education of any kind. Fifty percent obtained only a few years of elementary education, enough for them to read and write. Only 12 percent completed elementary school and another 17 percent went on to high school.

Two-thirds of the women headliners were the firstborn in their family, although ten percent of them were born after earlier infant deaths. In the families described above, firstborn children were expected to work. Selling newspapers, running errands and operating sidewalk stands brought in a few extra dollars each week.

The rest of these women were born either third, fourth or fifth in order. They had less responsibility to help support the family, but they were more likely to be ignored or left to be on their own.

While the early lives of these women were severe, their experiences made them more autonomous. Being a female in a male-dominated environment was obviously a challenge. At the time they were maturing, Victorian mores were in the process of eroding, the suffrage movement was becoming a viable alternative, and the concept of the "new woman" was being promoted in women's magazines and among the better classes of society.

These women obtained their first theatrical experiences by observing performances at neighborhood saloons and concert halls. Women already appearing at these questionable venues were employed and seemingly free of the limitations of the traditional feminine role. When these youngsters had a few coins, they visited local variety theaters and witnessed women actually performing on stage, in costume, to audience approval. Performers appeared to be equal to their male counterparts. Theater had many appealing elements.

The church was a focal point for warmth, social interaction and music education for many of these young women. The Catholics were persuaded to learn to sing and dance, to participate in the church choir and in amateur theatricals. Many of the women headliners began their career training by participating in church events. Those who demonstrated promise were encouraged to continue their training. Even though only teenagers, some were persuaded to enter vaudeville. Parents agreed to encourage their daughters to pursue a possible career in popular theater. After all, it meant more money to support the family.

For Jewish girls, the situation was entirely different. Religious traditions were strong and women had a perceived role to play. Most Jewish parents viewed the theater as evil and immoral. Young women had to learn to sing and dance surreptitiously, usually by copying the acts they had seen at local vaudeville houses or by appearing in amateur contests. When a young Jewish woman decided to enter the theater, she had to consciously make a break with traditions and, often, with family ties. It was a brave and precarious decision.

Most of these girls began performing as teenagers. Many began by appearing in melodramas and farce-comedies. Some were lucky enough to be hired as chorus members in a musical or comic opera. A few whose talent showed great promise were engaged to appear in supporting roles in vaudeville.

Seventeen was the average age that the women began performing. More than half of them began performing by the age of fifteen. Only four of the eighty had the luxury of stage mothers. Another four, born into performing families, remained with their parents as they learned the business. The majority, however, lived on their own while they sought to improve their stage skills. Those who survived the challenge laid the foundation for later success. These early experiences helped the women to overcome the barriers and pitfalls as they pursued a theatrical career.

The average age of entrance into vaudeville was nineteen. Two-thirds of these women had entered vaudeville before they were twenty years old. One-third had begun in vaudeville before they were fifteen.

Young women performers were faced with many problems related to their sex and age. Initially, there was considerable resistance to women playing in vaudeville. Men dominated as managers, agents and performers. Women earned lower salaries. They were given menial assignments. They were judged by a more stringent set of standards than men. Their early success relied more on audience approval than colleague acceptance. They also had to challenge the public image of women appearing on the popular stage, a profession viewed as dubious by some and immoral by harsher critics. Along with having to perform to higher expectations, these women had to build a reputation for respectability and learn what the proper parameters were for them in popular theater. Protecting themselves sexually was constant, particularly at their young ages.

Minstrel shows actually attacked women's roles. Men were the sole performers and, when a female role was written in the script, men dressed in female clothes and parodied their roles as part of the comedy. Farce-comedy contained female roles but they tended to be weak, frail, and indecisive, subject to the whims of men. Variety had women on their programs but they were relegated to singing popular songs. However, vaudeville welcomed women but, at the same time, put them in a position of having to compete with men for recognition and billing. By the turn of the century, almost as many women as men were headliners, but few of them were able to command equal salaries.

As women's roles began to dominate vaudeville programs, the medium itself gained popularity. This synergy helped vaudeville prosper and grow. Heterogeneous audiences filled the theater, with an equal number of women and men in attendance. From these beginnings, celebrities and star power were created, tying women performers even closer to their audiences and admirers.

Victorian notions were giving way to the "new woman" movement and the emancipation of women from their traditional roles. Not only were women attracted as theater patrons, many now openly aspired to follow theater careers. Women performers were on the forefront of changing women's lives. Theater gave women the opportunity to express assertiveness and sensuality, and audiences expressed their approval with enthusiasm. Feminine beauty and sexual display became important selling points and many women headliners added these elements to their performances. These factors contributed strongly to ultimate headliner status.

At the same time, however, fame also impacted their personal lives. The average age of marriage was twenty-two. More than a third of these women were married before they were eighteen, often to fellow cast members or agents who promised to guide their early careers. Most of these early marriages ended in divorce.

More than two-thirds of these women were married two or more times. One-third had three or more husbands. Subsequent marriages were also with theatrical people. Marriages were continually challenged by the clash of strong personalities, career paths, long separations due to touring, salary differences and publicity that cheerfully invaded privacy. Along with marriages came frequent broken engagements, secret liaisons and sensationalized divorces. With the rise of celebrity status, a woman headliner's entire life was on public display, and only a few of them were able to handle the additional pressure.

Once they became headliners, some women married men who appeared subservient to them. One-fifth married younger men, in some cases significantly younger. Whether it had to do with dominance or sex is hard to tell.

Considering the stress of headliner status, it is surprising that any of the women had children. Actually, two-thirds of them had no children. One-quarter had one child, usually the result of the first marriage when they were still teenagers. Unfortunately, these children lived dysfunctional lives, either put aside or remaining in the shadow of their larger-than-life mothers. Eight women had two children, usually later in their careers. One, Adele Astaire, had three children after she retired, but all three died in infancy.

During an era when life expectancy for women was forty-five to fifty years, women headliners were a robust group. The average age of death was almost seventy-four years. Twenty-two percent lived into their eighties; another 11 percent lived into their nineties. There is no question that the lives they led strongly contributed to their longevity.

But old age had its downside. A majority of these women retired from the stage when the medium died. Many were unable to get other jobs. Savings and a solid marriage helped some of them in their later years. But almost half of them died in poverty, ironically, similar to the way they had begun their lives.

A very few headliners were versatile enough to accommodate to new forms of entertainment and performed until they died. Others shifted to movies, recordings or television but age forced them into retirement and, often, into problematic living conditions.

Many of the women died in obscurity, their names and triumphs totally forgotten by the public. Some did not even warrant obituaries in *Variety* or *The New York Times*. After all, vaudeville was archaic, conjuring up dusty old theaters and an outdated form of entertainment. The world of popular theater had moved on.

Yet, the form is not dead. It has survived in many facets, from "The Muppet Show" to Monty Python, to halftime shows at sporting events, and to sitcoms. And which of us is not guilty of creating our own vaudeville show by surfing from TV channel to TV channel.

In the world of amusement, women vaudeville headliners were a unique group. They were independent, highly motivated risk-takers whose desire to get out of tenuous situations was strong. They possessed a drive to overcome considerable barriers on their way to stardom. Determination and perseverance led to success. They had a joy of performing and gave it all to their audiences.

They created a stage presence that captured audience attention and admiration. They built a reputation and a mythology that portrayed colorful lives, both on and off stage. And they worked hard at perfecting these skills.

More than anything, these women were pathfinders who provided inspiration for women, whether they be appreciative audiences or today's performers.

Selected Bibliography and Source Materials

Archives, Collections, Libraries

Academy of Motion Picture Arts and Sciences
British Music Hall Society
British Theater Museum
Friars Club
Harvard University, Houghton Library
Houdini Historical Center
Library of Congress
Los Angeles Central Library
Museum of the City of New York
National Archives
New York Public Library, Performing Arts Division
Newberry Library
Princeton University Library, Rare Books and Special Collections
San Francisco Public Library, Historical Center
University of California at Los Angeles, Theater Arts Division
University of Rochester, Rush Rhees Library
University of Southern California, Cinema Library
University of Southern California, Special Collections
University of Texas at Austin, Harry Ransom Humanities Research Center
Yale University, Sterling Memorial Library

Newspapers

New York Clipper, January 1865 to July 1923
New York Dramatic Mirror, January 1880 to December 1910
Variety, December 1905 to December 1960
ProQuest Internet file (courtesy of University of Southern California, Special Collections) for all newspaper articles on women vaudeville headliners in the *New York Times, Boston Globe, Washington Post, Chicago Tribune* and *Los Angeles Times*

Genealogical Sources

Ancestry.com http://www.ancestry.com
British Library Online Newspaper Archives — http://www.uk.olivesoftware.com
Brooklyn Genealogy Information Page Index — http://www.bklyn-genealogy-info.com
California Death Records & Certificates — http://www.vitalsearch-co.com

Family Search — http://www.familysearch.org
GenForum — http://genforum.genealogy.com
Godfrey Memorial Library — http://www.godfrey.org
Google — http://www.google.com
London Gazette Archives—
http://www.gazettes-online.co.uk/generalArchive.asp?webType=0
New England Historic Genealogical Society — http://www.newenglandancestors.org
New York Obituary Links — http://www.obitlinkspage.com/obit/ny.htm
New York Public Library, Digital Library — http://www.nypl.org/digital/digitcollsearch.htm
New York State Resource Links — http://www.connorsgenealogy.com/NewYorkState
Random Acts of Genealogical Kindness — http://www.raogk.org
Rootsweb — http://www.rootsweb.com
Searching Ellis Island Database in One Step — http://www.jewishgen.org/databases/EIDB/ellis.html
Social Security Death Index—
http://ssdi.genealogy.rootsweb.com/cgi-bin/ssdi.cgi
TopoZone — http://www.topozone.com
US Genweb — http://usgenweb.com/states/index.shtml
World Genweb — http://www.worldgenweb.org/countryindex.html

Books: Vaudeville, Popular Theater

Allen, R., *Horrible Prettiness: Burlesque and American Culture,* Chapel Hill: University of North Carolina Press, 1991.
Baral, R., *Revue: A Nostalgic Reprise of the Great Broadway Period,* New York: Fleet, 1962.
Bordman, G., *American Musical Theater,* New York: Oxford University Press, 1978.
Coffin, C., *Vaudeville,* New York: Mitchell Kennerie, 1914.
Davis, T.C., *Actresses as Working Women: Their Social Identity in Victorian Culture,* London: Routledge, 1991.
Erdman, A.L., *Blue Vaudeville,* Jefferson NC: McFarland, 2004.
Fields, A., and L.M. Fields, *From the Bowery to Broadway,* New York: Oxford University Press, 1993.
Gilbert, D., *American Vaudeville, Its Life and Times,* New York: Whittlesey House, 1940.
Glenn, S.A., *Female Spectacle,* Cambridge: Harvard University Press, 2000.
Green, A., and J. Laurie, Jr., *Show Biz from Vaude to Video,* New York: Henry Holt, 1951.
Hughes, L., and M. Meltzer, *Black Magic,* New York: Da Capo Press, 1967.
Jenkins, H., *What Made Pistachio Nuts? Early Sound Comedy and the Vaudeville Aesthetics,* New York: Columbia University Press, 1992.
Kibler, M.A., *Rank Ladies, Gender and Cultural Hierarchy in American Vaudeville,* Chapel Hill: University of North Carolina Press, 1999.
Laurie, J., Jr., *Vaudeville: From the Honky-Tonks to the Palace,* New York: Henry Holt, 1953.
Lewis, R.M. (ed.), *From Traveling Show to Vaudeville,* Baltimore: Johns Hopkins University Press, 2003.
McLean, A.F., Jr., *American Vaudeville as Ritual,* Lexington: University of Kentucky Press, 1965.
Marks, E.B., *They All Sang,* New York: Viking Press, 1935.
Peiss, K., *Cheap Amusements: Working Women and Leisure in Turn-of-the-Century New York*, Philadelphia: Temple University Press, 1986.
Rowe, K., *The Unruly Woman: Gender and the Genres of Laughter,* Austin: University of Texas Press, 1995.
Sampson, H.T., *Blacks in Blackface,* Metuchen NJ: The Scarecrow Press, 1980.
Samuels, C. and L., *Once Upon a Stage: The Merry World of Vaudeville,* New York: Dodd, Mead, 1974.
Short, E., *Fifty Years of Vaudeville,* London: Eyre and Spottiswoode, 1946.
Slide, A., *Encyclopaedia of Vaudeville,* Westport CT: Greenwood Press, 1994.
Smith, W., *The Vaudevillians,* New York: Macmillan, 1976.
Snyder, R.W., *The Voice of the City: Vaudeville and Popular Culture in New York,* New York: Oxford University Press, 1989.
Sobel, B., *A Pictorial History of Vaudeville,* New York: Citadel, 1961.
Spitzer, M., *The Palace,* New York: Atheneum, 1969.
Staples, S., *Male-Female Comedy Teams in American Vaudeville, 1865–1932,* Ann Arbor: UMI Research Press, 1984.
Stearns, M. and J., *Jazz Dance,* New York: Da Capo Press, 1994.

Stein, C.W. (ed.), *American Vaudeville as Seen by its Contemporaries,* New York: A.A. Knopf, 1984.
Toll, R.C., *On With the Show: The First Century of Show Business in America,* New York: Oxford University Press, 1976.

Books and Articles: Biographies, Autobiographies

Barnes, N., "Eva Tanguay," *Notable Women in American Theater,* New York: 1989.
Barrymore, E., *Memories, an Autobiography,* New York: Hulton Press, 1956.
Campbell, Mrs. Patrick, *My Life and Some Letters,* New York: Dodd, Mead, 1922.
Castle, I., *Castles in the Air,* New York: Doubleday, 1958.
Cohen-Straytner, B.N., "Gertrude Hoffman," *Biographical Dictionary of American Dance,* New York: 1982.
Cullen, F., "Charlotte Greenwood," *Vaudeville Times,* Vol. 3, Issue 1, Summer 2005.
____, "The Dancing Rooneys: A Vaudeville Dynasty," *Vaudeville Times,* Vol. 6, Issue 4, Winter 2003–04.
____, "Ethel Waters," *Vaudeville Times,* Vol. 1, Issue 1, Spring 1998.
____, "Rae Samuels," *Vaudeville Times,* Vol. 7, Issue 3, Fall 2004.
Egan, W., "Florence Mills," *Vaudeville Times,* Vol. 3, Issue 4, Winter 2000–01.
Kate Elinore Papers, University of Rochester, Rush Rhees Library.
"Ella Shields," *Call Boy, The Official Journal of the British Music Hall Society,* Vol. 39, No. 2, Summer 2002.
Fields, A., *Lillian Russell: A Biography of "America's Beauty,"* Jefferson NC: McFarland, 1999.
____, *Sophie Tucker: First Lady of Show Business,* Jefferson NC: McFarland, 2003.
Gallefont, E., *Astaire and Rogers,* New York: Columbia University Press, 2000.
Golden, E., *Anna Held and the Birth of Ziegfeld's Broadway,* Lexington: University of Kentucky Press, 2000.
Goldman, H.G., *Fanny Brice: The Original Funny Girl,* New York: Oxford University Press, 1992.
Hale, A., "So Bad They Were Good," *Coronet,* December 1944, pp. 92–96.
Janis, E., *So Far, So Good!,* New York: E.P. Dutton, 1932.
Keller, H., *The Story of My Life,* New York: Bantam Classics, 1990.
Kendall, R., "The Fabulous Duncan Sisters," *Hollywood Studio Magazine,* May 1976, pp. 28–29.
Kennedy, M., *Marie Dressler: A Biography,* Jefferson NC: McFarland, 1999.
Knapp, B., and M. Chipman, *That Was Yvette,* New York: Holt, Rinehart and Winston, 1964.
Macdonald, M., *Evelyn Nesbit and Stanford White: Love and Death in a Gilded Cage,* New York: William Morrow, 1976.
Marshalonis, E., and D. Soren, "Ada Reeve." *Vaudeville Times,* Vol. 5, Issue 3, Fall 2002.
Nation, C., *The Use and Need of the Life of Carrie A. Nation,* New York: IndyPublish.com, 2002.
Petrova, O., *Butter with My Bread,* New York: Bobbs-Merrill, 1942.
Picon, M., *Molly!,* New York: Simon and Schuster, 1980.
Shelton, S., *Divine Dancer,* New York: Doubleday, 1981.
Shirley, G., *"Hello Sucker!"; The Story of Texas Guinan,* New York: Eakin Press, 1990.
Simmons, C., "Maggie Cline," *Vaudeville Times,* Vol. 6, Issue 4, Winter 2003–04.
Skinner, C.O., *Madame Sarah,* New York: Houghton Mifflin, 1967.
Sudworth, G., *The Great Little Tilley: Vesta Tilley and Her Times,* London: Courtney, 1984.
Waters, E., *His Eye Is on the Sparrow,* New York: Doubleday, 1951.
Watts, J., *Mae West, An Icon in Black and White,* New York: Oxford University Press, 2001.
Wiley, B.H., *The Indescribable Phenomenon: The Life and Mysteries of Anna Eva Fay,* Seattle: Hermetic Press, 2005.
Wolf, R., "Nora Bayes," *Green Book Magazine,* April 1914.

Index

Abba Dabba Honeymoon 85–86
Actor's Equity Strike 7, 9, 72, 129, 198
Ade, George 150, 159
Adelphi Theater (London) 131, 232
Adler, Jacob 22, 93
After the Ball 149
Albee, E.A. 7, 21, 48, 50, 81, 94, 107, 138, 232, 252
Alexander's Ragtime Band 37
Alhambra Theater (New York) 76, 162, 173
All of Me 93
Am I Blue? 99
American Music Hall (New York) 130, 177
Astaire, Adele 199–201, 246, 262
Astaire, Fred 199–201, 213, 246
Atkinson, Brooks 28, 100–101

Baker, Belle 86, 92–95
Baker, Josephine 75, 99, 110–112
Baker, Phil 65, 81, 188
Barrymore, Ethel 8, 12, 158, 165, 181, 195, 233–236
Bayes, Nora 5, 9, 20, 23, 27, 37, 43, 47–51, 57, 59, 61, 64, 81, 89, 92, 97, 116, 153, 180, 190, 196, 202, 208
Beck, Martin 7, 235
Belasco, David 76, 182, 237
Belasco Theater (New York) 28, 46, 131, 142, 177
Bent, Marion 51–53
Berlin, Irving 27, 37, 44, 78–79, 84, 92–94, 100, 108, 115, 124, 135, 150, 159, 163, 168, 170, 206, 211
Bernard, Sam 43, 106, 133, 163, 179, 211
Bernhardt, Sarah 8, 12, 84–85, 93, 152, 190, 235–237
Bijou Theater (New York) 149, 228
Billy Rose 68, 170–172
The Black Crook 2–3
Blackface acts 26–28, 60, 88–89, 93, 137, 166, 222, 241, 245
Blue Skies 94
Bordoni, Irene 44, 105–109, 166
Brady, Diamond Jim 215, 217

Brice, Fanny 10, 78, 131, 168–172, 188, 217
Broadhurst Theater (New York) 50, 75
Broadway Theater (New York) 24, 27, 60, 84, 102–103, 133, 144–145, 177, 190, 196, 210, 229
Burns & Allen 62, 164, 209
Button Up Your Overcoat 116

Cahill, Marie 35–36, 62, 133, 142–146, 151
Campbell, Mrs. Patrick 231–233
Cantor, Eddie 115–116, 16, 169, 207, 222
Capitol Theater (New York) 53, 138
La Carmencita 5, 176–177
Carus, Emma 27, 35–38, 136, 196
Casino Theater (New York) 4, 37, 40, 43, 55, 131, 205, 254
Castle, Irene 131, 185, 187, 193, 210–213
Castle, Vernon 40, 49, 57, 185, 193, 210, 211–213
Century Theater (New York) 138, 187–188, 203
Cherry Sisters 12, 214–216
Chicago Tribune 21, 57
Claire, Ina 35, 130–132, 198
Clayton, Bessie 89, 177–181, 227, 234
Cline, Maggie 4, 13–15, 18, 211
Cohan, George M. 9, 19, 50, 53–55, 57–58, 123, 134, 149, 155, 158, 168, 178, 180, 190, 196, 241
Cohan Theater (New York) 41, 64, 106, 116
Collier, William 58, 145, 163, 180
Colonial Theater (New York) 46, 49, 72, 81, 111, 127, 138, 158, 165, 230
Come Josephine in My Flying Machine 41
Coon singing/shouting 4, 25–26, 37, 49, 59, 89, 126, 149, 242
Cotton Club 99, 112, 114
Criterion Theater (New York) 39, 130

Daly, Augustin 147–148, 182

Daly's Theater (New York) 57, 99, 139, 143, 180, 186, 227
Davis, Richard Harding 187, 234, 236
Dazie, Mlle. 202–204
De Angeles, Jefferson 40, 103, 120
De Mille, Cecil B. 135, 160, 228–230
Deslys, Gaby 78, 137, 203
Dillingham, Charles 83, 102–103, 129, 159, 178, 187, 200, 210, 212, 221
Dinah 99
Dockstater, Lew 81, 241
Dolly Sisters 5, 12, 137, 168, 187, 216–220, 237
Doner, Kitty 208, 244–246
D'Orsay, Fifi 237–239
Dramatic Mirror 66, 138, 245
Dresser, Louise 40, 56–59
Dressler, Marie 5, 7, 9, 26–27, 35–36, 119, 125–130, 134, 136, 151, 154, 179–180
Duncan Sisters 8, 10, 12, 109, 220–223

81st Street Theater (New York) 110, 194
Elinore, Kate 154–157, 166–167
Elinore Sisters 155–156
Erlanger, Abraham 7, 126, 202
Errol, Leon 44, 78, 106, 137, 159, 166, 168, 171, 187, 217–218, 243
Etting, Ruth 114–117

Fay, Anna Eva 247–249
Fay, Frank 101, 107, 161, 174, 200
Fields, Benny 45, 59, 61–63
Fields, Herbert 28, 145
Fields, Lew 27–28, 37–38, 40–41, 49, 57, 60, 84, 120, 126, 144, 157, 163, 179–180, 187, 193, 196, 198, 210, 212–213
Fields, W.C. 79, 131, 139, 169, 173, 234
Fifth Avenue Theater (New York) 66, 96, 202, 221, 252
44th Street Theater (New York) 120, 194, 200
14th Street Theater (New York) 54, 122, 143, 220–221, 225, 227, 232, 246, 262

Foy, Eddie 27, 37, 57, 120, 134, 143, 158, 190
Franklin, Irene 26, 79, 118–121, 134, 153
Friganza, Trixie 24, 57, 94, 120, 132–136, 205
Frohman, Charles 131, 148, 234, 237
Frohman, Daniel 153, 229–230
Fuller, Loie 178, 182, 190
Fulton Theater (New York) 96, 205

Gallagher & Shean 193, 237–238
Gerry Society 73, 158, 199
Gershwin, George 61–62, 76, 106–107, 109, 174, 188, 200, 224
Get Happy 116
Gilson, Lottie 4–5, 14, 16–18, 23, 29, 81
Globe Theater (New York) 49, 60, 106, 173, 193, 200, 221
Grand Opera House (Chicago) 82–83
Greenwood, Charlotte 10, 45, 62, 66, 104, 135, 164, 204–208, 245
Guilbert, Yvette 32, 45–47, 152
Guinan, Texas 65–68, 107

Hackett, Jenette 208–210
Hall, Adelaide 75, 110–114
Halperin, Nan 131, 164–167
Hammerstein, Oscar 45–46, 180, 190–191, 215, 236, 241
Hammerstein, Oscar II 56, 120
Hammerstein's Olympia Theater (New York) 123, 131, 143, 215
Hammerstein's Victoria Theater (New York) 19, 39, 45, 60, 81, 93, 120, 157, 177, 179, 190–191, 204, 211, 228, 250, 255
Has Anybody Here Seen Kelly 27, 47, 49
Hayes, Helen 49, 114
Held, Anna 5, 22–25, 57, 82, 126, 133–134, 158, 187, 190, 193, 259
Herald Square Theater (New York) 23, 39–40, 55, 57, 82, 120, 127, 133–134, 187, 193
Herbert, Victor 57, 83, 102–103, 143–144, 159, 178–179, 187, 212
Hilton Sisters 12, 224–225
Hippodrome Theater (New York) 68, 76, 97, 110, 186, 244, 253
Hitchcock, Raymond 44, 62, 106, 197, 206
Hoffman, Gertrude 8, 106, 189–192
Hopper, Edna Wallace 40, 57
How Ya Gonna Keep 'Em Down on the Farm 50
Howard, Willie & Eugene 135, 171, 205
Hoyt, Charles 23, 143, 178, 218

Hudson Theater (New York) 183–184, 199

I Can't Give You Anything But Love 112, 114
I Cried for You 61, 93
I Don't Care 20–22, 99
I'll Get By As Long As I Have You 64
I'm Just Wild About Harry 75, 111
I'm the Last of the Red Hot Mammas 91–92
Imperial Theater (New York) 108, 113
In the Good Old Summertime 36, 38–39
Influenza epidemic 9, 200, 206
Irwin, May 4–5, 27, 35, 136, 147–151
Irwin Sisters 4, 71, 147–148
It Had to Be You 64
I've Got Rings on My Fingers 40–41

Janis, Elsie 5, 9, 62, 151, 157–161, 164, 210
Japanese Sandman 50
Jolson, Al 27, 44, 58, 60, 62, 78, 93, 123, 137, 168, 222, 244–245

Keith circuit 7, 20–21, 32, 35, 37, 48, 52, 57, 61, 64, 72, 75, 78, 80–81, 83–84, 90, 93–94, 96, 109, 112–113, 119, 130, 138, 156, 165–167, 180–181, 190–191, 199, 202, 208–209, 224, 227, 241, 243, 252, 255
Keith-Orpheum circuit 61, 75, 110
Keller, Helen 257–258
Kellerman, Annette 5, 93, 251–254
Kelly, John T. 15, 27, 179–180, 196, 259
Kern, Jerome 58, 106, 120, 124–125, 131, 145, 187, 221
King, Charles 28, 62, 66, 137, 145, 206, 208, 218, 245
Kiss Me Again 103, 105
Knickerbocker Theater (New York) 39–40, 103, 196, 198, 211
Koster & Bial's Theater (New York) 19, 34, 46, 54, 152, 176–177

Lahr, Bert 75, 174
La Rue, Grace 37, 42–45, 78, 106, 136, 206
Lasky, Jesse 95–96
Laurie, Joe, Jr. 35, 151
Leslie, Lew 75, 93, 99, 112–113
Let's Do It 108
Levey, Ethel 43, 53–56
Lew Fields Theater (New York) 144, 180
Liberty Theater (New York) 54, 58, 112, 145, 200

Lightner, Winnie 172–175
Lloyd, Alice 80–82
Lloyd, Marie 80–82
Loew's circuit 163, 167, 224
Loew's State Theater (New York) 110, 210
Loftus, Cissie 35, 50, 62, 145, 151–154
Longacre Theater (New York) 56, 141, 167
Lorraine, Lillian 24, 89, 168, 188, 196, 217
Love Me or Leave Me 116–117
Lyceum Theater (New York) 46, 106–107
Lyric Theater (New York) 4, 103, 200

Majestic Theater (New York) 27, 40, 83, 108, 206, 250
Make Believe 50
Maurice & Walton 168, 192–194
Mayhew, Stella 25–29, 60, 136, 196
McCoy, Bessie 186–189, 217
Mean to Me 116
Meet Me in St. Louis, Louis 48
Mills, Florence 73–77, 99, 111–112
Mitchell, Julian 82–83, 178–181, 190, 193
Montogomery & Stone 83, 159, 210
Moore, Florence 162–164, 206
Morris, William 20, 81, 89–92, 206
Music Box Theater (New York) 44, 100, 107, 161, 163, 170, 206
My Gal Sal 57–58

Nation, Carrie 249–251
Nesbit, Evelyn 12, 254–257
New Amsterdam Theater (New York) 52, 115, 124, 131, 184, 202, 204, 211
New York Clipper 70, 89–90
New York Theater (New York) 36, 43, 123, 158, 193–194, 196, 202
New York Times 3, 44, 46, 85, 87, 93, 105, 108, 125, 162–163, 174, 186–188, 209, 215, 233, 243, 257, 262
Niblo's Garden (New York) 2–3, 176
Nobody's Sweetheart 64
Norworth, Jack 20, 27, 40, 43, 49, 56–57, 62, 89, 196, 202, 206, 211

Oh, How I Hate to Get Up in the Morning 78
Oh, You Beautiful Doll 37
Orpheum circuit 28, 57, 77–78, 90–91, 106, 130, 155–156, 170, 173, 180–181, 199, 209, 227, 235, 238
Orpheum Theater (New York) 150, 165–166
Over There 9, 50

Index

Oxford Theater/Music Hall (London) 151–152

Palace Theater (Chicago) 78, 97, 99
Palace Theater (London) 23–24, 44, 106, 127, 169
Palace Theater (New York) 8, 21, 25, 33, 35, 38, 41, 44, 47, 49–50, 52–53, 56, 58, 61–62, 64, 73, 76, 78–79, 81–82, 84–87, 90–91, 93–96, 99, 104–105, 107–110, 120, 124, 129, 131, 135, 140–141, 145, 150–151, 154, 157, 162, 164–167, 169–171, 173–174, 181, 191, 194, 198, 202–203, 206, 208–209, 211–212, 218, 223, 228, 231, 233–239, 242–243, 246, 253, 255, 257, 259
Palladium (London) 50, 109, 113, 141, 235
Pantages circuit 81–82, 109
Pastor, Tony 4, 16, 31, 70, 118, 147–148, 155
Patricola, Isabelle 109–110
Pavilion Theater (London) 34, 76, 95
Petrova, Olga 95–97
Picon, Molly 140–142, 259
Porter, Cole 106–108, 113, 120, 207, 219
Proctor circuit 130, 167, 191
Proctor's 58th Street Theater (New York) 127, 183

Reeve, Ada 33–35
Ring, Blanche 5, 7, 20, 36, 38–42, 136, 180, 205
Riverside Theater (New York) 209, 237, 243
Robinson, Bill "Bojangles" 78–79, 110, 112–113
Rodgers & Hart 28, 92, 94, 116, 145
Rogers, Will 41, 58, 61, 120, 131, 169, 194, 211, 238
Romberg, Sigmund 49, 53, 56, 120, 163, 194, 197, 200, 218, 221, 245
Rooney, Pat, Jr. 36, 51–53
Rooney and Bent 4, 52–53
Rose, Billy 68, 105, 108, 170–172
Royal Theater (Brooklyn) 136, 139
Roye, Ruth 59, 78, 85–87
Russell, Lillian 4–5, 7, 9, 25–26, 29, 57, 69–73, 123–124, 126, 128, 136, 148–149, 158, 166, 179–180, 187, 215, 230

St. Denis, Ruth 181–186, 190, 202
St. Louis Blues 99–100

Samuels, Ray 77–79, 92
Savoy, Bert 139, 187–188, 212
Scheff, Fritzi 102–105, 187, 195
Seeley, Blossom 8–9, 45, 59–63, 145, 206
Shields, Ella 242–244
Shine On Harvest Moon 43, 49, 116, 202
Shubert Theater (New York) 28, 57, 65, 138, 166, 169, 174, 197, 205, 218
The Shuberts 25, 27–28, 57, 60–62, 65–66, 68, 93, 96, 105, 134–135, 137, 159, 163–164, 166–167, 169, 174, 187, 191–192, 194, 197, 200, 203, 205, 208, 218, 221, 245
Smiles 61
Smith, Harry B. 20, 24, 55, 82, 103
Some of These Days 89
Somebody Loves Me 61, 63, 109
Stanley, Aileen 63–65
Stormy Weather 100
Summerville, Amelia 36, 122, 229
Suratt, Valeska 180, 226–229
The Syndicate 7–8, 15, 20, 26–27, 37, 81, 123

Take Me Out to the Ball Game 49
Takin a Chance on Love 101
Tanguay, Eva 5, 8, 18–22, 39, 84, 89, 99, 119, 158, 190, 196
Templeton, Fay 5, 121–125, 128, 143, 158, 179–180
Thornton, Bonnie 28–30, 78
Throw Him Down McClosky 13, 15
Tilley, Vesta 32, 240–242, 244, 246
Tinney, Frank 137, 218, 221
Tony Pastor's 14th Street Theater (New York) 14–16, 29, 31, 34, 118, 240, 244
Tony Pastor's New Theater (New York) 4, 70–71, 88
Tucker, Sophie 8, 10, 20, 22, 50, 59, 87–94, 114, 136, 164, 196, 206, 257

UBO circuit 21, 72, 145, 170, 202
Union Square Theater (New York) 54, 217
Urban, Joseph 115, 131, 159, 187, 200–201

Van & Schenck 159, 166–167, 169, 187, 212
Vanderbilt, Gertrude 27, 89, 195–198, 259
Variety 28, 59, 62, 77, 79, 81–82, 85, 87, 91, 97, 106, 108, 111, 150, 158, 168, 199

Victoria, Vesta 30–33, 158
Victoria Palace (London) 33, 245

Waiting for the Robert E. Lee 62, 85, 87
Wallack's Theater (New York) 27, 52
Walton, Florence 192–195
Ward, Fanny 229–231
Waring Fred 94, 145, 167
Waters, Ethel 98–102, 110–111
Way Down Yonder in New Orleans 61
Wayburn, Ned 27, 37, 61, 137, 187, 199, 208, 245
Weber, Joe 24, 40, 126, 128, 134, 180, 227
Weber & Fields 48, 53–54, 62, 71–72, 119, 123–124, 128, 151, 158, 163, 178–180, 187, 241, 259
Weber & Fields Music Hall (New York) 126, 227, 241
West, Mae 8, 10, 45, 136–140, 218
What'll I Do 93
When My Sugar Walks Down the Street 64
When You Were Sweet Sixteen 30
White, Stanford 182, 254–255, 257
White Rats 7, 18, 26, 123
Whiteman, Paul 62, 65, 76, 115, 173
Why Was I Born 120
Williams, Bert 78, 131, 153, 168–169, 187, 217
Williams, Percy 30, 49, 72, 127, 230
Winninger, Charles 41, 169
Winter Garden (New York) 27, 60–62, 66, 75, 78, 93, 106, 137, 159, 163, 166, 169, 174, 200, 203, 221, 245, 252
Woman's suffrage 2, 7, 37, 69, 72, 119, 128, 135, 150, 260
Wynn, Bessie 82–85
Wynn, Ed 131, 138, 163, 221

Yiddishe Mama 91–94
Yip-I-Addy-I-Ay 40
You Made Me Love You 44, 78

Ziegfeld, Flo 20, 22–24, 37, 43, 48–49, 75–76, 83, 89, 115–116, 126, 129, 131, 134, 159, 168, 170–171, 178, 187–188, 190, 193, 196–197, 201–202, 212, 217, 245
Ziegfeld Follies 9, 20, 24, 37, 43, 48–49, 78, 89, 115, 130–131, 169–172, 179, 185, 187, 196, 202, 209, 217, 245

www.ingramcontent.com/pod-product-compliance
Lightning Source LLC
Chambersburg PA
CBHW081546300426
44116CB00015B/2770